Fort Bowie, Arizona

Arnold Sweenberg

March 11, 2006

Ycenka

Fort Bowie, Arizona

COMBAT POST OF THE
SOUTHWEST, 1858–1894

Douglas C. McChristian

UNIVERSITY OF OKLAHOMA PRESS : NORMAN

Also by Douglas C. McChristian

An Army of Marksmen: The Development of United States Army Marksmanship during the Nineteenth Century (Fort Collins, Colo., 1981)

Garrison Tangles in the Friendless Tenth: The Journal of Lieutenant John Bigelow, Jr., Fort Davis, Texas (New York, 1985)

The U.S. Army in the West, 1870–1880: Uniforms, Weapons, and Equipment (Norman, 1995)

To Frances

Library of Congress Cataloging-in-Publication Data

McChristian, Douglas C.
    Fort Bowie, Arizona : combat post of the Southwest, 1858–1894 / Douglas C. McChristian.
        p. cm.
    Includes bibliographical references (p.) and index.
    ISBN 0-8061-3648-0 (cloth)
    ISBN 0-8061-3781-9 (paper)
        1. Fort Bowie (Ariz.)—History—19th century. 2. United States. Army—Military life—History—19th century. 3. Frontier and pioneer life—Arizona. 4. Apache Indians—Wars. 5. Indians of North America—Wars—1866–1895. I. Title.

    F819.F6M37 2005
    979.1'53—dc22

                                                            2004053729

2 3 4 5 6 7 8 9 10

Contents

Illustrations

FIGURES

MAPS

Acknowledgments

In the course of preparing this study, I have relied on the generous assistance of numerous individuals and institutions. I am particularly indebted to Larry L. Ludwig, park ranger in charge of Fort Bowie National Historic Site, who willingly shared with me his intimate knowledge of the Fort Bowie story. I especially enjoyed and benefited from the time we spent walking the environs of Apache Pass. Those hikes were invaluable in familiarizing me with the topography and historic sites in the vicinity of the post. Larry gave the draft report a careful reading, correcting numerous errors and offering many insightful comments. I also wish to thank park ranger Jeff Helmer at Fort Bowie, who responded with his usual promptness and enthusiasm to my many research requests.

A host of librarians in Arizona and elsewhere facilitated my research. Chief among these was the Library and Archives staff at the Arizona Historical Society Library. Those folks handled my numerous requests efficiently and professionally, in many instances suggesting sources I might not have otherwise discovered. Venice Besky and Priscilla Golden (now retired) of the Wyoming State Library went beyond the call, and always with good cheer, to assist me in accessing government publications. Others to whom I am indebted include: Mitch Yokelson and Carolyn Bernaski of the National Archives, Washington, D.C.; David T. Faust, Fort Lowell Museum, Tucson; and the courteous staff of the California State Archives in Sacramento. David Hayes, at the Western Historical Collections, Norlin Library, University of Colorado (Boulder), was most helpful with my work at that institution. Cynthia A. Wood, formerly at the Arizona Historical Foundation, was instrumental in facilitating access to the Henry Martyn Robert Papers. Colleague David F. Halaas, formerly historian at the Colorado Historical Society, contributed generously of his time in assisting with my research there. My friend Thomas R. Buecker, curator of the Fort Robinson Museum, generously loaned me microfilmed copies of the *Army and*

Navy Journal, which were not available to me locally at the time I did the research.

During the course of researching Fort Bowie, several of my National Park Service colleagues either contributed source materials or steered me to particular collections bearing on the subject. I am especially grateful to Jerome A. Greene, historian at the Denver Service Center, who will recognize information he generated in his "Historic Structures Report" many years earlier; historian Mary Williams at Fort Davis National Historic Site; Dr. Joseph P. Sanchez of the Spanish Colonial Research Center; and Johanna Alexander, librarian (since retired) and Khaleel Saba, archives technician, at the Western Archeological and Conservation Center in Tucson. Historians Robert L. Spude and Art Gomez at the Santa Fe office, provided me encouragement and administrative support throughout the course of preparing the original Fort Bowie Historic Resource Study, which was the foundation of this book.

Gordon Chappell, regional historian in the National Park Service's San Francisco office, contributed much by his deep personal and professional interest in Fort Bowie extending over several decades. His thorough review of the draft resulted in many improvements in the quality of the final manuscript. I am likewise indebted to Bruce J. Dinges, editor of the *Journal of Arizona History*, for his insightful comments and suggestions for reshaping the original report into a book treatment.

I owe special thanks to my long-time friend John Langellier, historian at the Ronald Reagan Library, for pointing me to a collection of previously unpublished Fort Bowie photographs, and to Marva R. Felchin, assistant director for research services at the Autry Museum of Western Heritage, for providing copies of those images.

Fort Bowie, Arizona

Introduction

Viewed from a distance, Apache Pass is unimposing—merely a shallow saddle separating southeastern Arizona's Chiricahua Mountains from the Doz Cabezas at the northern extremity of the range. The modern traveler, hastening along the interstate highway that now traverses the broad San Simon Valley, pays little if any attention to this seemingly unimportant feature on the horizon.

That would not have been the case in the nineteenth century. The pass, known to the Spanish as El Puerto del Dado, lay on a natural course between the Rio Grande settlements and a chain of missions along the Santa Cruz Valley. Although the trail may not have been used extensively as a continuous travel route, segments of it were undoubtedly employed by Spanish and, later, by Mexican military patrols.[1] Following United States acquisition of what had been Mexico's northern frontier, that corridor became nationally prominent as the Southern Overland Mail Road from "the States" to California. In its day, the stage road was every bit the equivalent of today's Interstate 10, which, like its predecessor, carries traffic to San Diego over approximately the same route. Unlike today's travelers, keen-eyed stage drivers and emigrants would have watched intently the point marking Apache Pass during their approach across the desert. Ever a place fraught with the danger of ambush, the passage through the mountains also promised a welcome respite from the unmerciful Arizona sun and, most important, an abundant source of refreshing water.

Apache Pass lay in the very heart of a region the Spanish aptly called Apacheria, an enormous area extending from western Texas to southern California and from Colorado well into Mexico. The reliable, though never superabundant, supply of water at Apache Spring made the location a favorite haunt of the Chiricahuas, who spent much of their time in their namesake range, as well as in the Dragoon Mountains to the west. The Indians sought relief from the summer heat of the desert floor by retreating

Eastern approach to Apache Pass as viewed from San Simon Station. Pass lies at the low point on the horizon. (Author's collection)

into the mountains, there to hunt game and to gather native fruits, berries, nuts, and roots. Although anthropologists disagree as to when Apaches may have appeared in what we know today as New Mexico and Arizona, the consensus is they were firmly established there by the mid-sixteenth century. The Chiricahuas, one of the so-called Western Apache tribes, were extremely hardy and warlike, equally at home in the mountains and the deserts. Their range extended from the Gila River, the great dividing line between northern and southern Arizona, southward to the Sierra Madre in Mexico, and from southwestern New Mexico, home of their closely allied cousins, the Mimbres Apaches, westward beyond the Santa Cruz River.[2]

The spring was the very thing that attracted John Butterfield to Apache Pass as he charted his mail route in 1858. A road around the mountains would have made for easier, faster travel, but no reliable source of water existed in the area north of the Dos Cabezas, and it was water that dictated where men traveled across the desert.

The establishment of that road had been a long time coming. The Mexican-American War, sparked by the annexation of Texas, offered a singular opportunity for the United States to extend dominion over the northern frontier of Mexico, thereby opening a southern, all-season route to ports on the Pacific coast. President James K. Polk directed Brigadier General Stephen Watts Kearny, hardened veteran of frontier service and leader of the first major military expedition over the Oregon Trail in 1845, to assemble a strong column at Fort Leavenworth for the purpose of capturing Santa Fe, and thereafter California.[3]

The first segment of Kearny's army, a mixed force of regulars and Missouri volunteers, started down the Santa Fe Trail in early summer 1846, quickly capturing the territory of New Mexico in a bloodless conquest. However, Kearny's plans for moving against Mexican forces in California were squelched when he learned that the provincial capital, Monterey, had already fallen to a United States naval force and was occupied by American rebels led by the noted military explorer, Lieutenant John Charles Frémont, who happened to be in the territory under still-mysterious circumstances.[4]

The crisis past and the urgency of his mission thus diminished, Kearny divided the Army of the West into two columns that would march by different routes to occupy California. One of those, led by his subordinate, Lieutenant Colonel Philip St. George Cooke, would explore a passable wagon route farther south, starting from the ancient Camino Real on the Rio Grande, through to San Diego. With the Pacific coast in U.S. hands, a continuous overland road connecting with the Santa Fe Trail would provide a vital supply link to the major military depot at Fort Leavenworth, as well as to commercial traders in Missouri. And, with Texas officially under the American flag , communication could be opened all the way from the Gulf of Mexico to the Pacific.

Although the region west of the Rio Grande had been traversed to some degree by American trappers, no reliable maps were available. Cooke therefore engaged two guides familiar with the Gila River country from their trapping days in that region and from having been members of the Jackson party that had journeyed to California via Tucson in 1831.[5] However, their limited experience in the desert west of the Santa Rita silver mines, in southern New Mexico caused them to believe that water was scarce in that region, a factor that probably influenced Cooke to diverge southwest, following a torturous trail leading to Sonora, rather than steering directly for Tucson. After a circuitous journey over hundreds of miles of rugged terrain, Cooke eventually reached Tucson in December, and from there attained his goal of reaching the coast six weeks later.

Much to Cooke's disappointment, however, he failed to establish an easily navigated wagon road to San Diego. In fact, the arduous nature of the terrain had utterly destroyed most of his own vehicles. Nevertheless, Cooke's route would be used by a few hardy California-bound emigrants in the years immediately after the war. Meantime, Apache Pass lay nearly forgotten by white men, but not the Chiricahuas, who continued to frequent the spring and camp nearby.

The military victory over Mexico resulted in a veritable land bonanza for the United States. The Treaty of Guadalupe Hidalgo ceded to the Americans California and nearly all the territory embraced by the present states of Nevada, Utah, Colorado, New Mexico, and Arizona.[6] In a single stroke of the pen, the young nation realized its ambition of Manifest Destiny. Bolstering that achievement, Major William H. Emory, a topographical engineer with Kearny's column, confirmed the feasibility of building a railroad across that vast tract to San Diego.

However, a surveying error caused government officials to discover too late that the new international boundary failed to include the potential railroad corridor. Political debate raged over the disputed territory for two more years before a solution was finally reached. A second agreement, termed the Gadsden Treaty, permitted the United States to purchase the disputed area for $3 million. The price proved to be a bargain. Southerners were satisfied to have secured a direct outlet to the Pacific, while expansionists in general were enthused with the idea of fleshing out the nation by the addition of thirty thousand square miles of new territory. Congress ratified the treaty on June 30, 1854.

As Texans rapidly established overland routes to the budding American town of El Paso during the years immediately following the war, conflicting sectional rivalries flared over New Mexico Territory. Southerners coveted a transcontinental railroad through that region, but northerners were opposed because they feared it portended the extension of slavery into the newly acquired region.

News of gold discoveries on the American River spurred more intense interest in establishing a rail route across the Southwest to the Pacific. To determine the feasibility of such a venture, Congress authorized several other army expeditions to chart potential railroad passages to California. The area between El Paso and Tucson remained unsettled and wild—the unchallenged domain of the Apaches. The few Americans who had ventured there saw no reason to return. The desolate region appeared to hold little potential for either agricultural or mining development; yet, to some, the territory was of vital importance.

By the mid-1850s, California and New Mexico boasted significant numbers of transplanted easterners, not to mention a sizable native Hispanic population, all of whom pleaded for mail service and overland roads. Moreover, the extension of U.S. economic and military interests throughout the Southwest vested the government with an interest in creating a regular system of communication. Despite an existing contract to carry the mail via the Isthmus of Panama, that arrangement was scorned by Californians as a government-protected monopoly.[7] To express that sentiment, Senator John B. Weller presented to his colleagues a memorial bearing seventy-five thousand signatures challenging Congress to improve lines of communication to the new state. The petition specifically demanded that a wagon road be constructed between Missouri and California and that regular overland mail service be established, since the prospect of a transcontinental railroad appeared remote. Weller, who considered the Topographical Engineers to be capable surveyors but inefficient road builders, pointedly called for this and other frontier roads to be developed by the Interior Department. By emphasizing a central route in his proposal, Weller ensured quick passage of the measure by the Northern-controlled Congress. Within a few months, the secretary of the interior created the Pacific Wagon Road Office in Washington, D.C., to supervise the contractors.[8]

As slavery became more hotly debated throughout the nation, so did the question of a transcontinental railroad. It was an expensive proposition; therefore the young nation could afford only one—but which was the best route? Sectional biases ran rampant, with northern, southern, and border states all vying for the honor of being the starting point. Even as the International Boundary Survey was underway, Congress passed legislation authorizing the Topographical Engineers to conduct a series of reconnaissance expeditions to examine all feasible routes across the West. Lieutenant John G. Parke was sent to retrace the route from San Diego across New Mexico to improve the data compiled during Emory's earlier work. Parke set out from California with fifty-four men in January 1854. Because the first segment of the road to Fort Yuma and beyond was already well established, Parke marched directly to the Pima Indian villages at the great bend of the Gila, near present-day Phoenix, then led his column southeast to Tucson.

Parke's expedition followed the old Spanish trace across the San Pedro directly to Apache Pass. The nearly straight line across the southern portion of New Mexico Territory (at that time encompassing both Arizona and New Mexico) confirmed the practicality of the route for anyone traveling from the Colorado River, via the Santa Cruz, to the Rio Grande. "There are no secondary rocks in the Puerto," Parke wrote of the pass itself, "the whole mountain is a mass of primary rock." He further noted that the pass crested three miles inside the west entrance, from which "the remaining distance, seven miles, is a slow descent through a narrow canon, tortuous and difficult for wagons."[9]

The maps prepared as a result of the Parke survey for the first time officially defined a trail across New Mexico Territory to the Rio Grande. Coupled with the Marcy-Pope Road from Dona Ana to Fort Smith, and connecting trails from El Paso to the Gulf Coast via San Antonio, the two-pronged southern pathway to the Pacific avoided the hardships of Cooke's trail through the Animas Mountains.

As a railroad corridor, however, it was politically doomed in the short term. Animosities between North and South intensified by the time Parke's surveys were published in the mid-1850s. Even though Secretary of War Jefferson Davis based much of his support for Parke's route on scientific data, his southern sympathies could not be discounted. In Davis's mind, the evidence merely supported widely held opinion that it was the best route, and Parke had merely confirmed that conclusion. By maintaining his stance, however, Davis inadvertently contributed to the measure's ultimate defeat.[10]

When it became obvious to Congress that factionalism would delay indefinitely the realization of a transcontinental railroad, the establishment of an overland mail route arose as a new obsession, and a new political issue on an old theme. On March 3, 1857, Congress passed legislation authorizing a contract to convey all letter mail from some point on the Mississippi to San Francisco for a period of six years. Additionally, the successful bidder was to use four-horse coaches or spring wagons suitable for carrying passengers. Stations were to be at least ten miles apart, and at each chosen site the company could claim 320 acres of land, provided it was not already privately owned or publicly reserved. The bidders were challenged to accomplish each one-way trip in no less than twenty-five days.[11]

Nine firms submitted bids in response to the invitation; most of them being variations of the thirty-fifth parallel route from Memphis to Albuquerque, thence west via the old Zuñi trail to southern California. Only two based their proposals on the more northerly central route crossing the

Rocky Mountains at South Pass in southwestern Wyoming. Aside from the usual biases expressed by slavery and antislavery advocates, the proponents of that road argued that the great waterless distances of the Southwest made the El Paso–Tucson portion impracticable for operating mail coaches. Postmaster General Aaron V. Brown nevertheless dismissed that point by countering, "There is no route between the Mississippi river and California against which the same objection may not be made. After much examination, we believe that the route selected [San Antonio–San Diego] is freer from this objection than almost any other."[12] He dispelled the myth of no water by citing the testimony of Lieutenant Sylvester Mowry, a Third Artillery officer who had been a member of Parke's military escort. "The country from El Paso to Tucson," Mowry wrote, "three hundred and forty miles, is susceptible of early settlement, and is, moreover, one of the finest routes ever opened towards our western possessions. In no part of it is there a distance of over thirty miles without water, and it is often found at distances of ten and fifteen, with plenty of good grazing throughout the entire distance."[13]

References to the other railroad survey reports revealed additional reasons for Brown's decision to award the contract to the southern route. The central route, to no one's surprise, was frequently closed when mountain passes, if not the plains, became choked with snow. Even the thirty-fifth parallel route was vulnerable to heavy snowfall, and average winter temperatures farther north, and at higher elevations, were markedly lower than along the southern route. The postmaster general envisioned passengers traveling during that season, "benumbed by the cold for more than a week [as they crossed the Rockies], overcome by the loss of sleep . . . which common sense will always suggest as to the suffering and exposures of stage traveling under circumstances so inauspicious. . . . The southern or El Paso route is eminently comfortable and desirable for winter emigration, which the Albuquerque one cannot be, whatever might be said in its favor as a route in the summer season."[14] Were those reasons not compelling enough, Brown capped his argument with the reminder that service on the contract had to begin within twelve months after the award. Since neither of the most promising routes had been developed to any degree, and that was particularly true of the whole region west of the Rio Grande, the course had to be one where terrain naturally favored wheeled vehicles. Time would not allow for the creation of a road requiring more than minor improvements. Brown added that the government's Pacific Wagon

Road was even then being pushed across southern New Mexico Territory. The matter was settled; the mail would go by way of El Paso and Tucson.

As it turned out, however, none of the bidders entered a proposal for the exact route Brown had in mind. More recent information produced by the Topographical Engineers convinced Brown that a trail from Fort Smith to El Paso, charted by Captain Randolph B. Marcy back in 1849, was the best one. However, to satisfy sectional interests, Brown wisely established dual starting points at Memphis and St. Louis, from which the coaches would converge at Little Rock (later adjusted to Ft. Smith), then course southwesterly below the Llano Estacado to the Rio Grande at Franklin (El Paso). From Mesilla, fifty miles north of Franklin, the new road would extend almost due west along Parke's route to Tucson and the Gila, thence to San Francisco. This great looping route, starting and ending on nearly the same latitude, traversed almost 2,700 miles and was aptly dubbed the "Oxbow Route."[15]

Declaring no successful bidder on the basis that none of the routes corresponded to his preference, Brown exercised unilateral authority by selecting the firm he considered to be the best qualified to undertake such a daunting enterprise.[16] Brown favored a partnership assembled under the head of an experienced stage man, John Butterfield.[17] A native New Yorker, Butterfield began his career as a driver, and by the early 1850s operated the American Express Company. The prospect of a transcontinental mail contract found Butterfield favorably positioned to act on the opportunity. A confident Butterfield originally submitted bids for all three of the Post Office Department's schedule options. Brown, therefore, assigned Butterfield the most challenging one—semiweekly service over the southern route, for an annual compensation of $600,000. Income from passenger rates would augment the company's proceeds.

At the same time, the Post Office Department elected to extend mail service from San Antonio to San Diego, awarding a contract to Sacramento resident James E. Birch on June 22, 1857. Birch began his stagecoaching career in Rhode Island during the Mexican War, but with the gold rush to California, he quickly perceived the opportunities awaiting a man of initiative. In 1849 young Birch inaugurated a stage line from Sacramento to the very seat of the strike at Sutter's Mill. Turning a fortune in only two years, he amassed sufficient capital to purchase and consolidate several lines under the banner of the California Stage Company. Birch's business and political associations also positioned him to snare the potentially lucrative Texas-to-California route.

With stations already in place along the road as far west as El Paso, Birch realized that by moving quickly he could provide the only through service all the way to California, thereby enjoying a temporary monopoly on the Pacific Coast traffic until Butterfield commenced operations. The first Birch mail run, soon known as the "Jackass Mail" for its exclusive use of hardy mule teams, left San Antonio on July 9, 1857, arriving in San Diego seven weeks later.[18] The occasion was hailed as a momentous national achievement.

In their race to take advantage of Butterfield's delay, Birch and his successor, George H. Giddings, chose not to establish stations along the road west of El Paso. In crossing the long stretches, coachmen sometimes took an extra team, driven along and grazed under the supervision of an outrider. Teams were rotated on the stage, giving the alternate animals time to rest and graze along the way. Drivers paused at water holes for a few hours at night, mainly to refresh the mules and themselves. Passengers were expected to bring their own provisions and bedrolls and to sleep on the ground. That no station was established at Apache Pass by the San Antonio–San Diego Mail is revealed in the diary of Phocion R. Way, who rode a Giddings coach over the trail in 1858. Arriving at Apache Pass on June 9, Way described the place as

> . . . a deep and wild looking dado pass. The mountains rise on either side from 600 to a thousand feet above our heads, and in many places it presented a perpendicular wall of rock for a great height, with only just space enough for one wagon to pass between. Near the end of this pass is the Apache Spring. This is a bad place for Indians. The spring is half a mile from the road in a canon [sic], and I and three others were appointed to stay and guard the wagon while the rest shouldered their rifles and went after the water.[19]

In the months after Butterfield and the Post Office Department signed their agreement, the company spared no effort to develop a first-class stage line over the Oxbow Route. It was a colossal job involving the purchase of some 250 coaches, construction and staffing of 141 stations, and the purchase of thousands of head of stock. Butterfield's construction crews took every advantage of extant towns and natural water sources

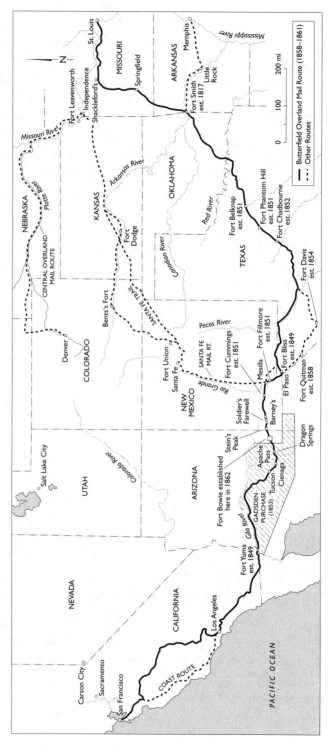

Central and southeastern overland mail routes

along the way, though they occasionally found it necessary to dig wells and build reservoirs to maintain reasonable distances between relays.[20] Distances between stations varied from eight to twenty-four miles in the more settled regions on either end of the line, but stretched to intervals of fourteen to fifty-two miles in the desolate segment between El Paso and Tucson.[21]

Butterfield established nine stations between Mesilla and Tucson, one of which occupied a site in Apache Canyon approximately six hundred yards west of the spring. Captain James H. Tevis arrived there with an army patrol in July, just as the station was nearing completion. He later described it as "a stone corral . . . with portholes in every stall. Inside, on the southwest corner, were built, in 'L' shape, the kitchen and sleeping rooms. At the west end, on the inside of the corral, a space about ten feet wide was apportioned for a grain room and store room, and here were kept the firearms and ammunition."[22]

Butterfield commenced service on September 15, 1858, just one day short of the contract deadline. Passengers paid $200 for a one-way through fare if they provided their own meals, or slightly more if they dined at designated company stations. Each passenger was allowed a maximum of forty pounds of baggage. Stages left each terminal on a biweekly schedule, the trip averaging only twenty-one days, though Butterfield urged his employees "to use every possible exertion to get the Stage through in quick time, even though ahead of this time."[23] A four-day tolerance allowed for breakdowns and other unforeseen delays along the way.

Hence, within a decade following the Mexican War, the United States had established the first tenuous threads of overland communication with California and the new territories in the Southwest. Following closely on the heels of the stage men would be the soldiers, who were only then arriving in southern New Mexico as the vanguard of government authority in that untamed land. Yet, as mail coaches and emigrant trains plied the new road across the desert, wary Apaches high in the Chiricahua Mountains watched the white intruders with great suspicion.

CHAPTER 1

The Army Meets Cochise

The ink was hardly dry on the Gadsden Purchase treaty when American citizens residing in the Santa Cruz Valley near Tucson petitioned Brevet Brigadier General John Garland, commanding the Department of New Mexico, for military protection. Despite their appeals, however, the United States was unable legally to exercise jurisdiction over the area until the Mexicans delivered their versions of the International Boundary maps. Meantime, Mexican troops posted at Tucson maintained a half-hearted presence in the territory they were about to relinquish, a circumstance providing little peace of mind to the inhabitants. Progress was agonizingly slow on the diplomatic front, and only in February 1856 were the maps finally verified and the boundary officially accepted. That done, the Mexican garrison at Tucson was only too happy to march south the following month, leaving the territory entirely devoid of any military presence, the very circumstance feared by the local populace.[1]

Only in fall of that year did the United States Army move to occupy the western portion of New Mexico Territory, what is today Arizona. Major Enoch Steen assembled four companies of the First Dragoons at Fort Thorn, situated on the Rio Grande approximately eighty miles above El Paso, and set out for Tucson following Parke's survey trail through Apache Pass.[2] An uneventful journey found the troops bivouacked near the brilliantly white-washed San Xavier del Bac mission, just a few miles south of the old presidio, on November 14. Although Steen immediately reconnoitered the area for a suitable location for an army post, he quickly decided that Tucson afforded no suitable buildings. Nor did he consider the surrounding vicinity conducive to the health of the troops, probably because of the proximity to cantinas and prostitutes. Whatever the reasons, Steen moved south, up the Santa Cruz River, to Calabasas, a sleepy village near the Mexican border, claiming better grazing was available in that vicinity. His choice nevertheless placed the troops some sixty miles from their principal objective, the new stage road to San Diego, not to mention further distancing the garrison from the more populated agricultural region of the central Santa Cruz Valley.[3]

A year later, higher authority ordered Steen to relocate his post nearer both the trail and Tucson. One of Steen's subordinates, veteran dragoon Captain Richard S. Ewell, suggested the lush Sonoita Valley on the southeastern slope of the Santa Rita Mountains, approximately forty-five miles from Tucson. Steen liked the location, and it satisfied the need to have troops nearer to the California road. The new post, christened Fort Buchanan after President James Buchanan, was occupied on March 7, 1857. Even though the location was more scenic, the site proved to be an unhealthy one and the post itself was rated as one of the worst in the entire Southwest. The miserable assortment of adobe and wood buildings, more nearly resembling a Mexican village than a fort, was poorly constructed by the unskilled troops. Despite its shortcomings, Fort Buchanan survived for several years as the only permanent military station in southeastern Arizona, the presence of U.S. troops serving to stimulate settlement along the Sonoita River.[4]

Two years afterward, an aging Colonel Benjamin L. E. Bonneville, Third Infantry, commanding the Department of New Mexico, conducted a twelve-hundred-mile tour of inspection of posts in the territory.[5] A four-day pause at Fort Buchanan convinced Bonneville that Steen's second choice still was "entirely out of position," being nearly forty miles off the mail route, too far from Tucson for economical supply, and too distant "from the homes of the Indians [sic] for a depot."[6] The officers at the post had previously voiced similar views, urging that the garrison be moved to a new site farther northeast on the San Pedro River, so as to offer better protection to both the mail route and a growing number of settlers in that valley.[7]

Even at that early date, the citizens of Arizona were keenly aware of the financial advantages to be gained by exaggerated reports of Indian depredations. Whenever the army could be induced to react to such alarms, the regional economy profited from additional troops, increased army payrolls, and lucrative government contracts for local residents. Stirring the army to action kept the Apaches on the defensive, and Indian troubles, real or fabricated, were good for business.

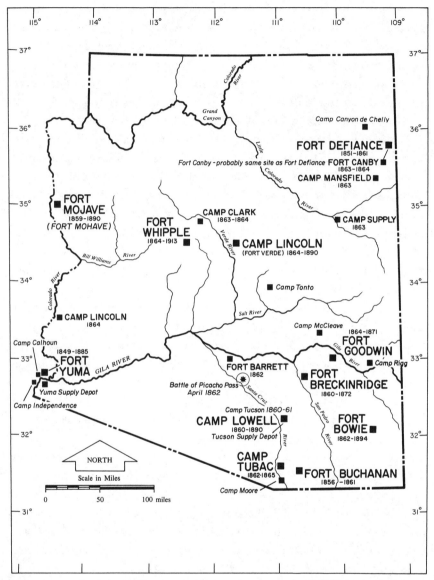

Military posts in Arizona Territory, 1849–1864 (Reprinted from Henry Pickering Walker and Don Bufkin, *Historical Atlas of Arizona,* copyright © 1979 University of Oklahoma Press)

The ploy was aptly demonstrated when civilian pleas for military protection prompted Bonneville to launch an offensive against the Pinal Apaches in fall 1859. During the resulting campaign, Captain Isaac V. D. Reeve and a mixed force of infantry and dragoons made two thrusts into the Apache homeland, killing a small number of warriors and capturing forty-three men, women, and children.

Although the Pinal Expedition was of dubious military value, it served to reinforce Bonneville's opinion that Fort Buchanan was too remote to carry out the army's mission. In fact, to shorten his supply line, Reeve established a depot on the San Pedro at the mouth of Aravaipa Creek, precisely where officers at Fort Buchanan had suggested a new post be constructed to protect the stage line. Accordingly, Captain Ewell led a company of the First Dragoons to the spot the following spring to establish Fort Breckinridge.

While the army focused most of its attention on the Apaches north of the Gila, Bonneville reported that the nearby Chiricahuas "appear to be exceedingly friendly [but] . . . it is impossible to say how long this state of things may last. In case they should break out, the Overland Mail company would require strong escorts to protect it through the Canons, and the settlements would be obliged to form themselves into to [sic] villages to protect themselves."[8]

Prior to the establishment of the Butterfield station in Apache Pass, the Chiricahuas had experienced few contacts with Americans until Ewell, scouting in the Chiricahua Mountains in June 1857, surprised and attacked a rancheria, capturing twenty horses. The next night, the Chiricahuas retaliated by jumping Ewell's camp, recovering most of their stock and, adding salt to the wound, taking two dragoon mounts as well. The next month, Chiricahuas pounced on a small emigrant train as it labored through Apache Pass. The warriors killed two men, wounded two women, and made off with thirty head of cattle. When the incident was reported to Major Steen at Fort Buchanan, he ordered out a detachment of dragoons in pursuit, but to no avail.[9] Beyond these and other minor occurrences, the Chiricahuas initially seemed more curious than hostile toward the Americans, evidenced by their tolerance of a stage station in one of their favorite haunts.

The restraint initially shown by the Chiricahuas was no doubt the influence of their principal chief, Cochise. Born about 1810, either in southeastern Arizona or northern Mexico, Cochise was described by a contemporary who knew him well as "fine a looking Indian as one ever saw. He was about six feet tall and as straight as an arrow, built, from the ground up, as perfect as

Typical Apache rancheria. (Arizona Historical Society/Tucson, AHS Photo Number 6211)

any man could be."[10] Beyond his commanding physical appearance, Cochise possessed intelligence, common sense, and years of experience as a warrior. Those qualities enabled him to rise to the leadership of his people by the late 1850s, just at the critical juncture when the Americans were making significant incursions into Apacheria.[11]

Concurrent with the army's efforts to exercise military authority over the Apaches, the Indian Bureau moved to expand its system of agents into western New Mexico Territory. James L. Collins, superintendent of Indian Affairs in Santa Fe, appointed Dr. Michael Steck as agent for the southern Apaches, with an enormous district extending some six hundred miles from the Pecos River all the way to the Colorado. One of Steck's first actions was to meet with the various bands to determine their dispositions and needs. Collins was particularly concerned about keeping open the U.S. Mail route to California. Well aware of the strategic importance of Apache Pass, he instructed Steck to schedule a talk with the Chiricahuas in December 1858. Steck later reported that the conference went exceedingly well and that no travelers had since been molested along the California road. Cochise, although not mentioned by name, no doubt figured prominently in that meeting.[12]

Cochise and his people apparently remained in the immediate vicinity of Apache Pass during the winter of 1859, camping in Goodwin Canyon, about a mile northwest of the station. That summer the Chiricahuas migrated to higher elevations in the mountains, but returned in October to receive the rations promised by Steck. Although Cochise and his warriors may have joined Mangas Coloradas, chief of the closely affiliated Warm Springs Apaches, on a raid into Sonora during December, few depredations were committed in southeastern Arizona. Those that did occur involved small numbers of horses or mules being stolen from ranches or the mines. As evidence of his continued friendly intentions toward the Americans, Cochise turned over three stolen animals to Steck, at the same time renewing his pledge not to cause any problems for travelers plying the overland road. In Cochise's view, his avoidance of the trail and the occasional return of stolen animals would be sufficient appeasement for the Americans to overlook other transgressions.[13]

However, the situation was becoming precarious. Even though Cochise apparently honored his word not to raid along the stage route, incessant Apache attacks south of the border in Sonora continued, and ever more frequently spilled over into Arizona. At about the same time that Steck rationed the Chiricahuas at Apache Pass, Captain Reeve was ordered to organize a punitive campaign against them in retaliation for recent depredations attributed to Cochise. Reeve was convinced of Cochise's guilt in these matters, yet was hesitant to open a war with the Chiricahuas when the Indian Bureau was professing the government's peaceful intentions. More to the point, Reeve lacked the troops to conduct offensive operations against both the Pinals and the Chiricahuas simultaneously. Thus, military action was temporarily forestalled.

An already smoldering public sentiment turned abruptly against the Chiricahuas during the closing weeks of 1859 and early 1860. Evidence increasingly pointed to Cochise's band as the perpetrators of raids on both sides of the border. In his annual report, Agent Steck was forced to label them as "the most warlike band west of the Rio Grande, and the least reliable."[14] More damning was a report that accused the Chiricahuas of using Apache Pass both as a sanctuary and as a place to dispose of their ill-gotten Mexican booty by trading it to the station-keepers and passengers.

Tensions heightened when Americans killed several Chiricahua warriors in three incidents during the same period. On one occasion, cattleman Thomas Smith pursued a raiding party from his ranch in Sonora northward into U.S. territory. Closely pressed, the Indians turned to fight it out. Smith and his men killed three warriors, forcing the others to flee and abandon the stolen mules. In a second confrontation, a man was shot as he attempted to

steal horses from a ranch near Patagonia. In January 1860, Cochise threatened the stage station at Apache Pass, and shortly thereafter the company
attendant shot a Mexican captive belonging to Cochise. Just as the incensed
Chiricahuas prepared to attack, a westbound freight train ascended the pass.
The Apaches promptly diverted their attention to the more lucrative prey,
killing some of the oxen, but no teamsters, before disappearing into the
mountains. Cochise's disenchantment with Americans further intensified
in the spring when he led an attack on the Dragoon Springs stage station,
closely following that with a raid on the Santa Rita Mining Company's herd
at Tubac. Ewell followed the marauders' trail to their stronghold in the
Chiricahua Mountains, leaving little doubt as to their identity. Late in June,
Ewell arranged a meeting with Cochise at Apache Pass to discuss the theft.
Faced with the accusation, Cochise admitted his band had taken some mules
from the miners at Tubac, whereupon he offered to return only two animals,
claiming the rest either had been traded away in Mexico or eaten by his
people. The effect of these incidents was to engender even further distrust
of the Chiricahuas among the Anglos. With both sides poised for conflict, it
would take only one incident to escalate the situation into a full-fledged war.

During following months, a combination of several events set the stage
for that eventuality. Ewell's aggressive field operations caused a major segment of the Chiricahuas to leave Arizona for what they perceived as the
comparative safety of Sonora. With the Americans growing ever more hostile north of the border, the time seemed right for the Indians to talk peace
with the Mexicans.

Cochise, however, returned to Apache Pass, where he once again assumed
a passive attitude with the Americans. Along with some 150 of his people,
he awaited the outcome of the peace overtures in Mexico. The Chiricahuas
remained at the pass throughout the summer and fall in anticipation of the
annual issue of rations and other material guaranteed by Agent Steck.
Delivery of the semiannual issue, promised in March, did not arrive until
November. At that, the quantity was deficient. Disenchanted with the Indian
Bureau, more of Cochise's people drifted south to join those already being
fed by Mexicans.

Cochise himself considered going to Mexico. So serious was he, in fact,
that he ventured south, sending a small delegation of men, women, and
children ahead to Fronteras to sound out Sonoran officials about the prospects for a peaceful coexistence. Both the journey and the Mexican response
required time. Frustrated by the delay, Cochise became impatient and suspicious

of his old antagonists. Departing without waiting for a response, he led his small band of followers back to the United States to once again take up residence in Apache Pass.[15]

The nature of the depredations attributed to the Chiricahuas in late 1860 altered relations with the Americans. No longer did the incidents merely involve stealing horses, mules, and occasionally cattle. According to the *Sacramento Daily Union*, "They had for several months been growing more and more daring and not only committed repeated depredations upon the settlers but took life when they could do so without incurring loss on their own side."[16] The garrison at Fort Buchanan, composed mostly of infantry at the time, was impotent to prevent the raids or punish the perpetrators. Even when the troops attempted to give chase, the Chiricahuas crossed the international border with impunity. Were that not enough, the Apaches were intimately familiar with the entire region, on both sides of the border, knowing exactly where to find convenient mountain passes and reliable water holes. These combined factors placed the troops at a distinct disadvantage.

Amid the growing turmoil in southeastern Arizona, the Chiricahuas lost perhaps the best friend they had among whites at that time. Michael Steck, a staunch advocate of the Apaches and the only agent they had known up to that time, resigned his position with the Indian Bureau after being elected to the Arizona territorial delegation. As events would later prove, Steck's departure for Washington was particularly unfortunate for relations between the U.S. government and the Chiricahuas.

Apache marauders struck again early the following year. On January 15 they reportedly ran off all the cattle from the Santa Rita Mining Company, and less than two weeks later, attacked John Ward's farm, located in the Sonoita Valley just eleven miles from Fort Buchanan. Two war parties swooped down on the ranch, one driving off a number of cattle, the other scooping up Ward's twelve-year-old adopted son, Felix Martinez, who was herding stock a few hundred yards from the house.[17] Ward himself was absent on business, but upon his return he learned that two men had pursued the raiders for some distance without catching them.

When news of the raid reached Fort Buchanan on January 28, Lieutenant Colonel Pitcairn Morrison, commanding the post, responded by ordering Second Lieutenant George N. Bascom to pursue the Indians and recover the boy if possible. An 1858 graduate of West Point, Bascom had been assigned to the Ninth Infantry as a brevet second lieutenant, a temporary rank accorded graduates when no vacancies existed in the officer corps.

Second Lieutenant George N. Bascom, Seventh Infantry. (Arizona Historical Society/Tucson, AHS Photo Number 28642)

The youthful lieutenant, cultivating a beard to assume a more mature appearance, spent the first ten months of his career at Fort Columbus, New York, awaiting permanent assignment. In April 1859, he was commissioned second lieutenant in the Seventh Infantry and posted in Utah as part of General Albert Sidney Johnston's expedition to quell the Mormons. Following a year of occupation duty, the Seventh was transferred to the Department of New Mexico, with Bascom assigned to isolated Fort Buchanan.[18]

Because Cochise's band had been culpable of some of the depredations in the region, Morrison assumed that the Chiricahuas were involved in the raid on Ward's ranch as well. He therefore directed Bascom to proceed eastward to Apache Pass in search of the boy and the stolen cattle.[19] Had the officers at Fort Buchanan been more familiar with the culture and habits of the Indians in their district, they might not have jumped to the conclusion that Cochise was responsible. The Chiricahuas, by no means innocent, had never been known to take American captives. The White Mountain Apaches, however, habitually kidnapped whites, primarily for use in bartering with other tribes or with the Mexicans. Despite Cochise's attempts to appease the government by professing his friendship and returning token numbers of animals ostensibly stolen by other bands, increasingly frequent raids on the Sonoita and Santa Cruz valleys had hardened the army's resolve toward the Chiricahuas. Morrison made it clear that, if Bascom succeeded in locating Cochise, he was to settle for nothing less than the boy's return, using force if necessary. John Ward, anxious about the boy's fate, accompanied the column as interpreter.[20]

On January 29, Lieutenant Bascom assembled the fifty-four available men from his own Company C, Seventh Infantry. Mounted on mules, they rode eastward.[21] Although Felix Martinez was probably not taken to the Chiricahua Mountains, Bascom elected to follow the Overland Road to Apache Pass. It was common knowledge that Cochise often wintered there, so it was a likely place for Bascom to begin his search. In fact, the army frequently sent patrols to the pass to query any Chiricahuas present about depredations in the region. A march of three days brought Bascom's column to the Butterfield station on February 3. Arriving at midday, Bascom had his men establish camp in the basin some two hundred yards east of the station. There he was greeted by Sergeant Daniel Robinson of his company, commanding an escort with a returning supply train of four wagons that had been sent from the depot at Fort Buchanan to recently established Fort McLane.[22] Robinson had parked his empty wagons off the road about halfway between the station and the spring for convenience in watering his mules. The lieutenant immediately consolidated Robinson's detachment under his command, directing the sergeant to move his men and train down to the new location.[23]

Before returning to the station, Bascom questioned Sergeant Robinson as to the whereabouts of the Chiricahua rancheria, since he had camped near Apache Spring a few days earlier on his way to Fort McLane. Cochise and a few members of his band had come to the soldiers' camp asking for something to eat and indicating their desire to play cards. Thus, Robinson was able to verify that the Chiricahuas were indeed camped in the vicinity of the pass.

While his men busied themselves at the bivouac, Bascom and Ward proceeded to the stage station. There they found three Butterfield employees—station keeper Charles W. Culver, Robert Walsh the hostler, and James F. Wallace, a relief driver awaiting the next coach—who informed him that Cochise was camped approximately two miles distant in Goodwin Canyon.[24] After explaining his mission to the attendants, and probably considering their views of the situation, Bascom sent word by two Apache women (probably Mexican captives) present at the station that he wished to speak with the chief.[25]

Cochise failed to respond immediately to Bascom's request. One historian has speculated that the delay indicated Cochise did not have the Martinez boy. By stalling for time, the chief may have sent runners to attempt to locate him among other bands.[26] It is altogether conceivable that Cochise had a fair idea of the boy's kidnapper. The lieutenant, uncertain of Cochise's motives, returned to the stage station late in the afternoon of February 4 to confer with Wallace and Culver about Cochise's failure to appear. Since the stage men were well acquainted with the Chiricahuas and appeared to be on friendly terms with them, Bascom asked Wallace to contact Cochise personally to reiterate his request for a parley. Wallace, at first hesitant, somewhat reluctantly agreed to go to the Chiricahua camp. Sergeant Robinson recalled that during his absence a Mexican freighter's train passed by their camp and halted for the night "in a ravine off the road some distance beyond us."[27] Wallace returned later that evening to inform Bascom that Cochise agreed to come to the station the next day at noon.

As promised, Cochise, along with his brother, three other male relatives, his wife, and two boys, arrived at Bascom's camp at midday, just as the cooks were serving dinner.[28] The presence of his immediate family members strongly suggests that Cochise sensed no danger in meeting with Bascom. Seated at a table in Bascom's tent, the officer and Ward invited Cochise and his brother, Coyuntura, to join them. The other members of the party, meantime, were conducted to the large conical Sibley tents where the enlisted men messed. Bascom quietly instructed the sergeant of the guard to post men in rear of the tents and not to permit any of the Indians to leave without his permission.[29]

When Bascom began questioning Cochise about the raid on Ward's farm, he denied any involvement, placing the blame instead on the neighboring White Mountain Apaches. As evidence of his good intentions, Cochise offered to try to find Felix, whom the chief suspected was being held at Black Mountain, and to secure his return. However, he cautioned Bascom that such negotiations would require at least ten days. Bascom's report did not clarify the details of the meeting, but he claimed to have consented to

Scene of the Bascom Affair. Ruin of Butterfield stage station lies in the right foreground. Bascom's camp was located at the base of the hill to the left. (Author's collection)

Cochise's terms. Bascom failed to report that he told the chief he and his family would be held hostage, except for Coyuntura, who would be permitted to negotiate for the boy. Cochise and his brother immediately drew their knives and slashed their way out of the tent. That alerted the nearby guards to surround the Indians waiting outside.[30] Coyuntura was immediately confronted by a soldier with fixed bayonet and compelled to surrender. Cochise, exiting through the rear of the tent, leaped through the cordon of startled soldiers and quickly bounded up the nearby hillside. Ward snapped off a pistol shot at the fleeing chief, perhaps wounding him in the leg, while the troops discharged a few more shots as he darted among the bushes and rocks and quickly disappeared. So hasty was Cochise's exodus that he arrived at the top of the hill still grasping his coffee cup.[31]

Earlier that morning, Bascom had directed Sergeant Robinson, whom he had placed in charge of transportation, to take the precaution of rounding up the mules then grazing about the camp. After dinner, Robinson was to drive the mules within the wagon corral, situated "on a little knoll, from which I could see all over the camp."[32] While Bascom entertained the Apaches in camp, Robinson proceeded to carry out his assignment. As Robinson made his way uphill toward the corral, the commotion in the camp caused him to turn just in time to see the Chiricahuas scampering in all directions. Robinson, unarmed at the time, watched in amazement as the remaining warrior, brandishing a knife, ran from the mess tent directly toward him. Close on his heels was a soldier bent on capturing the Apache. The defiant warrior turned occasionally to hurl stones back at his pursuer, until the soldier finally paused to reload. During that momentary interlude, as Robinson continued to watch the little drama unfold, the warrior concealed himself among the boulders. Apparently, the soldier advanced a short distance, then gave up the chase and turned back toward camp. Just then, the Apache jumped out from behind a rock, intent on stabbing the soldier. But, the man turned just in time to fire a fatal Minie ball through the warrior at close range.[33]

Bascom had failed in his attempt to capture Cochise, yet he was not entirely empty-handed. Six Apaches, all or most of them related to Cochise, remained in army custody. Although Bascom remained in a strong position to bargain with the chief, the lieutenant lost no time in improving his defenses. He immediately ordered his men to strike the camp at the wash and to move up to the stage station. The stone walls of the corral, six feet high with embrasures in the stalls, would provide a strong defensive position. The corral also would protect the mules from gunfire and from being stampeded by the Apaches. Bascom saw that a deep ravine approximately one hundred yards south posed an imminent threat to the station. If the Indians were to attack, the terrain would permit warriors to approach that side of the station undetected and to gain protected firing positions at close range. He therefore directed Sergeant Robinson to arrange the wagons end-to-end in a semicircle encompassing the south side of the station. Bascom further improved the barricade by having his men fill empty grain sacks with earth, then stack them around the inside perimeter of the line of wagons to form a breastwork high enough for the men to assume prone or kneeling positions from which to fire. While the defenses were being readied, other soldiers herded the stock to the spring for water, and filled all available kegs and canteens. Those preparations, along with an ample supply of musket ammunition and twenty days' rations, prepared the troops to withstand a siege if necessary. Apache signal fires observed on the neighboring peaks that night did not bode well for a peaceful resolution.

The following morning, Tuesday, February 5, a strong force of Chiricahuas assembled on the prominence several hundred yards south of the beleaguered station. After a brief demonstration, most of the warriors dispersed, leaving only a small party bearing a white flag. Bascom acknowledged the gesture by raising a white handkerchief, whereupon one warrior, bearing the flag, approached the station within earshot. Speaking in Spanish, the warrior called out that Cochise wished to talk with the soldier chief. Bascom arranged for the meeting to take place midway between the wagon corral and the nearest bend of the ravine south of the station. Each leader would be permitted to bring three men, all unarmed.

At the appointed time, apparently not long after the initial contact, Bascom cautiously stepped outside the barricade. He was accompanied by Ward and Sergeant William A. Smith, displaying a white flag. Robinson, also a member of the party, was assigned to keep watch over the adjacent ravine during the conference to prevent an ambush. Before leaving the station, Bascom instructed those left behind to stay within the defensive perimeter and keep close watch on the surrounding area.

Cochise and White Mountain chief Francisco, along with two others, cautiously emerged from the ravine to meet Bascom. Dispensing with ceremony, the officer brusquely asked Cochise what he wanted. The chief responded with "a long harangue about the treatment he had received in our camp, and made a strong appeal for the release of his captive friends."[34] Bascom responded that the captives would be released as soon as the Martinez boy was returned unharmed to his father. During the meeting, Sergeant Robinson spotted several Apaches moving up through the lower part of the ravine with bunches of bear grass tied to their backs and shoulders as camouflage. Robinson closely eyed the warriors, but did not react since both parties were under flags of truce.

At that juncture, two of the station men, Culver and Wallace, defied Bascom's instructions by approaching the conferring parties, apparently to intercede in the discussion. (Walsh evidently ventured out only partway.) The two women who had been at the station when Bascom arrived appeared at the edge of the ravine, somewhat farther up from the site of the meeting. Bascom ordered the company employees back immediately, for if they were captured, he could not exchange his prisoners for them. The pair continued toward the ravine, ignoring Bascom's instructions. Juanita, the younger of the two women, was seen communicating by sign language to Wallace as they approached. The girl, who may have had a romantic relationship with the driver, immediately embraced Wallace, then led him closer to the brink of the ravine. Several warriors then sprang up and, after a brief struggle, dragged both

Wallace and Culver into the gulch.[35] Culver was shot during the scuffle, but managed to break free and fled toward the station. At the same instant, Francisco dropped his flag and, pointing to Bascom's party, yelled "*Aqui!, aqui!*" Bascom commanded the men at the station to fire, and pulled down his white flag as Apaches hiding nearby fired a volley. Both sides opened fire as the lieutenant and his men turned and sprinted toward the station, taking an oblique course to avoid friendly fire. An Apache bullet nicked Sergeant Smith, but with help he was able to reach the station. Walsh was not so fortunate. Just as the hostler reached the station, a bullet smashed through his head, killing him instantly.[36] Both sides kept up intermittent firing throughout the remainder of the day, with no further casualties among Bascom's men.

All was quiet as the sun gradually illuminated Apache Pass the next morning. The soldiers at the station remained vigilant, nevertheless. Bascom took the precaution of sending out a patrol to reconnoiter the broken terrain south of the station. Ascending the hill, the party was able to scan the ravines used by the Apaches to approach the station the previous day, but they saw no signs of Indians. Robinson, meanwhile ordered to secure water for the teams, led another reconnaissance toward Apache Spring. En route, he detached one soldier to take position atop the hill on the left, known today as Overlook Ridge. From his vantage point, the sentinel could see both the spring and the station, enabling Robinson to communicate by signal that the way was clear to send the herd. Prudently, Bascom sent only half the animals at one time because the water supply was limited and, should the Apaches attack, he thought it better to lose half the herd than all of it. The sentinel was instructed to fire his rifle to warn Bascom if Indians appeared. But Cochise apparently wished to avoid further trouble, at least until he could again attempt to negotiate, and the day passed without incident.

While Robinson and his detail were tending the herd, Cochise appeared on a hill near the station. He informed Bascom that he would exchange Wallace, whom he displayed in full view with bound hands and a rope about his neck, along with sixteen stolen government mules for the Apache prisoners held at the station. Bascom replied that he would agree, on the condition Cochise would return Ward's boy as part of the deal. The parley ended inconclusively.[37]

Bascom could not have realized that events then unfolding were about to undermine his bargaining position. Cochise had posted lookouts at both the east and west ends of the pass. Knowing that a stage would be passing through that night, he directed the warriors to prepare an ambush in the narrowest part of Siphon Canyon. His men placed a barricade across the road to halt the coach and stacked hay nearby that could be set afire to illuminate the scene for more accurate shooting. Fortunately, the driver was running several hours ahead of schedule, which saw the coach enter the canyon during midafternoon. Seeing no need to remain at the ambush site during the day, the Apaches had departed with the intention of returning later that evening. The driver, A. B. Culver, brother of the station attendant, circumvented the barricade and proceeded to the station, arriving there with his passengers at about four o'clock. Upon learning of the confrontation with Cochise, Culver quickly decided to remain there under the protection of the troops.[38]

Late in the day, Cochise had Wallace scribble a note to Bascom stating that he now had three additional prisoners—Sam Whitfield, William Sanders, and Frank Brunner. These men had been with a train of five wagons loaded with flour eastbound for the Pinos Altos mines. The unsuspecting freighters had crossed the summit of the pass and gone into camp about two miles west of the station. After darkness fell, Cochise's warriors surrounded the wagons and pounced on the party without warning, instantly overwhelming the eleven men. Six of the Mexican teamsters were killed in the brief struggle. The Apaches summarily lashed two survivors to the wheels of the wagons before setting the vehicles ablaze. Cochise spared the three white men only because of their potential for strengthening his bargaining position with Bascom. His dictated note, stating that he would come to talk again the next day, was placed on a bush within sight of the stage station where it was sure to be found by the soldiers.[39]

The eastbound mail coach rattled along the winding road as it descended the pass between midnight and one o'clock on the morning of February 7. The nine occupants aboard the stage, no doubt looking forward to a respite at the station just ahead, were as yet unaware of the momentous events unfolding at Apache Pass. Warriors lying in wait near the smoldering wagon train unleashed a volley of shots at close range, one ball striking the driver, twenty-five-year-old King Lyon, in the leg. One of the mules fell dead from a bullet as another animal was seriously wounded. The passengers tumbled from the coach and prepared to defend themselves, although in the darkness they could see only the muzzle flashes of the Apaches' guns. After the initial fusillade of a dozen or more shots, however, the tribesmen vanished into the night. To their horror, the travelers discovered that they were in the midst of the debris and corpses left from the ambushed wagon train, the charred remains of the two teamsters still suspended in chains from the wheels. Wasting no time, some of the men immediately cut the harness from the dead mule, while others loaded the wounded Lyon into the stage. Conductor Nelson J. Davis mounted the box and hastily drove on toward the station. All along the way, Apaches continued to lurk in the brush, placing boulders in the road now and then to impede the stage, and occasionally firing a shot or two from concealment. The coach, with its passengers somewhat the worse for wear, but with no further casualities, pulled up to the station about an hour later.[40]

The rest of the day passed uneventfully. Cochise was concerned with moving his women, children, and elders farther south into the protective sanctuary of the Chiricahuas. Since the army had not cooperated in exchanging his people, the chief saw no alternative but to take them by force. To accomplish that, he induced Francisco and his band to join him, as well as Mangas Coloradas's band of Mimbres Apaches that also happened to be in the area. A plan was devised to decoy some of the troops away from Apache Pass Station, then attack the remainder with a second force concealed near the station. As was customary, the Apaches staged appropriate ceremonies and dances to invoke the spirits to ensure success of the venture.

Back at the station, things had become decidedly crowded with both Bascom's and Robinson's detachments and the passengers from the two stages, not to mention dozens of mules and horses. Complicating matters were the two wounded men, Culver and Lyon. They required medical assistance, and the nearest place to find it was Fort Buchanan. At least five soldiers volunteered to ride the dangerous gauntlet to the post to summon a doctor and to report the recent events at Apache Pass. Superintendent Buckley also sent A. B. Culver to go through to Tucson to alert the company about the delayed mail. The couriers, mounted on the available saddle mules, left the station in pairs at intervals before and after midnight on February 7, making their way cross-country to avoid Apaches certain to be lurking along the road. As a further precaution, they tied grain sacks around the mules' hooves to deaden the sound of iron shoes clattering on the rocks.[41]

Bascom made plans to water the animals on the 8th. Snow had fallen during the previous night, so First Sergeant James J. Huber, commanding the detail, delayed until nearly noon before venturing toward the spring. He hand-picked fifteen reliable men, including Sergeant Robinson, as a guard for the operation. Along the way, a sentinel was again posted on Overlook

Ridge to relay signals to the station. Noting that there were no signs of Indians in the newly fallen snow, Huber indicated to the soldier above to notify the men at the station to release the herd. Huber sent four or five men into the ravine to assist with the watering, while he and the rest of the detachment posted themselves on the knob just above the spring. From that vantage point, Huber could overlook the broken area forming the head of Siphon Canyon opposite his position. As the army mules under an escort of teamsters came trotting up the trail toward the spring, Sergeant Robinson was alarmed to see that the entire herd, including the Butterfield animals, had been turned loose. One of the extra stage drivers, Moses Lyon, rode ahead of the herd to guide the leaders to the spring. The plan had been to keep the company teams at the corral until the army mules returned. But, it was too late to try to turn them back.

Huber and his men had no sooner gained their position near the spring when they spotted some two hundred dismounted Apache warriors jogging northward down a ravine less than a quarter of a mile away. "At the gait they were coming," Sergeant Robinson later recalled, "it seemed as if they intended to sweep everything before them, both men and animals."[42] The troops near the crest of Overlook Ridge immediately opened fire on the Indians below, causing the war party to diverge eastward and take cover in rough terrain. Meantime, the soldiers reloaded their muskets and prepared for another assault. When the Apaches emerged once again, the troops leveled a volley at them. But the warriors kept advancing and, without firing a shot in return, gained the hill immediately south of the spring. Being on higher ground than Huber's men, the warriors suddenly had the advantage. Huber therefore ordered his men to fall back, uphill, to a rock outcropping about fifty yards away.[43]

As they were doing so, Sergeant Robinson darted to the brink of the hill overlooking the spring, calling out to the men below to drive the herd back to the station. A Chiricahua marksman across the ravine fired a shot that struck the sergeant in the right leg, knocking him to the ground. The soldiers returned fire overhead, while the incapacitated Robinson attempted to conceal himself under a nearby bush. The skirmish continued as the Apaches, seeing Robinson's vulnerability, tried to finish him. As he lay helpless and exposed, bullets kicked up snow and rocks all about him, some ripping through the skirts of his overcoat. Only when the fire of the tribesmen shifted to the herders below were Robinson's comrades able to rescue him.

Shooting as they bounded down the hillside, the Apaches mortally wounded Moses Lyon and drove off most of the mules, including forty-two head belonging to the army and another fourteen from the Overland Mail. Just then, Bascom sent out a relief force from the station. According to Daniel Robinson, Bascom had delayed sending out reinforcements because other warriors had been sighted on the ridge west of the station during the action. The lieutenant was concerned, and rightfully so, that another attack might be launched from that direction. Only when that threat failed to materialize did the lieutenant send out help to the herd guard. Huber's men, all of whom were dismounted, skirmished with the Indians through the hills for about a mile, reportedly killing five warriors by the time Huber eventually abandoned the chase.[44]

The messengers, meantime, made their way safely out of the pass. They parted company at Dragoon Springs Station the following morning, the soldiers pushing on to Fort Buchanan, arriving that evening. Culver continued to Tucson, and by changing horses at each station along the way, was able to make the entire 125-mile trip from Apache Pass in about twenty-four hours.[45]

There being no cavalry at Fort Buchanan, the assistant surgeon, Bernard John Dowling Irwin, volunteered to lead a picked detachment of Seventh Infantrymen to the relief of the beleaguered garrison at Apache Pass. As a medical officer, Irwin was under no obligation to assume that risk. However, the nearest dragoons were posted at Fort Breckenridge, a hundred miles to the northeast. To await an escort from that post would needlessly delay medical attention for Bascom's wounded men. Irwin selected eleven men from Company H to augment the couriers and, with his detachment mounted on mules, left the post the following morning.[46] Accompanying Irwin was James "Paddy" Graydon, an adventuresome ex-soldier residing in the area. Meanwhile, Lieutenant Colonel Morrison sent word of Bascom's situation to the commanding officer at Fort Breckenridge.

Irwin's detachment reached Dragoon Spring by nightfall, having ridden some sixty-five miles that day. Next morning, the 10th, he pressed on across Sulphur Springs Valley, east of the Dragoon Mountains. Along the way, Irwin spotted a dust cloud some miles away from the stage road. Assuming it was made by Apaches, he diverged from his course to investigate. It indeed proved to be three White Mountain Apaches driving a small herd of cattle and a couple of horses stolen in a recent raid. When the Apaches saw the soldiers, they made a run for the nearest mountains. Irwin gave chase for six or seven miles, finally catching up and surrounding the Apaches, one of whom proved to be a chief. Irwin then proceeded on to Apache Pass, with his captives and the cattle, arriving there later that day.[47]

Meantime, the courier from Fort Buchanan rode into Fort Breckenridge to alert the garrison that Bascom was surrounded at Apache Pass and that the U. S. Mail had been intercepted in both directions. First Lieutenant Isaiah N. Moore, commanding the post, immediately assembled a force of seventy men from Companies D and G, First Dragoons. Second Lieutenant Richard S. C. Lord served as second in command.

All remained quiet at Apache Pass after the skirmish on the 8th. Taking no unnecessary chances, Bascom waited until after dark each night before sending water parties to the spring. Had he sent out scouting parties, he might have learned that the Apaches had already left the pass. In his defense, however, he had only infantry at his disposal and, after the raid, too few animals to mount a sufficient scouting force to defend itself. Consequently, the troops waited and watched the nearby hills until the 10th, when Irwin and his odd cavalcade of mule-mounted doughboys, Indians, and cattle appeared descending the hill west of the station. The joyous mood at the station was dampened, however, when Irwin confirmed that a wagon train had indeed been destroyed just west of the station.

On February 14, the troops at the pass were further cheered by the arrival of Moore's dragoons. Even after the arrival of Irwin's mounted men, Bascom had inexplicably taken no action to examine the immediate vicinity to determine the whereabouts of the Apaches. Moore, now the senior officer present, immediately organized a reconnaissance-in-force, comprising all the dragoons and forty of Bascom's infantrymen. Leaving the station early on the 16th, the troops scoured the surrounding mountains for three days. Initially, they found no fresh Apache signs, but discovered a rancheria of ten to fifteen lodges on the third day out. Although the camp had been abandoned a few days previous, Moore took the precaution of burning the lodges and other property. Later, as the troops passed through the hills west of the station, they disturbed a flock of vultures from one side of the stage road. Upon investigation, they found the badly deteriorated remains of four human bodies. William Oury, who accompanied the troops, identified the gold fillings in the teeth in one of the skeletons as those of James Wallace. The others were presumed to be those of the three men taken by the Apaches at the wagon train. Moore sent a detail back to the station for spades, while the officers looked about for a suitable site to bury the men. They selected

William S. Oury, division superintendent for the Butterfield Overland Mail. (Arizona Historical Society/Tucson, AHS Photo Number 1932)

a spot in a small oak-studded basin north of the stage road, "and here sadly and silently we committed their mutilated bodies to mother earth, and upon the countenances of those who surrounded that sacred spot, could be read the resolve that the red fiends should pay for their barbarity."[48]

As the column wended its way back to the station, murmurs in the ranks developed into open propositions concerning the fate of the Indian captives. William Oury remembered that the comments began among the enlisted men and spread to the officers. Surgeon Irwin later claimed personal credit for suggesting that the hostages be hanged in reprisal for the murders of Wallace and the others. By the time the column arrived back at the station, the fate of the Indians was cast—they would be hanged from trees near the grave of the white men. Lieutenant Moore approached Bascom, in charge of the prisoners, stating his intention to execute the six men. Bascom objected, stating that the prisoners were his responsibility and he would be the one censured should they be killed. Moore rejoined that as the senior officer, the ultimate responsibility was his. Bascom conceded the point.

The tribesmen gone and nothing more to be accomplished at the pass, the combined commands departed the next morning. (The two coaches left the day before, February 18.) The column marched up the road to the west, halting near the mass grave of the murdered men. There, the warriors were quickly herded to a stand of oaks and summarily hanged as the woman and boy watched. The bodies were left swinging in the wind to ensure that Cochise would find them. The troops proceeded to the San Pedro, where Moore turned downstream toward his post, while Bascom continued to Fort Buchanan.

The Bascom Affair marked a significant turning point in relations between the Americans and the Chiricahua Apaches. It can be speculated that, if Lieutenant George Bascom not been duplicitous with Cochise at the outset, subsequent events might have been entirely different. Similarly, we now know that Felix Martinez, who later became an army scout called "Mickey Free," was alive and well and, presumably, Cochise could have produced the boy as proof of his good intentions for keeping peace with the whites. Patience on Bascom's part, while maintaining a constructive dialogue with Cochise, might have produced the desired result, though no one can ever be certain. Likewise, Cochise might have avoided fueling the situation during his second meeting with Bascom by not abducting Wallace and ambushing the soldiers.

Bascom is faulted for his apparent intransigence in negotiating with Cochise. To the latter's credit, the chief did make repeated attempts to communicate, even if he was not forthcoming with the one thing Bascom demanded— Felix Martinez. Too, there can be no question that Cochise escalated hostilities when he attacked the herd guard, and later killed the stage men. If the future of Apache-American relations was not cast prior to Cochise killing his white hostages, it certainly was after that moment. The officers responsible for hanging the warriors not only demonstrated a deplorable lack of good judgment, they allowed themselves to degenerate to the same level of savagery they perceived in Cochise. The murder of those innocent individuals destroyed forever any chance the army still may have had to recover Felix Martinez, whose welfare was lost sight of entirely in the seesaw of events. One thing is certain. The momentous events at Apache Pass in 1861 portended a bitterly hostile association between the Chiricahuas and Americans for the next twenty-five years.

CHAPTER 2

The March of the California Column

The army's confrontation with Cochise at Apache Pass could hardly have occurred at a more crucial moment. For months, the South had been threatening secession from the Union and early in 1861 talk turned to action as southern states began breaking away in rapid succession to form the Confederacy. Of critical importance to the Southwest was the Texas legislature's vote to secede on January 28, followed by public ratification six weeks later.

In months to follow, southern officials cast an eye to the West, a region of vital interest to the Confederacy. The Pacific Coast afforded advantageous access for Confederate shipping. Not only could the South maintain open trade for critical military supplies, but it would be virtually impossible for the Federals to impose a naval blockade of coastlines on opposite sides of the continent. Moreover, the South needed capital and the southwestern territories exhibited great potential for mineral wealth. The gold fields in California were already well established, and in 1858 Georgia prospectors discovered significant deposits along Colorado's Cherry Creek, causing a new flood of miners, many of them southerners, to the Intermountain West. Other strikes in Nevada portended a new bonanza there, while comparatively small numbers of prospectors searching the country south of the Gila were reporting rich deposits of silver near Tucson and Yuma. However, like the Spanish before them, they found that the Apaches made retrieving the precious ore a risky business. Regardless of the gamble, the opportunity for bolstering the treasury of the cash-starved Confederacy was irresistible.

Also motivating the South was the tantalizing prospect of capturing all of the military armaments and other supplies deposited at the posts throughout the Southwest. New Mexico alone boasted some fifteen military posts, in addition to several garrisoned towns. Although many of the forts were small and isolated, places like Fort Craig, Albuquerque, and Santa Fe offered major caches of materiel. The grand prize was Fort Union, anchoring the lower end of the Santa Fe Trail and supplying all of New Mexico. The acquisition of such enormous stockpiles would be of great benefit to Confederate forces in the West.

Looming war clouds spelled the end of the "Jackass Mail." Northerners had chafed over the selection of the Oxbow Route since its inception four years earlier. Concern that the mails would become a target for the disruption of communications with the west coast was borne out when southern elements began destroying equipment, animals, and bridges belonging to the Butterfield Overland Mail Company. Such activity effectively stopped regular through-mail service to and from California by early in March. The forced cessation of Butterfield service only added weight to the arguments already being voiced in Congress for the adoption of a central route across the Rocky Mountains. Legislation passed in March 1861 amended the overland mail contract to essentially follow the Oregon-California Trail from St. Joseph, Missouri, to Fort Bridger, where the coaches diverged to Salt Lake City and Sacramento. Butterfield suspended service over the Oxbow Route effective March 2, and when the last eastbound coach arrived in Missouri less than three weeks later, the southern route was effectively abandoned.[1]

The decision to alter the primary mail route threatened to leave southern California without any service whatever. To correct the oversight, George Giddings, through the influence of Postmaster General Montgomery Blair, secured a special contract for mail service over the southern route, from San Antonio to Los Angeles, beginning April 1. George and brother James immediately boarded a coach to Franklin for the purpose of organizing their new operation. The two completed their business at that key point a few days later and, arrangements having been made with the Butterfield company to purchase some of its unneeded stock and coaches on the eastern end of the line, George turned back to Fort Stockton to complete the negotiations. James continued west to inspect the stations along the line and to organize the new leg from Yuma to Los Angeles.[2]

Giddings may have been only vaguely aware of what had transpired recently in Apache Pass, but the news in Franklin (later called El Paso) was that the mood of the Indians in southern New Mexico had turned ugly. His business would not wait, however, so Giddings joined forces with two Butterfield employees, Michael Neiss and Sam Nealy, also traveling west to gather the company's stock and other assets for the shift to the central route. Just at dawn on April 28, the coach approached the station at Stein's Peak, near the present-day New Mexico–Arizona border.[3] Cochise and a number of his warriors had laid an ambush and opened fire at close range from a stone breastwork alongside the road. The first volley killed Briggs, the driver, and his conductor, Anthony Elder. With no one at the reins, the team bolted forward, running full-speed for a mile and a half until the stage wrecked near the foot of the mountain. Cochise purportedly scoffed later that Giddings and Neiss "had died like poor sick women," but that Nealy put up a fight, killing three Chiricahuas.[4]

That was only the beginning of Apache depredations along the stage road. Within a month after the attack at Stein's Pass (also known as Doubtful Canyon), Cochise led raids against nearly every station east of Tucson, including those at Mimbres River, Cow Springs, Soldier's Farewell, Barney's Station, Apache Pass, Dragoon Springs, and San Pedro Crossing. At San Simon Station, twenty-one miles east of Apache Pass, Indians ran off a herd of company and government mules, along with several horses belonging to Butterfield employees. John Jones, the plucky station-keeper, gave chase with five men, killing three warriors in a running fight and recovering most of the stock. Particularly devastating was an attack at Cooke's Spring, where Cochise and his men first destroyed the station, then prepared an ambush for the incoming stage. The Apaches wiped out the entire party of a dozen white men. During a period of just a few weeks, Cochise's warriors killed at least thirty men, destroyed six stagecoaches and tons of forage, and ran off hundreds of horses and mules. They also acquired dozens of Sharps rifles, Colt revolvers, and other firearms taken as booty from the Overland Mail Company stations.[5]

While the Apaches plundered the mail route, talk of secession was rife among the civilian populace in New Mexico. Only fifteen years had passed since the Southwest had been annexed by the United States, and during that time Democratic officials in the territory had used their positions to influence the residents to embrace slavery. Miguel Otero, the territorial representative in Washington, blatantly encouraged his constituents to support secession. Once the Union began unraveling, southern sympathizers met in Mesilla on March 16, 1861, to pledge their loyalty to the Confederate States of America. Those in the western part of the territory held a subsequent convention in Tucson in August. Those assemblies swore to resist federal authority over the territory and proceeded to elect a delegate to the Confederate Congress. Although the attendees purported to represent a majority of the populace, their claim later proved to be exaggerated.

The far western territories may have had little political impact on the coming war; nevertheless, Federal military officials, occupied with events in the East, failed to appreciate their strategic value. Illustrating this was Secretary of War Simon Cameron's decision early in 1861 to withdraw most of the regulars from New Mexico Territory. However, the importance of the area was not lost on the secretary of the interior, Caleb Smith, who no doubt had a keen appreciation for the transportation routes to California, the mineral potential on that enormous region, as well as the Indian situation in the West. Although Cameron noted Smith's views, he nevertheless concurred with the army's decision to transfer 3,400 soldiers to eastern commands.

In Texas, meanwhile, the federal military establishment crumbled during February when General David E. Twiggs, commanding that department, surrendered the Union forces throughout the state. Twiggs, whose sympathies lay with the South, used Washington's lack of direction as the excuse for his treasonous act. Although most of the troops escaped, or were paroled on their oath not to take up arms against the South, huge amounts of arms, ammunition, clothing, food, and other supplies fell into the hands of the Confederates.

The roster of southern-born regular army officers joining the Confederacy that spring included Henry Hopkins Sibley, a native of Louisiana and a West Point graduate. Sibley subsequently served in the Second Dragoons, distinguishing himself during the Mexican War and earning a brevet to major for his conduct at Medelin. He spent the 1850s campaigning against Indians on the New Mexico frontier, gaining a familiarity with the region that was later to prove useful. On May 13, 1861, Sibley resigned his commission and rode east to meet with Confederate States President Jefferson Davis to promote a bold plan for conquering New Mexico.[6]

Meeting with Davis in Richmond, Sibley outlined a strategy calling for the organization of a Texas brigade, utilizing captured Federal stores already on hand there, with himself in command. Sibley pointed out the many advantages to the Confederacy. Beyond gaining a Pacific outlet, mineral resources, and military supplies, the South stood to extend slavery into the new territory, perhaps even into California. Sibley's personal plans actually extended beyond the conquest of New Mexico Territory, though he apparently did not confide his ultimate goal to Davis. Once he captured the territorial capital of Santa Fe, and forced the Federals to abandon Fort Union, Sibley intended to march on the gold fields of Colorado. Even though he assumed that the majority of the miners there were loyal to the Union, it was reported that as many as seventy-five hundred secessionists resided in the territory and could be counted upon to support the invasion. Then, living off the land, Sibley's army would turn west to capture Salt Lake City. Presumably, the disaffected Saints would be only too happy to help force the Federals out of Utah, considering that they had endured an army of occupation since 1858. In the end, Sibley would crown his grandiose plan with the seizure of California.

Sibley's scheme was doomed by several factors. After leaving Texas, he proposed subsisting his troops on whatever the Rio Grande Valley afforded. Although the region supported some subsistence farming, it was by no means capable of supporting three thousand troops and their animals. Sibley also seriously miscalculated the sentiments of Hispanic New Mexicans. His service in the territory should have convinced him that they had by no means forgotten the Texan invasion of 1841 and continued to harbor an intense hatred for their expansionist neighbors. Even had those conditions not existed, Henry Hopkins Sibley personally lacked the leadership and organizational skills to carry off the plan. His addiction to alcohol and his general ill health by that time seriously detracted from his ability to function effectively as a field commander. Nevertheless, President Davis saw little risk or financial investment in the proposal. At the very least, it promised to secure the all-season southern route to California, and would open the way for the South to eventually construct a transcontinental railroad.[7]

While Sibley promoted his campaign in Richmond, events were already unfolding in New Mexico that were to affect the impending invasion, and the future of the territory. As summer approached, the California mail was in disarray as the result of the change in contractors and Giddings's precarious hold on a route spanning both Union and Confederate territories. Compounding the situation were Cochise's unrelenting raids all along the line across southern New Mexico and southeastern Arizona. Canby's far-flung garrisons were unable to conduct offensive operations. Even the forts were not immune from attack. In June, for example, Cochise and twenty-five warriors struck Fort Buchanan, driving off most of the post's beef herd. Lieutenant Bascom led a detachment in pursuit and, after a thirty-mile chase, killed four Indians, but failed to recover the stock.

In June, Canby learned of the mobilization of Texas forces. Despite the intensity of Apache raiding, he considered the threat of invasion from the south a greater danger than that posed by the Indians. Were the Confederates to capture the territory, the Indian situation would be of little consequence. He therefore ordered the abandonment of Forts Buchanan, Breckinridge, and McLane in July, and those garrisons were redeployed to Forts Fillmore and Craig to bolster defenses on the Rio Grande. At the same time, Canby petitioned the territorial governors of New Mexico and Colorado to raise eleven companies of volunteers to reinforce the remaining twenty-four hundred regulars still at his disposal.

The Confederate vanguard made its appearance at Franklin on July 23 when Lieutenant Colonel John R. Baylor and the Second Texas Mounted Rifles occupied abandoned Fort Bliss. Baylor moved quickly on Fort Fillmore, upriver some forty miles, just below Mesilla. Major Isaac Lynde, commanding the post, confronted Baylor's Texans in a brief skirmish, but quickly retired within his defensive works. Lynde, whose courage, if not his loyalties, have been questioned, grew faint of heart and summarily evacuated Fort Fillmore for a retreat to Fort Stanton, 150 miles northeast. When Baylor's mounted men overtook the Federals, Lynde immediately surrendered his superior force of eleven companies and two artillery pieces.[8] The Confederates thus scored an easy victory, thereby gaining control of the Rio Grande Valley below Fort Craig. That turn of events, combined with the earlier abandonment of the posts in southeastern Arizona, confirmed the Confederate claim to southern New Mexico Territory, and cleared the way for Sibley's intended thrust northward.

Meantime, Southern sympathizers met in Tucson to proclaim Arizona for the Confederacy. The fact that the decision rested on the votes of only sixty-eight citizens hardly made a compelling statement about the sentiments of the general populace. It nevertheless encouraged Baylor to declare on August 1, 1861, that all of the area south of the thirty-fourth parallel from Texas to California, be designated as the Territory of Arizona. Baylor imposed martial law over the new territory and established himself as governor.

Lynde's defeat, coupled with Baylor's declaration, roused the citizens of New Mexico from their complacency about the war. The governor published a proclamation calling the citizens to fight for the Union and, just a day after Baylor declared martial law, Canby requested additional volunteer companies from both New Mexico and Colorado. When the units failed to recruit up to strength as rapidly as Canby had hoped, he wrote to Army Headquarters to request that the regulars still posted in the territory be left there as the reliable core of his forces. Army Headquarters in Washington, finally awakening to the reality that the Confederates stood a very real chance of annexing the entire Southwest, consented to his request.

While Baylor secured his gains on the Rio Grande, Sibley was busy organizing his brigade in San Antonio. During August, he assembled three regiments of cavalry and a battery of mountain howitzers for the invasion of New Mexico. The men were mustered into service early that fall, briefly trained, and then set in motion on the road to Franklin during October and November.[9] When Sibley reached abandoned Fort Thorn on January 27, 1862, he detached a company of cavalry under the command of Captain Sherod Hunter to march west to Tucson.[10] As far as anyone knew, there were no Federal forces between the Rio Grande and Fort Yuma on the Colorado River. Sibley saw an opportunity to consolidate Confederate authority over the region, and at the same time protect his supply line by posting Hunter's company at Tucson. Hunter would be in a position to confirm whether or not the citizens in the Santa Cruz Valley were indeed pro-Southern, and he could help protect the "Jackass Mail," which had been under contract with the Confederate government since August.[11]

The Confederate government also seriously underestimated the degree of Union sentiment in California. Most of the state's population resided in the north after the 1849 gold discovery. Those who had responded to the siren song of quick riches were primarily from the northern and northeastern states. On the eve of the Civil War, consequently, virtually all communities of any size raised companies of pro-Union Home Guards, to be ready to answer the national government's call should it come. Shortly after the firing on Fort Sumter, Secretary of War Cameron assessed the Californians to provide an infantry regiment and five companies of cavalry to defend the vital central overland mail route. A month later, perhaps in reaction to the Texan threat to New Mexico, Cameron increased the assessment by an additional four regiments of infantry and one of cavalry.

Since few regulars remained on the West Coast, the California volunteer forces assumed even greater importance. The secretary of war thus suggested to the California governor that Major James Carleton, a regular officer of twenty years' experience, be appointed to command the First Infantry, California Volunteers. Carleton began his career as a member of the Maine militia during the international boundary dispute with Canada in 1838–39. His natural aptitude for and attraction to military life prompted him to apply for a commission in the Regular Army, and he was soon wearing the straps of a second lieutenant in the First Dragoons. Serving under Edwin Vose Sumner at the Cavalry School of Practice, Carleton quickly became a stern practitioner

General James H. Carleton. (Courtesy of the Museum of New Mexico, neg. no. 22938)

of Old Army discipline. By 1842 he was posted at Fort Leavenworth, where he joined Colonel Stephen Watts Kearny's expedition up the Oregon Trail to South Pass in 1844–45. Two years later, he participated in the invasion of Mexico. Returning to the plains after the war, Carlton led patrols down the Santa Fe Trail and, still later, was selected to analyze reports rendered by American military observers of the Crimean War. When the Civil War opened, Carleton was stationed at Los Angeles. Coincidentally, the Department of the Pacific was commanded by his old dragoon comrade, Sumner, who further supported Secretary Cameron's recommendation that Carleton head the volunteers. The California governor yielded to the pressure by confirming Carleton's appointment on August 19.[12]

Another old regular, Colonel George Wright, Ninth Infantry, was promoted to the rank of brigadier general of volunteers the following month, and placed in command of the District of Southern California. Wright, a Vermonter and an 1822 graduate of West Point, had compiled a distinguished record as an infantry officer in both the Seminole War and the Mexican War, earning three brevets to higher rank for his gallant conduct.[13]

Sumner formulated a plan to make a thrust across Arizona to counter the Southern incursion into New Mexico. But he had no sooner begun training his troops when he was summoned to Washington to assume new duties. Wright was selected to fill his vacancy as department commander, while Carleton was elevated to command the District of Southern California. Command of the First California Infantry fell to a Mexican War veteran, Lieutenant Colonel Joseph Rodman West, whose shiny pate prompted the men in the ranks to refer to him as "the Bald Eagle." The regiment rendez-voused at Oakland to begin training.

Although the California Volunteers had been organized primarily to protect the central overland mail route, secessionist activity in the southern part of the state dictated that the First be sent down the coast to reinforce Union authority. Assembling his troops at a camp of instruction near Los Angeles, Carleton introduced his citizen soldiers to a rigorous schedule of Regular Army training. Drilling often lasted up to eight hours a day, with officers of the guard required to conduct grand rounds nightly. Carleton also man-dated that officers conduct frequent inspections, a duty he often performed personally, and insisted that the officers maintain a proper gulf between themselves and their men.[14]

News of the Confederate occupation of southern New Mexico and Ari-zona lent purpose and urgency to Carleton's relentless training schedule. Coincident with Sibley's arrival in El Paso in December, Army Headquarters granted General Wright permission to organize an expedition to march toward the Rio Grande, via Fort Yuma, to fall on the Confederate flank, thereby cutting Sibley's supply line. The other part of Wright's dual mission was to reopen the southern mail route by reclaiming the posts that had either been abandoned or captured by the Texans.[15] To accomplish this, Carleton was directed to organize a column comprised of the First California Infantry, a five-company battalion of the First California Cavalry under Lieutenant Colonel Edward E. Eyre; and Company B, Second California Cavalry. The brigade was to be augmented by Light Battery A, Third U.S. Artillery, which had been stationed on the coast prior to the war and had not been transferred to the eastern theater of operations. The strength of the brigade totaled approximately fifteen hundred men.[16]

As Carleton mustered his forces, yet undetected by the Confederates, General Sibley marched on Fort Craig in hopes of reducing it and capturing much-needed supplies to support the continuation of his campaign north to Fort Union. Yet, Sibley wanted to avoid the costly prospect of directly attacking the Federals in their defensive works at Fort Craig, choosing instead to bypass the fort in a successful ploy to lure the enemy into the open by threatening their supply line to Albuquerque. Canby took the bait and met the Texans in the Rio Grande Valley about five miles north of Fort Craig on

February 21, 1862. The day-long Battle of Valverde ended indecisively on the field, but the Union troops were content to lick their wounds within the relative safety of the fort, leaving the way open for Sibley to march on Santa Fe. Among the three officers and sixty-five Union men killed in action that day was recently promoted Captain George Nicholas Bascom.[17]

Despite the potential danger posed by leaving a Union force on his own line of supply, Sibley gambled on capturing large stockpiles of goods at Albuquerque and Fort Union. In March, his Texas Brigade occupied the territorial capital without firing a shot, but as he marched eastward to attack Fort Union, he was confronted by an imposing force of Colorado volunteers that had force-marched from Denver to block the Texans. The two forces collided in a pivotal action at Glorieta Pass on March 26. Sibley, initially seizing the advantage in the ensuring engagement, was later compelled to fall back when Federal cavalry, outflanking his lines, intercepted his wagon train. Although the Federals failed to exploit the victory by immediately attacking Sibley's main body, the Texans eventually retraced their steps all the way back down the Rio Grande.

Meantime, Captain Hunter and his Texas troopers arrived in Tucson on February 28, just two weeks after President Jefferson Davis declared a separate Confederate Territory of Arizona. Finding a hospitable reception there, Hunter settled down to await events.

Reports of a Confederate presence in Tucson prompted the Californians to dispatch a reconnaissance force to capture the town. Leaving Fort Yuma on March 19, Captain William Calloway led a mixed force of infantry and cavalry, along with two mountain howitzers, up the Gila.[18] Along the way they discovered still-smoldering hay stacks burned by the Confederates, but the raiders had already departed. Calloway reached the Pima villages at the great bend of the Gila without encountering any of Hunter's men. Proceeding south on the road to Tucson, Calloway's scouts reported sighting a party of Confederates ahead at the abandoned Picacho Pass stage station. He immediately sent Lieutenant James Barrett and a small cavalry detachment around the supposed enemy flank. Calloway advanced some distance farther without meeting any Texans, nor did he find Barrett. Eventually, they arrived at the scene of a brief, but costly, skirmish between Barrett's men and Hunter's. The Union loss included Barrett himself and two soldiers killed, plus three others wounded. Calloway camped overnight on the battlefield, then turned on his back-trail, leaving Hunter in possession of Tucson.[19]

The unexpectedly aggressive Confederate actions in Arizona induced Carleton to request reinforcements shortly before beginning his offensive to the Rio Grande. Wright concurred, assigning him the Fifth California Infantry, which had been training for the previous six months under the command of Colonel George W. Bowie. A lawyer by profession, Bowie was considered a gentleman, "but no soldier" because discipline was lacking, according to one of his soldiers.[20] The Fifth nevertheless increased the strength of the California Column to fifteen companies of infantry, in addition to the five companies of cavalry and a four-gun battery of howitzers, giving Carleton a total strength of 2,350 men.[21]

The limited sources of water available in the southern California desert dictated that Carleton move his army by battalions composed of several companies during March and April 1862, each one setting out a day or two apart. The troops at Camp Wright, being nearest Fort Yuma, were to proceed first. After they were on the road, the remainder of the First Infantry would take up the march from San Diego, followed in turn by the Fifth, from its camps in the vicinity of Sacramento. The column reached Fort Yuma in mid-April, pausing only briefly before setting out on the desolate road to Tucson.

West's battalion remained in the van, with instructions from Carleton to capture Tucson, considered to be the most important point between Fort Yuma and the Rio Grande. As West cautiously entered the unimposing sun-baked village on May 20, he learned from local residents that Hunter's troopers had departed two days earlier, heading east along the stage road. With Sibley defeated and limping his way back toward Franklin, Hunter's position in Arizona was no longer tenable. Tucson was reclaimed for the Union without a shot being fired.[22]

The absence of rebel troops at Tucson made Carleton's task in Arizona suddenly much simpler. By early June, the entire California Column (with the exception of some companies of the Fifth Infantry left behind to guard Forts Yuma and Barrett) had assembled in the town for a much-needed rest before making the arduous trek eastward through Apacheria.

Uppermost in Carleton's mind was determining the whereabouts of Sibley's Confederates, and for that matter, Canby's Union troops. The best information available, mostly rumor at that, indicated the Texans had evacuated Arizona entirely. Carleton sent a three-man scouting party eastward on June 15, to reconnoiter the road and endeavor to open communication with Canby. He hired frontiersman and former Butterfield employee John Jones to serve as the principal messenger, along with a Hispanic guide named Chavez, who was also familiar with the country. Sergeant William Wheeling of the First California Infantry went along as escort. Chiricahua warriors jumped the couriers in the vicinity of Apache Pass on the 18th, severely wounding Chavez in the hip with their first shots. As the men attempted to mount their mules, Wheeling was thrown and the escape attempt was temporarily aborted. Jones convinced Wheeling that their only chance was to ride out of the ever-tightening circle of Apaches, leaving Chavez to his fate. With the guide pleading not to be left behind, Jones and the sergeant once again mounted to make their escape. Wheeling was immediately pulled from his mount and killed, but Jones managed to flee, with several warriors close on his heels. In a running fight of nearly twenty miles across the San Simon Valley, Jones wounded two Apaches and finally managed to outdistance the others by sundown. Two days later, Jones accidentally stumbled into the hands of the Confederates near Mesilla and was taken prisoner. Not only did Carleton fail to establish a link with Union forces in New Mexico, the Texans at once gained vital information about the strength and plans of the California Column. Despite that setback, Carleton remained determined to accomplish his mission by marching the California Column across 350 miles of desert, the heretofore undisputed domain of the Chiricahua and Mimbres Apaches.[23]

CHAPTER 3

A Sharp Little Contest: The Battle of Apache Pass

Carleton paused at Tucson for nearly a month to give his troops time to rest and refit before advancing to the Rio Grande. Congress, meantime, passed legislation officially establishing the federal Territory of Arizona. On June 8, 1862, Carleton announced that, in the absence of any civil authority, he was assuming the role of military governor, "so that when a man does have his throat cut, his house robbed, or his fields ravaged, he may at least have the consolation of knowing there is some law that will reach him who does the injury."[1] He also imposed a requirement that all male residents take an oath of allegiance to the United States and have a legitimate means of supporting themselves. In short, Carleton wanted no Southern sympathizers hanging around the territory to threaten its stability or his supply line to California.[2]

Only toward the end of June, with the start of the rainy season "to fill the natural tanks between here and the Rio Grande," did Carleton resume his march.[3] The limited capacity of the springs, coupled with abnormally dry conditions that year, dictated that the California Column continue to march by battalions of a few companies each, departing Tucson a day or two apart. Much of the marching was done from early morning until midday to avoid afternoon heat.[4]

In another attempt to open contact with General Canby in New Mexico, Carleton dispatched Lieutenant Colonel Edward E. Eyre and a strong reconnaissance force toward the Rio Grande in advance of the California Column. Eyre, with two companies of the First California Cavalry and three wagons, was to move as swiftly as possible toward old Fort Thorn to determine the strength and disposition of Sibley's Confederates.[5] It would also be an opportunity to establish communication with Federal forces believed to be in the vicinity of Fort Craig. Accordingly, Eyre led 140 troopers out of Tucson at 3 o'clock A.M. on June 21, following the Overland Mail Road eastward. The cavalrymen camped for the night at the burned-out station at Ciénaga de los Pinos, an intermittent source of water thirty-five miles from Tucson,. The next day's march brought the column to the crossing of the San Pedro, where Eyre discovered the Butterfield bridge still intact near the vacant station. Some of Eyre's men found the carved name or initials of Jones, the courier who had departed Tucson six days earlier. Camping at Dragoon Spring on the 24th, Eyre roused his men in the middle of the night for another early start. At about 6 o'clock, the troopers trotted up the winding road through Apache Pass, where they found "water scarce and no grass."[6] Halting at Apache Spring a few hours later, the soldiers began a slow process of watering their mounts by using their tin cups to dip the water from small pools among the rocks. As the horses were watered, Eyre had the men lead the animals out of the ravine and turn them loose, under guard, to graze on the hills to the southwest. Although no Indians had been sighted up to that time, some of the men reported seeing fresh tracks in the area. Confident that the Apaches would not dare attack such a strong force of soldiers, Eyre took few other security measures. "Horses were scattered over the hills and ravines, and men [were] wandering carelessly everywhere," one soldier recorded.[7] Had they been aware of Bascom's experience, and the mood of the Apaches since that time, the Californians might have been more prudent.

Then, someone reported that a horse was missing. Within minutes, several shots were fired up the ravine and, simultaneously, someone yelled, "Indians!" A soldier recalled: "The camp became a scene of wild excitement and confusion—horses were driven in, and the men rushed promiscuously to the spot from whence the alarm proceeded—upon reaching which, I saw the Indians dodging about on the hill and rising ground, several hundred yards off and the men standing about on the heights ready for a fight."[8]

Captain Emil Fritz immediately responded by mounting twenty-five men of B Company and had them standing at the ready when Eyre arrived. He informed the colonel that a number of Apaches were in plain sight and were displaying a white flag. Denying Fritz's plea to charge the tribesmen, Eyre fastened a white cloth to the tip of his saber and, accompanied by an interpreter, started toward the Apaches. Just at that moment, a corporal ran up breathlessly to report that three soldiers had been overwhelmed by Indians only a short distance behind him in the hills. He had narrowly escaped being caught himself. Eyre, surprisingly, scoffed at the story, expressing his determination to speak with the Apaches. Nearly an hour later, the colonel and Newcomb, the interpreter, worked their way up the head of Siphon Canyon until they finally got near enough to one warrior to express their desire to meet with the Indian leader. Some seventy-five to a hundred mounted warriors, all heavily armed with rifles, revolvers, and shotguns, were arrayed on the surrounding hills. The warrior motioned for the interpreter to come farther up the ravine, which he did, with Eyre following at a distance. As the two cautiously approached, Cochise and about a dozen of his men came down to parley. As Eyre described the exchange:

> When the chief came forward, I told him we were Americans, and that our great Captain lived at Washington; that we wished to be friends of the Apaches; that at present I was only traveling through their country, and desired that he would not interfere with my men or animals; that a great Captain was at Tucson with a large number of soldiers; that he wished to have a talk with all the Apache chiefs and to make peace with them and make them presents. He professed a great desire to be friendly with the Americans, and assured me that neither my men nor animals should be molested.[9]

When Cochise asked for tobacco and food, Eyre produced a large can of pemmican, a nonstandard ration that had been procured especially for the troops on the Pacific coast in lieu of the regulation salt pork and beef. One soldier described the pemmican as "the most unpalatable and unhealthy diet, having been made of rotten old dried beef and the refuse of a soap factory. . . . the lot furnished to our command is certainly the meanest food ever served up to a hungry man."[10] Just what the Apaches thought of the gift can only be imagined. Concluding what the soldiers quickly dubbed the "Pemmican Treaty," Eyre and Cochise agreed to meet again at sunset.

When Eyre returned to camp, he ordered a search be made for the missing men. About an hour later, the stripped bodies of Privates Albert Schmidt, James F. Keith, and Peter Maloney, all B Company men, were discovered in a nearby ravine. Each had been shot through the chest, then lanced in the neck as a coup de grace. Schmidt and Maloney were scalped. The evidence indicated that the men had led their horses over a ridge into a gulch, isolating themselves from the rest of the command, and thus became "victims to their own imprudence," according to Eyre.[11]

Apaches on the surrounding heights observed the troops as they discovered the bodies of their comrades. Eyre directed Fritz to lead a detachment against these warriors, visible on a hill half a mile distant. It proved to be a fruitless effort when the Apaches dispersed into the rugged terrain. Late that afternoon, the slain soldiers were buried about three hundred yards from the old Butterfield station in a simple ceremony attended by the entire command. Eyre then marched out of Apache Pass to establish a dry camp on the plain two miles below, where grass was more abundant.[12]

Cochise punctuated his message to Eyre later that night by firing a volley of shots into the camp. One bullet struck the acting assistant surgeon, Kittridge, over the left eye, and another killed a cavalry mount on the picket line as the startled troops sprang from their blankets to return fire at the phantom raiders. After things settled down, "We had the ball taken from the Doctor's head," a soldier reported. "He is now getting along nicely."[13]

Eyre and his cavalry proceeded without encountering any other enemy forces, Apaches or Confederates. On the road between Soldier's Farewell and Cow Springs, they were met by a party of couriers sent out from Fort Craig by Colonel John M. Chivington, commanding the Southern District of New Mexico, who was attempting to open communication with Carleton. From these men, Eyre learned of courier Jones's hair-raising escapes from both the Indians and the Texans, and of Sibley's withdrawal below Fort Thorn. Eyre dispatched the couriers to Chivington with word that Carleton and his Californians would be arriving in only a matter of days.

Eyre arrived on the Rio Grande three miles above Fort Thorn on July 4. In recognition of Independence Day, he had the colors raised "amid the long and continued cheers of the assembled command."[14] The impromptu ceremony signaled the reestablishment of Federal authority over Arizona and all of New Mexico, except for the southernmost section in the vicinity of Fort Fillmore and Mesilla. But, it would only be a matter of time before the Texans evacuated entirely. The coming of the Californians ended forever Southern designs for the conquest of the Southwest.[15]

Back in Tucson, Carleton, still unaware that his advance party had encountered opposition at Apache Pass, issued orders setting the main body of the California Column in motion toward the Rio Grande.[16] The first contingent, originally composed of Companies B, C, E, and K, First California Infantry; Company G, Fifth California; and Lieutenant William A. Thompson's two-howitzer "Jackass Battery," was scheduled to leave Tucson on July 20. The next day they would be followed by Company A of the First and Company B,

Fifth California, supported by a regular battery under the command of First Lieutenant John B. Shinn. A third battalion, consisting of the remaining four companies of the First Infantry (D, F, I, and H), would depart on the 23rd. As a concession to desert marching, Carleton permitted the infantry-men to transport their knapsacks by wagon. Each command was provided with a small train to haul the knapsacks, a few tents, ammunition, and rations for thirty days. In addition, each column included an all-important water wagon having a capacity of six hundred gallons, along with spare kegs that could be filled whenever springs were found. Following the cavalcade on July 31 would be a train of all the remaining wagons to transport the reserve ammunition and quartermaster supplies. The train and a herd of cattle would be escorted by a company of infantry and a company of cavalry.[17]

Carleton could only assume that Sibley's Texas forces still held the Rio Grande below Fort Craig and that Eyre's cavalry might well collide with them. Faced with those odds, Eyre might be forced to fall back toward Tucson. In any event, he expected Eyre to return from his mission to the Rio Grande, and when he did, his battalion would need provisions.[18] Planning for those contingencies, Carleton ordered Lieutenant Colonel West to send a party to establish a supply depot, protected by entrenchments, at San Simon Station. West selected Captain Thomas L. Roberts and his E Company, First California Infantry, to carry out that mission.[19] Roberts's company would be reinforced by a detachment from Captain John C. Cremony 's B Company, Second California, and the mountain howitzers.[20] Once established at the crossing of the San Simon River, Roberts was to scout eastward along the road for the purpose of contacting Eyre.

Along the way, Roberts was to detach Lieutenant Alexander B. MacGowan and ten men at San Pedro Crossing to guard a quantity of forage that Carle-ton's quartermaster was depositing there. Cremony was to leave three reliable cavalrymen there as couriers. Roberts was instructed that once the new camp was established at San Simon, he was to send the empty wagons back to Tucson where they would be reloaded and returned to the column. Cremony and his cavalry would escort them at least as far as the San Pedro.[21]

The prevailing drought that year prompted West to advise Roberts to divide his command to allow the springs time to replenish between detach-ments. He also suggested that Roberts place his infantry and the wagon train in the lead, along with a few cavalrymen. When the advance element finished watering, a trooper could be sent back to notify the cavalry and artillery to advance. West cautioned Roberts to be constantly on guard and ready to fight at all times, but to avoid initiating a confrontation with the Apaches. In other words, Roberts was to keep in mind that the primary objective was to defeat the Confederates, not to start an Indian war.

The battalion left Tucson early on the morning of July 10, arriving on the San Pedro two days later. There, heeding West's advice, he divided his command, taking with him sixty infantrymen and the howitzers, plus eight cavalry troopers in the charge of Sergeant Titus Mitchell. He also took along two wagons for the company's equipment, provisions, and reserve ammunition, along with a water tank. Captain Cremony was left in command of the remaining cavalry, the train, and a detachment from E Company, along with the beef herd.[22] Roberts planned to use three of his troopers as messengers to Cremony; the others as scouts. At 1 o'clock on the morning of July 13, as a torrential rain fell from lightning-streaked skies, Roberts and his men marched off into the murky darkness, leaving MacGowen and his detachment to guard the crossing.

Captain Roberts's mud-caked doughboys trudged up to Dragoon Springs seven hours later. The drought now broken, they found an abundant water supply at the spring, whereupon Roberts immediately dispatched two troopers back to Cremony with instructions to move forward. While those couriers retraced the route to the San Pedro, Sergeant Mitchell and the others advanced to reconnoiter Ewell Spring. The weary infantry, meantime, ate and rested until 5 o'clock before taking up the forty-mile march to Apache Pass. By the time they were ready to depart, Cremony and a fourteen-man detachment had arrived to secure the spring in advance of the train.[23]

Cochise, meanwhile, was watching the progress of the column with great interest. Just as Eyre had said, more soldiers were coming. Knowing that the troops could not avoid stopping at Apache Spring, Cochise proposed to Mangas Coloradas that his Mimbres join forces with the Chiricahuas to lay a trap for the unsuspecting newcomers. Assembling a combined force of some 150 to 200 warriors, the Apache leaders placed their men in two advantageous positions. West of the old stage station, the road passed through a series of hills and ravines forming the drainage from a low mountain on the south. There the soldiers would be forced to go slowly and would be at a disadvantage for maneuvering. Warriors would be placed in dense cover on both sides of the road, yet would have clear escape routes over the ridges. A larger force would lie in wait on the hills commanding the spring itself. The soldiers, just like Bascom's men the year before, would be isolated in the barren basin formed by the mountains surrounding the old Butterfield station.[24]

Marching all night, at times through mud and water halfway to their knees, the leading element of Roberts's small column finally descended the last ridge west of Apache Pass Station shortly after noon on July 15. The wagons and the "Jackass Battery," encountering rough going through the arroyos on the east slope of the pass, had fallen behind the infantry approximately half a mile. Just as the battery was crossing a narrow ravine, approximately one hundred Apaches concealed behind boulders and brush fired on the rear of the column. Private Charles M. O'Brian, a member of the battery's rear guard, fell dead with a ball through his head. Two other men, teamster Andrew Sawyer and a hospital steward, were wounded in the initial volley. The rest of the men hastened to catch up with the rest of the command.[25]

The infantry battalion had just broken ranks at the station when the firing began. Roberts, quickly recovering from his initial surprise, ordered E Company soldiers to fall in and load their muskets. Deployed in a skirmish line, the company rushed back up the ridge, opening fire on the Apaches as it reached the summit. The tribesmen immediately dispersed, many of them taking to the high ground south of the road.

As Apache fire slackened, Lieutenant Thompson advanced his howitzers to the relatively flat ridge top just above the ambush site. His well-drilled crews quickly loaded the guns and fired a few explosive case shot at the warriors bounding up the ridge.[26] The infantry pursued them for a short distance before Roberts recalled them and reassembled his force at the station. "We were now foot sore and weary with a good appetite [sic] and no water, the spring being about three quarters of a mile from the station up a narrow ravine," Private Eli Hazen recalled.[27] O'Brian's comrades found his stripped and mutilated body some distance from the ambush site and brought it to the station. Roberts claimed that his men killed four Apaches in the fight.[28]

Roberts next moved to secure Apache Spring, where he anticipated another ambush. Two hills, one on the north side of the spring, the other on the south, formed a narrow gorge in which lay the spring. Early in the afternoon, he divided E Company into two platoons, one of them commanded by First Sergeant Albert J. Fountain, who was instructed to deploy his men as skirmishers and to lead an advance on the spring.[29] The second platoon, under Roberts's personal direction, followed in reserve, supported by one of the howitzers. "Proceeding up the canon cautiously," Roberts reported, "[we] found the Indians posted high above us, from where they kept a rattling fire upon us."[30] Dashing forward into the gorge, the first platoon got within fifty yards of the spring as the Apaches fired down on them from

Apache Pass battlefield. Cochise's warriors occupied the hill in the center; Apache Spring lies in the swale to the right. (Author's collection)

vantage points on both flanks, killing Private John Barr. Fountain's men fell back a short distance, then rallied briskly to return the fire, scattering the warriors occupying the immediate vicinity of the spring. However, their muskets could not effectively reach the warriors positioned higher up in the rocks.[31] Thompson, seeing an opportunity to use his howitzer, sent a round hissing over the heads the infantrymen. A soldier recounted: "The loud report of this gun attracted the attention of the Indians, and from their actions they knew not what to make of it. At the first report they rose up with a yell, and when the shell exploded in their rear, great was their consternation and surprise, fleeing over the hill 'like scared sheep.'"[32]

Artillery was something new and awesome to the Apaches. Those who had been concealed on the slopes just above the spring quickly retreated to higher ground, joining their kinsmen in the rocks and behind the breastworks. Assessing the vulnerability of Fountain's position in the wash, Roberts directed a bugler to sound "recall" as a signal for the first platoon to fall back out of range. Cochise remained in control of the spring, and Roberts could see that taking it would not be easy so long as the warriors occupied the high ground. He therefore directed Thompson to move his howitzers up the wash to shell the breastworks and other Apache concentrations in an attempt to dislodge them from their positions. The terrain, however, made it impossible for the gunners to elevate the muzzles enough to reach the higher positions, although they did lob several shells into the Indian positions lower down. The gunners attempted to attain greater elevation by positioning the guns on reverse sloping ground, thereby lowering the stock trails. It worked, after a fashion, but the recoil flipped one howitzer over on its back.[33] With bullets kicking up sand all around them, the panicked gunners fled, abandoning their piece. Sergeant Mitchell, in charge of the cavalry detachment accompanying Roberts command, saw the crew's predicament and dashed forward with his five troopers. The cavalrymen righted the gun and moved it to a better position, all the while exposed to fire from the Apaches. The gun crew, no doubt chagrined by their own behavior, returned and resumed firing. Still, the howitzers were unable to range the positions atop the hills.[34]

Roberts reformed his men for a second attack. This time the platoons would assault each of the hills separately. Using his field glasses to study intently the higher ridge to the left (today's Overlook Ridge), Roberts turned to Fountain. "We must have that hill," said Roberts, "and you must take it, it can be done. Take twenty men and storm it."[35] Fountain promptly rejoined his company and asked for volunteers; every man responded. Taking the first twenty, he instructed the men to form two squads of skirmishers. Under the supervision of the other noncoms, the squads would alternately advance by rushes, one providing covering fire for the other. With the rest of the parched command looking on, awaiting their chance to dash to the spring, Fountain led his men up the hill. Progress was slow at first as the squads threaded their way up through boulders and brush that clawed at their uniforms. The tribesmen above, detectable only by puffs of smoke, kept up a steady fire on Fountain's determined little force. When they finally reached an area below the breastworks where the Apaches could not see them, the men lay down for a brief rest before making a final charge. Sergeant Fountain later remembered that during this lull he raised his canteen to his mouth, and immediately a bullet tore it from his hand. Writing of the event years later, he recalled:

> I ordered the men to fix bayonets and make one dash for the summit.
> As engaged, fifty rifle shots came from the breastworks. They overshot
> us, and the next moment we were over a rough stone wall and on the
> inside of a circular fortification some thirty feet in diameter; fifty or

more Indians were going out and down the hill on the opposite side . . .
the men became demons; with savage yells and curses they hurled
themselves upon the flying foe and slaked their vengeance in blood.[36]

The remainder of the company pressed forward as Apaches on the
opposite hill continued to fire. But Fountain's detachment now had the
upper hand and began shooting at the warriors clearly visible on the lower
hill south of the gorge. The "Jackass Battery" also moved up with the
troops, pausing from place to place and throwing explosive shells into the
Indian positions. Fountain watched as the Apaches, caught in the crossfire,
broke—"we could see hundreds of Indians scampering to the hills to escape
the bursting shells."[37]

By five o'clock, the troops were in possession of the spring. As soon as
the cavalry horses had been watered, Roberts ordered Sergeant Mitchell
and his men to ride back down the road to meet the train and inform Cremony of the day's events. It would be dark within a few hours, and Cremony
needed to know that there were large numbers of Apaches occupying the
pass. Roberts assured Cremony that reinforcements would be sent to accompany the train the rest of the way.

After the couriers departed, Roberts had his men fill their canteens and
the tank wagon at the spring before returning to the station to camp for the
night. Roberts considered holding the hard-won spring, and he probably
should have, but having only one company at his disposal, he concluded that
he could not defend both the spring and the camp, and still assist Cremony
if necessary.

Meantime, Sergeant Fountain paused on the ridge to gaze westward
beyond the pass. The sun was low in the sky by that time and he expected
to glimpse Cremony's train coming along at any time. Instead, he observed
a small number of riders galloping westward, followed by another larger
group. Puffs of smoke indicated the parties were shooting at each other. He
then scurried down the steep slope to inform Roberts that Mitchell's
detachment appeared to be in trouble. Roberts hurriedly selected twenty-
eight men, telling them to refresh themselves with a cup of coffee and be
ready to march right away. Leaving Lieutenant Thompson in command of
the camp, Roberts himself led the detachment down the road just at sunset.

Earlier that day, while the troops were engaged with Cochise and Mangas
at Apache Pass, Cremony was plodding along the stage road toward Ewell
Station, thirteen miles west of the pass. Arriving there at about 7:30 that

evening, Cremony halted to rest the men and animals before completing the journey. The train had barely stopped when Sergeant Mitchell, with Privates King, Maynard, and Young rode in on lathered mounts, two of the wide-eyed troopers riding double. Mitchell informed Cremony that they had been ambushed as they left the pass, and presumably Private John Teal had been killed. Private Jesse T. Maynard clutched a bloody right arm, a bullet having torn through it just below the elbow. Mitchell related that the detachment had spotted the Indians in the hills west of the station, but had ridden fast enough over the pass to maintain a safe distance. Once they were out on the plain, where it was more difficult for the Apaches to get near them without being seen, they slowed to a walk. In fact, Teal decided to rest his horse by dismounting and leading him for a time. Although Mitchell should have insisted that the men stay together, he nevertheless permitted Teal to fall some two to three hundred yards behind the others. The Apaches waited until the cavalrymen passed between two slight swells, where about forty warriors lay in ambush. The tribesmen opened fire at close range from behind rocks alongside the road. Maynard was hit in the initial volley, as was his horse and Private Keim's. Teal was simultaneously cut off from his comrades. Mitchell realized that he and the remaining four men could do nothing to help Teal, considering that he already had one man and one horse wounded, and another horse dead. They had little choice but to leave Teal to his fate and attempt to reach the train with Roberts's message. When they were within a mile of the train, Keim's horse, too, dropped dead from its wound. Keim, displaying remarkable coolness and presence of mind, tarried long enough to recover his horse equipment, arriving at the train a few minutes after the others.

As Cremony's men assisted the cavalrymen, the captain weighed the situation. With only sixty men, the odds were against getting a score of wagons through the pass on a moonlit night. Better to wait for Roberts and enter the pass at daylight.

A few hours later, to everyone's amazement, Teal appeared out of the darkness alive and well. Teal recounted that his comrades "looked back at me but self preservation the first instinct of nature getting the better of their valor they galloped off, leaving me to take care of myself. The Indians turned toward me."[38] Seeing that he was being cut off, Teal leaped into the saddle, got off a shot with his Sharps carbine at the warriors closing on him, then attempted to run the gauntlet. For a time, he outdistanced the fifteen warriors galloping after him, but other warriors in front of him, one of whom Teal thought was a chief, took up positions in the brush. The soldier suddenly turned on his pursuers as if to fire again, causing the Apaches to scatter for cover. Turning his attention once again to the leader, the trooper glimpsed the Apache taking aim from behind a clump of bear grass. Teal rolled out of the saddle just in time—the bullet struck his horse, mortally wounding the animal. Dismounted and surrounded, Teal took cover behind the body of his mount and prepared to make a last-ditch stand. The Apaches soon closed in, probably assuming that Teal's principal weapon was a muzzle-loader. "I expect they had never run against a breech-loader before, and the rapidity of my fire must have astonished them," Teal wrote later.[39] The Apaches maneuvered for over an hour, firing occasionally, yet keeping their distance. Teal held his fire for awhile, inducing the Indians to approach more closely. When they came within point-blank range, Teal fired, knocking one man from his horse and causing the others to make a precipitous retreat carrying the wounded warrior. It was later determined that the man Teal shot was none other than Mangas Coloradas. Only Teal's aggressive actions saved his life. After darkness fell, the plucky trooper stripped the equipment from his horse and struck out for the wagon train, eight miles distant.[40]

Captain Roberts and his men reached the train at about 11:30 that night. By that time, they had marched a total of nearly sixty miles and had engaged the Indians in a four-hour fight. Cremony's men treated the exhausted infantrymen to coffee, the lack of wood precluding more extensive cooking. Pickets stood guard while everyone else stretched out on the ground to catch a few hours' sleep.

The command broke camp at daybreak without eating, a file of infantry skirmishers guarding each flank of the train, while half the cavalry were deployed dismounted three hundred yards to the front. The rest of Cremony's men acted as a rear guard. Three infantrymen and three cavalry troopers, mounted, herded the cattle behind the wagons. Large parties of Apaches were sighted from time to time as the column approached Apache Pass, but seeing that the troops were well prepared, they stayed beyond rifle range. The train arrived at the station by noon on July 16 without incident. Only then did Roberts's famished men finally have time to cook a meal.

Overnight the Apaches had again occupied the heights above the spring. The soldiers at the station could see them plainly atop the hills and realized that they would again have to dislodge the tribesmen in order to obtain water. But this time the troops were better prepared. Not only was Apache resistance expected, the soldiers were now familiar with the terrain. The arrival of the train also assured that there would be no shortage of either food or ammunition. Roberts ordered that the wagons be arranged in a hollow square and chained together to form a corral for the mules. To avoid having to detail men from his effective force to guard the train, Roberts issued arms and ammunition to the civilian teamsters.

Roberts prepared another frontal assault on the spring. He anchored his line on the mountain howitzers, both of which were positioned in the middle of the canyon. Twenty doughboys were assigned to protect the gun crews to avoid the near-disaster of the day before. The remaining fifty-odd infantrymen were deployed in skirmish order on either side of the guns. Following behind the line was Cremony's cavalry as a reserve.

Cremony, however, had not yet been engaged and desired a more prominent role in the coming fight. Approaching Roberts, he suggested the gunners shell the hilltops, while he and his troopers mounted and charged up the slopes to disperse the Apaches. Roberts declined the offer. Not only were the hillsides extremely steep and rocky, which would seriously impede the momentum of a mounted charge, but the cavalry was already committed to escorting the empty train back to San Pedro Crossing after Roberts established the depot at San Simon Station. An attack on the Apache positions might well decimate the cavalry, or at the least ruin the horses for any further service. Roberts could not take those risks with such a small mounted force. Cremony was not to be denied, however. After returning to his men, he prevailed upon his subaltern, Lieutenant Muller, to further plead the case with Roberts. Muller argued so adamantly that the captain finally lost his patience, telling him "to either obey or be placed under arrest. This ended the colloquy."[41]

As the line advanced, the gun crews pushed the little howitzers along, stopping periodically to lob a shell or two into the Apache positions. As the platoons separated to begin ascending the hills, the battery moved along the wash, firing ahead of the infantrymen to break up warrior concentrations. "The shells burst splendidly," Fountain recorded, "starting the concealed foes from behind their breastworks, and as they fled the skirmish line accelerated their speed with volleys of minnie [sic] balls."[42] The fight was brief. Within twenty minutes, the Sacramento men had cleared the Apaches from the hilltops and from around the spring itself. When the warriors broke, Cremony's two dozen cavalrymen dashed through the infantry line to route and scatter the tribesmen.

The Battle of Apache Pass resulted in few casualties on either side. The few recorded Apache recollections of the fight both minimized casualties and distorted the magnitude of the incident. Conversely, Captain Roberts claimed that his men killed a combined total of nine warriors in all phases of the battle, and he suspected that more dead and wounded warriors were carried off. The troops lost Privates O'Brian and Barr killed, and Private Maynard and a teamster wounded.[43]

The only other military casualty recorded was "Butch," the nine-year-old canine mascot of the California Volunteers, who lost a toe to an Apache bullet. Butch had accompanied the column all the way from San Diego and was a veteran in every sense of the word. The dog had previously belonged to the regulars, who had no choice but to leave him behind when they departed for the East at the beginning of the Civil War. He assumed his own place with the unit at all guard mounts, musters, and parades, and stationed himself with Post Number 1 every night, where he would challenge anyone not having proper business at the guard tent. During the Battle of Apache Pass, Butch went with the Jackass Battery, chasing through the brush ferreting out Indians and barking all the while.[44]

Roberts immediately secured the area and put his men to work digging out the spring to improve its flow. They walled up a portion of it to form a small reservoir for filling canteens, kegs, and the tank wagons. Captain Cremony recalled the moment: "In peace and quiet we partook of the precious fountain. Our horses and mules, which had not tasted water for forty-eight hours, and were nearly famished from so dusty a road and so long a journey under the hottest of suns, drank as if they would never be satisfied."[45] Before moving the command back to the stage station for the night, Roberts posted a detachment of infantry to guard the water hole. He was not about to have to fight for water a third time. Later that evening, sixteen cavalrymen relieved the infantry for the remainder of the night and until the column moved out of the pass the following day.[46]

The volunteers buried the bodies of O'Brian and Barr beside the graves of Eyre's men and broke camp at 8:00 on the morning of the 17th. After wending their way down Siphon Canyon and out onto the plain below for about two miles, they discovered several corpses near the road. A short distance down the trail, Roberts came upon what he presumed was the site of Eyre's bivouac, and somewhat beyond that a heavy blood stain on the ground. In the same area, his men recovered a bloodied holster bearing the initials "N. W."—or "M. W."—along with several small articles of both white and Indian origins.[47]

The bodies were not identified but were presumed to be those of men belonging to a party of nine miners that had left Pinos Altos a few days previous. Captain John C. Cremony later offered a conjectural reconstruction of the incident using the evidence at the scene. He assumed that while Cochise and Mangas awaited Carleton's column to arrive from the west, they observed the miners riding toward the pass from the opposite direction. The Apaches quickly prepared an ambush, concealing warrriors in a deep gully alongside the road. The gully, even though it cut across the open plain beyond the mouth of the canyon, was so abrupt that it was nearly invisible to the hapless miners until they came within fifty yards of it. Although the Americans were experienced frontiersmen and well armed, they were immediately cut down when the Apaches arose, seemingly from nowhere.[48]

The train continued along the stage road for fifteen miles, arriving at San Simon Station that evening. The next day Roberts carried out Carleton's orders by having some of his men begin digging a defensive entrenchment in the rock-solid ground around the adobe station house. Others off-loaded the supplies from the wagons and generally improved the camp. The only water available was alkaline run-off, "as thick as cream," that had collected among the rocks along the otherwise dry wash.[49] Roberts allowed the cavalry, whose horses had eaten nothing for more than forty-eight hours, to rest and recuperate somewhat on the meager forage in the vicinity of the station. Early on the evening of July 19, Cremony and his men, reinforced by a detachment of twenty infantrymen, started back to the San Pedro with the train and a water wagon. Rather than risk another encounter with the Apaches, Cremony circumvented the pass by taking a less well-watered trail around the Dos Cabezas Mountains to intersect the Butterfield road fifteen miles east of San Pedro Crossing. Arriving there three days later, Cremony met West's contingent of the California Column and informed them of the recent encounter.[50]

Although West experienced no problems with the Apaches, both Roberts and Cremony advised Carleton that the Indians posed a serious threat to the California Column and its supply line. "I deem it highly important that a force sufficient to hold the water and pass should be stationed there," Roberts wrote to Carleton, "otherwise every command will have to fight for the water, and, not knowing the ground are almost certain to lose some lives." Lieutenant Colonel Eyre was even more specific in recommending that at least two companies of infantry be posted in Apache Pass because "that corps would be far more effective against the Indians in the rugged mountains . . . than cavalry; besides, horses could not be kept in flesh on the dry grass alone; they would be utterly useless in two weeks' riding."[51] The route Cremony had used between San Simon Station and the San Pedro, while comparatively flat and easy to traverse, was somewhat longer and less practical because of its lack of water. The army was left with little choice but to rely on Apache Spring, and to contend with Cochise.

To the aggressive Carleton's profound disappointment, Eyre confirmed that the Confederates had evacuated the upper Rio Grande Valley and were even then retreating into Texas. Any chance for glory in fighting Rebels in the Southwest had vanished. Although Arizona and New Mexico were once again firmly in Union hands, Carleton hoped that the high command might want him to threaten the South by making a counterinvasion across Texas. However, the volunteers were destined for the more mundane role of reoccupying the Rio Grande posts and establishing a line of communication to California along the southern overland route.

CHAPTER 4

The Post at Apache Pass

The battalions of the California Column were already on the road to the Rio Grande by the time Roberts's report reached Carleton at his headquarters in the field on July 27. After making a cursory examination of Apache Pass on his way through, and concurring with his subordinate's assessment of the dangers posed by continued Indian control of the spring, the general paused at the stage station to pen orders establishing a post in close proximity to the spring. Lieutenant Colonel West was directed to detach Captain Hugh L. Hind's Company G, Fifth California Infantry, from his command for that purpose. He further stipulated that when the main supply train came up in a few days, a detachment of A Company, Fifth Infantry, would reinforce Hinds, increasing the garrison to one hundred enlisted men. Major Theodore A. Coult, attached to West's column, would assume command of the new post, which Carleton christened Fort Bowie in honor of Colonel George W. Bowie, commanding the Fifth California Infantry. Carleton assured Coult that when the first empty wagons were sent back to Tucson for additional supplies, part of the cavalry escort would be assigned to him for scouting purposes.[1]

Carleton made it clear to Coult that he was not there on a peace mission and that he should "cause the Apache Indians to be attacked whenever and wherever he may find them near his post unless they bear flags of truce."[2] Carleton underscored his instructions by authorizing an issue of twenty-two thousand rounds of musket ammunition for Coult's men. The command was rationed for eighty days on a diet that included the hated canned pemmican, in addition to fresh beef, on the hoof.[3]

In obedience to Carleton's orders, Coult immediately reconnoitered the area surrounding Apache Spring to find a suitable location for the post, one that would comply with Carleton's directive to hold the spring and protect travelers on the road. Unfortunately, neither of the two available defensive positions lent themselves to a permanent camp. Although the higher ridge to the north commanded the entire site, as the volunteers had proven in the recent battle, it was far too steep and rugged to accommodate a garrison. The lower hill directly south of the spring, while being far from perfect, afforded the only defensible terrain suitable for a bivouac.[4]

Carleton considered Fort Bowie to be one of the most important points for a military post in Arizona Territory, correctly predicting that it would be occupied for many years to come. The fort not only commanded Apache Pass and its all-important water supply along the southern transcontinental route, it was situated squarely in Chiricahua Apache country. Still, the establishment of permanent forts along his line of supply was unanticipated and lay beyond the scope of his instructions to cooperate with Canby in ousting the Confederates from New Mexico. Realizing that he had no funds for the construction of buildings at Fort Bowie, Carleton informed Coult that his men would have to get along in tents for the foreseeable future. He also advised his subordinate to build a fieldwork for defense. Since the Apaches had shown no reluctance to confront a sizeable body of troops, Carleton assumed they would not hesitate to attack an isolated garrison.[5]

Two miles beyond the north entrance of the pass, near where the messengers had been ambushed and where Eyre's command found four bodies three weeks earlier, Carleton's advance party discovered further evidence that Cochise would show no quarter. Scattered in the brush were the bodies of nine men, presumed to be miners from Pinos Altos, a developing gold mining district in the Mimbres Mountains in the vicinity of the old Santa Rita copper deposits. The disposition of the bodies suggested that the Apaches had employed a favorite tactic by surprising the miners on the open flat, probably jumping up from a nearby ravine, then shooting the men down before they had time to react. Carleton's men concluded from charred bones and burned fragments of rope that one of the miners had been captured and burned alive. Carlton had the bodies buried in a common grave near the road.[6]

The challenge Coult faced at Apache Pass was a daunting one. It would have been difficult to imagine a more unlikely place for a military post, even on the frontier. The ground selected for the new post was rugged—hardly a flat spot in the entire area—and strewn with rocks and brush. Nevertheless, the men of G Company settled in as best they could, clearing some of the debris and using it to lay up stone breastworks crowning all four sides of the hill. The tiny garrison, of course, could not have manned the entire perimeter at any one time, but Coult relied on his advantage of interior lines to reinforce whichever side might be threatened at a given time. Coult reported on August 9:

> I am building, as defenses, out-works on four faces of the hill, but sufficiently near that either of them being attacked can be readily and safely re-enforced from the others. My breastworks are four feet and a half high and built of large stone, three feet wide at the bottom and from eighteen inches to two feet on top. They are substantial and will afford ample protection, against all kinds of small arms. I have one already completed eighty feet in length, covering the rear of my position, and another, over 100 feet long, nearly done. The latter protects my most exposed flank.[7]

For a time at least, Coult maintained an outlying picket guard on Overlook Ridge to the north, as well as another on an elevated position on the south side of the ravine above the spring. Coult also advised Carleton that, because of "the large number of hostile Indians represented to be in the neighborhood," he was sending to Tucson for two mountain howitzers to augment Fort Bowie's arsenal.[8]

Coult's concerns about defense were not unfounded. Only the previous day, Private McFarland, assigned to watch over the cattle, had tracked a missing cow up a ravine just six hundred yards from camp. After losing her trail, McFarland turned around to retrace his steps when an Apache warrior appeared from behind a large boulder only twenty feet away. McFarland, contrary to orders and common sense, had gone out unarmed, and now stood helpless as the Apache fired, hitting him in the chest. Mortally wounded, McFarland ran back to the post with two warriors close on his heels. Meantime, the guard turned out the garrison and a party started out to the soldier's assistance; however, the Apaches retreated after pursuing McFarland for only a couple of hundred yards. Coult, clearly disgusted that a soldier would leave camp unarmed, viewed the incident as being instructive to the other men by arousing them from "a state of false security into which, from the non-appearance of Indians, they were rapidly falling."[9]

Adding to Coult's frustrations, the very next night eight head of cattle panicked during a thunderstorm and ran off into the darkness. Although

Indians appeared to have played no part in the incident, a party sent out to retrieve them came back empty-handed. Apaches were obviously lurking near the post and had no doubt scooped up the free cattle. Coult blamed the loss on his small garrison of only forty infantrymen, twenty-one of whom were constantly detailed on guard duty. He still had no cavalry at that time.[10]

Only a day later, the supply train arrived, along with a few men of A Company, Fifth California Infantry. A detachment from Coult's own company, previously assigned to guarding the Mowry Mine south of Tucson, returned to Fort Bowie as well. His labor force bolstered by these additions, Coult was able to complete the breastworks by mid-August, when he proudly announced that

> Alcatraz (I give the names applied to them by the men who built them, and to whom as they worked well and faithfully, I allowed that privilege) is on the left [west] flank of the camp, 150 feet in length, and commands every point within musket range, in the canon toward the road and camping ground of trains. Fort Point, on a slight elevation, covers the rear of the camp [south] and the wagon road up the hill. It is ninety-five feet in length. Bule Battery over looks the country and the approaches to the hill on the southeast, or right flank of the camp. It is ninety-seven feet long, and effectually covers and protects the cattle corral and picket rope of the cavalry detachment. Spring Garden (guarding) overlooks the spring and commands the ravine in which it is situated and every point within musket-range around the spring. This wall is seventy feet long. The total length of wall around the post 412 feet, the height four to four and a half, and thickness from two and a half feet to three feet at bottom, tapering to eighteen inches to two feet at top, and built of stones weighing from twenty-five to 500 pounds. . . . In addition to the wall defenses I have built the walls of a guard-house on one end of the front wall, and will have it roofed in a few days. It is fourteen feet square, and loop-holed on two sides.[11]

Coult's defenses were simply dry-laid stone redans, probably built with a salient toward the front in order to provide for mutually supportive fire.[12]

About the same time, a sergeant and a dozen troopers of the First California Cavalry arrived at the post to provide escorts for the express men maintaining communications between Tucson and Mesilla. Although Coult certainly could have benefited by having mounted men for scouting duty, there simply were not enough cavalry in the district for that luxury. The Apaches continued to frequent the area around the pass and along the road to such an extent that mail riders would not venture out without an escort.[13]

Administrative changes spared Major Coult from having to endure for long the hardships of living at Fort Bowie. Early in September, Carleton ordered Fort Bowie's first commander to Tucson to relieve Major David Fergusson, First California Cavalry, as commander of the Western District of Arizona. Carleton had established that district prior to departing Tucson in July to facilitate the management of his ever-lengthening supply line to California.[14] However, the district lay within the Department of the Pacific, which included all of Arizona Territory, but not New Mexico. That technicality was to be a recurring annoyance to General Carlton.[15]

As the ranking officer in the territory, Carleton replaced Canby as commander of the Department of New Mexico. That meant that Carleton had to surrender command of the First California Infantry, a unit whose stamina and soldierly qualities he had come to admire during the long, hard march across the desert. The hard-bitten old dragoon, whose stern hand had molded the volunteers into a well-disciplined and effective fighting force, revealed his respect for the miners-turned-soldiers in his farewell remarks. "The Southern Overland Mail Route has been opened, and the military posts in Arizona, Southern New Mexico, and Northwestern Texas have been reoccupied by troops composing the Column from California . . . . California has reason to be proud of the sons she has sent across the continent to assist in the great struggle in which our country is now engaged."[16]

Carleton also relinquished immediate command of the District of Arizona, another of his own creations, while retaining authority over the Column from California. Fort Bowie was placed under the jurisdiction of what was briefly called the Eastern District of Arizona, commanded by Colonel Joseph R. West and headquartered at Mesilla, which by that time boasted "a plaza, an adobe church, and some five thousand inhabitants."[17] A subsequent realignment authorized at Army Headquarters consolidated Arizona, formerly under the Department of the Pacific, with Carleton's Department of New Mexico. Renamed simply the District of Arizona, the new organization comprised all of Arizona Territory and that portion of New Mexico lying south of an east-west line through Fort Thorn, near present-day Hatch.[18] This realignment ensured that Carleton would maintain unified control over the entire area occupied by the California Column, particularly his overextended supply line to the Pacific.

There was no question that the Californians were dedicated soldiers, yet they had their limits. Prior to leaving Fort Bowie, Coult recommended that the post be abandoned during the winter months. He complained to West: "The locality is decidedly unhealthy, and I am informed by reliable persons that during the winter season the snow falls there from three to five feet in depth. During the period of my stay at Fort Bowie I do no think a single man escaped having an attack of fever, and some came very near dying. The garrison there have no protection save tents . . . . The place can be dismantled, and, if necessary, reoccupied in the spring."[19]

Coult was only too happy to exchange life at Fort Bowie for the comparative comforts of Tucson, leaving the fort in charge of Captain Hugh L. Hinds. Within days, Hinds forwarded his own plea to Coult, telling him that the high winds coursing through the pass were whipping the tents to pieces and that, if the troops were to remain there, some sort of more permanent quarters would have to be built, and soon. Hinds added that he had no tent stoves and clothing supplies were low, "not enough to make the men comfortable for the winter months."[20] Even more critical was the fresh beef supply, which was only enough for ten days. When Hinds's letter eventually reached Carleton, the general bristled at the mere suggestion that Fort Bowie be vacated, even for a few months. He had fought for the spring and he intended to keep it. Reiterating his instructions that the garrison should initiate offensive operations against the Apaches, Carleton stated unequivocally that the troops were not to be withdrawn.[21] Preoccupied with more pressing wartime needs, Congress was hardly concerned with appropriating funds for the comfort of troops posted at temporary stations in the far-off Southwest. Accordingly, there was little Carelton could do about improving the quarters, the men would have to get by as best they could, but he did authorize Hinds to appropriate enough cattle from a large herd being driven toward the Rio Grande to supply his men for sixty days.[22]

The soldiers at Fort Bowie were thus faced with a grim existence, but to their advantage nearly all of them were hardy, independent men who had migrated to California to become miners. They were accustomed to the deprivations and hardships of an outdoor life. Utilizing whatever materials they could lay hands on, the men set to work sheltering themselves as well as circumstances would permit. The soldiers excavated holes in the southeast side of the hill, where they would be somewhat sheltered from prevailing winds, lining them with crude stone walls elevated above ground level. Roofs were fabricated by covering the structures with brush and earth, and perhaps an occasional piece of canvas. A year later, a disgusted post commander lamented: "The quarters if it is not an abuse of language to call them such, have been constructed without system, regard to health, defense, or convenience. Those occupied by the men are mere hovels, mostly excavations in the side hill, damp, illy ventilated, and covered with the decomposed granite taken from the excavation, through which the rain passes very much as it would through a sieve. By the removal of a few tents, the place would present more the appearance of a California Digger Indian rancheria than a military post."[23]

Hinds's small garrison faced many demands that fall. Not only did they perform all of the usual garrison functions, such as guard duty and surveillance of the cattle and mule herds, but they provided a ten-man detail to protect San Pedro Crossing as well. Three others were assigned to quartermaster duties at the depot in Tucson. "My company has been divided and subdivided so much and so long," Hinds complained to Coult, "that I hope you will order all of them to join their company whilst you have it in your power."[24]

Cochise and his band continued to frequent the area, harassing the soldiers at Apache Pass whenever an opportunity presented itself, including several nighttime alarms that disrupted sleep but otherwise caused no harm. Hinds, nevertheless, was alert to the possibility of an attack and became especially suspicious that the Apaches were up to something during the first week in October. As a precaution, he began sending out a stronger than normal guard party with the herd. His caution paid dividends when a large number of warriors crawled down the mountain and into the basin below the fort in an attempt to drive off the stock. Their plan was for one party to rush the sentinels while the other captured the herd. But the ten soldiers assigned to the herd discovered the ruse and opened fire. Hinds had two other parties of men in readiness to reinforce the herd guard if necessary. As soon as the firing started, Lieutenant Lafayette Hammond and seventeen infantrymen dropped what they were doing, shouldered their muskets, and double-timed out of camp to the scene of the action. The Chiricahuas, one of whom paused long enough to taunt the soldiers by poking his rifle at them, began withdrawing as soon as they saw the reinforcements approaching. Hammond and his men immediately charged up the mountain after them. Meantime, Hinds organized a second relief party of twenty-five men led by Lieutenant Benjamin F. Harrover and sent them around the mountain by another route in an attempt to cut off the Indians' retreat. But the soldiers arrived just minutes too late. Harrover pursued the raiders for ten miles, without getting close enough to engage them. Hinds kept the herd out all day, hoping to entice the Apaches to try again, but they failed to reappear.[25]

Cochise, who probably led the raid, demonstrated that he was not intimidated by either the fortifications or the soldiers at Apache Pass. Although it was highly unlikely that the Apaches would ever attempt to attack the fort directly, they were still quite willing to confront the troops on their own terms. Similarly, Hinds had shown that he was both eager and prepared to engage the tribesmen. In reporting the incident to Coult, the captain noted that Apaches were in sight of the post every night. "We will have to whip them after this winter," he predicted.[26]

Hinds was not alone in his opinion. Major Coult also reported from his Tucson headquarters that "the Apaches are committing great depredations near the Sonora line, and certainly need punishing, but I have not the force to make a campaign against them."[27] Coult went on to say that Apaches were committing depredations in all parts of the territory, having stolen forty horses from San Xavier, the old mission village just south of Tucson, that very morning. Since Coult had only twenty-three cavalrymen at his disposal, and the Apaches had a ten-hour head start, he did not bother to mount a pursuit. However, the incident reinforced his complaint that his available force in the district was "scarcely sufficient for garrison duty and to furnish necessary escorts."[28]

But Coult had an idea for overcoming those shortages. Knowing that there were many experienced frontiersmen in the Tucson area "who would gladly go on a campaign if supported by regular troops," he proposed that a company of partisans, consisting of sixty to eighty picked men, be raised and armed by the government. Whether or not the army was desperate enough to turn loose an armed mob on the countryside was a moot point because the governor of California had already been authorized to enlist enough men to organize the remaining seven companies of the First California Cavalry. Brigadier General George Wright notified Carleton in mid-December that the units would be sent east and placed at his disposal as soon as the men could be recruited and trained. He also reminded Carleton that the rest of Colonel Bowie's Fifth California Infantry had been relieved of duty in southern California and was even then on the road east of Fort Yuma. Wright may have been more concerned about precluding another Confederate attempt to overrun the Southwest; nevertheless, the reinforcements would certainly augment the skeletal forces then in Arizona, giving the army the ability to launch offensives against the Apaches.[29]

After the Confederate threat subsided, Carleton reverted to his former role as a ruthless Indian fighter. His experience on the frontier before the war had provided him with both a rare understanding of western Indians and what one historian has characterized as "a psychopathic hatred of Apaches."[30] Carleton's attitude was reflected in his standing orders that officers and soldiers were to reject all attempts on the part of the Indians to parley, that the Apaches were to be attacked at every opportunity, and that all males capable of bearing arms were to be summarily killed. It was a blatant policy bordering on extermination that was manifested in the murder of Mangas Coloradas near Pinos Altos in January 1863. To the discredit of the California Volunteers, West lured Mangas to a parley, then took him prisoner. West later claimed that he could not in good conscience kill the chief because he had voluntarily come in to talk. But a civilian who was present testified that soldiers tortured Mangas with red-hot bayonets and, when the Apache attempted to fight back, they shot him down. That act simply intensified the hatred the Chiricahuas had already assumed for the Americans invading their homeland.[31]

Continued Apache attacks along the old Butterfield Road discouraged civilian mail riders from hazarding the trip, even with military escorts. The difficulty in hiring men to carry the mail caused West to devise an alternate arrangement to ensure that military communications in the district were not disrupted. For reasons that are not entirely understood, West decided to move his headquarters to Hart's Mill (formerly Franklin, i.e., El Paso), Texas during March.[32] The next month, West inaugurated a system of cavalry vedettes to carry army dispatches between key points. He assigned the duty to Company F, First California, directing that detachments consisting of a noncommissioned officer and nine men be stationed at Las Cruces, the crossing of the Mimbres River, Fort Bowie, San Pedro Crossing, and at Tucson. Runs were to leave the respective termini on the first and fifteenth day of each month, with the exchange of mail occurring wherever the two parties met on the road between Fort Bowie and the Mimbres. West specified that each relay would be composed of all of the available men at each station, except for one who would remain behind to watch over the station. "As those stations will be constantly exposed to attack by Indians," West cautioned the men, "great care must be observed to prevent surprise and loss of animals."[33] It was indeed hazardous duty, especially for lone station guards, since most of the old Butterfield facilities were quite isolated.

Just ten days after the first military express passed over the trail, the Chiricahuas again made their appearance near Fort Bowie.[34] When sentries sighted approximately two hundred warriors, thirty of them mounted, approaching the post from the north on the morning of April 25, Captain Benjamin F. Harrover sent out a detachment of twenty-five men to intercept them. "On reaching the spring north of the post," Harrover reported, "the Indians were discovered within range, and I ordered my men to fire. The Indians commenced to retreat but returned our fire."[35] Harrover pressed the war party in a skirmish lasting three hours over a distance of four miles, during which he observed several warriors hit by the fire of his men. The Apaches, reportedly armed with a mixture of army rifle muskets and other arms of large caliber, wounded one soldier, Private Marvin B. Wilcox of Company E. This seriously wounded soldier probably owed his life to the skill of Edward L. Watson, the surgeon who accompanied the detachment.

Not all of the depredations in the region could be blamed on Cochise and his band, although they certainly committed their share. White Mountain and Pinal Apaches still swept out of their strongholds in the Gila country to descend on the easy prey along the San Pedro and Santa Cruz valleys. In May, Captain Thomas T. Tidball acted on Carleton's directive by organizing a small expedition of twenty enlisted men and a handful of civilians familiar with the region. Employing tactics that would be used successfully by similarly aggressive officers in following decades, Tidball trailed the Indians by night and concealed his force during the day. He allowed no fires for cooking and insisted that his men maintain silence. That his tactics were effective was evidenced when he located the Apaches at Canada de Arivaipa. Approaching to within striking distance, the little expedition quietly broke camp in the evening to undertake a sixteen-hour march over extremely rugged terrain to strike at the rancheria. The attack caught the Apaches completely unaware. The troops claimed to have killed over fifty Indians and wounded as many more. The victors returned to Tucson with ten prisoners and several dozen head of stock as proof of their achievement. Tidball's force suffered the loss of only one civilian killed. The success of the expedition proved that small numbers of determined men, using caution and common sense, could operate quite successfully against the Apaches.[36]

The area in the immediate vicinity of Fort Bowie remained quiet, probably because Cochise was back in Sonora that spring of 1863. The Chiricahuas found themselves in the uncomfortable situation of being at war with both the Americans and the Mexicans simultaneously. Officials at Fronteras were once again offering substantial bounties for Apache scalps. Nevertheless, Cochise sought to placate the Sonorans by offering to trade loot stolen north of the border for more guns and ammunition. But the Mexicans betrayed the wary Apache by attempting to steal his stock and kill his people, an act that caused Cochise to resume raiding his old antagonists.[37]

The Chiricahuas slipped back across the international border and secluded themselves in the mountains to rest and gather food, satisfied to avoid their enemies for a time. Whether or not Cochise allied his band with the Mimbres in June is unclear, but Apaches seeking to avenge the death of Mangas gathered at Cooke's Peak, then launched a series of raids in New Mexico. In a wanton attack on a small party of soldiers on the Rio Grande, the Apaches killed First Lieutenant L. A. Bargie and two of his men. Bargie's headless body was later found with the chest cut open and the heart removed. Although it is unlikely the chief was directly involved in that incident, he had nevertheless colluded with the guilty bands.[38]

During July a combined force of some 150 to 200 Chiricahua warriors led by Cochise, Luis, and Victorio rampaged along the road between Tucson and Las Cruces. The Apaches struck first at a government train bound for Las Cruces. Preparing an ambush in Cooke's Canyon, the Chiricahuas fired on the train and its eight-man cavalry escort, wounding four soldiers. Despite their disadvantage, however, the troopers managed to kill four warriors before the Indians withdrew. Less than two weeks later, the Apaches struck near the same place, this time engaging a train escort in a five-hour fight. The soldiers had just abandoned the wagons in the hope of escaping when another detachment came to their relief and dispersed the Apaches. At about the same time, raiders put in an appearance at Fort Bowie, where they made off with five head of cattle.[39]

When West launched a campaign in southern New Mexico to rid it of Apaches, Cochise avoided contact by shifting his attention to the area around Fort Bowie. A party of eleven Apaches boldly dashed down the river bed at San Pedro Crossing on the morning of August 22, just as the cavalry picket guard there was turning out its horses to graze. Sergeant George W. Yager, Company E, First California, correctly guessed that the Indians intended to stampede some of the horses that were picketed near the haystacks. However, the soldiers opened fire with their Sharps carbines, causing the Indians to diverge from their intended course. The party managed to get away with only two Spanish horses and a mule. Sergeant Yager and one of his men quickly saddled their mounts and gave chase. Although the troopers got near enough to fire a few pistol shots at the fleeing Apaches, they failed to stop them.[40]

Only five days after the raid at San Pedro Crossing, Apaches struck again at Fort Bowie. A member of the cavalry express party, Private Creeden, watched over the horses as they grazed approximately a thousand yards below the post. Almost before he realized what was happening, twenty-five or thirty Indians galloped down the road from the west, surrounded the herd, and swept it off down the old road through Siphon Canyon. All the while, Creeden was firing at them with his carbine, wounding one warrior. The sentinel at the fort, reacting slowly to the emergency unfolding in the basin below, finally sounded the alarm by firing his rifle to alert the garrison. Captain Tidball, who had successfully engaged the Indians at Aravaipa Canyon in May and now commanded Fort Bowie, led a pursuit party consisting of almost every man in the garrison. They were too late; the Apaches escaped with all six horses belonging to the mail express. A mule, apparently ridden by Private Chappins as a personal preference, was left behind. Tidball later discovered the tracks of two other sizable war parties that had been concealed behind nearby hills, indicating that the raid had been well planned.

An embarrassed Sergeant Kuhl, in charge of the mail party, afterward explained to his company commander that the animals were allowed to graze for only an hour or two each morning after being watered at the spring, and he did not anticipate any trouble. Apparently, General West's admonishment to make certain always that the horses were secure had been lost on the sergeant. Still, Kuhl attempted to fulfill his duty by mounting his "expressmen" on team mules, the only other animals available at the post. The mules, however, were not receptive to becoming cavalry mounts. In what must have been a hilarious exhibition to the onlookers, the mules bucked, kicked, and bit the troopers, broke saddle girths, and in a final protest, lay down in the road and refused to move. Sergeant Kuhl finally gave up and hitched them to a wagon. One can only imagine the chiding the troopers must have received from their comrades when they arrived by wagon at the next relay station.[41]

At the beginning of September, Captain James H. Whitlock led a force of the Fifth California into the Chiricahua Mountains south of Fort Bowie, where he suspected the Apaches were operating. Whitlock indeed found and attacked a camp just a few days later. Although the inhabitants escaped, Whitlock's men captured a large quantity of food, along with two mules, a government carbine, and other property implicating the Apaches' involvement in the attack on Lambert's train back in July.[42]

Field offensives by both the U. S. Army and Sonoran military forces during summer and fall 1863 kept the Apaches from feeling very secure on either side of the border. Expeditions launched by both governments dogged the Indians' trails, forcing them to keep on the move.[43] Consequently, the opportunities either for plundering or for trading were comparatively few, nor could they spend the usual amount of time gathering and preparing traditional foods in the mountains. Losses from attacks on their rancherias compounded shortages of ammunition and food, which probably compelled Cochise and his people to hide out in southeastern Arizona that winter.

Hostilities intensified during 1864 as both Mexican and American troops increased their efforts to exterminate the Apaches. In February, for example, Mexican cavalry followed an Indian trail into their Chiricahua Mountain stronghold, and upon locating the camp, launched an attack from three sides. Six warriors were reported killed in the fight, along with fifteen noncombatants. Later that same month, in response to a raid on Pinos Altos, a mixed command of California troops and miners lashed back, all but annihilating Luis's band.

The Apaches had their turn in March when they attacked a government supply train at Camp Mimbres, a temporary cantonment at the crossing of the stream by the same name. Captain Whitlock, then stationed there, delayed his pursuit long enough to make the Apaches believe the troops were going to remain in camp. Five days later, he set out with seventy-two men and eventually located a large Apache camp, perhaps that of Cochise, in the Graham Mountains. In the surprise assault that followed, Whitlock's troops killed twenty-one Indians.

While the army and the Apaches struggled over control of southeastern Arizona, developments elsewhere in the territory were about to add new impetus to Carleton's preoccupation with ridding the region of Indians he classed as hostile. A few mountain men and prospectors had suspected for some time that Arizona offered the potential for rich gold and silver deposits beyond the limited Spanish silver lodes around Tubac and Ajo. Placer discoveries above Fort Yuma manifested that potential, and Arizona's hard-won ascendancy to territorial status, finally signed into law by President Lincoln on February 24, 1863, had been justified in large measure on its undeveloped mineral wealth.[44] The territory's infant mining industry first began to take shape above Fort Yuma. Carleton was also keenly aware of the discovery of new placer deposits along the Colorado River at La Paz, a camp that had burgeoned to some sixteen hundred inhabitants, as well as even more recent strikes in the Bradshaw Mountains in the territory's interior. He therefore perceived the protection of the miners as a key military mission supporting national interests. Having no Confederates left to fight in the Southwest, Carleton felt he could nevertheless contribute to the war effort by making the territory safe so that mining might flourish. Just as Sibley had perceived the treasure of the Southwest as important for the southern cause, so too did Carleton appreciate its value to the Union. The Apaches, to Carleton's way of thinking, posed the greatest obstacle to the development of those resources. Articulating this from his headquarters in Santa Fe, Carleton wrote, "The Apaches in Arizona are very hostile, and unless vigorous measures are pursued against them right away the miners will become panic-stricken and leave the country."[45]

Carleton considered this adequate justification for a coordinated plan of action designed to finally conquer all of the Apaches. He therefore directed Colonel Bowie, who had replaced West as commander of the District of Arizona, to prepare his men for active field operations. Ever attentive to details, Carleton coached Bowie to make sure that the soldiers' arms were in good condition and to conduct "careful and systematic target practice to the extent of twenty rounds per man with musket and carbine and eighteen rounds with revolver, and have careful drills at skirmishing at least two hours a day for all troops."[46] The old campaigner nevertheless betrayed a lack of confidence in Bowie's abilities by adding that he planned to go to Franklin to assist personally with the preparations.

Carleton planned a general offensive involving not only his own troops but civilians and Indian auxiliaries as well. He suggested to Territorial Governor John N. Goodwin that he issue a proclamation encouraging every able-bodied man with a gun to join in the effort. Additionally, Carleton authorized the issue of enough arms to equip four companies of Pima and Maricopa allies. The miners also organized partisan groups and offered their services to Carleton. Hoping to deny the Apaches their usual sanctuary in Mexico, Carleton probably overstepped his authority by soliciting the cooperation of the governors of Sonora and Chihuahua to mount similar expeditions on their side of the border.[47] Ideally, the Apaches would be caught between and decisively defeated by one force or the other.

The campaign was to be spearheaded by a five-hundred-man expedition marching west from Las Cruces. Commanded by Colonel Edwin A. Rigg, the column comprised elements of both the First and Fifth California Infantry, the First New Mexico Infantry, and the First California Cavalry. Carleton's strategy called for Rigg to establish a base of operations on the upper Gila at a place selected by his inspector general, Lieutenant Colonel Nelson

Davis. The new post would bear the name of Governor Goodwin. From that cantonment, Rigg was to send out small, lightly equipped columns into the mountains to search the eastern part of the territory. The plan also called for other columns to scout both northeast and southeast from Tucson and from Fort Whipple, near the new mining camp of Prescott, down across the Salt River with the objective of blocking the movements of any Apaches flushed by Riggs's detachments. On the east, other troops marching in a pincer movement south from Fort Canby would prevent the hostiles from escaping in that direction.[48]

Two companies of the First New Mexico Infantry were assigned to duty in Arizona as a result of this campaign. Company A was posted at Fort Bowie in July 1864, while Company I joined the Apache Expedition at Fort Goodwin. Company A had been raised in Santa Fe during early fall 1863, after which it was sent to Fort Union to help protect the Santa Fe Trail. Like the other components of the regiment, most of its members were Hispanic farmers and common laborers having no formal education. Although they may have been unfamiliar with army ways, their heritage instilled in them a practical knowledge of Indians and how to take care of themselves in the desert environment. They were also men unaccustomed to many comforts. Consequently, when the New Mexico Volunteers replaced the Californians, soon to be mustered out of service, they were probably not affected by the primitive conditions they found at Fort Bowie.[49]

Fort Bowie itself also figured into Carleton's plan. It was the logical point from which Lieutenant Colonel Davis could secure an escort for his reconnaissance to the Gila River. Since the post still had no cavalry, other than the mail express, Carleton saw to it that a platoon of the First California, under the command of Lieutenant Henry Stevens, was sent there from New Mexico. But, as Stevens and his sixty troopers rode through Doubtful Canyon on May 4, Cochise ambushed them from concealed positions. The lieutenant quickly recovered from his initial surprise, rallied his men, and counterattacked, driving the Apaches back. In a fight lasting about forty-five minutes, Stevens accounted for ten warriors killed and left on the ground, plus an estimated twenty more wounded. It was a costly fight for Cochise, who made his way back to the Gila country to live near his White Mountain cousins. The cavalrymen proceeded to Fort Bowie without further incident.[50]

Arriving at the post a few days later, Stevens joined forces with most of Tidball's infantry company as an escort for Davis. They departed on the ninth, leaving only eighteen men to hold Fort Bowie. What began as a reconnaissance to locate a site for Fort Goodwin turned into one of the most noteworthy army victories of the entire campaign. Davis examined the general area suggested by Carleton and eventually selected a site on the south bank of the Gila about eighty miles northeast of Tucson. By that time, however, Davis had begun seeing fresh Indian trails and set out in pursuit. A few days later, on May 29, his men surprised a camp in the Mescal Mountains and attacked immediately before the Apaches had time to escape. The band of more than four dozen was all but annihilated.[51]

Shortly after Tidball's return from the expedition, one of the companies of the First New Mexico joined the garrison at Fort Bowie. Tidball lost no time employing these reinforcements to carry out Carleton's orders to scout the Chiricahua Mountains south of the post. He marched out of the post on July 10 at the head of thirty-two soldiers from his own company and twenty-five New Mexicans. A few days later, the column encountered a recent Indian trail, which they followed for seven miles. Approaching the Apache camp without being detected, Tidball attacked. The leader of the group, a minor chief named Plume, was killed in the ensuing skirmish. The troops afterward scouted west across Sulphur Spring Valley to the Dragoon Mountains, but finding no other signs of Apaches, they returned to the post.

The rest of Carleton's summer campaign proved anticlimactic. A few of the columns sent out by Rigg, as well as from other posts, resulted in minor successes, but none equaled Davis's early victory. Although the volunteers performed hard service in scorching desert heat all that summer, they accomplished little beyond stirring up the Apaches and killing only enough "to enrage and irritate them without breaking their spirit," according to one civilian.[52] With the California Volunteers nearing the end of their enlistment term, it would be Carleton's last opportunity to mount a large-scale operation.

Even though Carleton's campaign had failed to achieve its goal, some of the Apaches, Cochise's band among them, were so discouraged that they migrated back to northern Mexico, only to be hounded by troops there. By January 1865, the Chiricahuas had been on the run for so long that they began to consider negotiating a peace with the Americans. When word reached Carleton, he flatly stated that his terms still stood—surrender and go to Bosque Redondo, or be exterminated.[53] Consequently, a few dozen Apaches led by Nana approached an officer at Fort Webster, New Mexico, to broach the subject of surrender. Satisfied that the soldiers were receptive to peace, Nana convinced Victorio to come in. The latter consented to give up, provided he and his people could settle in familiar country on the Gila or the Mimbres, not Bosque Redondo. The army rejected the overture, however; there could be no conditions.[54] Aside from short periods during the following decade when he would temporarily submit to reservation life, Victorio was to remain one of the terrors of the borderlands.

Cochise and his people refused to consider any sort of truce with the whites. Soon he was at the head of a large number of tribesmen operating in the vicinity of the upper San Pedro. His warriors surprised two westbound cavalry couriers near San Pedro Crossing on January 4, capturing both their horses and the mail, but the soldiers managed to escape. Other attacks followed in quick succession. A few days later, Apaches appeared at Tubac, where they waylaid a wagon, killing one man and wounding another. The raiders struck at the ancient town several more times during the following month. They murdered two more men, William Wrighter and Gilbert W. Hopkins, in the vicinity of the Santa Rita mines on February 17 and attacked a nearby ranch. The few troops stationed in the region gave Cochise almost complete freedom to raid at will. Growing ever bolder, he planned an attack on the cavalry vedette station at old Fort Buchanan, which was part of the military communications system across southern Arizona. Only a corporal and two privates were at the station when the Apaches struck. Corporal Buckley was shot through the thigh in the opening volley, yet he and Private Berry effectively returned fire, each felling a warrior. After the Indians set fire to the station, the two men ran for their lives and were successful in breaking through the Apache lines to safety. Striking once more at Tubac on their way south, the Chiricahuas crossed into Mexico to take up a series of bloody raids in Chihuahua.[55]

Major General Irvin McDowell, who had led Union forces to defeat at the Battle of Bull Run in the opening act of the Civil War, was subsequently placed in command of the Department of the Pacific during summer 1864. By early the following year, it was obvious to McDowell that, since supplies for troops in Arizona were provided from quartermaster and ordnance depots at San Francisco, that district would be more logically placed under his administration. Army headquarters approved the change, and on January 20 Brigadier General John S. Mason was assigned to command the District of Arizona. Just a month later, prior to his departure to assume his new command, Mason met with both McDowell and Governor Goodwin to discuss the Indian situation in the territory. Goodwin conveyed the impression that the Apaches wielded almost total control over the territory and were permitted to cross back and forth over the international border whenever they chose

Merijildo Grijalva served as post guide and interpreter at Fort Bowie during most of its active years. (Arizona Historical Society/ Tucson, AHS Photo Number 1815)

to do so. Therefore, when Mason arrived in Arizona early in June, he immediately conducted a personal tour of inspection to determine the condition of the posts and troops under his command, and to assess the Apache situation for himself.

Mason proceeded from Tucson to Fort Bowie, taking a circuitous route via Tubac and old Fort Buchanan, where he was greeted with a howitzer salute in his honor. There he learned from Second Lieutenant Thomas Caghlan, commanding the one-company garrison of New Mexico Volunteers, that the Apaches under Cochise were probably in the vicinity of Mount Graham, near where Whitlock had found them the previous March. Upon his return to Tucson, Mason ordered Lieutenant Colonel Clarence E. Bennett, First California Cavalry, to lead an expedition from Fort Bowie to the Gila River country to find and attack Cochise. Bennett assembled a small cavalry force of forty-three men from Companies E, L, and M and marched out of Fort Bowie at 7:00 in the evening of June 26. Accompanying Bennett's column were three civilians—George Cox, Charles Kenyon, and a Mr. Dysart—who volunteered their services. Guiding the expedition were Merijildo Grijalva, a civilian employed at Fort Bowie, and an Apache boy named Lojinio. Bennett, following the advice of his guides, marched at night and rested during the day to reduce the chances of being discovered by the Apaches.

Bennett proceeded west from Fort Bowie following the stage road over the pass, then turned northward past the Dos Cabezas. All went well until the third night's march, when Bennett discovered one of his men missing while the column halted. When last seen, the man had paused to tighten his saddle. Bennett sent back a party to locate the soldier, but they found no trace of him. Moving from one water hole to another, approaching the Apaches before sunrise, Bennett hoped to surprise them in a rancheria, but discovered only signs that were more than a week old. The little column eventually struck the Gila about thirty miles from Fort Goodwin, whereupon Bennett decided to go into the post for supplies and to have his horses reshod before continuing his scout. That accomplished, Bennett again set out southward on July 2. The next morning, near Cottonwood Creek, he encountered fresh footprints left by Apaches who were apparently out hunting. He followed these to a rancheria situated at a point where the mouths of three canyons converged. Bennett, having no choice but to attack in daylight, deployed his men along a ridge, then charged down on the camp. Their noisy approach down the rocky slope alerted the Indians, who immediately scattered into the surrounding oaks. The troopers fired at the fleeing Indians, but apparently hit none. Booty left behind in the camp revealed that the band had been involved in some of the recent raids, including the one on the Fort Buchanan express station.

Bennett's men destroyed the camp and moved on, circling the Penaleno Mountains to the west before turning back south toward Fort Bowie. As the troops crossed Sulphur Spring Valley, they cut another trail that led them directly to a rancheria in a nearby canyon. Bennett, fearing that his men would be discovered if he attempted to reconnoiter along the flanks of the camp, ordered them to charge directly into what Bennett was to name Cavalry Canyon. As it turned out, the camp was situated three miles up the canyon, and the clatter of shod hooves on the rocky ground again gave the Apaches time to escape. The soldiers exchanged some long-range fire at up to a thousand yards, but the distance was too great to be effective. At the same time, Francisco, the leader of the band, yelled down from the mountainside "and abused everybody," according to Bennett.[56]

Although Bennett had harassed the Indians, his expedition caused them no great damage. Shortly afterward, Cochise and Francisco launched another series of raids into Arizona from one of their hideouts in Sonora. The force of 150 warriors first fell on the Ochoa Ranch, killing several persons there, then proceeded to wipe out a family of German emigrants, along with several Mexicans, camped at Ciénaga de los Pinos on the road east of Tucson.

Encountering continued devastation, Bennett urged that "vigorous efforts should be made to annihilate the bands of Cochise and Francisco and the other Indians infesting those mountains west of Fort Goodwin."[57] The persistent lack of enough troops, especially cavalry, to deal effectively with Apaches roaming over such a vast area, placed the army at a disadvantage for many years to come.

Bennett's experience in the field that summer gave him a better appreciation for the necessity of assigning cavalry at Fort Bowie. Therefore, at the end of the Gila campaign, he sent Company L, First California, to reinforce the New Mexico Volunteers at Apache Pass. Even the addition of only one mounted company increased the ability of the post commander to patrol the surrounding area and to respond more effectively to Indian depredations. Bennett, in obedience to Mason's orders, left Fort Bowie on July 10 with the remainder of his command to "examine, measure, and report upon" the wagon road between Croton Spring and Maricopa Wells, via Fort Breckinridge.[58]

Meantime, Mason sent out Captain Hiram A. Messenger and thirty men from the Mowry Mine, near Tubac, to reconnoiter the Huachuca Mountains and the adjacent San Pedro Valley. Messenger accidentally stumbled across the trail of the marauders and gave chase into Sonora. Failing to catch up with Cochise and Francisco, Messenger circled to the west and camped fifteen miles east of Santa Cruz. When two of his men failed to return from a hunt, Messenger led a search party out of camp in an attempt to find them, but was promptly ambushed by the full Apache force. The would-be rescuers fought a rear guard action all the way back to camp. No casualties were recorded on either side as a result of the skirmish, but the corpses of the two hapless hunters were later found in the mountains.[59]

Mason's inspection of Fort Bowie impressed on him the rude nature of the quarters and other buildings at the post. He reported to department headquarters that he found the men living in hovels, and had therefore directed the commanding officer to construct new barracks in an elevated basin a few hundred yards east of the post. The larger number of soldiers at the post finally permitted detachments to be sent to Ojo del Carrizo, approximately twenty miles south, to establish a lumber camp.[60] Other men were put to work hauling and burning limestone in kilns to make lime for mortar. Soon after assuming command of the post in August, Major James Gorman devoted his full attention to construction by assigning all men not on essential military duties to the lumber camp and lime operations, making shingles and hauling stone for the new buildings.[61]

Image taken by D. P. Flanders in 1874 looking west from the new fort toward Apache Pass. The buildings of old Fort Bowie are on the hill to the left and the second stage station stands at the base of the hill in the middle ground. (Arizona Historical Society/Tucson, AHS Photo Number 21355)

Gorman's plans were progressing nicely when Cochise suddenly showed up in the hills above the post during October. As he had done on numerous occasions in the past, the chief displayed a white flag and indicated his desire to talk. Since Francisco and Victorio had recently gone in to Fort Goodwin and Pinos Altos, respectively, to discuss truces, Cochise may have been influenced to make similar arrangements before the coming winter. Whatever the reason, Gorman knew very well that Carleton's order regarding such overtures was still in effect. Resisting his own inclination to open fire on the Apaches, Gorman nonetheless consented to allow one of his officers and Grijalva to have a brief talk with Cochise to determine his intentions. Had Gorman still been under Carleton's command, there would have been no ambivalence. But, with Fort Bowie answering to a new headquarters in San Francisco, Gorman agreed to contact Mason and to meet again with Cochise in twelve days.

Gorman afterwards reconsidered this decision, perhaps after discussing it with others at the post. He decided not to wait for an answer from Mason, but to plan a surprise attack on Cochise. Loading thirty-four soldiers aboard wagons ostensibly bound for the pinery, the detachment camped during daylight hours and traveled by night. Moving by stealth, the soldiers discovered a rancheria in Mescal Canyon, about forty-five miles from Fort Bowie, on November 5. Gorman concealed his wagons and teams some distance from the camp and approached on foot. The troops were surprised to discover not one, but two rancherias about a half-mile distant from each other. Gorman quietly moved his men into position, then attacked both camps simultaneously. The volleys unleashed by the soldiers killed seven Apaches outright; the rest fled. As on previous occasions, the troops found numerous articles in the camp that implicated the band's involvement in the raid on the vedette station at Fort Buchanan and the subsequent attack on the German emigrants at Ciénaga.[62]

Gorman's treachery did nothing to improve relations with the Apaches. It was evident that Cochise wished to secure a peaceful winter camp in the vicinity of Apache Pass. However, the many depredations he and his band had committed during the past several years indicated to the army that the Chiricahuas would abide by a truce only so long as it suited them. The following spring they would no doubt resume raiding on one side of the border or the other, and probably both. But distrust existed on both sides. Gorman's surprise attack only confirmed in Cochise's mind that Americans could not be trusted any more than Mexicans. For the Apaches, that truth was confirmed with the unwarranted slaying of Francisco at Fort Goodwin on November 10 and the attempted murder of Victorio at Pinos Altos.

General Mason tacitly approved his subordinate's actions by organizing a winter campaign against Cochise, who, despite Gorman's attack, had elected to remain in the Chiricahua Mountains. Even though winters were nothing like those encountered on the plains farther north, the Apaches did not expect the soldiers to hunt them at that season. A column commanded by Colonel Charles W. Lewis, Seventh California Infantry, marched out of Fort Mason in December with the intent of scouting the Huachuca Mountains and the area eastward to the Sulphur Spring Valley.[63] Mason also directed other columns to scout both sides of the Dragoons for the purpose of denying the

Apaches that sanctuary for the coming winter. One of the columns, under Captain Porfirio Jimeno, found and attacked a camp near Sulphur Springs, but the others returned without success. The more determined Lewis decided to make a reconnaissance of the Chiricahua Mountains, arriving at Fort Bowie early in January. There he exchanged his guide for the intrepid Merijildo Grijalva, who was intimately familiar with the area to be penetrated. Lewis, leading his column southward through the mountains, discovered a recently abandoned rancheria and sighted sixty or more Indians riding far ahead toward the border. Although Lewis pursued them into Sonora, he finally gave up and returned to Fort Mason.

The next few months would see the volunteer troops mustered out of service. Although many state and territorial units had been organized specifically to keep the Indians in check for the duration of the Civil War, the Californians enlisted for the purpose of countering the Confederate threat to the Southwest. It can be speculated that Carleton's California Column would have assured Union success in the West given the opportunity, but events relegated his troops to a secondary, yet critical, mission of controlling the Indians throughout southern New Mexico and Arizona. Perhaps because of Carleton's frontier experience and his no-quarter approach to dealing with Indians, or because the soldiers themselves were largely frontiersmen, the Californians proved more adept at their task than most other volunteer organizations. Carleton's leadership abilities and prewar experience as a dragoon clearly reduced the time it normally would have taken for such troops to abandon conventional tactics in favor of those adapted to hunting down the elusive Apaches. But the end of the Civil War signaled the disbanding of the volunteers, resulting in the loss of their valuable frontier experience. The Regular Army would soon return to the Southwest, but would have to learn again many of those same lessons.

CHAPTER 5

Neither Life nor Property Is Secure in Arizona

The effect of the Confederate surrender at Appomattox was slow in rippling west to far-off Arizona. While the end of the Civil War signaled the rapid demobilization of the huge Union war machine in the East, the army's mission beyond the Mississippi had grown more complex than it had been in 1861. The lure of gold, silver, and fertile farming lands drew thousands of Americans to the West, necessitating additional routes of travel and communication requiring protection. Not surprisingly, the increasing numbers of whites flooding across the plains alarmed the Indians. If anything, the Federal government's distraction of the previous four years, coupled with inconsistent treatment by volunteer forces, had left the western tribes in a more warlike mood. By 1864–65, the state units posted on the frontier, whose members wanted nothing more than to go home, found themselves engaged in a full-blown Indian war across the central and northern plains. And in southeastern Arizona, Cochise was as unrelenting in exacting his revenge on the Americans as Carleton was in prosecuting his own brand of Indian pacification. Consequently, there was to be no immediate reprieve in store for the volunteers, including the Californians posted in the Southwest.

The Regular Army was ill prepared to resume its responsibilities in the western territories at the end of the Civil War. While the bulk of the army remained in the South on Reconstruction duty, many line officers anticipated a respite from field service. Artillerymen could rest assured they would be posted along the seacoasts, but most cavalry and infantry officers faced the prospect of reassignment in the hinterlands of the Far West. Arizona, in particular, had the reputation for being hardship duty, and for good reason.

Still worse, a war-weary Congress was hardly in a mood to be generous with military appropriations, a factor that all but doomed major construction and other improvements at most frontier stations.

An effect of this belt-tightening was the redesignation of many western forts, particularly those established by the volunteers during the war, as "camps." The exercise, in many respects, was one of semantics to satisfy Congress that many of the forts on the army's inventory were not really forts, only impermanent cantonments. The army apparently reasoned that forts were permanent installations, whereas camps were intended only to serve temporary needs and, once those were met, they would be abandoned. Thus, Fort Bowie was officially demoted to "Camp Bowie" in 1866.[1]

The army's next move was to divide Carleton's Department of New Mexico into three new geographical commands. The Territory of New Mexico itself became a district within Major General John Pope's Department of the Missouri, an enormous area embracing much of the Great Plains. West Texas, a part of the Confederacy since 1861, had fallen to Carleton by virtue of his conquest of southern New Mexico, though he exercised little responsibility for it beyond symbolically reclaiming the abandoned forts along the old Butterfield mail route as far east as Fort Davis. The 1865 reorganization unified the entire Lone Star State under a separate Department of Texas.

The administration of Arizona was shifted to the new Department of California, under the jurisdiction of the Division of the Pacific, both headquartered in San Francisco, and commanded by Major General Irvin McDowell, a man "of unexceptional habits and great physical powers."[2] Although the new boundaries may have seemed logical administratively, they at once destroyed the unity of command that "General Jimmy" Carleton had exercised over Apacheria.[3] To better facilitate the management of affairs in Arizona, McDowell subsequently subdivided the territory into four military districts, with the posts in the southeast placed under a headquarters in Tucson.

The postwar reduction in the size of the army left it with more officers than there were units to command. Most of those who chose to remain in service were forced to accept rank far beneath their wartime commands with the volunteers. Regular Army officers reverted to the lineal grades they would have achieved had the war not intervened. As a result, Carleton was offered a lieutenant colonelcy in the Fourth Cavalry, though he was allowed to exercise command temporarily over New Mexico by virtue of his brevet rank as a brigadier.

Meanwhile, Brigadier General John S. Mason, a West Pointer who had served as an artillerist in Mexico and had led an Ohio infantry regiment during the Civil War, was placed in command of the District of Arizona. Mason's troop dispositions reflected the wisdom of Carleton's decisions concerning the defense of the territory. Like his predecessor, Mason considered Fort Bowie to be essential for the protection of the California road. He further bolstered the defense system by reactivating certain strategic antebellum posts that had been abandoned, to the delight of the Apaches, at the outset of the war. Recognizing that the White Mountain tribe would continue to pose a threat from beyond the Gila, he sent troops to old Fort Breckinridge, which he renamed Camp Grant, to open the way for settlement of the lush bottomlands along the lower San Pedro Valley. Farther up the Gila and almost directly north of Camp Bowie, Camp Goodwin stood watch over the Apache reservation. Old Fort Buchanan also remained important for protecting the Tubac mines, as well as the agricultural regions along Sonoita Creek and the Santa Cruz Valley. But the low ground on which the dilapidated post stood had always been a source of disease for the troops; therefore, new Camp Crittenden was established on a hill a half-mile northeast. Mason took the further step of improving the district supply depot at Tucson, which he rechristened Camp Lowell.

During the winter of 1866, McDowell sent Inspector General Charles A. Whittier to report on the condition of the troops in Arizona. Arriving at Camp Bowie on February 27, Whittier found the post well situated to protect Apache Pass, but noted that its lack of adequate grazing made it a poor station for cavalry. He nevertheless considered a mounted detachment to be absolutely essential for carrying the military mail. Whittier also found the quarters appallingly inadequate.

> The men live in excavations made in the hillside, which are dark, confining and at some seasons very damp. The place is naturally so very healthy from its elevated position that no great amount of sickness has existed at the post at any time, but they are not the kind of quarters which should be given men to live in. I think it of great importance that quarters for one company of Infantry (all the force which I consider necessary to be kept here) should be at once constructed.[4]

Whittier further noted that no less than three post commanders at Camp Bowie had been charged with constructing new barracks for the men, and still they lived in hovels. The only accomplishment of any importance had

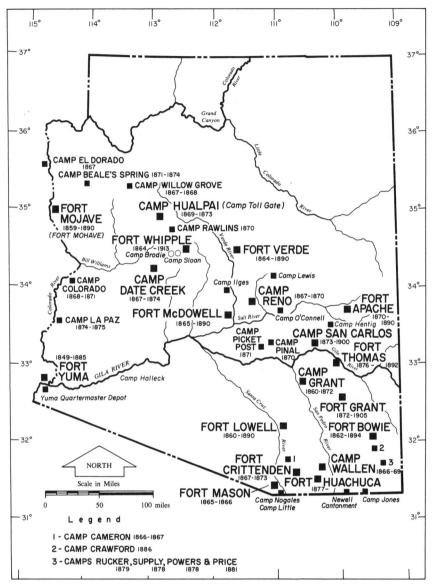

Military posts in Arizona Territory, 1865–1920. (Reprinted from Henry Pickering Walker and Don Bufkin, *Historical Atlas of Arizona*, copyright © 1979 University of Oklahoma Press)

been the erection of a small stone and canvas storehouse to protect food, clothing, and ammunition supplies from the elements. The current post commander, Major James Gorman, attributed his own lack of progress to insufficient transportation for hauling building stone to the site. Only two of the eleven wagons at the fort were in serviceable condition, a deficiency Whittier sought to correct by alerting General Mason himself to the immediate need for tire iron, felloes, and spokes. He suggested that Gorman, meanwhile, make all the progress possible by appropriating any empty wagons that might arrive with passing supply trains.

Of even greater concern to Whittier was the fact that the terms of service for most of the two-company garrison would expire within the next few months. More than half the men belonging to Company L, First California Cavalry, were due to be discharged that spring, with the remainder scheduled for mustering out within a year. The New Mexico Volunteers were obligated to serve only until fall 1866. Whittier felt that that these soldiers should be returned to their home states prior to discharge and "not turned loose in the desert with an allowance of mileage totally inadequate to the expense of getting to their homes."[5] He emphasized that it was imperative that regular troops be sent to relieve them as quickly as possible.

Whittier probably knew that a regular regiment, the Fourteenth Infantry, already was en route to Arizona. The Fourteenth, one of the large three-battalion regiments authorized at the beginning of the Civil War, had compiled a distinguished combat record with the Army of the Potomac. War's end found the regiment assigned to provost duty in Richmond, Virginia, where it remained for several months until being ordered to the Pacific Coast. Each battalion was recruited to full strength before it shipped out for San Francisco, the Third Battalion being the last to arrive in California early in December. Orders had already been issued directing the eight companies of the battalion to take station in Arizona, with its headquarters at Camp Goodwin. In the weeks to follow, several of the companies were distributed to Camps Crittenden, Lowell, Grant, and Bowie. Company E marched into Apache Pass in May.[6]

Cochise unwittingly gave the newly arrived regulars time to settle in by remaining below the border in Chihuahua throughout most of 1866. Even though the flurry of expeditions sent against him during the previous year had done him little harm, the constant harassment by the troops made hiding out in Mexico more appealing than remaining in the United States. Moreover, the murder of one of his most faithful allies, the Eastern White Mountain chief Francisco, at Camp Goodwin the previous November had the effect of further distancing the Chiricahuas from the White Mountain and Pinal Apaches. Relations with those tribes had already deteriorated because they felt wrongfully blamed for many of Cochise's raids. At the same time, both the Pinals and the previously troublesome White Mountain people made peace overtures to the Americans at Camp Goodwin, prompting some of the men to hire out later as trackers for the army. The last straw came when Victorio and a few of his Mimbres warriors returned to Pinos Altos to discuss the possibility of securing peace without being exiled at Bosque Redondo. When some of the residents of the mining town attempted to assassinate the chief and his party while they were being entertained in a home, the incident simply reinforced in Cochise's mind the folly of attempting any reconciliation with the whites. Nevertheless, his absence from southeastern Arizona gave the army a welcome respite and time enough to muster out the volunteers.

Not all of the California men left the territory, however. Many of them were already experienced miners and their practiced eyes detected the region's mineral potential. Earlier prospectors had discovered placer deposits along the Gila and the Colorado, and by 1863 mining districts sprang up farther upstream on the Colorado, giving rise to camps at Ehrenberg and La Paz. Others were soon drawn across the desert to discoveries at Wickenburg and in the Sierra Prieta. In the south, small-scale copper, gold, and silver mining had attracted a few Americans to the Tubac area prior to the war, but the lack of smelting facilities and adequate transportation stifled any significant development. The exodus of the Regular Army and Cochise's subsequent unbridled raiding at the outbreak of the war quickly swept the few whites from the Santa Cruz Valley.

With little else to occupy their off-duty time, numerous California soldiers prowled the mountain slopes in the vicinity of Camp Bowie to see what they might discover in the form of mineral deposits. Shortly before they were due to be mustered out of service, a party discovered a "gold ledge in the side of the mountain just back of this post, distant from the post less than one mile and in full view from the parade ground."[7] Another source claimed that the find was located about fifteen hundred yards east of the old stage station, probably in one of the hillsides above the second fort.[8] Exactly what transpired after the initial discovery is not known, but in all probability the soldiers had little time to develop their claim before their unit left for California. Subsequently, a partnership known as the Apache Pass Mining Company acquired the rights to what was dubbed the "Harris Lode," after one of its discoverers. The *Weekly Arizonian* described the new company as "a party without capital or organization . . . more properly [a] mining mob."[9] Never mind the character of the investors, Camp Bowie could at least boast its own gold strike.

The end of the Civil War also prompted other changes at Camp Bowie. While the California mail contract continued in force over the central route via Salt Lake City to Sacramento, there was renewed interest in reopening an overland corridor from the Gulf of Mexico and Texas to California. After the reoccupation of New Mexico by Federal forces in 1862, the U.S. Mail had followed an established route from Missouri along the Santa Fe Trail and down the Rio Grande to Franklin. By 1865, the Santa Fe Stage Company was operating a mail and passenger line from the booming settlement of Prescott directly to the New Mexico capital, with extended service to Denver and Kansas City. West of El Paso to the Colorado, however, communications were in a shambles. Except for a none-too-reliable mail connection between Prescott and Tucson following the appointment of a postmaster at the latter place in July, southern Arizona remained largely isolated from the world. Mail service was haphazard at best, with private mail being transported between points by travelers and freighters, and at times surreptitiously by military couriers. An enterprising Confederate veteran, Bethel Coopwood, organized a freighting operation from San Antonio to El Paso and Chihuahua. When he discovered that no coaches ran west of Mesilla, Coopwood quickly seized the opportunity and began advertising a passenger service in the form of a train of several vehicles having a combined capacity of fifty people. Although the record is unclear as to whether Coopwood had any official status as a mail carrier, he nevertheless provided the service for a time all the way to Los Angeles.[10] So acute was the communications problem that the territorial legislature appealed to Congress in late 1866 to reestablish the Fort Yuma-to-Mesilla mail route.[11] The petition prompted no immediate action, however. If the absence of regular mail service was hardship enough for the budding civilian population, it severely hampered military operations. Inspector General Roger Jones complained that even routine messages from the far-flung posts below the Gila sometimes took up to three months to reach San Francisco, making it "impossible for the department commander to know of any particular transaction in Arizona until long after it has transpired."[12]

The abandoned Southern Overland Mail Route west of the Rio Grande lay open to any entrepreneur having the capital, and the courage, to undertake the risks. The first of those was J. W. Davis, who secured a mail contract within a year after the war ended and began operating passenger coaches between Mesilla and Tucson. That prompted the erection of a post office at the foot of the hill occupied by Camp Bowie, with ex-California volunteer George Hand appointed as postmaster, in December 1866. The site selected was a more logical location than the abandoned Butterfield station because the trail branching from the main Overland Road to Apache Spring had been improved and re-routed over the hill upon which the second fort was eventually built. From that point, the road turned northward down an unnamed canyon to intersect the old route on the desert below. The location of the new station placed it conveniently close to both the post and the spring.[13]

A series of three express riders, purportedly paid $200 a month to make the dangerous weekly runs, carried the mail in relays from Tucson to Mesilla, where it connected with mails bound for Santa Fe and San Antonio. At times when mail was light, the rider would carry the bags on his own mount, either a horse or mule; other times the mail would be packed on an additional mule led behind. The riders exchanged bags at Camp Bowie and at Soldier's Farewell, one of the old stone-walled Butterfield stations located just west of the Continental Divide in New Mexico. Each rider then returned to his former station. The expensive express system, relying on riders courageous enough to risk their lives, gave way to weekly and, later still, tri-weekly delivery using buckboards and light passenger coaches, at times escorted by two or three soldiers. The Tucson–Los Angeles connection eventually was renewed in 1867. No more would the California-bound mail from Arizona be required to take the frustratingly circuitous route via St. Joseph, Missouri.[14]

Dampening the spirits of Arizona residents was Cochise's return to the territory early that same year. Although the Chiricahuas initially avoided contact with the whites, preferring instead to take refuge deep in the Animas Mountains of New Mexico, as well as in their own Chiricahua range, the mail riders plying the Overland Road made inviting and vulnerable targets that proved irresistible. In late February warriors surprised and killed mail carrier Charles A. B. Fisher a few miles east of Camp Bowie. Later investigation of the scene revealed that the Apaches pounced on the lone rider after he had reached the flats some distance beyond the mouth of the canyon. Fisher instantly turned back toward the post, putting spurs to his horse in an attempt to outrun the Apaches. During the chase, an Indian bullet struck Fisher, severely wounding him, causing the expressman to drop from his horse about halfway back to the fort. The Apaches took both Fisher's horse and the packmule bearing the mail. Soldiers later recovered the rider's scalped and mutilated body and took it to the post cemetery for burial.[15]

The single company of infantry then comprising the garrison at Camp Bowie was impotent to do anything about such attacks, a fact that did not escape Cochise.[16] Nor were the other posts in the Tucson district any better prepared to deal with the Chiricahuas. Living up to his reputation as "the terror of the Southern Country," Cochise next struck one of his traditional targets—the Mowry Mine, where he hoped to plunder the company's arsenal of small arms and ammunition.[17] After a fight lasting several hours, during which the mine employees kept up a heavy defensive fire from the main building, Cochise withdrew to his old haunts in the Chiricahua Mountains. That spring, both the United States and Mexico mounted concerted efforts to subdue the Apaches, including reinforcement of the garrisons along the northern frontier of Sonora.

Camp Bowie would have been the most logical post for the U.S. Army to use as a base for offensive operations in the region, but the new district commander, Colonel Thomas L. Crittenden, was unable to conduct them. Some of his meager cavalry forces scouted from Camps Lowell and Wallen, but because Crittenden had to contend with numerous Apache bands throughout the district, he simply did not have sufficient mounted forces to spare for Camp Bowie. Consequently, it continued to be manned by only the one company of infantry. The forty-five-man garrison had its hands full performing the necessary garrison duties, escorting supply trains, and doing what little it could to protect mail couriers and travelers on the road. An offensive was simply out of the question.

Before the army could organize a force strong enough to pursue the Apaches into the mountains, Cochise struck again near Tubac. In only two day's time, his warriors shot up a wagon train and stole its cattle, pillaged a nearby ranch, and stampeded the horses of a Papago scout detachment stationed at Calabasas. A cavalry troop, sent out after the Chiricahuas, managed to surprise a rancheria of approximately seventy warriors in the mountains south of Camp Bowie. The troops killed three of them and burned the village. When the army subsequently tried to trap Cochise and his band between separate columns sent out from Tubac and Camp Grant, the chief and his party slipped back into Sonora, where they remained for the remainder of the summer and into fall 1867.

A few months earlier, a new railroad survey party, retracing the course laid out by Lieutenant Parke in the 1850s, set out toward California to confirm

Second Lieutenant John Cuthbert Carroll, Thirty-second Infantry, killed by Apaches near Fort Bowie on November 5, 1867. (Wendall Lang Collection, U.S. Army Military History Institute)

Camp Bowie, November 6, 1867. The flag appears at half-staff in honor of Post Commander John C. Carroll, killed by Apaches the previous day and buried the morning William A. Bell took this image. (Arizona Historical Society/Tucson, AHS Photo Number 28840)

the route for a southern link along the thirty-second parallel. Arriving at Apache Pass in early November, one of the surveyors, Englishman William A. Bell, described the fort as "a small collection of adobe houses, built on the summit of a hill, which rises as a natural lookout station in the centre of the defile, and commands the road both ways for two or three miles of its length."[18] The three officers at the post, starved for new company and the latest news, invited the surveyors to spend the night. The following afternoon, Bell, the official photographer with the expedition, ascended Overlook Ridge with his camera to capture an image of the post. While seated on the summit taking in the view of the surrounding mountains, Bell heard shots to the west and observed a commotion among the men in the garrison as the sentinels strained to observe what was happening out toward the old stage stand. From his perch, Bell watched as the westbound mail carrier, John Slater, raced back past the beef herd grazing near the road. Bell watched intently as a pair of Apache warriors appeared in close proximity to the cattle, apparently intending to drive them off. Just then, a detachment of soldiers joined the expressman and started out toward the herd.

Post commander Captain John C. Carroll, a still-youthful veteran of the war with nearly five year's service, saddled his horse and minutes later dashed off down the winding road from the fort. According to a cattle drover who arrived at the pass a short time after the event, Carroll "could not believe that there existed such a thing as a hostile Indian . . . he had never been close to one."[19] Bell last saw the captain as he caught up with the courier and the two disappeared over the hills to the west. Observing these events, First Lieutenant Joseph Lawson, commander of a six-man detachment of the Third Cavalry escorting the survey party, could not resist the opportunity to engage the Indians. Although their mounts were jaded by the long journey from the Rio Grande, the troopers trotted down the road after Carroll until they, too, disappeared from view.

Later that afternoon, the soldiers began straggling back to the post a few at a time. They reported that, after searching for several hours, they had neither caught up with the Indians, nor even sighted them again. Ominously, neither had anyone seen anything of Carroll and the mail rider. Those men who had gone farthest west had heard gunshots out toward the plain beyond the pass, portending a grim fate for the two men. A nine-man search party immediately set out, taking a shortcut southwesterly over the base of Helen's Dome. Reaching the plains shortly before sunset, the party spread out in skirmish order in an attempt to intersect the trail left by the two men. They eventually found tracks of shod horses and, following them for some three miles, discovered Slater's nude and mutilated body. The Apaches had scalped both his head and the long sideburns from one cheek. Farther along, with barely enough light to see, the party found Carroll's corpse in a similar condition. Both bodies were returned to the post and buried during a brief ceremony the next morning. The surveyors continued on their way shortly thereafter. For Bell and his comrades, their side-trip to Apache Pass had been a most memorable one.[20]

The administration of Camp Bowie by the Regular Army resulted in few improvements, even as late as 1868. When Major Henry Martyn Robert made an inspection of the Arizona forts during January and February of that year, he found that at Apache Pass

> [m]ost of the buildings excepting the officers quarters are on the side hill so that one side is partially underground thus [sketch]. The buildings are either dry stone or stone with adobe mud for mortar or of Adobe mud (as the Barracks and Comdg. Officer's qrts.) The roofs

are all Adobe & leak. The houses are generally damp and especially Com. Store room so that the stores have to be removed to be dried after every rain.[21]

The rest of the post was equally dismal. The cramped parade ground, occupying the nose of the hill overlooking the spring and surrounded by a cluster of shacks that served as officers' quarters, was hardly worthy of being called a fort. Boasting four beds, the hospital was housed in a rock-walled subterranean room somewhat removed from parade ground activity, yet was situated near the sounds and odors of the quartermaster corral. Additionally, there were at least seven, perhaps as many as ten, small huts each quartering a few enlisted men. Camp Bowie clearly ranked as one of the most primitive posts anywhere in the West.

Robert's report echoed the recommendation made by Lieutenant Colonel Bennett three years earlier.

My opinion is that it would be better to remove the Post three hundred yards to the plateau where a fine large building 150' x 30' was begun by Col. Bennet [*sic*] & raised several feet high. To attempt to repair the existing buildings and build new ones where they sink into the hill side so far as to keep them damp would in my judgment cost more in the end than the building of a new post on a far better site for building, where there has already been done a great deal of work.[22]

The comparatively large, open area some five hundred yards east of the original fort site, although not ideal terrain for a fort, was considerably better than the one Carleton had selected. It could be argued that Camp Bowie should have been built there in the frst place, but for Carleton's overriding concern that the Apaches might capture the all-important water supply. Still, the immediate presence of troops, and the ease of maintaining a picket post nearer the spring if necessary, probably would have discouraged any such attempt.

In any event, Robert's recommendations tipped the scales in favor of the new location. The army recognized by that time that the fort's role had grown beyond Carleton's mandate of protecting the spring and the travel route to the Rio Grande. Camp Bowie by then formed part of the defense network in southeastern Arizona that was intended to control the Apaches through constant military presence in their homeland. The role of the army also extended to promoting transcontinental communication and emigration from Texas to California. Also of concern to the government were the mineral resources in the territory that remained largely untapped, and would remain so as long as the Apaches continued to discourage settlement through incessant raiding.

Not long after Major Robert's visit, the garrison began constructing new buildings around a 500-feet-square parade ground higher up in the basin to the east. The first of these was a building 150 feet long by 33 feet wide, the one mentioned in Robert's report, which had been started but never finished while the California Volunteers occupied the site. Although the structure had been designed as a barracks, the regulars modified it for use as a stable and forage house, since the post afforded no other place to shelter animals. Other structures followed as the garrison made a gradual transition to the "New Post" site. The troops, therefore, were occupied primarily with construction throughout the remainder of the year.[23]

While the soldiers labored to improve living conditions at Camp Bowie, Cochise remained secluded in the Peloncillo Mountains north of the California Road near the New Mexico border. His warriors occasionally ventured out to lurk near Camp Bowie, awaiting another chance to steal livestock or ambush a careless white man. During those months, troops from Sonora and Chihuahua demonstrated unusual cooperation with each other in patrolling the border and pursuing any Apaches discovered in the region, regardless of Mexican or American boundaries. A force of Mexican cavalry crossing into Arizona managed to surprise Cochise's camp during February, but the Chiricahuas escaped after fighting a minor rear guard skirmish. Following that incident, the region remained relatively quiet until spring.

Then, shortly after noon on May 13, 1868, Cochise paid another visit to Camp Bowie. Leading a party of approximately fifty warriors, he swept down on the herd grazing a mile or two below the post. However, he was unaware that the soldiers were no longer armed with muzzle-loading rifle muskets. Two years earlier, Congress approved the conversion of twenty-five thousand Civil War muskets into single-shot breechloaders firing a powerful .50-caliber metallic cartridge. The new arms, which had only recently reached the Thirty-second Infantry, increased the soldier's firepower considerably—from a maximum of three shots per minute with a musket to more than a dozen rounds with the breech-loading rifle.[24]

At the sound of the first shots, a detachment of infantry sprinted off from the post to assist the dozen soldiers comprising the herd guard. Meanwhile, the guard surprised the Chiricahuas with both the volume of fire and range. Post Surgeon Joseph P. Widney, who accompanied the first relief party, commented, "The new breech-loaders with which the men are now armed undoubtedly saved them."[25] Somewhat bewildered when the soldiers failed to draw ramrods after their first shots, the Apaches kept their distance rather than closing in quickly as they normally would have done. A short time later, a second detachment left the fort to reinforce the first. As these parties were making their way down to the flats, the Apaches thwarted the herders' attempt to drive the animals up the stage road canyon. The herders, meantime, keeping the warriors at bay, moved the stock around to an alternate canyon (probably Siphon Canyon), and returned safely to the post. Cochise and his men retreated, satisfied to leave the soldiers alone for the moment. The troops suffered no casualties in the skirmish and Indian losses, if any, were not determined.[26]

It was not long after this "rude rebuff" that the Apaches had an opportunity to acquire a couple of the new rifles for themselves.[27] Two weeks after the frustrated raid on the fort, members of Cochise's band still hovering in the area laid a trap for the eastbound mail coach. After making its usual stop at the Camp Bowie post office on May 26, the coach rolled out of the mountains toward Barney's Station. Aboard were driver Charles "Tennessee" Hadsell, teamster John Brownley, and an escort of two infantrymen, Privates Robert King and George Knowles. As the stage reached the ambush site about ten miles from the fort, the Apaches began shooting from a ravine near the road. Hadsell reacted quickly to turn the coach and whip the mules into a run back toward Camp Bowie, as the other men returned fire. During the flight, Brownley was shot through the heart and collapsed within the stage. The Apaches gave chase for five miles, eventually surrounding the coach and capturing the remaining three men, who would have been better off had they heeded the frontier creed of not being taken alive. The warriors subsequently drew the coach off the road some 150 yards, where they proceeded to cut open the mailbags and scatter the contents about the desert. Before leaving with the team and their hostages, the Apaches scalped Brownley and dragged his bloody corpse away from the road where it would not be readily discovered.

Later that day, the westbound stage arrived at the designated transfer point, Barney's Station. When Hadsell's coach failed to appear, the driver pressed on, hoping to meet the other party farther up the road. The second coach rattled into Bowie just at sunset on the 28th, the driver reporting to commanding officer Captain Homer J. Ripley that he had seen nothing of

Hadsell or the other stage. Ripley immediately dispatched a detachment to investigate, but nightfall prevented them from finding the bullet-riddled coach and the dead teamster until the following morning. The men searched the area for miles around, but found no trace of the other three men.

Two days after the incident, Lieutenant Edward B. Hubbard left the post with a second party of thirty men, plus surgeon Widney and two civilian guides, in an attempt to strike the trail of the marauders and to recover the missing men, or determine their fate. They already knew there was little chance of finding them alive. Hubbard picked up the Indian trail near the place where the coach was abandoned and followed it southward toward the mountains to a canyon approximately eight miles from Camp Bowie. There he discovered the site of a recently occupied rancheria and, nearby, "a huge flat rock upon which the men had been tortured and suffered such a death as only an Apache Indian can invent."[28] Surgeon Widney later claimed that the two men had been made to walk in a circle for many hours, after which they were tortured to death. Before burying the remains, the doctor made the members of the detachment view the dead bodies, admonishing the soldiers, "That is what you may expect if ever you surrender; so fight to the last, and make them kill you." Afterwards, the men used their bayonets to scrape out a shallow grave for the putrid bodies, then piled rocks on top to keep coyotes from digging them up. Hubbard pursued the war party for several more days, but finally abandoned the chase when, predictably, the Apaches dispersed into small groups.[29]

Hadsell's body, mutilated almost beyond recognition and partially burned, was discovered several months later in an abandoned rancheria near the Mexican border by a scouting detachment from Camp Bowie. According to one account, "His face and body was [sic] burned and otherwise mutilated and his feet were badly cut up as if he had been compelled to run or been dragged over sharp rocks."[30] The Apaches apparently executed Hadsell when Sonoran troops attacked the camp.

An uncertain calm again settled over southeastern Arizona in late summer. Cochise and his Chiricahuas migrated back to northern Mexico following their earlier raids on the Americans. The chief hoped he could play his old game of currying favor with the Mexicans, perhaps even negotiating a temporary truce at Janos or Fronteras. The Apaches often had been successful in playing off Sonora against Chihuahua, and vice versa, but this time neither governor was inclined to be lenient. Troops from both states hounded the Chiricahuas incessantly, and when small bands ventured north to trade in

New Mexico, they were attacked by U.S. troops from Forts McRae and Cummings. Although American forces were too few and too scattered to conduct any major offensives against the Apaches, the effect of these actions caused Cochise to seek refuge farther north in the Mogollon Mountains, an area the Chiricahuas had not frequented for many years. His departure from Sonora was none too soon, for Mexican troops struck hard at related Chiricahua bands that chose to remain south of the international border. Cochise later acknowledged the loss of over one hundred of his people to Mexican attacks during 1868.[31]

The garrison at Camp Bowie could be thankful that Cochise was occupying himself elsewhere. It gave the troops time to continue the sorely needed improvements aimed at making life at the isolated post a bit more bearable. However, influences far beyond Apache Pass slowed that progress. The army's responsibilities for Reconstruction duty in the South drained off many troops that otherwise would have been available for frontier service. Compounding the situation was an 1866 congressional reorganization act that reduced the army to an actual strength of only slightly more than 38,500 men.[32] Additionally, the job of controlling the Plains tribes along more vital transportation arteries, particularly the Oregon-California Road and the Santa Fe Trail, had assumed critical proportions by 1868. Arizona boasted no less than fifteen forts and temporary cantonments at that time, scattered over an area of 104,000 square miles. Even though Major General Henry W. Halleck, commanding the Division of the Pacific, committed two full regiments of infantry and nine companies of cavalry (a total of twenty-nine companies) to the defense of Arizona, the force was thinly spread.[33] Consequently, Camp Bowie was still occupied by only a single company of the Thirty-second Infantry. Like previous garrisons, Company D, having an average strength of about fifty men, was hard-pressed to perform the required garrison duties, provide escorts for the mails, and still have enough men available for construction work on the new post.

While part of this meager force cleared brush and large rocks from the basin overshadowed by Bowie Mountain, other men were detailed to cut and haul timber from the pinery eighteen miles south of the post. The site was ready for construction to begin by fall. Captain Ripley, recognizing that the small number of soldiers at his disposal could not accomplish everything at once, assigned priorities to building a combined quartermaster storehouse and barracks to provide adequate shelter for both the supplies and the men. Attention was given also to erecting a bakery to provide fresh bread, a dietary necessity as well as an important morale factor. The troops also completed two small officers' quarters and a granary by early the following year. These structures, along with the stable finished previously, accommodated the garrison's basic functions, though the hospital remained temporarily at the first fort until spring. The garrison gradually transitioned to the higher plateau during winter and by early 1869 the new fort was fully occupied. The original fort was relegated to married soldiers and civilian employees. Even by contemporary standards, Camp Bowie was still a relatively primitive station because of its remote location. Nevertheless, the new buildings afforded the troops a degree of comfort they had not previously enjoyed.[34]

CHAPTER 6

Capture and Root Out the Apache

The Quartermaster General's Office had taken a hand in designing the new post; consequently, it conformed more closely to the standard arrangement commonly associated with frontier forts. The primary buildings were positioned around the perimeter of a parade ground measuring approximately three hundred by four hundred feet, though it certainly failed to meet the usual criterion for being flat. Situated at the foot of Bowie Mountain, the south end of the parade was considerably higher than the north end, and the uneven surface was strewn with rocks. The two adobe officers' quarters stood on the south, facing directly across the parade toward the combination barracks and commissary storehouse. Flanking the east side was a stable, with attached corral and forage house, and lining the other was the quartermaster warehouse. Near the end of January, the post trader's store, operated by former California Volunteer Sidney R. De Long, advertised "new goods at reduced prices."[1] First Lieutenant George M. Wheeler arrived at the post soon thereafter for the purpose of officially surveying the boundary of a military reservation. Up to that time, the army had laid claim to the property merely by right of occupancy in the public domain, but times were changing. Wheeler marked off a plot measuring one square mile, measured from the flagstaff, to preclude homesteaders from settling too near the garrison, and perhaps gain title to the land.[2]

The economic development of Arizona was perpetually retarded by two principal factors—the Apaches and poor transportation facilities. Despite efforts by the volunteer regiments to bring order to the territory, the Chiricahua and other Western Apache tribes raided almost at will south of the Gila.

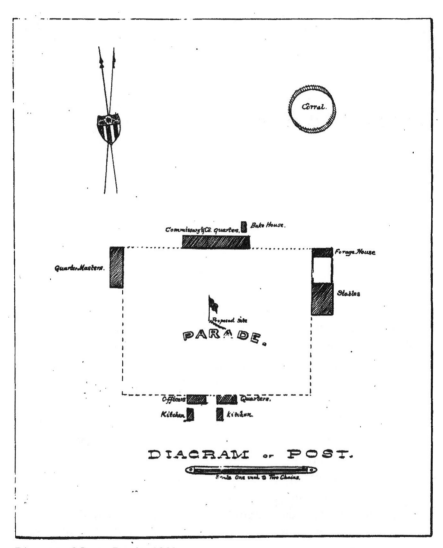

Diagram of Camp Bowie, 1869

Mining, the only significant industry in Arizona up to that time, suffered as a result. The territory was still unable to boast a single railroad by 1869, and even wagon transportation was a risky proposition, made more uncertain by the Apaches. The brief boom of placer gold mining subsided by the end of the Civil War, except for a brief resurgence in the Bradshaw Mountains during 1868–69, after which efforts shifted to more complex lode mining involving the extraction of metals from raw ore. Unlike the rich and easily accessed placers, lode mining called for heavy equipment and substantial capital investment. The absence of rail connections made the shipment of such machinery to the territory slow and extremely difficult. Equally difficult was the transportation of ore to the few crushers and stamp mills established in the mining regions. Moreover, smelting had to be done in California, the ore being moved to the coast by steamers operating on the Colorado River. The modest boom in Arizona thus faltered when potential eastern investors became discouraged by the constant Apache menace to both travel and mining operations in the territory.[3]

Mining interests may have been the most vocal in their outcry for protection, but there were those in military circles, like Major General Henry W. "Old Brains" Halleck, commanding the Division of the Pacific, who questioned just how rich Arizona's mineral resources really were: "I do not mean to say that there are no valuable mines in Arizona, but simply that the products of these mines have never equaled the sanguine anticipations and presentations of their owners, and that the failure of expected dividends to anxious stockholders has not been entirely due to the want of military protection."[4]

In Halleck's view, Arizona afforded superior opportunities for farming and stock-growing, prompting him to predict that "it will become one of the most prosperous countries on the Pacific slope." Indeed, the stagnation of mining translated to some degree into corresponding slumps in agriculture and other businesses that relied on a population large enough to support profitable ventures. The budding town of Tucson offered a market outlet for a small number of farmers and cattle ranchers courageous enough to reside in the Santa Cruz Valley and along Sonoita Creek. However, the very presence of livestock at those farms and ranches likewise made them enticing prey for Apache raids, and it was stockmen, according to Halleck, who deserved more military protection than the miners. "The farmer's wealth," Halleck reasoned, "consists in his cattle and crops; and if these are destroyed, he is often utterly ruined. The miner's principal wealth is in his mines, which the Indians cannot destroy, although they may cripple his operations for a time by robbing him of his work animals, tools, and supplies."[5] Less vulnerable, perhaps, but nonetheless tempting were cattle and horse herds at military posts. Emigrant parties following the Southern Overland Mail Road to the Pacific Coast, as well as cattle herds being driven from Texas to lucrative markets in California, also presented Indian marauders new sources of livestock.

Apache depredations in Pima County alone accounted for the deaths of fifty-two people, with another eighteen wounded, and the loss of one thousand head of stock during a one-year period ending in July 1869. In another example, the Tucson freighting firm of Tully, Ochoa & Company suffered losses amounting to at least $18,500 in only two years. Needless to say, the Apache-Mexican trade in stolen livestock had not diminished.[6]

At that time, the white population of the territory totaled only about 9,500 people, over twenty percent of whom were U.S. soldiers stationed at fourteen posts scattered throughout the territory. An undocumented but nevertheless significant portion of the population was directly dependent on those same forts. They included contractors supplying beef, hay, and wood to the army, as well as guides, blacksmiths, teamsters, and other civilian employees. Virtually every fort, including Bowie, had a licensed post trader (with his own employees) catering to the needs of the garrison. On a broader field were freighters, farmers, and a variety of merchants, all profiting to some degree by the army's presence. Most of the supplies for the army posts in Arizona Territory, including Camp Bowie, were shipped from San Francisco to Yuma via steamer up the Gulf of California, then freighted overland. The combined effect, according to Major General Edward O. C. Ord, who had inherited the Department of California from Halleck in April 1868, was that "almost the only paying business . . . in that Territory is supplying the troops . . . . I am informed from every quarter that if the paymasters and quartermasters of the army were to stop payment in Arizona, a great majority of the white settlers would be compelled to quit it. Hostilities are therefore kept up with a view to protecting inhabitants most of whom are supported by the hostilities."[7]

Recently arrived reinforcements for the Thirty-second Infantry were just settling into their new quarters at Camp Bowie when a detachment of their comrades under the command of Captain Frank W. Perry from Camp Goodwin arrived at the post. Perry reported that he had just come from the Dragoon Mountains, where he had met with Cochise to discuss peace. The council had resulted from an extraordinary and quite unexpected overture by the chief, something Cochise had not risked with any Americans since the Bascom debacle. Perry had contacted Cochise through a self-appointed White Mountain emissary offering to lead him to the Chiricahua camp. Surprisingly enough, Cochise was inclined to talk of peace, but was nevertheless reluctant to subject his people to the abhorrent living conditions and disease prevalent at the Camp Goodwin reservation. Cochise remained uncommitted to giving up the free life as a result of his interview with Perry.[8] Whether or not Cochise seriously considered the matter made little difference. Ord, who had a reputation as an unrelenting campaigner, directed his field commanders in Arizona to "capture and root out the Apache by every means, and to hunt them as they would wild animals."[9]

District of Arizona commander Colonel Thomas C. Devin, Third Cavalry, conveyed Ord's instructions to his subordinates in the field, directing them to begin offensive operations as soon as possible. One of the most capable officers in the district was Captain Reuben F. Bernard, only recently arrived in Arizona from two years of recruiting duty in the East. Bernard eagerly embraced Ord's strategy, and had the advantage of possessing an intimate knowledge of the region. As a sergeant in the Dragoons prior to the Civil War, he had served at both Forts Buchanan and Breckenridge and had been a member of the column sent to relieve Lieutenant Bascom at Apache Pass in 1861. When Sibley invaded New Mexico, Bernard's troop of the First Cavalry (redesignated from Dragoons) engaged the Confederates at Valverde and Glorieta before being attached to the Army of the Potomac in the East. Bernard quickly rose to commissioned rank and participated in some sixty-five actions during the Civil War. Although he was promoted to captain of G Company in 1866, Bernard's detail to the recruit depot at Carlisle Barracks prevented him from joining his unit for nearly three years.[10]

Only two days later, the old dragoon led his company and four Indians scouts northward out of Camp Lowell, departing after nightfall to conceal his movements. Bernard marched to Camp Grant, where he spoke with an Apache woman who provided information on the whereabouts of Chiquito's band. Learning that some of the hostiles were probably camped in the Arivaipa Mountains, Bernard obtained reinforcements from the garrison and proceded south along the San Pedro. A short time later, the cavalrymen discovered some rancherias, recented deserted. Bernard realized that his chances of catching up with the Apaches might be better if his force were smaller, so he arranged to have more than half the men return to Camp Grant as a ruse to make the Apaches believe the entire column had turned back. It worked. On February 4, Bernard and his remaining thirty men found and attacked the unsuspecting camp high in the mountains. When the Apaches saw the soldiers charging, they immediately fled, making a running fight of several miles up snow-covered slopes. The troopers exchanged fire with the Indians for several hours, during which "nearly every man emptied his Spencer carbine three times," according to Bernard. The fight

As a sergeant of dragoons, Captain Reuben F. Bernard (shown here circa 1885) was present at the conclusion of the famed Bascom Affair. He served throughout the Civil War as an officer in the First Cavalry and was afterward posted on the western frontier. While stationed at Camp Bowie, Bernard conducted tenacious pursuits of Cochise and his warriors. His success at the Battle of Chiricahua Pass in 1869, and in other Indian engagements, eventually earned him a brevet to brigadier general. (S. B. M. Young Collection, U.S. Army Military History Institute)

continued for a mile or so down the opposite side of the mountain, until the Apaches scattered and vanished. Bernard tallied eight Indians killed and six taken prisoner. [11]

Returning to Camp Lowell, Bernard immediately refitted his company and made ready to take the field again just two weeks later. His force consisted of twenty-eight men of Company G, plus a ten-man detachment from Company E, Thirty-second Infantry. Bernard scoured the eastern edge of the Dragoon Mountains, then crossed Sulpher Springs Valley and ascended Apache Pass, arriving at Bowie on March 7, where he and his men bivouacked for the night before proceeding north toward Mount Graham. There he struck a fresh trail and followed it northwest, eighty miles beyond Camp Goodwin. Eventually locating the rancheria, Bernard and his men attacked, but again the Indians stampeded at first sight of the soldiers and the only firing was at long range. Nevertheless, they captured and destroyed the contents of the village and took one prisoner.[12]

It was obvious by May that Camp Bowie's location made it a logical station from which to launch protective cavalry patrols along the stage road toward New Mexico. Likewise, a body of cavalry at that point would enable the army to scout the surrounding area in hopes of preventing depredations by keeping the Apaches off-balance. When Bernard and G Company arrived at the post on the 21st, they were disappointed to find that the infantry occupied the only barracks available. They had no alternative but to make themselves as comfortable as possible at "Camp Merijilda," as the old fort was known among the soldiers.[13]

Meantime, the men of the Thirty-second Infantry continued their work on the new post. A better pinery had been found in the mountains some twenty-five to thirty miles south of Bowie, and by July they had a steam-powered sawmill operating there. Captain Bernard, now post commander, formed daily armed details from the old guard to escort the wagons to and from the pinery and inaugurated weekly target practice to improve the garrison's proficiency.[14]

Bernard's men had little time to lament their poor quarters because their energetic commander soon had them back in the saddle in search of Apaches. During the following month, he led two scouting parties, one to the south approximately a hundred miles and another to the Stein's Peak area. Neither party found any Indians, nor did yet another detachment during a three-hundred-mile reconnaissance to the Burro Mountains.[15]

That the Apaches were not intimidated by the troops at Camp Bowie was evidenced by a series of raids Cochise conducted from his headquarters in the nearby Dragoon Mountains. During June and July his warriors struck southwest, descending on farms and ranches in the Santa Cruz and Sonoita valleys, before turning their attention once again to the Tucson–El Paso road. On one occasion, they killed a civilian and wounded another near Apache Pass, and followed that with an attack on one of the mail riders, shooting his horse but missing the rider himself. At about the same time, warriors stole a horse from under the noses of two civilians sleeping near the Apache Pass ore mill, and the next day broke into a company warehouse to destroy acids, belting, and other property. Indians also attacked a party of three miners driving a wagon loaded with supplies bound for the mine. When the warriors rushed the wagon in the fading light of dusk, the men fled and escaped, leaving all the tools, provisions, and mules in the hands of the Apaches.[16]

Bernard retaliated early in August with another expedition to the Mount Graham area, where his company approached a rancheria, but were too late to engage the occupants. The Apaches detected the troops before they could deploy and escaped into the mountains, taking all of their property with them. The Apaches outdistanced the troops and a disappointed Bernard was compelled to return to Camp Bowie with nothing to show for a march of 260 miles.[17]

The arrival of a company of the Twenty-first Infantry at Camp Bowie shortly after Bernard's return was the effect of events in far-off Washington, D.C. In an effort to further reduce military appropriations in the wake of the Civil War, Congress passed an act on March 3 calling for another army downsizing. The unfortunate infantry bore the brunt of the reorganization. The forty-five foot regiments mandated only three years earlier were further reduced to only twenty-five. The army relied on normal attrition to eventually decrease the number of enlisted men to meet its total new paper strength of twenty-five thousand. Accordingly, the Thirty-second Infantry was merged with the Twenty-first, causing the latter regiment to exchange its comfortable quarters in Virginia for the wilds of Arizona.[18] The men of D Company trudged into Apache Pass on August 21 to join their comrades of the former Thirty-second. A Texas woman traveling to California with a party of emigrants about that time probably had a higher opinion of Camp Bowie than the recently arrived soldiers did when she described it as "a pretty, romantic place." All the soldiers, she claimed, were "gentlemanly and nice."[19]

The Apaches soon introduced the new troops to the uncertainties of life in Arizona. Still camped in the Dragoons, Cochise sighted two prey along the road to Tucson on October 6. The westbound mail coach, with thirty-three-year-old John Finkel Stone aboard, wended its way through a herd of cattle plodding toward California. Stone, a stout, bearded man who was universally addressed as "colonel," was president of the Apache Pass Mining Company, heir to the Harris Lode. He and his partners had purchased the claim from the "mining mob" in the spring of 1869 and afterwards established a stamp mill at the foot of Overlook Ridge, just below the spring. By early September, the company was advertising to crush ore at $25 per ton and had only recently concluded a contract with the Pinos Altos Mine to process one thousand tons. Stone, having personally overseen the erection of the mill, was en route to Tucson when Cochise's warriors ambushed the stage three miles east of Dragoon Springs.[20]

The first volley fired by the Apaches must have disabled the driver, thus stopping the coach. Riding aboard the stage were four privates—W. H. Bates, M. Blake, D. B. Shallaberger, and J. W. Slocum—who had joined it at Camp Bowie as escort for the mail. The fight was probably a short one. Evidence of the attack indicated that a large party of warriors had sprung up and fired point-blank into the stage, quickly killing all of those aboard. Apparently, the startled soldiers had no time to put up a defense.

John Finkel Stone, owner of the Apache Pass Mining Company, was killed by Apaches at Dragoon Pass in October 1869. (Arizona Historical Society/Tucson, AHS Photo Number 1721)

After ransacking the mail and mutilating the bodies of their victims, the Apaches attacked the herd coming along behind the stage. They failed to stampede the cattle, but did make off with 120 of the 500 head, killing one of the six drovers in the process. One of the survivors later claimed that the cowboys unknowingly camped that night on the scene of the stagecoach ambush, for the next morning, they discovered "the Intrells [*sic*] and lims [*sic*] of human beings strewn over the ground."[21]

Word of the attacks reached Camp Bowie later that day, whereupon Captain Thomas S. Dunn, commanding the post, ordered out Lieutenant William H. Winters and twenty-two Third Cavalrymen to take up Cochise's trail. The following day, Winters notified Dunn that he was "hot upon the trail and hope to be up with the cattle by daylight tomorrow."[22] Winters correctly predicted that the Apaches were headed for Chiricahua Pass, some fifty miles south of the post, and that if a second force could be sent along the east side of the mountains, they might be able to intercept the Indians. Dunn immediately dispatched Bernard with a makeshift force consisting of the eighteen cavalrymen, two infantry soldiers, and five civilian volunteers. Seven hours later, at a point about forty-five miles south of the post, Bernard encountered Winters, driving the stolen cattle back toward the post. Winters informed Bernard that he managed to overtake the tribes-men when they reached the mountains and engaged them in a running fight for seven miles. The troopers had killed twelve warriors, with a loss to themselves of only two men wounded.[23]

Never content with allowing the Apaches to go unmolested, the tenacious Bernard mounted another patrol consisting of an officer and twenty-five men to continue the pursuit of Cochise and his band. This time he took twenty-six of his own troopers, along with a detachment of twenty-four men from G Company, Eighth Cavalry, which had been sent to Camp Bowie for temporary duty. First Lieutenant John Lafferty accompanied Bernard as second-in-command. Also present with the expedition were Second Lieutenant John Q. Adams, First Cavalry, and Acting Assistant Surgeon H. G. Tidemann, six civilian packers, and a guide.

Bernard departed the post after dark on October 16 and marched directly to the place where Winters had skirmished with the Apaches. There he picked up the trail and followed it high into the Chiricahua Mountains, where he discovered a recently abandoned campsite on the twentieth. When the guide eventually detected the faint Indian trail, the troops followed it westward for about ten miles through intermittent rain and hail. Just when Bernard thought they had lost the trail and had dispersed his men in an attempt to locate it, the Apaches opened fire from among boulders surrounding the summit of a low mesa, or "thumb," extending southward from a nearby moun-tain. Deep rocky canyons flanked the mesa on the east and west sides. The captain directed his men to dismount and to advance up a steep, rocky slope under heavy fire the whole distance. The men scrambled up the mesa until they found cover behind a low ledge only thirty yards from the Apaches, "where every man who showed his head was shot at by several Indians at once."[24] Using both guns and bows in the close-range fight, the warriors killed Sergeant Stephen S. Fuller and Private Thomas Collins, and wounded another man. Bernard deployed his men in the surrounding rocks and engaged the Indians briefly until he discovered that his horses stood exposed to enemy fire. With three men down and the troop horses threatened, Bernard ordered Lafferty to collect the bodies of the two dead soldiers and fall back. But the lieutenant found it impossible to remove the corpses from their exposed position without incurring additional casualties. The Apaches seemed to be well supplied with ammunition and unleashed a hail of fire at any-thing that moved. Finally, Lafferty and a few men took cover at the bottom of the hill to prevent the bodies from falling into the hands of the Apaches.

Meantime, Bernard led thirty mounted men behind a hill and around the left flank of the Indians in an attempt to assault their position on the mesa above. His plan was frustrated, however, when he encountered a canyon across his intended route, with Apache sharpshooters controlling the entire area from high ground above. His only recourse was to post his first sergeant and fifteen men on an even higher knoll from which they could fire into the Apaches. Returning to his former position, Bernard ordered Lieutenant Adams and a detail of men to reinforce Lafferty in a dismounted charge in an attempt to secure the bodies of the two fallen troopers. But, just as Adams reached the line, a bullet tore through the right side of Lafferty's face, "breaking and carrying away the greater portion of the lower jawbone, the bullet and broken bones greatly lacerating the lower portion of the face."[25] This caused Bernard to reassess his situation. He had no place to camp that was not exposed to Apache fire, and he had two seriously wounded men, plus another who had fallen and broken his leg during the fight. Moreover, the Apaches held an almost impregnable position and "were recklessly brave." In a gesture of respect unusual for those times, Bernard credited Cochise with being "one of the most intelligent hostile Indians on this continent."[26] Although it chafed him to break off the fight, especially when he had to leave two of his men on the field, Bernard had little choice but to withdraw, for the moment anyway. His men nevertheless accounted for eighteen Apaches killed during the fight.

According to Acting Assistant Surgeon Levi L. Dorr, who later treated Lieutenant Lafferty, the wound "healed kindly without much deformity." Dorr, however, did not have a high regard for Dr. Tidemann's professional abilities, calling him "a crazy dutchman [who] knew little of wounds & their proper dressing."[27] Bernard recommended both Lafferty and Adams for brevets for their bravery, but only Lafferty received one, and that was not approved until 1890, twelve years after his retirement from the army. At that late date, Lafferty was awarded the honorable promotion to captain in recognition of his actions at Chiricahua Pass as well as for gallant and meritorious service in action at Black Slate Mountains, Nevada, on February 15, 1867.[28]

Only two days after his return to Camp Bowie, Bernard assembled another mixed command of two officers and forty-nine men, augmented by eight enlisted Indian scouts. This was the first of many instances in which scouts were employed at the post. Again departing under cover of darkness, Bernard's column reached Chiricahua Pass at about midnight on the 26th. He immediately sent out the scouts with a detachment of twelve soldiers to locate the trail. After a search that lasted well into the next morning, the scouts failed to find any fresh sign, but did report seeing horses in a deep, narrow canyon nearby. However, the scouts were of the opinion that the horses were merely decoys tied there to lure the troops into an ambush. Bernard scoured the area during the rest of that day, and finding no other indication of the Apaches, he decided to enter the defile early the following morning. Lieutenant Winters and the packtrain remained outside the mouth of the canyon.

Bernard, with flankers out, had no sooner entered the canyon and proceeded a short distance when he observed warriors sprinting along the mountainside on his flank, apparently heading toward the entrance. His experienced eye perceived that the Indians were attempting to gain the advantage offered by a particular cliff, from which they could fire on his rear, hoping to trap him within the canyon. Although the range was extreme, Bernard ordered his men to open fire in hopes of thwarting their movement. Simultaneously, Winters' troops began shooting at other warriors he observed from the opposite side of the mountain. The tribesmen were quickly forced to take cover in the rocks before reaching their objective. Withdrawing from the canyon, Bernard combined forces with Winters and commenced an assault on the ridge where the Apaches were concealed. The opposing forces exchanged fire for a brief time, until the Indians fell back to a higher position on the mountain beyond range of the troops.

Soon thereafter, the scouts opened a dialogue with Cochise, while the troops went into camp a safe distance below. Later that evening, a party of Chiricahuas bearing a white flag came to the foot of the mountain to discuss where they would be allowed to live in the event they surrendered. Bernard was careful to make no commitments, but advised them that if they surrendered, they would have to accept whatever terms were presented at that time. Meanwhile, he sent a messenger back to Camp Bowie to summon Dunn to his assistance with any cavalry that might be available. Having none, Captain Dunn upheld the honor of the infantry by marching a detachment of nineteen men to Bernard's camp by the next morning, covering fifty miles in less than twenty hours. Bernard and Dunn concurred that, even with the reinforcements, they probably could not dislodge the Apaches from their superior position. Dunn himself returned to the post with a small cavalry escort, leaving his doughboys with Bernard.

Bernard and Winters remained in camp until the morning of the 29th, when more reinforcements arrived from Camp Crittenden. Captain Harrison

Moulton rode in at the head of thirty-one men belonging to C Troop, First Cavalry, bolstering Bernard's force to a total of 118 men. Doctor Dorr also accompanied Moulton's platoon.[29]

After conferring with his fellow officers, Bernard decided to launch another assault against the Indian position. Lieutenant Adams and twenty-five men would be left to guard the camp and the packtrain, while the other officers and the remaining ninety-three enlisted men would make a night attack. The troops left camp at 2 o'clock, just as the moon rose, on the morning of the 31st, advancing over the ridge where the Indians had been engaged earlier. The troops cautiously approached the summit at sunrise. To their astonishment, they found no Apaches, but discovered a series of low stone breastworks with firing embrasures. Bernard estimated that, had the Indians held the position, they could have defended it against five times their own number.

The troops remained on the mountaintop until broad daylight, peering down into the canyon beyond, but were unable to see anything of Cochise's force. Bernard, still cautious, detailed Winters to post detachments on high points from which the infantry, with their longer-range rifles would be especially effective in providing covering fire for the remainder of the command, which Bernard was leading down the slope into the canyon.

About halfway down, the troops sighted a number of horses in the bottom. Bernard quickly directed the scouts, followed by Moulton's platoon, to capture the ponies. At the same time, he sent G Troop, First Cavalry, led by First Sergeant Francis Oliver, around to the left to provide protective fire. By the time the troops reached the canyon floor, warriors had mounted their ponies and ridden up the canyon some distance before opening fire. Bernard's command responded, immediately killing two warriors who had crept down to get closer shots at the soldiers. Winters and his sharpshooters commanded the opposite slope, pinning the Indians to their positions. While the Apaches rolled boulders down the mountainside to hold back the troops, Bernard studied the situation and concluded that a frontal attack was not feasible. Nor could he outflank the Indians without driving them back to one mountain after another. Considering the exhausted condition of his men, Bernard chose to break off the engagement and return to Camp Bowie in the hope of obtaining fresh troops with which to renew the campaign.[30]

Arriving at the post on November 2, Bernard was encouraged to find that Dunn had arranged for L Troop, First Cavalry, under the command of Captain John Barry, to come from Camp Goodwin. Even more unexpected was the appearance of a detachment of twenty-one Mexican cavalrymen, also operating north of the border, who offered to accompany Bernard on his pursuit of Cochise. Bernard briefed Barry as to where he had left the Apaches and instructed him, along with a guide and the Mexican regulars, to delay Cochise until the rest of the command could join them. Barry left that same evening, while Bernard's troopers refitted for an early morning departure.

Assembling a combined command of 156 men at Chiricahua Pass, where the fight of October 31 had occurred, Bernard took up the Indian trail on a treacherous course through the mountains. It proved to be the most difficult sort of stern chase imaginable. For days, Cochise's party led the cavalry "over the worst country they possibly could," hoping to shake off their pursuers.[31] The Apaches subsisted by killing and eating their own horses, which would only slow them down anyway in such rugged terrain, while the troops soon exhausted the five days' rations they brought with them. Worse yet, the trackers noted that Cochise's force was steadily dwindling by the departure of two or three warriors leaving the main body each day. Bernard lost a great deal of time checking out those false trails, and in recovering troopers' horses that lost their footing and tumbled down the steep slopes.

When the trail disappeared altogether, Bernard sent out two detachments in opposite directions in hopes of relocating it, but without success. By that time, both men and horses were near exhaustion; Bernard had no choice but to curtail the eleven-day pursuit. Back at Fort Bowie, Bernard reported a tally of thirty-three warriors killed and an undetermined number wounded in the four skirmishes of the previous month. His troops had also captured twenty Indian horses, in addition to recovering the cattle stolen from the drovers in early October. Although he could not claim complete success for his campaign, the ever-determined Bernard was by no means willing to concede defeat by "this wily Indian, Coches [*sic*]." More cavalry was on the way, and Bernard intended to use it to run him down once and for all.[32]

The arrival of the new year saw the posting of G Troop, Eighth Cavalry, at Fort Bowie as a permanent addition to the garrison. With these reinforcements, Bernard lost no time in making good on his pledge to give Cochise no rest. On January 26, after learning that Apaches were in the mountains west of the post, he led a force composed of fifty-five soldiers, five scouts, guide Merijildo Grijalva, and three civilian packers toward the Dragoon Range, the Chiricahua's traditional stronghold. However, Cochise himself probably remained on Bonita Creek, in White Mountain territory to the north, where he had taken refuge following Bernard's previous campaign.

Captain Gerald Russell, Third Cavalry (circa 1885). An Irish-born immigrant, Russell served in the Regiment of Mounted Rifles on the frontier until his promotion to lieutenant in 1862. He subsequently served through the Civil War in the Third Cavalry and later proved to be one of Camp Bowie's most aggressive Indian fighters. (S. B. M. Young Collection, U.S. Army Military History Institute)

Two days later, the troops surprised a rancheria and attacked. In the ensuing fight, Bernard's men killed thirteen Apaches and captured two. Found in the camp was a bar of gold said to have been taken from the body of Colonel Stone four months earlier.[33]

A few days later, other Apaches attacked the mail stage in Doubtful Canyon. On this occasion, the three Camp Bowie infantrymen, knowing full well the fate that awaited them if they were captured, put up a bold defense, even though the team was disabled when one mule was killed. The desperate soldiers aboard the slow-moving coach continued to keep the sixteen warriors at bay until the mail arrived safely at the post.[34] Patrols sent out during the next several weeks failed to discover any Apaches, probably because Cochise and most of his people were still far away in the vicinity of the Gila.[35]

The arrival of yet a third troop of cavalry at Bowie in March brought to the garrison another officer of Bernard's ilk. Captain Gerald Russell, a native-born Irishman, had begun his army career as a private in the Regiment of Mounted Riflemen in 1851. He served in the ranks for eleven years, fighting Apaches in both Texas and New Mexico prior to the Civil War. On the eve of the war the regiment was redesignated as the Third Cavalry, and thereafter saw service against Sibley's Texans at the Battles of Valverde and Glorieta before being sent to the eastern theater of operations. When the exigencies of the war enabled intelligent, experienced noncoms like Russell to cross the gulf to the officer corps, he donned the shoulder straps of a second lieutenant in 1862. The Third Cavalry later provided part of the cavalry screen for General William T. Sherman's famous March to the Sea to divide the Confederacy. After the war, the regiment returned to its old home in New Mexico, where Russell again campaigned against the Mimbres Apaches for a year prior to transferring to Camp Bowie.[36]

Russell needed no time to warm up before taking the field on his first scouting mission hardly a week after his arrival at Apache Pass. His troop, accompanied by some of Bernard's men, now familiar with the country, spent ten days scouring the Dragoons hoping to find Cochise back in his old haunt. The Chiricahuas had recently committed several depredations in the Sonoita Valley, after which troops from Camp Crittenden had chased them to the mountains, yet Russell found no trace of the Apaches after scouting for nearly two hundred miles.[37]

Reuben Bernard apparently stung Cochise severely enough that he preferred to avoid further contact with the army for the present. Risking the scalp bounty revived by the Sonoran government, the chief moved his operations south of the border in spring 1870, but found the Mexicans no more receptive to peaceful coexistence than the Americans had been. The Mexican Army immediately organized a two-hundred-man column to operate against the marauders. Nevertheless, beyond a few minor raids into the most southern reaches of Arizona, Cochise was content to remain in Mexico for the present.

The War Department took a positive step in resolving the Apache problem when it elevated Arizona to full department status on April 15, 1870. This was something the various district commanders had requested for years because of slow communications with distant San Francisco, and the resulting delays in decisions by higher headquarters. Having a commander several hundred miles removed from district operations, and often preoccupied with problems elsewhere in his department, only made matters worse. Selected to head the new department was Brevet Major General George Stoneman, who had been promoted to the permanent rank of colonel of the Twenty-first Infantry three years earlier. Stoneman was no stranger to Arizona or its problems, for he had commanded the district for the previous eight months. Earlier in his career, he had been assigned to the First Dragoons following his graduation from West Point in 1846, and accompanied the Army of the West to New Mexico. He was afterward detailed as quartermaster officer with Philip St. George Cooke's Mormon Battalion on its march to California, and still later, he again crossed the territory with a survey party traveling from California to San Antonio.

Although the press initially welcomed Stoneman as the man of the hour, he soon dashed public enthusiasm by declaring that no quarters suitable for a department commander were available at Prescott, the territorial capital. He therefore spent the first few months of his tenure at Drum Barracks, California. Late that summer, he returned to Arizona to conduct an inspection tour of the posts in his department, but at once incensed the citizens of the territory by recommending that eight of the fifteen forts be abandoned for the sake of the economy. (Camp Bowie was among those to be retained.) He fanned that flame into a blaze of criticism by establishing Indian "feeding stations" in the territory, one of which, Camp Grant, was designated for the Apaches. Neither the public nor the press could fathom why anyone would create sanctuaries for enemies who had been the scourge of the territory for as long as anyone could remember. Stoneman nevertheless ignored the outcry and proceeded with his plans, calculating that the availability of government rations would induce the Indians to remain near the agencies, and off the warpath.[38]

The temporary calm in the Camp Bowie patrol area afforded the troops a respite from field service during which they could once again devote full attention to building construction. Of critical importance was the completion of more quarters for the enlisted men, by that time numbering about 180. To achieve that end, the obvious next step was to create a dormitory in the warehouse section of the combined barracks and commissary storehouse at the north end of the parade. However, before that could be accomplished, room had to be made elsewhere for the foodstuffs. The troops therefore constructed a new building, adjoining the existing storehouse on the west side of the parade ground, to house both commissary and quartermaster supplies. In what became a sort of "musical chairs" exercise, the previous quartermaster storehouse was adapted for use as the post hospital, which finally allowed the medical function to be transferred from the first fort on the hill below. Further living space was created by reconverting the stables and granary (originally designed as a barracks by the California Volunteers) at the northeast corner of the parade. Consisting of two squad rooms each measuring fifty by thirty feet, plus attendant orderly room, dayroom, and storage area, the building became home to Bernard's company. A third barracks, an entirely new structure, was erected in a vacant space on the north side of the parade ground. Beyond the two barracks on that side were stables for the cavalry horses and quartermaster mules. Another officers' quarters was staked out near the southeast corner of the parade ground, adjacent to a large building that had been intended as the hospital. However, a change of plans located the hospital in the converted storehouse, as previously

View northwest across parade ground. Buildings shown are (l. to r.) school; old hospital (1868–1889), later converted for use as first post canteen; subsistence storehouse; and granary. (Fort Bowie Photo Album, Paper, 1858-1894, Museum of American West Collection, Autry National Center)

noted, while the proposed hospital was remodeled into apartments for three bachelor officers. Additional support facilities included mess halls and kitchens for the enlisted men, as well as a bakery, guardhouse, and butcher shop. The rambling post trader's complex stood a short distance west of the parade ground. By July, the entire garrison was consolidated on the new site.[39]

The lull in Indian activity was short-lived. Cochise's warriors attacked the westbound mail coach, with two Twenty-first Infantrymen on board as escort, near San Pedro Crossing on August 18, killing Privates Lawrence Moore and Washington Peabody, as well as the driver and the conductor. The Apaches destroyed the entire contents of the mail at the scene. Ironically, the company to which Moore and Peabody belonged was scheduled to transfer to Camp Lowell less than a week later. Bernard dispatched a patrol northwestward to scout the east slopes of the Santa Catalina Mountains and the Galiuros east of the San Pedro Valley, while another scoured the west slopes of the Chiricahuas, the Dos Cabezas Range, and Mt. Graham. The detachments were unable to locate the war party after several hundred miles of fruitless searching, leading to the desertion of nine troopers who failed to share their commander's enthusiasm for such work.[40]

In other raids, Cochise and his men struck terror once again through the Sonoita Valley. On one occasion they pillaged and burned the Blanchard Ranch, and on another they looted Tubac. Continuing their rampage, they killed two civilians at Davis Springs, near Camp Crittenden, then ambushed a detachment of the Eighth Cavalry sent on their trail. When the troops withdrew, the Apaches boldly raided yet another ranch at the Ciénaga San Simon north of the post.[41]

The brief flurry of Apache raiding abated as quickly as it had begun. Cochise, perhaps because he knew the army would intensify its efforts to defeat him, suddenly decided to attempt another peace talk. In early August he sent an emissary to Camp Mogollon (later renamed Fort Apache) to test the mood of the Americans. The incredulous camp commander hardly knew how to respond to the request, deferring instead to his superiors, who granted Cochise permission to come in for further negotiations. Although details of the conference with Major John Green later that month differ among sources, the most credible version suggests that, after a decade of unremitting war with the Americans, Cochise was simply tired of fighting, tired of being constantly on the run. Having committed so many depredations south of the Gila, he could hardly risk going to any of the forts in that region. He confided to Green that "he was treated very badly at Camp Bowie

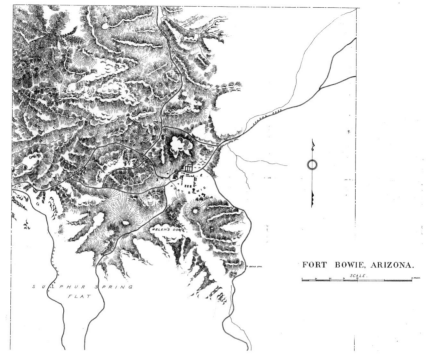

Fort Bowie vicinity, 1893

some years ago [Bascom Affair] but thinks he has killed about as many as he has lost and now that he is about even."[42] Nevertheless, the discussion was inconclusive. Cochise was unwilling to surrender his band and live among the White Mountain Apaches because his relations with them had deteriorated since they had accepted the hand of the government. Green allowed the chief to leave, much to the consternation of the Arizona press, with the suggestion that he simply stop raiding and return to his traditional home in the Chiricahua Mountains. He must have done so, because with the exception of a minor theft of cattle near Camp Bowie in November, all remained quiet in that vicinity for the next few months.[43]

Just before Christmas, however, a small band of Cochise's people left the Chiricahua Mountains and rode northward toward the White Mountain country, perhaps to visit relatives at Camp Grant and partake of government rations at the same time. Bernard mounted a pursuit that was to demonstrate again his tenacity once he struck an Indian trail. The Apaches veered northwest, away from Camp Bowie, thinking they would be safe once they crossed the Gila, but they underestimated Bernard. He dogged their trail for nearly 150 miles until he finally caught up with them in the Pinal Mountains, southwest of present-day Globe, on New Year's Day 1871. His men stealthily approached the rancheria before opening fire, killing nine Indians and wounding many more. Bernard's troops suffered no casualties, but the brutal 450-mile winter march may have provided the inducement for five more soldiers to desert soon after returning from the field. Captain Russell subsequently conducted a scouting party through the Chiricahua Mountains searching for the main camp from which Bernard's Indians had come, but failed to locate it.[44]

The trek to the Pinals proved to be G Troop's last patrol from Camp Bowie. Only three weeks after their return from the field, the men were cheered to receive orders transferring the company to the Presidio of San Francisco. Bernard and his troopers had performed arduous and continuous field service in southern Arizona, and had performed it with exceptional skill, dedication, and bravery. Their new assignment to the comparatively cool, tranquil surroundings of the Bay area was a justly deserved reward.

Even though Cochise apparently tried to avoid further confrontations with troops, he needed horses and mules to replace the many animals lost the previous fall. On February 1, some of his warriors raided a civilian herd near Camp Bowie and escaped before a Third Cavalry detachment could catch up. The following month, Apache raiders descended on Hispanic woodcutters supplying fuel to the post and made off with three animals. Russell and a few soldiers, accompanied by two Mexican trackers and a civilian volunteer, were soon hot on the trail, which led across the Dos Cabezas and the San Simon Valley to the Peloncillo Mountains. They found the rancheria with little difficulty and immediately attacked. Although Russell surprised the Indians and killed three early in the fight, the Apaches withdrew to a strong position from which they could not be dislodged. Like Bernard, Russell was not easily discouraged. He returned to the post for reinforcements and countermarched to the scene of the action with thirty men. By then, the Chiricahuas had ridden north to the Gila, where Russell again attacked and defeated them, killing fifteen.[45]

The approach of spring found Cochise back at his usual occupation, despite the destruction of a rancheria (though not occupied by Cochise's immediate band) high in the Chiricahuas by troops from Fort Bayard, New Mexico Territory, in mid-February. The loss of fourteen warriors, including a son of Mangas Coloradas, in a subsequent fight near the San Francisco

View from the post northward across the San Simon Valley, scene of numerous Indian attacks. (Fort Bowie Photo Album, Paper, 1858–1894, Museum of American West Collection, Autry National Center)

River was a further setback for Cochise, but not for long.[46] In April, he exacted retribution by conducting a raid through the ranches of the San Pedro Valley, murdering one civilian and driving off a herd of cattle, then surrounding and killing three members of a five-man posse that dared to follow.[47]

The very next morning, Cochise's men intercepted the eastbound mail wagon about twelve miles east of the San Pedro. When the driver of the westbound mail from Camp Bowie failed to meet his counterpart on the road as expected, he became leery and turned back to Sulphur Springs. The station-keeper then dispatched a messenger to the fort, whereupon Captain Russell rode out with a thirty-man patrol to investigate. Near Dragoon Springs, they found the wrecked and burned buckboard, along with the dismembered body of driver Mark "Brigham" Revelin. The mail was found shredded and scattered alongside the trail.[48] Russell took only enough time to bury Revelin's butchered remains before giving chase. At dusk the following evening, he found and engaged approximately one hundred warriors, whom he believed were led by Cochise himself. The opposing forces exchanged fire until it was too dark to see, when Russell fell back to San Pedro Crossing and sent to Camp Bowie for reinforcements. In the absence of Bernard's troop, the garrison was smaller than it had been for several years. Nevertheless,

Captain Dunn scraped together nineteen men and fifteen civilian volunteers to go to Russell's aid. Returning to the scene of the skirmish, the troops found that the Apaches had left and again took up the pursuit. Three days later, Russell became incapacitated with inflammatory rheumatism and was forced to return to the post, prematurely terminating the expedition. Russell later learned that a force of thirty-six Sonoran National Guard troops from Fronteras, under the command of Lieutenant Colonel C. S. Escalante, had arrived at Apache Pass on the 20th, and had offered to go to his assistance if only Dunn could spare them some rations. As it turned out, Escalante lost his nerve by the time he reached Sulphur Springs and countermarched to Camp Bowie. After enjoying the hospitality of the post for another night, the Mexicans departed directly for the border.[49]

By that time, Cochise was probably back in Mexico, but he was nevertheless credited with leading an encounter with F Troop, Third Cavalry, near the Whetstone Mountains on May 5, 1871. The Indians probably belonged to Juh's band of Southern Apaches. Killed in the fight was First Lieutenant Howard B. Cushing, an aggressive young Civil War veteran obsessed with making his mark by defeating Cochise. Captain Russell was summoned to assist, but arrived too late to be of any help. Other troops from nearby Camp Crittenden had preceded him to the scene of the fight and had pressed on after the perpetrators.[50]

Later that month, Cochise returned to southeastern Arizona through the Patagonia Mountains, where he committed several depredations before swinging eastward toward the San Pedro Valley. Before reaching its stream, he divided his band, part of them taking refuge in the Huachucas, while he led the remainder to his stronghold in the Dragoons. From that lofty vantage point, Cochise could keep an eye on both the Sulpher Springs and San Pedro Valleys. He was met there by Thomas J. Jeffords. Tall and lean with a generous crop of reddish whiskers, Jeffords was one of the few white men who could contact Cochise with any assurance that he would live to tell about it. He had resided in New Mexico in the years immediately after the Civil War, and probably became acquainted with Cochise in 1870 when he was authorized to trade with the central Apaches at the Canada Alamosa reservation. Brigadier General John Pope, commanding the Department of the Missouri, worked through his agent to hire Jeffords to make contact with Cochise for the purpose of convincing him to bring his people to the reservation.[51]

Jeffords, despite his credibility with Cochise, was unable to convince the Chiricahua chief to live at Canada Alamosa. Although the chief seemed sincere in his desire for peace, he was reluctant to move his people through the country occupied by so many soldiers and hostile civilians. His fears probably stemmed from the recent "Camp Grant Massacre," in which scores of Apaches, primarily women and children, had been murdered in cold blood by a mixed force of Papago Indians, Mexicans, and a few Anglo-Americans.[52] Still, Cochise had not entirely rejected the idea of concluding a peace with the Americans; he simply preferred to do it at a more opportune time. That in mind, he maintained a low profile into the summer of 1871. At long last, Captain Dunn at Camp Bowie could report with some relief that there was "no scouting this month; nor any Indian depredations committed."[53]

CHAPTER 7

We Will Make Peace

Prior to Ulysses S. Grant's election to the presidency in 1868, Indian policy in the United States took a dual approach to the challenge of assimilating native tribes into American society. The Department of the Interior, charged with the management of Indian affairs since its creation in 1849, relied on confining the tribes to defined reservations and there converting them to Christianity as the essential requisite for making the transition from savagery to civilization, as defined by the whites. Reformers saw Christianity as one leg of a triad, the other two being formal education and agricultural training, whereby the Indians would become self-supporting members of the population at large. On the other hand, the military "wanted to acculturate the nomads of the plains at the point of the bayonet," thus forcing them to live on reservations and abide by standards of behavior acceptable to whites.[1] In return for their good conduct, the Indians would become wards of the government. Regardless of methods, or reputed motives, the result would be the same—exploit the Indians and swindle them out of their lands. As general-in-chief of the army until his inauguration, Grant had naturally leaned toward a military solution, though his entrance on the political stage after the Civil War influenced him to keep an open mind to the possibility that Indians might be acculturated through peaceful means.

Grant had hardly warmed his seat in the White House when he was descended upon by a delegation of the Society of Friends, fresh from a spiritually invigorating national convention held recently in nearby Baltimore. The Quakers arranged an audience with the new president to persuade him to formalize an Indian policy firmly rooted in Christianity. Rather than using the sword to force the natives onto reservations, the government would employ the olive branch to coerce the Indians to embrace the blessings of Euro-American civilization. Church-nominated agents in charge of the reservations would ensure that the basic tenants of the policy were carried out. Grant chafed at the idea, but agreed to support the Quaker proposal in limited measure. The appropriations act of 1869 authorized him to appoint a board of ten unpaid humanitarians who would share control of the Indian funds with the secretary of the interior. Vincent Colyer, a self-righteous philanthropist with political influence, was named as the secretary of the Board of Indian Commissioners. But Grant still faced the problem of what to do with excess army officers left jobless by the consolidations mandated by Congress since the end of the war. He therefore retained his prerogative to name army men as Indian agents (appointing no fewer than sixty-eight), a move that would ensure continued heavy military involvement in matters relating to the western tribes. In short, the authorized agents of the Indian Bureau would exercise exclusive jurisdiction over the tribesmen so long as they were within the confines of their established reservations; outside the reservations, they were fair game for the army.

Grant, in fact, wanted the Indian Bureau to be transferred to the War Department, a proposal that attracted considerable support in Congress. However, Major Edward M. Baker's unwarranted attack on an innocent Piegan village in Montana early in 1870, and the resulting slaughter of the inhabitants, altered the mood of the legislators, ultimately causing the measure to fail. So incensed was Congress that it passed legislation a few months later prohibiting army officers from serving as Indian agents, much to the president's displeasure. Yet, Congress essentially abdicated its responsibilities by bestowing on the churches the responsibility for implementing the new Indian policy, causing Grant to fear that the aggressive Quakers would dominate control of the reservations. In a countermove, he ordered that supervision of the agencies be divided among the various religious denominations. So it was that the Dutch Reform Church gained authority over the tribes in Arizona, exclusive of the Navajos.[2]

The formulation of Grant's Peace Policy happened to coincide with Cochise's desire to call a truce. The Mimbres people under Loco and Victorio had already settled at Canada Alamosa, as had the Mogollons and the Gilas. The constant pressures exerted by both the army and no-holds-barred civilian posses, not to mention the Mexicans and their scalp bounties, simply wore down the Apaches. The prospect of having sufficient food and clothing, and not living under the fear of surprise attack, were strong inducements to accept the government's offers. Still, many of Cochise's people were wary, preferring to remain free and take their chances.

The atrocity at Camp Grant caused General William Tecumseh Sherman, commanding the army since Grant's inauguration, to relieve General Stoneman as commander of the Department of Arizona. In the eyes of the citizenry, particularly those who had suffered from Apache raiding along the Santa Cruz River, the Camp Grant massacre was justified because Stoneman and his subordinate, Lieutenant Royal E. Whitman, had been too lenient with the Indians at the Camp Grant reservation. The reservation, they claimed, served merely as a government-protected base of operations whereby the Indians could continue to sack ranches and farms south of the Gila. The department commander thus became the scapegoat for the continuing Indian problem and, consequently, the territory's retarded economic development. More to the point, perhaps, was the public's continuing dependency on the army's presence. Indian hostilities, real or fabricated, meant the retention in Arizona of large numbers of troops that had to be supplied, and who in turn spent large sums of money on goods and services in the territory. If allowed to succeed, the reservation experiment could mean the exodus of the military goose and its golden eggs. Stoneman's recommendation to close five military posts was the final straw. Governor Anson P. K. Safford, disgusted with Stoneman's policies, called for the general's expeditious removal.[3]

Stoneman's replacement was an experienced West Pointer, Lieutenant Colonel George Crook, recently jumped to brigadier general over the heads of several other officers his senior. Crook, an unpretentious, notably taciturn man, with a record of frontier service prior to the Civil War (he had more recently subdued the Paiutes in Oregon), was considered by Safford as the perfect man for the job in Arizona. Without Crook's knowledge, the governor used his influence with the California congressional delegation to persuade Grant to make the appointment, despite the objections of Sherman and the secretary of war.[4] Crook and his staff arrived in Arizona on June 4, to the fanfare of the press and no doubt to the embarrassment of the self-effacing general. But, if there was an officer who would apply a firm hand to the Apache situation, and do it through active field operations, it was George Crook. Unlike Stoneman, who preferred to manage the department from his comfortable headquarters at Drum Barracks near Los Angeles, Crook appreciated the advantages of maintaining direct control over affairs in Arizona. He therefore established his offices at Whipple

Barracks, just outside Prescott, to be centrally located for purposes of coordinating troop movements and maintaining ready access to territorial officials.

The new department commander immediately ordered officers in the Southern District of Arizona to provide him every shred of information that might be of use in conducting future operations. He wanted to know details about the Apaches themselves and their tactics, the locations of the all-important sources of water, where the county was accessible by roads and where trails crossed the mountains, as well as the latest intelligence about routes habitually used by the Indians. Crook also compiled data about climate, soils, weather, and vegetation to provide his troops with every possible advantage. And, to deprive the Apaches of succor formerly provided by the army, Crook ordered that Indians would no longer be fed at military posts, unless as prisoners of war.

Wasting no time, Crook departed Tucson on July 11 with five companies of cavalry and fifty Indian scouts he called "Destroying Angels" to conduct a personal reconnaissance of the southeastern portion of the territory, to impress the renegades with a display of strength. Crook also took advantage of the trip as "a 'practice march,' of the best kind in which the officers and men could become acquainted with each other and with the country in which . . . they should have to work in earnest," according to Second Lieutenant John G. Bourke, the general's aide-de-camp.[5]

Arriving at Apache Pass three days later, Crook learned that Cochise had recently made his presence known in the vicinity of the post. On July 8, the mail rider from Tucson, Julian Aguiera, failed to appear on time. Captain Russell had led a patrol to determine the whereabouts of the man, and did not have to search far. They found his body in the pass just a few miles west of the post. Russell promptly set out to cut the trail of the culprits by entirely circling the post, but failed to find anything except fragments of the mail near the Dos Cabezas. Nevertheless, the brazen attack reinforced Crook's conviction that the time had come to "to iron all the wrinkles out of Cochise's band of Indians."[6]

In an attempt to conceal his intentions, Crook led his column from Camp Bowie after dark on the 17th, bound for Mount Graham and Camp Grant. Turning north after debouching from Apache Pass, they marched only a few miles along the base of the Dos Cabezas Mountains before making a dry camp. At dawn the next morning, a packer out searching for water observed some horses—Apache horses—grazing lower down the ravine in which the cavalry was camped. The man immediately reported his discovery to Crook, but the warriors had already spotted the packer and made good their escape before a pursuit could be organized.[7]

Crook continued his survey of the country by making a circuitous march via Camps Grant, Apache, and Verde before reaching his new headquarters at Whipple Barracks. Along the way he proved his theory of fighting Apaches by sending out a small expedition composed of both cavalry and Indian scouts to find and strike a rancheria in the vicinity of Camp McDowell. Having gained a good understanding of the situation, and having seen much of the territory with his own eyes, Crook was convinced his strategy was sound. He lost no time in planning several similar expeditions. Each column would rely heavily on native guides to track and match wits with the Apaches. They would be supplied by packtrains that could follow wherever the trails led over Arizona's torturous terrain. Crook impressed on his officers that they were to stick to the trails and remain out as long as it took to run the Apaches to ground. He would settle for no half-hearted measures.

Crook's column was the largest body of troops to occupy Apache Pass for some time, nevertheless, it failed to intimidate Cochise. On July 18, the day after Crook left the area, the Chiricahuas laid an ambush for a company of the Twenty-first Infantry en route from Tucson to take station at Camp Bowie. After pausing for water at Ciénaga de los Pinos, Captain Henry E. Smith allowed most of his company to take up the march while his teamsters finished watering the mules. His mistake was just the opportunity Cochise had hoped for. When the command had outdistanced the wagons by about two miles, the Apaches attacked the train from the rear. The soldiers escorting the wagons opened fire at the onrushing Apaches, checking them long enough for Smith and the remainder of G Company to double-time back to their relief. Deploying his men in a skirmish line, Smith charged. Cochise's men faced the advance head-on, engaging the soldiers in a pitched fight before finally giving way under the disciplined fire of the troops. The Apaches left behind twenty-five dead warriors and Smith claimed another thirty or forty were wounded. His own loss was one soldier killed and three wounded. A civilian traveling with the command also was wounded.[8]

The company arrived at the post that night, only to be summoned to arms the very next afternoon when the Apaches raided the beef contractor's herd near Bear Spring, just a half mile southeast of the fort. At about three o'clock, some 100 to 150 warriors assailed the civilian herders, killing the butcher and another man and driving off the cattle. Since Russell was

absent with forty men of K Troop, Third Cavalry, on his scout to the Peloncillo Mountains, only a few cavalrymen remained at the post. Nevertheless,
Post Commander Dunn sent his orderly to First Sergeant John F. Farley
with instructions to mount every available man to take up the chase. The
infantry would follow as rapidly as possible to Farley's support, provided his
detachment could force them into a fight. Farley quickly scoured the post,
but found only five troopers not on sick call or occupied with some essential
duty. Undaunted, the sergeant mounted his squad and galloped after the herd.

Five miles from the post, the trail crossed over a low hill. His horses winded
by that time, Farley dismounted his men and they proceeded to walk up
the grade in single file. When they had gone about halfway, a single shot
split the air, the heavy slug striking Farley in the hip and knocking him to
the ground. The Apache delaying force then unleashed a volley, but their
aim was too high and the bullets whizzed over the heads of the troopers,
doing no harm. Sergeant Farley attempted to mount his horse, but could
not. At the same time, some of the warriors rode down off the crest, circling
the detachment in an attempt to cut them off. Four of the troopers on foot,
including Farley, turned their horses loose in order to shoot, while the
other two spurred their mounts back toward the safety of the post with a
dozen or more Apaches in hot pursuit. Meantime, six or eight dismounted
tribesmen descended the hill, firing all the while at the sergeant and his
three comrades. The exposed hillside was no place to make a stand, so Farley
directed his men to take cover in a brush-filled arroyo a few hundred yards
away. While the mounted party was away, the soldiers exchanged fire with
the remaining warriors, keeping them at bay for about an hour. The others
eventually returned, adding their guns to the fight, but the soldiers were
too well protected in the arroyo to be dislodged. Nor, were the Apaches
bold enough to rush them. The Indians finally broke off the skirmish at
about six o'clock in order to catch up with the rest of their band.

By that time, Farley was unable to walk at all and still no relief had come
from the fort. The men remained under cover of the arroyo until long after
dark, when they sighted figures cautiously approaching. Farley barked out
a challenge, which was answered by a surprised, but friendly, response. It was
a detail sent out with an ambulance, expecting to recover only the corpses
of the four men.[9]

This raiding party, probably led by Cochise himself, moved south into the
Chiricahua Mountains and eventually went into camp near the Mexican
border. They intended to retain the four prized cavalry horses, of course,
but the cattle could be eaten or readily exchanged in Sonora for ammunition,

tobacco, and liquor. But first, Cochise moved west to the Santa Rita Mountains, where he could secure more horses from the settlements before acting on his decision to seek a truce at Cañada Alamosa. Stealing stock from white men was one thing, but raiding a Papago village just across the line in Sonora proved to be a mistake. The Papagos backtracked Cochise's warriors and surprised his rancheria the next morning at sunrise. The Chiricahuas put up only a token fight, losing five or six people, before scattering into the mountains. The attack confirmed Cochise's realization that life for his band was becoming decidedly precarious and that survival for his people meant going to a reservation. He knew full well that his old enemies the Mexicans could never be trusted, nor could civilians in Arizona be expected to show any him any mercy. Despite his inherent distrust of the U.S. Army extending back to Bascom's treachery, Cochise concluded that his best chance for peace rested with the American government.[10]

An effect of the Camp Grant Massacre was to give impetus to applying Grant's peace policy to the Apaches. The government was not bound by existing treaties with the Apaches, as it was with many of the Plains tribes, and several of the leaders had already submitted to living near General Stoneman's "feeding stations." Others, like Cochise, had indicated an interest in discussing peace as the result of increasing pressure by the military. The massacre had sent an unmistakable signal to the Apaches that living under or near army supervision was poor insurance against attacks by civilians bent on Indian extermination.

As Crook was touring Arizona laying his plans to conquer the Apaches by force, Indian Commissioner Vincent Colyer, given the derogatory sobriquet "Vincent the Good" by the white populace of the territory, set forth to the Southwest to test the effects of kindness in subduing the Apaches. When the idealistic Colyer learned of Crook's intentions, however, he used his influence with Grant to suspend the new department commander's campaign. Crook learned of Colyer's enterprise "to make peace with the Apaches by the grace of God" through the newspapers, a slight that doubly irritated the general.[11] The general realized, however, that if he continued his operations, and if Colyer failed in his attempt to pacify the Apaches, the press would crucify him. Crook remained convinced that the nature of the Apaches was such that they would only be subdued by superior strength and force of arms. But, faced with the political realities, he was obliged to cease operations and to render Colyer any assistance he required.

Colyer's first act was to establish a reservation in New Mexico for the Mimbres Apaches, whom he labeled as "the most scary Indians I have ever seen." Then he made a whirlwind tour through Arizona laying out temporary reservations for the other Apache bands at Camps Apache, Grant, and Verde, as well as at Date Creek and Beale Springs.[12] The Apache-Mojaves were given an agency at Camp McDowell. Although he was greeted by some two hundred armed and belligerent Tucson citizens upon his arrival at Grant, Colyer remained undeterred in his crusade. By the time he arrived at Crook's headquarters at Camp Whipple, Colyer had convinced himself that he had resolved the entire Apache situation. His vanity further prompted him to add that he was glad to have Crook's full support in that effort, but Crook was not about to be led down that path.

> I disabused his mind of this impression by informing him that I had no confidence in his peace policy, but as he came out to Arizona clothed with powers from my superiors . . . and as I was directed by this authority to give him all the assistance at my command, I proposed to do so conscientiously, so that in case his policy was a failure, none of it could be laid at my door.[13]

Cochise, meantime, had traveled with his band to New Mexico, arriving in the vicinity of Canada Alamosa in mid-September. Unfortunately, Colyer had already left for Arizona, thus missing his only opportunity to meet the greatest, if not the most troublesome, of all the Apache headmen. Cochise may have been disappointed that he had likewise missed the Great Father's representative, but he did not allow that to stand in the way of his mission to secure peace for his people. He immediately sent for his old friend, Tom Jeffords, to seek his advice and assistance.

Jeffords arranged for Cochise to meet with the local agent, Orlando F. Piper, near the end of the month. Piper established friendly relations with Cochise, eventually coaxing the wary chief and some of his followers to the agency for further talks with his superiors from Santa Fe. As Cochise grew more comfortable with the situation and word spread, other bands began drifting to the reservation. Within a month after Cochise's arrival, some 450 Apaches had assembled in camps along the nearby Cuchillo Negro River.

To no one's surprise in Arizona, least of all Crook's, the peace wrought by "that spawn of hell," Colyer, barely survived his exodus from the territory. On the evening of October 22, R. M. Gilbert, bleeding from the groin, stumbled into Camp Bowie. Gilbert related that the day before a party of sixty to eighty Apache warriors had attacked O'Neil's Ranch near Ciénaga San Simon about thirty miles east of the post, killing Richard Barnes and setting fire to the house. Gilbert himself was shot while bringing his fatally wounded companion back into the building. After holding off the Apaches for awhile with his Henry rifle, Gilbert was able to escape into the brushy ciénaga, where he hid out until nightfall. As usual, the territorial press was quick to blame Cochise for the raid, although he and most of his people were far away in New Mexico at the time.[14]

The indomitable Captain Russell assembled twenty-five men of K Troop, who trotted out of the post that very night bound for the ciénaga. Also with the detachment were Robert Whitney and O'Neil himself, who volunteered to accompany Russell's detachment as guides. Arriving there a few hours later, the soldiers buried Barnes's body near the smoldering ruins of the house and immediately took up the southbound trail of the raiders. Two days later Russell entered Horseshoe Canyon, on the east slope of the Chiricahua Mountains, where he expected to find water for his horses. The command proceeded approximately three miles up the cañon before they located a spring sufficient to supply their needs. The troops had just begun watering their mounts at about one o'clock in the afternoon when Apaches opened fire from the surrounding heights. Whitney fell in the first volley with a bullet through the heart and Private Blockhaus was severely wounded. As the soldiers took cover among nearby boulders, "The Indians certain of victory attacked from all directions with the most fiendish yells they formed a complete cordon around the party, and opened a double crossfire." Russell and his men fought continuously for the next four hours, while the Apaches peppered their position with Henry repeating rifles and .50-caliber Springfields captured from the army in past encounters. Although the Indians ceased firing, Russell took no chances and kept his men concealed until after darkness fell. They packed up the wounded, along with Whitney's body, and quietly left the canyon during the night. Although the Apaches detected the command's exodus and fired a few parting shots in the dark, the troops returned to Camp Bowie without further loss.[15]

Just a few days after Russell's fight at Horseshoe Canyon, other Apaches, probably from the Date Creek reservation, fell upon a stagecoach near Wickenburg. Seven of the eight passengers, including three members of a government surveying party, died in the attack.

Crook could not have received less surprising news. The Indians accused of the incident at Wickenburg were some of the very ones with whom Colyer had just made peace. And, whether or not Cochise was involved with the events near Bowie, the mere fact that he was credited with them

Soldiers unloading the mail at the Quartermaster's Office at Fort Bowie. The arrival of the mail was always an eagerly anticipated event at isolated frontier posts. With the arrival of the railroad in 1879, mail was picked up at Bowie Station and transported to the post by buckboard. (Arizona Historical Society/ Tucson, AHS Photo Number 4472)

was what mattered. "By the time Colyer reached San Francisco," gloated Crook, "his confidence was considerably shaken, and by the time he reached Washington, his head was chopped off."[16] Colyer's failure signaled that Crook was once again unleashed to prosecute his campaign. In December he proclaimed that any Apaches found off the reservations by mid-February would be treated as hostile and punished accordingly.[17]

The white populace of Arizona welcomed such news because some Apache factions were demonstrating clearly that they would not be quelled by kindness and government rations alone.[18] Their actions, however, were not entirely without provocation. The Apaches had understood from Colyer's visit that they would have a permanent home at Canada Alamosa, but Colyer candidly had other ideas regarding their fate. Upon his return to Washington, the commissioner met with Grant and his secretaries of war and the interior to discuss the establishment of a new reservation for the Chiricahuas near Tularosa, New Mexico, rather than at the place the Indians preferred. When orders were promulgated in December 1871 to effect the move of the Indians, many renounced reservation life in favor of returning to the free life or living with their relatives the Mescaleros in southeastern New Mexico.

Some of those who left New Mexico proceeded directly for familiar haunts in the Dragoon and the Chiricahua ranges of southeastern Arizona. Shortly thereafter, on January 24, hostilities resumed in the vicinity of Apache Pass when both east and west mails were waylaid within a few hours of each other. Using time-proven tactics, a party of Apaches arranged an ambush along the road five miles west of Camp Bowie. A. F. Bice was at the reins of the buckboard, and accompanying him was John Petty, who had recently resigned from the mail company (apparently at Camp Bowie) and was en route to Tucson. A dozen warriors rose up and fired as the buckboard passed through an arroyo, whereupon both Bice and Petty leaped from the vehicle and ran for their lives. They did not get far. About a hundred yards from the road, Bice fell with a bullet through his chest. Petty was gut-shot, the bullet leaving "an opening into which your three fingers could easily be inserted."[19] The Apaches stripped both bodies.

Later that afternoon John Bedford, driving the mail to the Rio Grande, and Thomas Dunham, a discharged soldier riding alongside bound for Texas, discovered the grizzly evidence of the attack. Despite the obvious danger, the two men decided to remain especially alert and to take their chances getting through the pass. Only three miles from the fort, they lost their gamble when the same party of Apaches struck again. Dunham was killed outright, while another bullet grazed one of Bedford's fingers as he jumped from the buckboard. Bedford somehow escaped and made his way to the post. A patrol later recovered the bodies of the three dead men, along with the bullet-splintered vehicles and mail that had not been destroyed by the Apaches.

The attacks could not have come at a more inopportune time for Captain Harry M. Smith, commanding the post. Russell and his troop had been transferred to Nebraska in mid-December, leaving Smith only his own company of infantry to perform all of the usual garrison and escort duties. Worse still, there were only three horses and a few mules at the post, making it impossible for him to consider mounting a force to track the war party. In the wake of the two incidents, mail carriers refused to proceed west without an escort, which Smith endeavored to provide with the small force available, but the eastbound dispatches were compelled to rely on the cover of darkness as their only security. The renewed trouble at Apache Pass prompted

department headquarters to send a company of the Fifth Cavalry to reinforce the garrison.[20]

The decade-long grudge the Chiricahuas held against Camp Bowie was
manifested again on February 26, when warriors pounced on the beef herd
grazing near Bear Spring only a short distance east of the post. One of the
herders, John McWilliams, was killed in the attack, while the other, John
Dobbs, suffered wounds in both arms. A detachment guarding the herd
repulsed the Indians and recovered the animals before the Apaches could
make off with them.[21]

Just as Crook was reorganizing his forces to round up the recalcitrant
bands, his plans were again subverted by the advocates of the peace policy
in Washington. This time, Grant appointed Brigadier General Oliver Otis
Howard, an old wartime colleague, to negotiate peace with the Apaches.
Howard was an 1854 graduate of West Point who had compiled a solid combat
record during the Civil War. He had distinguished himself at Gettysburg
and during Sherman's Atlanta campaign, losing his right arm from wounds
received in the Battle of Fair Oaks in 1862. Considered sanctimonious by
many of his contemporaries, Howard was a devout (some would say fanatical)
Christian and self-styled humanitarian. After the war, as head of the Freed-
men's Bureau, Howard became convinced that "the Creator had placed
him on earth to be the Moses to the Negro" through aiding and educating
former slaves.[22] Once anointed as the official commissioner for the Apaches,
Howard was charged by the secretary of war with ensuring "that the policy
to civilize and elevate the Indians should prove successful."[23]

Howard, in company with Reverend E. P. Smith and a military aide, took
the train from Washington on March 7, arriving two weeks later in San
Francisco, where he met with General Schofield to discuss his intentions to
secure a formal peace with the Apaches. From there, he took a stage to
Crook's headquarters at Prescott, experiencing en route the miserable state
of transportation still plaguing Arizona. "I was glad to take it," Howard
later wrote, "for it gives a clearer idea of the difficulties under which any
campaign against hostile Indians must be carried on in this country."[24] His
meeting with Crook was congenial enough, though Howard pulled rank by
making it clear to Crook that he was cloaked with the authority to override
the department commander's decisions if necessary. His hesitancy to do so,
however, probably stemmed from news of the recent depredations committed
by the Apaches. To verify those reports, Howard arranged for his aide-de-
camp, First Lieutenant M. C. Wilkinson, to accompany Governor Safford on
an inspection tour through the Santa Cruz, Sonoita, and San Pedro valleys.

General Oliver O. Howard negotiated a lasting truce with Cochise.
(Arizona Historical Society/Tuc-
son, AHS Photo Number 48187)

Wilkinson accompanied the governor's entourage during visits to the homes
of several ranchers and settlers who were attempting to eke out a living in
those areas, despite Apache resistance. Along the way, Wilkinson observed
fresh Indian trails near the Huachuca Mountains, southwest of Bowie, and
noted "empty ranches, each one with its story of desolation" and abandoned
mines, "once worked with success."[25] These and other similar reports persuaded even Howard that military operations were necessary to protect citizens and to finally convince the still-hostile Apache bands, Cochise's in
particular, that submitting to reservation life was preferable to continued
fighting. He therefore dropped his opposition to a campaign against any
incorrigibles determined to stay out, much to Crook's satisfaction.[26]

Howard continued his journey to Camp Grant, where he visited the site
of the infamous massacre before entering into talks with the leaders of some
one thousand Apaches of various bands, primarily Aravaipas, who had
gradually come in to settle on the reservation. The May 21, 1872, conference
had important results for both the Apaches and the future of Arizona Territory. Despite the pessimism of an apprehensive citizenry, Howard secured
a pledge from the Apaches that they would reside on the reservation and
would forever cease warring against the Americans and the Mexicans, as
well as their neighbors the Papago and Pima tribes. In return, they would
be fed, clothed, taught to farm—and, perhaps uppermost in Howard's mind,

converted to Christianity. Unlike the pacifist Colyer, however, Howard supported taking military action against those bands that refused to accept reservation life. Moreover, Crook was delighted to learn that the bands settling on the Gila would supply him with native scouts willing to cooperate with the army against their kinsmen. Crook saw the combination of conventional troops and Indian auxiliaries as key to resolving the Apache situation once and for all.[27]

Howard's agreement with the Apaches also stipulated that the temporary reservation on the San Pedro near Camp Grant be abolished in favor of expanding the area formerly designated for the White Mountain bands. The new reservation, named San Carlos, would extend from somewhat south of the Gila northward to a common boundary with the Camp Apache Reservation. The motive behind the decision, of course, was not only to concentrate the various Apache tribes but to further distance them from the developing regions of the territory.

After his return to Washington later that spring, Howard rendered a lengthy report to Secretary of War Columbus Delano concerning his recent mission. Summarizing his recommendations, he noted especially that no depredations had been committed recently in the vicinity of Camp Bowie. Howard was justifiably proud of his accomplishment; still, he was realistic enough to admit that he did "not believe that what are called Cochise men, who report to nobody, consider themselves embraced in the terms of peace, into which so many of the Apaches have entered."[28]

He could not have been more correct in his assessment. Cochise was determined not to move to Tularosa, nor was he on friendly terms with the bands at Camp Grant, especially in view of their recent willingness to enlist as army scouts. The proposed relocation, in fact, disturbed many individuals among the Central Chiricahuas and the Mimbres. When it came down to moving, government officials were able to attract only 350 people, mostly from the Mimbres bands, to Tularosa. That meant that more than 1,500 had scattered to the winds by spring 1872. Perhaps a majority of those went only as far as southern New Mexico, while others went to live with their Mescalero relatives east of the Rio Grande at Fort Stanton. Cochise led his people, now numbering only about three hundred men, women and children, to the familiar country near the Arizona-Sonora border. Cochise may have even considered attempting a truce with the Mexicans, but if he did, troops there quickly dissuaded him from that notion.[29]

Even before Howard left the territory, Cochise's followers had already resumed their usual "dance of death," as one Arizona newspaper put it. Henry

Abrahams, a Las Cruces mail carrier on the route from the Mimbres River to Camp Bowie, departed on what he had announced as his last run early in May. Having concluded there were less dangerous ways to make a living, Abrahams told his friends that he planned to keep going right on to Tucson to find a new occupation. But some of Cochise's men cut short his plans by murdering him as he drove through Doubtful Canyon. After destroying the mailbags, the Apaches burned the carrier's mutilated body on a fire built from his buckboard. Fifth Cavalrymen sent out from Bowie buried Abraham's charred remains, punctured by several bullets and two arrows, where they found them beside the road about a mile west of the old Butterfield station.[30]

Intermittent raiding continued throughout the summer, although the now ailing chief himself may not have personally participated in the depredations. Age had relegated to him the role of selecting targets and planning strategy, and of grooming his eldest son to succeed him according to Apache custom. Cochise and his band apparently spent part of June and July in Mexico, which probably accounts for a lull in activity along the mail route. However, Cochise scurried back to Arizona in the wake of a surprise attack by Mexican troops that utterly destroyed Juh's camp. Safely north of the border, probably ensconced in the Dragoon Mountains, just west of Bowie, Cochise sent raiders to the Sonoita and Santa Cruz valleys, which were always lucrative sources of stock, food, and other plunder. The commanding officer at Camp Bowie dispatched troopers all the way to Calabasas during August at the request of farmers fearful of being attacked in their fields during harvest.[31]

The threat was by no means an imaginary one. The Chircahuas were watching when youthful Second Lieutenant Reed T. Stewart and Corporal Joseph P. G. Black set out in a buckboard from Camp Crittenden bound for Tucson, where Stewart was to sit on a court-martial. Another corporal and six soldiers were sent along as escort, but Stewart, sensing no danger, quickly outdistanced them. As they approached Davidson Canyon, the more-experienced corporal advised Stewart not to enter the defile until after dark, but Stewart scoffed at the warning. The two had no sooner entered the canyon when concealed Apaches opened fire, one of their bullets striking Stewart in the forehead, another boring through his body. Corporal Black jumped and ran for his life, but was caught and tortured to death on a high point in plain sight of the escort that arrived on the scene about an hour later.[32]

The military noose drawn around the border region was tightening, however. A Third Cavalry patrol operating from New Mexico in July struck what was in all likelihood one of Cochise's rancherias near Mount Graham. The troops destroyed all of the equipment in the camp, as well as sixteen lodges and a large supply of food. Additional columns from Camp Grant searched the ranges as far south as the Dragoons, while still others from Camp Crittenden scouted the area between the upper San Pedro and the Santa Cruz. Mexican cavalry also combed the ranges south of the border, and sometimes into the U.S. as well, without locating Cochise's main camp.[33]

Late that summer, in the midst of Cochise's raiding, Camp Bowie hosted harbingers of a new era in Arizona. Yet another railroad surveying party, this one representing the Texas and Pacific line, came to Apache Pass on August 21 to rest and replenish their supplies. The surveyors unexpectedly lingered at the post for a month awaiting a new cavalry escort to arrive from Camp Grant before resuming their trek toward Tucson.[34] The vision of a transcontinental railroad extending across the territory meant that Arizona's great potential as a mining region might yet be realized. For the army, a railroad portended rapid transportation of both supplies and troops, and an end at last to long, agonizingly slow overland travel.

On September 28, Jacob May, General Howard's interpreter, arrived at the fort with a detachment of five Eighth Cavalrymen from Fort Bayard. May brought the news that Howard was again in the field, this time with ambitions of treating with Cochise in hopes of finally ending hostilities. The general had arrived at Tularosa in July, where he was introduced to Tom Jeffords, who said he could take Howard to Cochise, but only on the condition that they travel without an escort. Jeffords knew they would never get close to the chief if he saw soldiers with them. A plan was therefore laid for Howard and Jeffords to be accompanied only by Howard's aide, Captain Joseph A. Sladen, two Indian guides, a cook, and an experienced packer. When Cochise was rumored to be camped somewhere in the vicinity of Mount Graham, Howard detached May with the ambulance on a circuitous trip via the few existing roads to Camp Bowie, where it was expected he would rendezvous with the rest of the party coming cross-country from New Mexico. May alerted the post commander, Major A. W. Evans, to expect Howard at the post upon the completion of his mission.[35]

Howard set out from Tularosa in mid-September on his quest to find Cochise. His route initially followed an eastward course circumventing the Black Range, before swinging southwest past Fort Bayard, where the party replenished supplies needed for continuing the trek into Arizona. Near the border of New Mexico, the guides discovered a fresh trail they were certain had been made by some of Cochise's people. The trail became more evident as they approached the Pelocillo Mountains, but then it suddenly vanished. The guides, nevertheless, thought it best to continue toward Stein's Peak. While the party was camped at a spring in the foothills, a scout sent by Cochise appeared and spoke with Howard's guides. He informed them that the main camp was located more than a hundred miles southwest of there, in the Dragoon Mountains, and that Cochise might be willing to talk, provided Howard came with even fewer white men. Howard readily agreed, selecting only Sladen, Jeffords, and the two Apaches to accompany him; the packer and the cook he sent to Bowie to join May.

Howard followed his Indian guides southwesterly across the barren San Simon Valley, pausing at Sulphur Springs Station on September 29. There, on the open plain east of the Dragoons, Captain Sladen suddenly realized, "how ineffectual had been the operations of our troops against this hostile band. It was practically impossible for any body of men to approach within a day's march of these Indians without discovery, and if the danger was threatening, it was with the greatest ease that the savages could steal away without discovery . . . long before the hostile party could possibly reach their vacated camp."[36]

After making a dry camp in the foothills that night, Howard's party wound their way through a gap in the Dragoons (known today as Middlemarch Canyon) to reach the west slope the following day. Chie, one of the guides and a nephew of Cochise, pointed out an area high above where he thought the chief might be found, and subsequently bounded off in that direction without a word. Just as Howard and the others were making camp on the evening of the 30th, two Chiricahua boys arrived with a message that Chie was in Cochise's camp and he wanted Howard to join him right away.

The boys guided Howard up a meandering streambed for several miles to a "natural fortification; the bottom was a rolling plat of thirty or forty acres of grassland" with a spring-fed ciénaga near the center.[37] He was greeted by a throng of curious and unexpectedly cordial Chiricahuas. Only the next day did the famed chief make his appearance. Riding up to the whites, Cochise greeted his friend Jeffords, who in turn introduced Howard. The general described Cochise as "fully six feet in height, well-proportioned, with large eyes; his face was slightly colored with vermilion, hair straight and black, with a few silver threads."[38] Closely studying Howard's face for any sign of insincerity, Cochise shook hands and extended a friendly salutation.

Thus began a lengthy series of discussions in which Cochise recounted the many wrongs done him and his people, emphasizing that Apache Pass was the worst place of all because of the murder of his brother and the other members of his band in 1861. Despite past grievances, however, Cochise expressed his earnest desire for peace with the Americans because continued war was taking a steady toll on his dwindling band. Howard, in turn, acknowledged past misdeeds by both sides, and proceeded to lay out his plan for creating a reservation in New Mexico for all the Apaches, including Cochise's people. The chief initially rejected that notion on the grounds that not all of his people were willing to live on a reservation, although he himself would, and that any agreement by him to go to New Mexico would make an irreparable breach among his people. Furthermore, he could not be responsible for the actions of those who might choose to remain out. Cochise countered that an acceptable solution would be to assign the Chiricahuas a reservation in their native region of southeastern Arizona, where his people would cooperate in protecting the white man's roads and preserving the peace. The proposal caught Howard unprepared, yet he exercised cool diplomacy by not rejecting it out of hand. The conversations remained positive, and Howard was especially pleased to learn that Cochise had already sent runners to notify the widely scattered Chiricahua bands of the council.

Still distrustful of the army, Cochise expressed to Howard his concern that the other leaders and their bands might be attacked on their way to the Dragoons. Howard reassured him that he would dispatch Sladen to Camp Bowie to prevent such a contingency from occurring, but the chief insisted that Howard go in person to make certain there were no misunderstandings. The general eventually assented to go, taking Chie as his guide and leaving behind Sladen and Jeffords at the Apache rancheria as a gesture of good faith.

The general arrived at the post on the morning of October 2 and immediately issued instructions for Captain Samuel S. Sumner to alert all forces in the region that any Apaches moving toward the Dragoons should not be molested. He likewise secured a quantity of supplies for Cochise's people and directed that they be hauled back to the stronghold in his ambulance. May and the other members of the expedition who had been waiting at Camp Bowie accompanied Howard on his return. Now that they knew the location of Cochise's camp, they followed the stage road around the north end of the Dragoons, then turned directly south.

Following Howard's return, Cochise moved his camp to a pleasant site somewhat north of the previous one, and there the leaders entered into protracted negotiations lasting several days. During that time, other Apache leaders arrived to join in the discussions, each presenting his own list of grievances and demands.

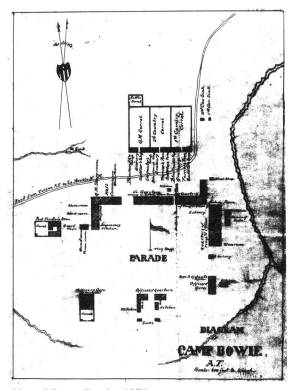

Plat of Camp Bowie, 1871

The final meeting took place in the shade of an overhanging tree and was attended by virtually everyone in camp. Cochise and several other headmen sat on the ground facing Howard, Jeffords, Jake May, and Sladen. The rest of the Apaches were crowded around in several concentric circles surrounding them. Discussions continued for several hours, the conversations being carefully translated from Apache into Spanish, the universal language of the Southwest, and finally into English. In the end, Howard had to concede his intention to relocate the Chiricahuas at Tularosa, an idea the Apaches almost universally rejected, rather than grant them an exclusive reservation in the Chiricahua homeland. The Apache leaders then held their own conference, invoking spiritual guidance to arrive at a final decision. Those ceremonies concluded, Cochise announced to Howard, "Hereafter the white man and the Indian are to drink of the same water, eat of the same bread, and be at peace."[39]

To avoid any misunderstanding about the terms agreed to at the council, Cochise demanded that the officers at Camp Bowie be summoned to hear the same words in his presence. Howard accordingly sent word for Captain Sumner and his officers to meet them at Dragoon Springs the next day. Much of what transpired during that four-hour meeting with Cochise was a repetition of the previous day's peace talk. However, by that time Howard and Cochise had refined the boundaries of the proposed reservation. The agency would be headquartered at Sulphur Springs, with Jeffords in charge. Howard later justified his departure from the established practice of appointing church-approved agents on the basis that Jeffords was the only white man in whom the Chiricahuas had complete confidence. He feared that if anyone else were placed in the position, the results might be disastrous, and he was probably correct.[40]

The new reservation became the focus of controversy as soon as word of the agreement spread. Crook, in particular, was displeased with the generous terms Howard had granted. He was not alone in his reaction that the "Christian Soldier" had virtually bowed to Cochise's every wish. Not only did they have their friend Jeffords as an agent, but the reservation embraced all of the Chiricahua Mountains, including Camp Bowie and a lengthy segment of the Southern Overland Mail Road, termed by Jeffords as "a grave yard for Cochise's victims."[41] Bounded on the east by New Mexico and on the west by the San Pedro, the Chiricahuas shared a common boundary with their archenemies the Sonorans. If that circumstance alone was not discomforting enough, Cochise made it chillingly clear that he had made peace only with the Americans, not the Mexicans. Consequently, the arrangement created a situation that Crook correctly predicted would lead to international tensions and military intervention.

For the moment, however, all was well in southeastern Arizona for the first time in anyone's memory. Jeffords announced on October 1 that Cochise and three hundred of his followers had settled on the reservation, and the agent himself had induced others to come in as well. Jeffords made his first ration issue later that month, claiming to have fed 450 people. The approach of winter made reservation life all the more appealing to those groups still roaming the desert. By the end of 1872, Jeffords had assembled some 1,000 to 1,150 Chiricahuas at the agency. They represented the central bands and so many of the southern and Mimbres people as well that Jeffords concluded there were no other large bands still out, only a few small parties scattered about the region. Had the Chiricahuas been content to remain on the reservation and to cease hostilities against the Mexicans, a lasting peace might have prevailed in the vicinity of Camp Bowie.

CHAPTER 8

This Sedentary Life

While Howard's truce with Cochise brought an unprecedented calm to southeastern Arizona, things were not so peaceful elsewhere in the territory. Many Apaches and Yavapais north of the Gila were content enough to live on the reservations, but renegade groups quickly resumed their old habits of raiding the settled regions. The agents found it difficult to maintain accountability of individuals, and many warriors took full advantage of the situation by slipping in and out of the government-sponsored sanctuaries. Proof of their complicity, however, was reflected in a one-year tally of fifty-four raids in which forty-four citizens were killed and at least five hundred head of stock were run off. Not unpredictably, the white populace of Arizona, ever-bent on eliminating the recalcitrant elements from the territory, clamored for the army to take action, threatening at the same time to take matters into their own hands. Even the Indian Bureau was forced to admit that military assistance was needed; yet officials remained adamant that restraint was necessary to punish only the guilty and to herd them back to the reservations.

In fall 1872, Crook was finally unleashed to deal with the recalcitrant tribes. One of his first actions was to reissue a previous order instituting frequent roll calls at the agencies to determine how many Apaches were absent and to declare that all those not on their designated reservations would be subject to military action.

Using the army's time-tested strategy of operating against the Indians during winter when they were most vulnerable, he relied on strike forces comprised of light columns of cavalry augmented by enlisted Indian scouts, rather than civilian guides. Crook was convinced that Indians were more adept at trailing their kinsmen and predicting their actions because "scouting is the business of their lives. They learn all the signs of a trail as a child learns the alphabet; it becomes instinct. With a white man the knowledge is acquired in after life."[1] In fact, he preferred recently hostile individuals, the wilder the better, who had voluntarily come over to the army side because they were knowledgeable of the routes and tactics used by particular leaders. Too, Indian scouts had a great psychological effect on the renegades, a factor that often made them capitulate sooner than they might have otherwise, if at all. Crook saw this as a way to shorten campaigns and, in the long run, save the lives of both soldiers and Indians.

Another of Crook's methods was the use of mule packtrains, which he spared no expense to outfit and have managed by competent frontiersmen, assigning them to small columns that could move swiftly, independent of the others. Only rations, ammunition, and small quantities of medical supplies were considered essential; all other amenities, including tents, were left behind. Packtrains eliminated the need for slow and cumbersome supply wagons, and the mules could follow the columns anywhere the Indian trails might lead. Crook charged his officers with pursuing renegades without regard to terrain or weather and pack trains afforded them the necessary mobility to do just that, even if the troops had to abandon their horses and continue on foot. Such determined pursuits, with Indian auxiliaries, eventually demoralized the hostiles and caused them to surrender. It was a method Crook would use with success in Arizona, and later on the northern plains.

In November, Crook launched several troop-strength columns from the posts surrounding central Arizona's Tonto Basin. His strategy called for the troops to sweep the surrounding country to drive the hostiles into the basin area while constantly crisscrossing it with cavalry patrols, and finally, to converge on the Verde River country, where he expected the Indians to take refuge. In so doing, he hoped to force the Indians into a few decisive engagements, rather than numerous inconclusive skirmishes. The campaign that followed confirmed the effectiveness of Crook's methods. The faithful scouts led the troops unerringly to the rancherias. In a series of some twenty actions, units of the First and Fifth Cavalry killed more than two hundred Tonto Apaches and Yavapais and destroyed numerous camps. A conclusive battle at Turret Peak in March 1873 caused the collapse of all resistance. By fall, more than six thousand Indians of various tribes were reported to be on the reservations at San Carlos, Camp Apache, Camp Verde, and at Camp Bowie. Headlines lauded Crook and his men, and both civilian and military authorities expressed

General George Crook, Department of Arizona commander, with Apache scouts Dutchy and Alchisay, circa 1883. (Arizona Historical Society/Tucson, AHS Photo Number 19775)

their satisfaction with the results of the campaign. Crook, still a lieutenant colonel despite his departmental command, was rewarded with a belated promotion to the rank of brigadier general.

Tom Jeffords, meantime, struggled to place the Chiricahua Agency on an operational footing. Despite Howard's promises, the Indian Bureau initially lacked congressional authority to issue rations or other annuities, or to construct habitations for Cochise's band. Howard had to rely on his position as special commissioner to direct the commanding officer at Camp Bowie to supply Jeffords with enough commissary goods to feed the Apaches for sixty days. He also rented a small adobe shack from Nick Rogers, the station-keeper at Sulphur Springs, for use as a combined office, storeroom, and quarters, and hired Frederick G. Hughes as his clerk and assistant. The English-born Hughes had previously settled in the Santa Rita Mountains, where he had taken up mining and married a Hispanic woman. A second employee, Horace Alden, functioned as laborer and cook.[2]

By early 1873, the Chiricahuas and the army were enjoying surprisingly amicable relations. The sudden contrast was indeed remarkable as the former enemies developed a semblance of mutual trust. Post surgeon Samuel L.

Orr, for example, visited the agency in February and returned two days later "after having interviewed Cachise [*sic*] and his Band, and administering to the wants of the sick in his camp."[3] The following month, Cochise himself made an all-day visit to the post, the first time he had journeyed there peacefully since the Bascom tragedy. His level of comfort was reflected in his bringing along twenty members of his band, many of them women and children, including his immediate family.[4]

The development of Arizona Territory likewise benefited by the relative tranquility that had settled over the region. Prospectors at last felt safe enough to push out into the mountains to exploit the districts previously established in the vicinity of Prescott and Tubac, and to search for new deposits elsewhere. The potential of the Harris Lode in Apache Pass could not be realized, however, because by that time it lay within the confines of the Chiricahua Reservation. The limitations posed by wagon transportation, in addition to a shortage of water in quantities required for mining, continued to frustrate efforts to develop that industry throughout the territory. A few especially rich mines survived during the post–Civil War era only because they were profitable enough for the owners to absorb the costs of shipping the ore by steamer down the Colorado River to smelters in California. Other deposits that would have been considered worth exploiting in more remote regions of the West were ignored simply because ore could neither be hauled out profitably nor machinery brought in to process it locally.

Although previous railroad surveys across southern New Mexico and Arizona had not resulted in construction, Congress had authorized the Texas and Pacific Railroad to build westward to El Paso, thence across the Jornada del Muerto along the thirty-second parallel to Yuma and San Diego. The proposed route passed only a few miles north of Camp Bowie and the recently created Chiricahua Reservation. The promise of a railroad spanning the territory would at last promote mining on a large scale by bringing in heavy equipment and shipping out ore to be smelted. An added benefit, declared the commissioner of Indian Affairs, was that the railroad would eventually "settle the Indian question in that quarter. Indians cannot fight near a railroad."[5] Crook's campaign in the Tonto Basin, coupled with Cochise's retirement, had already done much to resolve the situation, yet if hostilities were to break out again, the availability of a railroad would greatly expedite the mobility of troops and supplies to the places where they were required. Moreover, a railroad would reduce drastically the high costs of freighting army supplies by wagon to Bowie and other remote military installations.[6]

The U.S. Mail, meanwhile, continued to traverse the well-worn ruts of the Southern Overland Mail Road from the Rio Grande to California. In 1873, Camp Bowie was designated as a transfer station for mail going to Camp Grant via the old Goodwin road, and just two years later service on the mail line would be increased to three runs weekly using light two-horse vehicles. The same year would witness the final act of transcontinental stagecoaching through Arizona with the establishment of connections between Fort Worth and San Diego by the Texas and California Stage Company.[7]

The telegraph, by no means a novelty when it finally arrived in Arizona Territory, quickly surpassed conventional mail as the state-of-the-art means of communication for the army. The completion of a military line from San Diego to Prescott and Tucson in November 1873 gave Crook instant access to his superiors at Division of the Pacific Headquarters in San Francisco, as well as to his district commander in Tucson. When Crook and Schofield discovered that the line had actually been constructed for less money than had been appropriated, they immediately asked permission to use the excess funds to extend connections to Camps Verde and Apache, both well off the beaten paths of travel, "thus bringing all the military posts in Arizona within telegraphic communications."[8]

The absence of Indian depredations in southern Arizona encouraged an occasional Texas cattleman to avail himself of the lush grasslands along the Santa Cruz, the Rillito Valley southeast of Tucson, the San Pedro, and in the vicinity of the Whetstone Mountains, west of Camp Bowie. Most of the hardy individuals who had attempted to raise stock in those areas prior to Cochise's surrender were now dead or they had lost too many animals to continue profitable ranching. Apache raids during and after the Civil War had, in fact, driven out most of the Americans who had attempted to settle those areas. However, the situation changed dramatically by 1873, when over two thousand head of cattle were recorded on lands within just the first twenty miles south of Tucson.[9] The earliest herds to be driven into southern Arizona included cattle from California, as well as Texas. Drought conditions in southern California forced some stock growers to send their cattle by rail to Yuma, where they were unloaded and driven up the Gila to migrate eventually along the open-range tributaries all the way to the Mexican border. The many military posts in the region, including Camp Bowie, along with the Indian reservations, afforded lucrative markets for government beef contracts.

The expansion of commerce corresponded with a population boom. Between 1870 and 1880, the number of residents in Arizona increased by more than

318 percent—to 40,440 persons. In Pima County alone, wherein Fort Bowie was located at that time, the population leaped from 5,716 to slightly more than 17,000 during that decade. The problem was, most of those people did not consider themselves to be permanent residents. An army officer inspecting posts in 1873 reported that he had encountered "only one man who says he proposes to live and die in Arizona. All design leaving the country as soon as they can get money enough together to get away. Were the troops to be removed from the country tomorrow, not a hundred white men would remain in it. Nine tenths of those here live upon what they can make or steal off the Government."[10] He added that living conditions were so miserable that even discharged soldiers having a desire to reenlist traveled elsewhere to do so.

Cochise's pledge to keep the peace, and the confinement of the Chiricahuas to the seventy-square-mile reservation at Sulphur Springs, was perhaps the single most significant factor in promoting the development of southern Arizona during the mid-1870s. Still, Howard's hastily negotiated accord with Cochise overlooked several important factors that portended trouble. In fact, many of the understandings arrived at, or presumed by Cochise, were never officially documented. While Cochise seems to have been absolutely sincere in committing to peace with the Americans, he had made no such pledge to the Mexicans. Howard had seen to it that the presumably peaceful Cochise Chiricahuas were exempted from military authority, including roll calls, yet Crook remained skeptical, especially in view of the raiding that persisted south of their reservation in Sonora. Governor Ignacio Pesquiera complained repeatedly and bitterly to Crook that action should be taken to contain Cochise's warriors. While Crook strongly suspected that Cochise's band was at least partly culpable, but at the same time he could not be certain that southern Chiricahuas operating from the Sierra Madre were blameless.

There can be no doubt that a reservation having a common and largely uncontrolled border with Mexico was a dream-come-true for Cochise's warriors. Not only could they raid into Sonora with impunity, the Mexicans were prohibited from following them into the reserve. If that was not advantageous enough, those Chiricahuas still operating from the Sierra Madre, and not under Cochise's control, had a safe haven in which to escape pursuing Mexican troops. A further oversight on Howard's part—or perhaps he preferred not to address it during his talks with Cochise—was the matter of firearms. In point of fact, the Chiricahuas had not surrendered, nor were they disarmed. The "treaty" actually amounted to nothing more than a truce with the Americans, in exchange for being fed and clothed at government expense, and they were permitted to reside in their traditional homeland. Crook pulled no punches in exposing Howard's agreement for what it was: "Cachise [*sic*] only sees in this transaction that the President sent a General Officer to hunt him up and make peace with him on his own terms, which terms he understands to mean 'feed and protect me while I raid on Mexico and I will let you alone.'"[11]

In his defense, Cochise exercised no control over bands other than his own. Southern Chiricahuas in Mexico, led by Juh and other lesser chiefs, were not parties to the agreement with Howard. Even though Cochise allegedly had promised to help round up those Apaches, "his failure to do anything of the kind has established the impression that he is more familiar with the perpetrators of these outrages than he cares to admit and that he completely misled our commissioner in the conference, " wrote Crook.[12] It made little difference whether or not the raiders actually belonged to Cochise's band— the crux of the problem was that they were allowed to take advantage of the reservation at Sulphur Springs as a protected base of operations. As Crook and others were well aware, the Sonorans were rapidly losing stock, while Chiricahua cattle herds at Apache Pass were correspondingly increasing.

No love was lost between Crook and Thomas Jeffords, yet the agent recognized that his charges were abiding by the letter, though not the spirit, of the agreement when he reported there were few depredations north of the Arizona-Sonora line. He admitted, however, that the Mexicans were complaining of continual raiding and that "these reports have had too much foundation, and although I have made every endeavor to stop this raiding I have not met with success. Neither do I believe it can be stopped as long as the Chiricahua Reservation exists, and its present incumbents are allowed to roam over it at will."[13]

Moreover, the raids inevitably occurred outside U.S. jurisdiction, though the U.S. government had promised Mexico that it would prevent Indian raids from originating within its territory. Crook therefore felt justified in taking punitive action against the Chiricahuas on that score alone, though he probably recognized that he would be on political thin ice. Regardless, Crook distrusted Cochise on general principles, assuming it would be only a matter of time before his warriors again committed depredations in Arizona, and when that happened, the army would be poised to hammer him. Accordingly, during January 1873, Crook assembled a strong force of cavalry at the new Camp Grant, recently relocated to a more strategic position at

the base of Mount Graham, expressly "to watch Cochise's camp."[14] On the
eve of his offensive, however, Crook hesitated and decided to send a representative to call upon Cochise for the purpose of clarifying his understanding
of the terms of the accord, since Crook himself had never been provided a copy.

The department commander dispatched Captain William H. Brown, inspector general for the Department of Arizona, along with Lieutenant John G.
Bourke, Crook's personal aide, to call on Cochise near the end of the month.
Brown's detachment made camp at Sulphur Springs on the 29th, whereupon he sent word to Agent Jeffords that he desired a meeting with Cochise.
After learning the officer's intent, Jeffords arranged for him to talk with the
chief at today's Middlemarch Canyon in the Dragoon Mountains on February 3. Cochise courteously received the two officers and their party, along
with Jeffords as interpreter, immediately reiterating his desire for continued
peace. He assured Brown that soldiers were at liberty to cross the Chiricahua
Reservation at any time according to need, but that no whites were allowed
to reside there. As to the relationship with Mexico, Cochise initially attempted
to evade Brown's inquiry, but when pressed, finally responded:

> The Mexicans are on one side in this matter and the Americans on
> another. There are many young people here whose parents and rela-
> tives have been killed by the Mexicans, and now these young people
> are liable to go down . . . and do a little damage to the Mexicans. I
> don't want to lie about this thing; they go, but I don't send them. I
> made peace with the Americans, but the Mexicans did not come to
> ask peace from me as the Americans have done . . . . I consider myself
> at peace with Mexico, but my young men, like those at all the other
> reservations, are liable to occasionally make raids . . . . I can't prevent
> it. There are bad people everywhere. A great many of us were one
> time at peace at Fronteras and some of the Mexicans used to tell us to
> come up here and steal American horses, which are big and worth a
> great deal of money in Mexico. But when our people came back there
> with them, they killed them and took the horses and cattle away.[15]

The situation could not have been summarized more succinctly. In those
few words, Cochise laid bare the heart of the conflict, a trait the forthright
Crook could undoubtedly admire, even in an adversary. Jeffords also assured
Brown that if Crook attempted to force roll calls on his charges, the Chiricahuas would leave immediately. Back at his headquarters, Crook weighed these
factors carefully and finally elected to take no action for fear of needlessly

stirring up the Cochise Apaches. The Mexicans would have to contend with them as best they could.

Jeffords fully appreciated the deep animosities existing between Cochise's Apaches and the Mexicans and doubted there could be any lasting reconciliation. He stopped short of directly criticizing Howard, yet he openly predicted that the Apaches would continue raiding into Sonora and Chihuahua so long as they were armed, mounted, and separated from mortal enemies by only an invisible boundary line. As for removal to one of the more northerly reservations, Jeffords thought only about half of the Chiricahuas would consider joining their Mescalero cousins at Tularosa, New Mexico. (The Ojo Caliente reservation at Canada Alamosa had been abandoned in 1872 as being unsuitable for agriculture.) The others, however, might be persuaded to go if the government gave them enough presents. Once there, they would be in the midst of a number of military posts and, consequently, would not have the liberty to pass back and forth into Mexico.

Crook and Jeffords agreed on that point. The department commander was clearly peeved that Cochise had been allowed to negotiate such liberal terms for himself (not to mention that Howard took full credit for ending the war) and in so doing had placed the U.S. Government in a most difficult situation. "There is no process of reasoning short of subjugation," Crook argued, "which can convince Cochise that we are not afraid of him—I am satisfied any attempt on our part to prevent his raiding into Mexico will be regarded as a violation of the terms of his peace with General Howard and will provoke his outbreak."[16]

Jeffords subsequently became the target of vehement public criticism for his leniency, but the evidence suggests that he earnestly attempted to curb the raiding into Mexico by the limited means at his disposal. In late summer 1873, he requested and gained approval to move the agency headquarters from Sulphur Springs to Ciénaga San Simon, fourteen miles east of Camp Bowie, primarily because it offered better grazing and plenty of water but also because it was farther from the border. The soils, too, were better adapted to agriculture, and if the Apaches were going to be transformed into subsistence farmers, they had to be given every advantage. In any event, the experiment proved to be a failure when many members of the band fell ill, and five children died, within two months after settling at the ciénaga. The agent did not detail the specific conditions contributing to the illnesses, but indicated that they stemmed from stagnant pools of water standing in the bottomlands. In November, Jeffords again gained permission to move the Chiricahuas, this time to Pinery Canyon, "a favorite resort of the Apaches" south of Camp Bowie, where the army had established its lumber camp a decade earlier.[17] It was not, however, an area suited to farming.

Jeffords was also plagued by freeloaders from the reservations at San Carlos, White Mountain, and Tularosa, who showed up at his agency requesting to live with their relatives. He had no choice but to refuse, if for no other reason than they were not registered there, consequently, he could not ration them without depriving Cochise's people. Jeffords probably also feared that those factions would only compound the problems he was already experiencing. Commissioner of Indian Affairs Smith also weighed in with a threat to turn the matter over to the military, a move that would bring troops to the reservation and a requirement that the Chiricahuas submit to periodic roll calls. Cochise came to Jeffords's assistance by summoning all of the headmen and warriors to inform them in no uncertain terms that he still headed the reserve at Apache Pass and that those choosing to live there, whether of his band or not, must abide by the terms of his truce with Howard. He emphasized that the forays into Sonora must cease, lest they all suffer under a military occupation and perhaps be forced to move to Tularosa, or worse, to the hated San Carlos Reservation. Effectively evicted from the Chiricahua Reservation, the refractory groups proceeded to pillage their way south into Sonora. When the raids were laid at Cochise's doorstep, Jeffords defended him by explaining that the trails of the outlaws naturally led toward his reservation because the culprits were returning to their proper homes at San Carlos.[18]

The difficulties with maintaining the Chiricahua Reservation became even more evident to Levi E. Dudley, superintendent of Indian Affairs for New Mexico, when he visited Jeffords in May 1874. Dudley's primary purpose in coming, in fact, was to convince Cochise that his band would be better off by moving to Tularosa. Cochise, who was suffering the effects of a long and hard life by that time, countered that he would not oppose such a move because he would not live long enough for it to matter. But others in the band were adamant that "the Government had not enough troops to move them, as they would rather die here than live there."[19]

True to his own prophecy, the great chief of the Chiricahuas died only two weeks later in his alternate stronghold on the east side of the Dragoon Mountains. His band deeply mourned the loss, and, so did his friend Jeffords. "He was the most reliable and honorable Indian it has ever been my fortune to meet," Jeffords lamented. "He gave me more assistance than I thought it possible for any man to do, and compelled the other Indians to recognize me as their agent in every sense."[20] According to Apache custom, his body was dressed in his best clothing and, accompanied by a procession consisting of nearly everyone in the band, taken to a secret location where it was placed in a deep crevasse in the rocks. As Cochise's biographer aptly notes, "It was ironic that this courageous Apache leader, who could always be found leading his men into battle, died a natural death on a reservation."[21] Cochise's hatred for the Mexicans never abated; his eventual limited trust of the Americans developed as he came to the realization that he faced a choice between seeing his people exterminated or confined to a reservation. His decision to negotiate and abide by a lasting peace was a tribute to his wisdom.

Taza, Cochise's eldest son, succeeded him as head of the band. Although he had experienced many of the events associated with the American occupation of southern Arizona, and had been carefully tutored by his father, Taza had not attained Cochise's status in the tribe. Even in his own band, Taza had detractors, though most of the people accepted his leadership out of habit and respect for Cochise.

During the year following Cochise's death, intermittent raiding continued in Mexico. Most of the depredations, however, were committed by nontreaty groups still residing in Mexico and by outlaw Apaches from San Carlos, Tularosa, and the reactivated Apache reserve at Ojo Caliente, where most of the Chiricahuas had been relocated in late 1874. Jeffords wanted to retire to a less stressful life than that of an Indian agent, but was persuaded to stay by those in the band declaring that they would honor the peace only if he stayed. Jeffords also realized that Taza would need his help and counsel if the band were to survive on the reservation and, hopefully, make a successful transition to the white man's way of life. Submitting his annual report for 1874, Jeffords took satisfaction in notifying his superiors that he had the 930 members of the band completely under his control and that he was certain they had committed no depredations during the past year. He added that, in his opinion, the Chiricahuas were becoming reconciled "with this, to them, sedentary life."[22]

Military authorities nevertheless suspected that Jeffords's Indians were guilty of attacks in Mexico. Major General John M. Schofield reported from his San Francisco headquarters that although Arizona had experienced no depredations during the latter part of 1873 and 1874, the Sonorans were not so fortunate. Schofield thought that the Chiricahua Reservation needed to be brought under military control. In so doing, each adult male would be tagged with a numbered metal disk and his name officially recorded, along with the names of his family members. Ration issues were then based on those registered. Of even more importance to agency officials and the army, any Indians leaving the reservation could be discovered and identified quickly. Jeffords had resisted such controls, however. He held no roll calls, but as Crook put it, "claims to have counted them in their rancherias, an absurdity which is apparent on its face, as any person familiar with the subject must know that the approximation even to the correct number of a band of Indians scattered around in the rocks and mountains of a large reservation is an impossibility."[23]

The potential for Apaches to stray from the reservation was not Jeffords's only problem. In May he discovered that two Mexicans had trespassed on the reservation and had traded whiskey to some Apaches in exchange for a horse. Although Jeffords had troops from Camp Bowie arrest the two men and eventually transport them to Tucson for prosecution, the justice of the peace released the pair, claiming there was insufficient evidence on which to try the case. Such incidents influenced Jeffords to propose again moving the agency, this time to Apache Pass itself. Justifying his request, Jeffords explained to the commissioner of Indian Affairs that Pinery Canyon was "so far from the road and camping grounds of passing wagon trains and travelers that it was impossible for me to keep the necessary surveillance over the intercourse between the Indians and passers-by."[24] He also noted another advantage. Still standing below the spring was the adobe quartz mill building, abandoned since 1869 when Colonel John Stone was killed by some of the same Apaches Jeffords now sought to protect. Smith granted permission to relocate the agency on May 14, 1875.[25]

But, Jeffords' troubles did not end there. In July, a detachment of Mexican troops crossed into the reservation and opened fire on a party of Chiricahuas out gathering nuts fifteen miles within the boundary. To their credit, the Apaches fled and took cover without returning fire. Some of them later rode to Apache Pass to report the incident to Jeffords. Too, small groups of White Mountain Apaches continued to come to the reservation claiming they could not abide the old family feuds with the Pinal Apaches that continued to disrupt life at San Carlos. Jeffords, of course, had no authority to allow the refugees to stay at Apache Pass, and was forced to send them back. However, he took the precaution of provisioning them for the return trip to keep them from raiding for subsistence along the way. "These Indians being very unsettled," he reported, "are very dangerous to the peace of the reservation, taking every opportunity to slip away upon thieving expeditions."[26]

His claim was not an exaggeration, for the problems did not end there. Visiting Indians sometimes proved to be a bad influence on Cochise's band of Chiricahuas. In one instance, two of the latter joined a Mimbres raiding party on the Rio Grande that subsequently stole a number of horses near Las Cruces. In fall 1875, a number of White Mountain people arrived at the reservation to plead once again with Jeffords to allow them to remain because of the unbearable conditions at San Carlos. But before Jeffords could persuade the visitors to leave, a fight ensued in which a minor Chiricahua chief was murdered. Jeffords promptly sent the band packing back to San Carlos on Christmas Day in the hope of preventing his charges from exacting vengeance for their loss.[27] Jeffords's efforts notwithstanding, the Chiricahua Reservation continued to be plagued by hangers-on from both sides of the border.

The problems experienced on the reservation were relatively minor and were looked upon as the normal course of events by both the Indian Bureau and the army. Military officials, in fact, were so confident that the Indian situation in southeastern Arizona Territory had been resolved that they proposed abandoning Camp Bowie. As early as 1874, orders were promulgated to that effect, and had they been implemented, the secretary of the interior stood ready to take over the buildings for use as the Chiricahua Indian Agency. But, the army changed its mind at the last moment and suspended the directive because Bowie remained the only military post of any consequence in the entire region southeast of Tucson. A niggardly Congress was ever watchful for ways to economize, and was especially prone to reduce the army's budget in the post–Civil War era. Consequently, a second proposal to abandon Camp Bowie arose the very next year, but again the army stalled by pointing out that even peaceful Indians occasionally required a firm hand to keep them in line. With the army gone, the chances were good that troops would be called back from time to time. Again, the proposal was tabled.[28]

Jeffords began experiencing critical food shortages in early 1876. Although the cause is not clear, the beef supply to the reservation apparently was reduced at a time when the interlopers were already imposing stresses on the meat ration. By February the situation had become so critical that Jeffords instructed the men to resort to hunting to augment their subsistence. The expedition resulted in an unexpected tragedy that was to have far-reaching effects. When some of the warriors got into an argument, a gunfight ensued in which two of them were killed, along with a grandchild of Cochise. The incident rent the band, causing Taza and most of the people to return to Apache Pass, while twelve other families led by Skin-ya hid out in the Dragoons.

Some of Skin-ya's group joined forces with outlaw White Mountain Apaches passing through from San Carlos about a month afterward on their way to raid in Sonora. A few days later, the party returned with about one hundred dollars in silver and gold. Some of the men discovered that Nick Rogers had whiskey for sale at Sulphur Springs. The temptation was too great for the Apaches to resist. Jeffords had learned previously that Rogers was covertly dispensing whiskey to the Indians on the reserve and had warned him to desist or be prosecuted, an admonition Rogers apparently heeded for most of a year.[29] But when the Apaches showed up at his ranch on April 6 with hard money in hand, Rogers immediately went back on his word and opened a keg of the fiery liquid, which was laced with tobacco and other ingredients "to give it strength." Two men, Pi-hon-se-nay and his nephew, returned the next day to demand more liquor, but Rogers refused, probably because he feared being discovered by Jeffords. Since Rogers regularly supplied liquor to the Camp Bowie garrison, a charge of selling whiskey to the Indians could put an end to the most lucrative aspect of his livelihood. Pi-hon-se-nay was angered by the rebuff and immediately shot Rogers to death, along with his cook, O. O. Spence, the only other white man present at the ranch at the time. The two Apaches helped themselves to whiskey, guns, and ammunition before returning to the mountains. On the 8th, the same day that Jeffords learned of the murders at Sulphur Springs, intoxicated Apaches raided a ranch in the San Pedro Valley, killing a man named Lewis and stealing four horses.[30]

Jeffords immediately petitioned the commanding officer at Camp Bowie, Captain C. B. McLellan, for assistance in arresting the renegades. A cavalry detachment led by First Lieutenant Austin Henely rode directly to Sulphur Springs, where they found the bodies of Rogers and Spence.[31] The trail left by the two murderers led toward the mountains. Jeffords and Henely were both under the impression that the murder resulted from nothing more than a drunken row, therefore they agreed that it would be best if only the agent and his interpreter went to the rancheria. Because the appearance of troops would probably cause the Indians to open fire, or stampede, Jeffords suggested that the detachment proceed directly to Sulphur Springs and stand by. Meantime, he found the Apaches and attempted to reason with them. Four eventually agreed to give up and return with him to the station. The cavalry picked up Skin-ya's trail again on the 10th and followed the party to the west side of the Chiricahua Mountains south of the post. Skin-ya and his men opened fire from a prominence, causing the troopers to seek cover. Assessing the situation, Lieutenant Henely considered his force too small to dislodge the Apaches from their superior position, and to attack would only waste the lives of his men.[32] After their return to Camp Bowie, Jeffords and McLellan moved the Chiricahuas still at the agency to the east side of the mountains so as to isolate the renegades on the west slope from receiving any assistance. However, subsequent patrols failed to locate the outlaws and nothing more was heard from them until spring.

In early June, the outlaws showed up at Taza's camp about fifteen miles from Camp Bowie. The brothers, Skin-ya and Pi-hon-se-nay, attempted to persuade Taza and Naiche and their men to join them on the warpath, but the sons of Cochise rejected the notion of renewing the war with the whites. The talk then turned ugly and a fight broke out in which six men, including Skin-ya, were killed and three others were wounded. Taza dispatched a messenger to Jeffords with the news. Jeffords and Fred Hughes responded with a detachment of thirty cavalrymen, but the trouble had passed for the moment and the renegades had vanished into the mountains.[33]

It was a fortuitous coincidence when John P. Clum, the young agent at San Carlos, arrived at Apache Pass the next day with ten troops of the Sixth Cavalry, two companies of Indian scouts, and as an additional precaution, a personal bodyguard of fifty-four trusted Arivaipa and White Mountain Apaches. The troops were under the personal command of Colonel August V. Kautz, a veteran of both the Mexican and Civil Wars and author of military manuals who had replaced Crook as head of the Department of Arizona. Kautz posted his cavalry at Sulphur Springs and in the San Simon Valley to block any attempt the Apaches might make to escape. By the time Clum's force arrived on the scene, however, Taza and his people had moved to the agency to forestall any further trouble with Skin-ya's followers. Pi-honse-nay, mortally wounded in the June 4 fight, sent a message to Jeffords asking that he be allowed to come to the agency to die. His request granted, Pi-hon-se-nay came in, along with all the women and children from Skin-ya's band. Their men either had been killed or had fled the reservation, and the families had nowhere else to go.[34]

Clum called together the headmen to propose that the Chiricahuas move to San Carlos. The many problems associated with the Chiricahua Reservation had become known at high levels of the government and Taza's band was being watched closely. News of the murders of Rogers and Spence was the last straw needed to convince Congress that Howard's plan for a separate and lightly regulated reservation had failed. On May 5, the secretary of the interior directed Clum to proceed to the Apache Pass agency, collect the

Chiricahuas, and take them to San Carlos. There was to be no debate this time. The recent conflicts between Taza's band and Skin-ya's renegades worked to Clum's advantage because they served to convince Taza that going to San Carlos was, after all, the best alternative for his people. Their proximity to Mexico would always pose a strong temptation to continue raiding, and access to liquor obtained from whites residing on the Camp Bowie Military Reservation, or from passing travelers, would be an increasing source of trouble. It was a tremendous sacrifice for the Chiricahuas. They fully understood that they were being forced from their own reservation by the acts of a few malcontents and that they were being exiled to a place they dreaded.[35]

The cavalcade of 42 men and 280 women and children, accompanied by the ever-present menagerie of ponies and barking dogs, made its exodus down the dusty road leading out of Apache Pass on June 12. However, about 140 Chiricahuas who had always resisted the idea of living at San Carlos made their own way to New Mexico, showing up at Ojo Caliente a short time later. Unaccounted for were some 400 hundred central and southern Apaches led by Juh, and a new figure—Geronimo—who had vanished into their old homeland between the Mimbres and the Santa Cruz. The Indian Bureau thus absolved itself of any responsibility for the renegades and gave permission for the army to treat them as hostile.[36]

Despite the escape of Juh and Geronimo, the removal of the Cochise Apaches and the abolition of the Chiricahua Agency created a false sense of security for the citizens in the region surrounding Camp Bowie. Taza and his band had been gone only a short time before miners invaded the former reservation in search of gold and silver. Confident that the Apache menace had finally subsided, two prospectors, Todenworth and Keho (or Cadotte), entered the Chiricahua Mountains searching for quartz veins in July. Lurking renegades surprised and killed them about twenty-five miles south of the post.[37] A sergeant and detachment of cavalry pursued the offenders as far as the international boundary, where the soldiers stopped and turned back to the post.

Kautz was hopping mad. Demanding to know why a mere sergeant had been entrusted with such an important mission, he reminded Captain McLellan of the unofficial but standing policy that allowed the troops of both nations to pursue Indians into each others' territories. Kautz directed McLellan to send Henely and his Sixth Cavalrymen on "a vigorous campaign . . . against the renegade Chiricahua Indians . . . that [they] may be immediately destroyed and that loss of any further lives at their hands may be prevented."

The department commander concluded by instructing McLellan to support Henely in every way possible and to make certain the troops understood that "No imaginary boundary line should stop such a pursuit[,] for the service is as much in the interest of Mexico as our own Government."[38]

The Camp Bowie garrison at that time included only two companies of cavalry, augmented by a company of White Mountain Apache scouts, but Lieutenant Henely made the most of them. During the rest of the summer and into the fall of 1876, he conducted a series of scouts throughout southeastern Arizona, southwestern New Mexico, and into Mexico as far south as Janos. He was ably assisted by Lieutenant John A. Rucker, who had dropped out of West Point after completing two years of study, but had nevertheless secured a commission in the Sixth Cavalry. Both men were aggressive and eager to prove their worth in the field. However, after marching for weeks on end, and covering hundreds of miles through the winter of 1876–77, they had little to show for their efforts except a pile of worn-out equipment.

The once-promising state of affairs in Arizona continued to deteriorate as Apache raiding continued almost unabated. Two men were killed on the San Pedro in September and a number of horses and colts were stolen from Samuel Hughes's ranch near Camp Crittenden.[39] By February, a despondent commissioner of Indian Affairs concluded that "the old reign of terror seemed to have returned to the southeastern portion of Arizona."[40]

Indeed, the renegade Chiricahuas became even bolder as they returned to their familiar haunts around Camp Bowie. Apaches were blamed for the theft of stock from a ranch on the San Pedro early in February, but after following the trail of the raiders all the way to the Frisco River in New Mexico, Lieutenant Rucker was forced to abandon the chase when his horses became too feeble to keep up. Just two months later, the Apaches made another appearance, this time at the San Simon stage station, where they again ran off stock. During May, Sixth Cavalry troopers and scouts pursued a party of renegades from the Tularosa reservation into Chihuahua, a total distance of four hundred miles, without catching sight of them.[41]

That spring the Indian Bureau, relying on information supplied by army patrols, determined that some of the Apaches were taking adavantage of the Ojo Caliente Reservation much as they had the Chiricahua agency in previous years. Trails leading to and from the reservation were convincing evidence that it was serving to harbor renegades as a base for their forays. The raiders also recruited additional members from among the Mimbres and other Chiricahua bands living there. Clum was ordered to break up the operation in May. Taking a force of reliable Indian policemen with him, Clum disarmed and dismounted over 450 warriors suspected of participating in the raids, among them Victorio, Geronimo, Gordo, Francisco, and others whose names were to become famous during the years to come. These Clum had escorted to San Carlos, where he could keep an eye on them. The consolidation thus gave Clum exclusive jurisdiction over all of the Western Apaches. However, what Clum and his associates in the Indian Bureau did not fully comprehend were the differences and animosities that existed among the diverse bands of the Apache people. This lack of understanding and Clum's personal desire to concentrate the Apaches at San Carlos were to have serious consequences for the region.[42]

Of real advantage in controlling the Indians was the completion of the U.S. Military Telegraph Line to Camp Bowie on March 1, 1877, and afterward to Camps Apache and Thomas. In following months, the system was extended eastward to Ralston, New Mexico, where it connected with lines from Santa Fe and El Paso, thus completing a transcontinental network. The *Army and Navy Journal* announced that "the line will almost encircle the San Carlos reservation and will be of great service in case of a disturbance by the Indians . . . besides being invaluable in the progress of the territory."[43]

Confining most of the recognized outlaw leaders on the San Carlos Reservation did not entirely curtail raiding south of the Gila. In fact, within a month after Clum's roundup, Indians absconded with horses from Bowie and killed mail rider Jackson Tait at a favorite ambush site just three miles east of the post.[44] The driver of the eastbound mail encountered Tait's horse shot dead in the road. Realizing that it was foolhardy to search for the rider, the driver lost no time in turning back toward the post to report his discovery. First Lieutenant Frank West led out a detachment of six soldiers, five citizen volunteers, and two scouts to investigate. They soon discovered Tait's body, shot twice through the chest clad only in the blood-soaked shirt, lying in the brush about three hundred yards from the road. West sent the remains back to the post with the next buckboard mail, which happened by about that time, then took up the trail of the Indians. Uncharacteristically, the half-dozen renegades stopped and took up a position along a ridge top only two miles from the scene of the murder. The Chiricahuas engaged the approaching troopers in the usual manner—one shot as a signal, followed by a volley—probably thinking they could achieve an easy victory. West and his men returned only a few shots before withdrawing in the face of what he believed were superior numbers (later determined to be only six warriors).

Nearing Fort Bowie, West encountered a relief party of forty-five men sent out to reinforce him, but the Apaches were long gone by that time.[45]

Some of the same Apaches had also attacked the next Las Cruces–bound mail buckboard at a point about five miles west of the post, on May 30. An alert driver, spotting one of the warriors changing position just before the trap was sprung, had time to turn around and backtrack to a defensible position. A three-hour fight ensued before a telegraph construction crew from Camp Grant happened along and relieved the party. Regardless, Apaches boldly demonstrated no particular fear of the nearby fort by remaining in the area and murdering the next mail rider, Sam Ward, in nearly the same location as he galloped west from the pass on May 31.[46]

Lieutenant Rucker, who had been out scouting for three weeks and was then camped on Turkey Creek with seventy-five men, was summoned via the new telegraph system to take up the chase. Rucker arrived the next day and immediately sent a detachment of scouts on the trail of the marauders. Reporting back that evening, they found that the Apaches had gone toward Stein's Peak, but by that time they had a long lead. The scouts recovered only a few pieces of mail along the way, some of it punctured with bullet holes.[47]

Throughout the remainder of 1877, the renegades remained at large in the almost uninhabited region southeast of Camp Bowie. Some of them joined forces with Victorio, successor to Mangas, after he led over three hundred Mimbres and Cochise Chiricahuas in a break from San Carlos early in September to return to southern New Mexico. Consequently, elements of the Sixth Cavalry and the Apache scouts operating from Bowie continued to patrol the vast area from the San Simon Valley southward to the Animas Mountains in New Mexico. No longer could they cross the international border, however, because the Mexican government had changed its mind in regard to the reciprocal agreement.[48]

Although the patrols occasionally discovered trails left by the phantom raiders, they made few contacts until December, when the persistent Lieutenant Rucker finally got lucky. On the 16th, and again on the 18th, Rucker struck rancherias on Ralston Flat and in the Animas Range. His men accounted for a total of sixteen Apaches killed and an undetermined number wounded. They also captured sixty head of horses. The Apaches then fled to the mountains and, according to Colonel Orlando B. Willcox, who succeeded Kautz as commander of the Department of Arizona in March 1878, "such was the terror of their name and fear of their raids that whole valleys and ranges of

Company of Apache scouts posed on the Fort Bowie parade ground. (Arizona Historical Society/Tucson, AHS Photo Number 20806)

mountains and roads in Southeastern Arizona were practically abandoned by the whites except under escort of troops."[49]

Willcox had his work cut out. If the rampaging Apaches were not enough, he also had to contend with unscrupulous businessmen, dubbed by the army the "Tucson Ring," who placed profits above the lives of their fellow Arizonans. The army accused the ring of using the territorial newspapers to their own advantage, claiming that members exaggerated and sometimes blatantly fabricated Indian depredations to justify the retention of needlessly large numbers of troops in the region. Moreover, citizens openly criticized army officers for their lack of success in the field, thereby attempting to induce the army to deploy even more troops in the territory. Supplying the troops, especially those in the field, continued to be a lucrative occupation. Equally profitable was the provisioning of Indians at San Carlos. The "ring" continually fostered bad relations between the army and the Indian Bureau, "for it is not at all to the interests of contractors for Indian supplies that Indian agents and officers of the Army should harmonize."[50] Concentrating the Apaches at San Carlos was an unworkable concept, one that ring members fully appreciated, simply because the Apaches were nomadic people unaccustomed to living within such a confined area. Too, they belonged to distinctive groups that did not get along well when forced to reside in close contact with each other. The predictable outcome was that groups became disenchanted and left the reservation to join the renegade factions. Indian agents often were loath to admit such losses and continued to report the full complement of Indians on the reservation to justify full supply contracts.

Surpluses could be sold off in black market operations, for the benefit of both the contractors and the agents.[51]

Willcox's first move was to improve the effectiveness of scouting operations by combining them under a single officer, a post he delegated to Major Charles E. Compton, Sixth Cavalry. He also transferred a company of scouts from Camp Apache to Fort Bayard to act in concert with Rucker, who was assigned to reconnoiter on a broad front southeast of Camp Bowie. Troops from Camp Huachuca, a new post located near the San Pedro River southwest of Bowie, were directed to operate on Rucker's flank. The object was either to flush out the Apaches or to drive them across the border, where Mexican troops were waiting. Although the effort failed to corral the renegades into a decisive action, they were nevertheless forced to hide in the Sierra Madre or join forces with Victorio, who was then operating back and forth across the Mexican line from New Mexico to well below El Paso. In response to the establishment of Camp Huachuca, the Mexicans increased the garrisons on their side of the border and renewed efforts to track down the hostile bands. By the end of the year, Willcox was able to report: "Trading communications between Tucson and Mexican frontier towns were resumed, and on our side the lately hostile country soon became the scene of peaceful pursuits, ranches taken up, and mining districts formed, busy with explorers and miners."[52]

In 1877, a principal new mining district in the vicinity of Camp Bowie developed around a silver lode dubbed "Tombstone." Pennsylvania-born Ed Schieffelen had prospected in Nevada, Utah, and Idaho before trying his luck in Arizona. After years of failure, Schiefflelen found himself working for wages at Camp Huachuca to make ends meet, but continued to search in his spare time for the strike that would make him wealthy. At the peak of the 1876–77 Apache outbreak, he stumbled onto a rich silver deposit approximately fifty miles southwest of Camp Bowie and staked his claim. As the Apache troubles subsided, others followed and Tombstone quickly became one of the most active mining districts in the territory, producing not only silver but also paying quantities of gold, copper, lead, and zinc.

Geronimo, whose name was increasingly associated with the recalcitrant factions, had been captured in New Mexico during the previous year and returned to San Carlos. He did not remain there for long, however. Almost a year later to the day, he led yet another outbreak from the reservation, perhaps as the result of a tizwin drunk, or because his nephew had committed suicide. Maybe it was a combination of both.[53] Whatever the reason, Geronimo combined his followers with those of Juh, and struck out for the Sierra Madre in Mexico, where they soon made life hazardous for the inhabitants of western Chihuahua and Sonora. Victorio, meantime, led both the American and Mexican armies on a merry chase throughout eastern Chihuahua, southern New Mexico, and west Texas. But, for the moment at least, southeastern Arizona remained quiet.[54]

The cessation of hostilities fortuitously coincided with the long-awaited construction of a railroad across the Southwest. The Southern Pacific, building eastward from Los Angeles, had reached Yuma at the end of September 1877, but then suffered a year's delay. Intense desert heat further slowed progress, but a locomotive eventually chugged into Tucson amid a wild celebration some two and a half years later. The company president, Charles Crocker, gave an obligatory speech and was presented with, appropriately, a spike of Arizona silver from Tombstone's Tough Nut Mine. Not long afterward, Willcox announced the abandonment of the former military supply route from the railhead at Pueblo, Colorado, from which goods had been hauled overland by wagon via New Mexico, in favor of rail transportation direct from San Francisco.[55] The poor roads that still retarded travel from the railroad to most of the posts in Arizona became inconsequential to Camp Bowie, since it now lay only fifteen miles off the main line. "The completion of so many miles of the Southern Pacific Railroad has already had a marked effect on the supply of the troops," wrote an elated General Irvin McDowell, "and its near completion to New Mexico will still further reduce our expenses and add to the efficiency of the service."[56]

Graders and track layers pushed on, passing through the San Simon Valley until end-of-track reached New Mexico near the close of 1880. The plumes of smoke emitted by this latest symbol of progress were clearly visible to the soldiers stationed high up in Apache Pass. The nation had its second transcontinental railroad by March the following year when the Southern Pacific linked with the Atchison, Topeka, and Santa Fe at Deming. Buckboard mail runs, the less glamorous descendants of John Butterfield's famed "Jackass Mail" across the formerly deadly overland route, suddenly ceased, to be replaced by a network of short lines connecting the railroad with more remote points. Daily coaches plied the road between Camp Bowie and the station, and by 1882 mail coaches made runs to Willcox three times weekly.[57] It was truly the dawn of a new age in Arizona.

The completion of the railroad across Arizona witnessed the rapid development of mining at Tombstone and elsewhere in the territory when heavy

Military stage that operated between the fort and Bowie Station, thirteen miles distant. (Arizona Historical Society/Tucson, AHS Photo Number 44727)

ore processing machinery could finally be transported within reasonable distances of the deposits. The railroad also gave rise to other new towns. Benson, for example, sprang up at the old crossing of the San Pedro and by June 1880 wagons were plying a new road connecting the depot there with Tombstone.[58] Willcox was established soon thereafter just west of Railroad Pass at the junction of the road connecting Camp Bowie with Camp Grant. Lying twenty-four miles east of Willcox, and directly north of Apache Pass, was Bowie Station, a hamlet later renamed "Bean City" by the Post Office Department because of the similarity of the original name to that of the fort. The place was initially nothing more than a whistle stop, but by 1881 it boasted a forty-by-hundred-foot depot and freight warehouse, a two-story hotel with dining room, a boarding house, and a few stores. The railroad also made plans to construct a roundhouse, machine shop, and a nine-room bunkhouse for employees.[59]

Southern Pacific construction crews, meanwhile, completed the line's eastern division across the Trans-Pecos frontier in Texas. When the rails were joined near the Pecos River in January 1883, the nation at last achieved the all-weather transcontinental railroad that had been envisioned for nearly three decades. Freight and passengers could travel uninterrupted from the gulf port of New Orleans all the way to the Pacific in a matter of days.

The so-called Apache problem seemed almost a thing of the past by 1880. After a brief time on the warpath, operating mainly in Mexico, Geronimo and Juh made peace with the Chihuahuans at Casas Grande. But the fragile agreement quickly succumbed to the treachery that repeatedly marked relations between the Apaches and the Mexicans. When Mexican troops from another presidio attacked the Chiricahuas, they fled back to the United States to hide in the Animas Mountains of southwestern New Mexico. From there they sent word to the army that they were ready to surrender. The two leaders and over a hundred of their followers returned once again to San Carlos. By the end of 1879, the commissioner of Indian Affairs was able to report that Juh and Geronimo were "fat and contented" on the reservation.[60]

Victorio did not submit so easily. He had hoped to find a home for his people either at Ojo Caliente or at the Tularosa Agency, but neither attempt succeeded. Operating independently from Juh and Geronimo, he spent most of 1879 and 1880 crisscrossing the border in a protracted series of raids and skirmishes with the Ninth and Tenth Cavalry regiments as well as with the Mexican Army. Presidents Rutherford B. Hayes and Porfirio Díaz agreed to cooperate in a joint campaign, once again permitting each other's forces to cross the border when in pursuit of hostile Indians. Colonel Eugene A. Carr, the new commander of the Department of Arizona, sent Sixth Cavalry troops from Fort Bowie into the field numerous times that year as part of the combined effort to corral Victorio. Although they were involved in a couple of small skirmishes, the troopers of the Sixth served primarily as a blocking force to contain the Apaches east of the New Mexico line and prevent them from entering Arizona. The Mexicans eventually claimed victory when they surprised the Apaches in their camp at Tres Castillos in October 1880. Victorio himself was among those killed in the fight.[61]

The arrival of the railroad and the general progress in southeastern Arizona at the turn of the decade corresponded with improvements to the buildings at Fort Bowie. Lumber for flooring the barracks and other buildings was obtained from Pinery Canyon, as well as from Camp Grant. When a rail connection became available at Willcox, the Quartermaster Department began contracting for lumber from California firms as far away as San Francisco. In addition to an extension on the adobe hospital, the troops constructed an adjutant's office and another officer's quarters along the east side of the parade ground. Two barracks formed the angle at the northeast corner of the parade, though by early in 1879 the roofs of both structures leaked so badly that soldiers resorted to living in tents pitched on the parade. Shingle roofs were added to both barracks later that year. In recent years, the old adobe barracks on the north side of the parade had been converted for use as a quartermaster warehouse, while the old combination quartermaster-commissary building adjacent at the northwest corner of the parade was dedicated solely for subsistence stores. The addition of reading rooms and

Camp Bowie as it appeared in 1874 when photographer D. P. Flanders visited the post. Three adobe officers' quarters are visible beyond the flagstaff. Additional officers quarters, along with the adjutant's office, bakery, and a barracks, stand along the east (left) side of the parade ground. The long buildings just below the flagstaff are the quartermaster storehouse (left) and commissary storehouse (right). Adobe walled corrals appear in the left foreground. (Arizona Historical Society/Tucson, AHS Photo Number 46895)

bathing facilities for the men, as well as a tailor shop for fitting uniforms, signified that Bowie was indeed not the isolated post it once had been.[62]

Of greater significance than the amenities afforded by the railroad was the strategic importance that accrued to the fort. Its unique geographical position made it the only installation in the region, other than Fort Lowell at Tucson, directly serviced by rail. That meant that troops and supplies could be rapidly dispatched deep in the heart of the Chiricahua domain. Accordingly, on April 5, 1879, Army Headquarters approved its redesignation as Fort Bowie, thus giving it the stature of a permanent installation.[63]

CHAPTER 9

To End This Annual Apache Stampede Right Now

"People who desire to visit any portion of Southern Arizona can take the train at Kansas City and be in Tombstone or Tucson inside of three days," announced territorial governor John C. Frémont in 1881. The completion of the transcontinental railroad through the territory indeed wrought many changes in Arizona. He went on to cite the "wonderful mines of Tombstone district," noting that "where the city of Tombstone now stands (with a population of 7,000) was a barren waste two years ago."[1] Heralding greater things to come, construction crews were even then laying a railroad up the San Pedro Valley to link Benson with Sonora, while another extended from Benson southwestward to the port at Guaymas. Economical transportation was the principal factor boosting Arizona's precious metals production from fifth in the nation in 1879 to first place only three years later. The number of beef cattle rapidly expanded to over 280,000 head as stock growers discovered the fine grazing lands and the absence of hard winters in the region. Throughout the entire southern part of the territory, stage lines connected the burgeoning number of mining camps with the railroad. By 1880, the territory boasted over forty thousand non-Indian inhabitants, a figure that increased by over ten thousand persons each year.[2]

The Apaches may have ceased being a problem for the citizens of Arizona, but the booming economic condition of the territory attracted a new menace in the form of lawless gangs, known as "cowboys." These desperados "have rifled the mails, robbed the express, and deprived the passengers of all their valuables; and not unfrequently [*sic*] have they committed murder in connection with these robberies—always where any resistance has been offered."

Another more subtle scheme indulged in by the "cowboys" was to take advantage of the many military posts and Indian reservations in the territory by contracting to supply beef to the government. Taking a lesson from the Apaches, they then rustled the stock from ranches in Mexico to supply unsuspecting customers north of the border. The similarities in depredations were so uncanny, in fact, one might easily conclude that only the race of the perpetrators had changed.[3] So extensive did the raids become that it was not long before the governor was making a familiar plea for military assistance, this time petitioning Congress, unsuccessfully as it turned out, to lift the restrictions on federal troops aiding civil law enforcement authorities.[4]

With Victorio dead, and Juh and Geronimo once again ensconced on the reservation at San Carlos, Colonel Eugene A. Carr happily declared an end to field operations in southern Arizona. The garrison at Fort Bowie, now comfortably distanced from the nearest reservation, enjoyed a welcome reprieve from the grueling pursuits and patrols of previous several years.

Nevertheless, by summer 1881 trouble again brewed at San Carlos when a small, fair-skinned medicine man named Noch-ay-del-klinne began preaching a doctrine born of desperation. The mystic, a man in his late thirties who had served as one of Crook's scouts a decade earlier, had once visited the national capital as a delegation member and later attended boarding school in Santa Fe. It was there that he began combining elements of Christianity with traditional Apache religion into a prophecy promising that the Indian dead could be resurrected and that the whites would be eradicated. Learning of Noch-ay-del-klinne's activities, agent J. C. Tiffany became alarmed that the medicine man would incite others to an uprising and requested Carr, in command of Fort Apache, to arrest him. Carr, however, did not perceive a serious threat and was loathe to use his troops to effect an arrest. Brevet Major General Orlando B. Willcox, Carr's superior in Prescott, likewise wished to avoid precipitating another Apache outbreak, but if it came, he wanted to ensure that any blame fell on the shoulders of the Indian Bureau. There was no love lost between the army and the bureaucrats of the Interior Department, and Willcox was keenly aware that the tenures of department commanders in Arizona rested largely on public perceptions.

Carr maintained his position that Noch-ay-del-klinne posed an internal problem that was properly handled by reservation police, but a flurry of telegrams between Tiffany and Willcox resulted in Carr's being ordered to proceed to San Carlos with regular troops to make the arrest. The colonel resigned himself to carrying out the task by assembling two troops of the

Sixth Cavalry, along with a detachment of White Mountain scouts. The command easily found Noch-ay-del-klinne at his rancheria on Cibicu Creek, thirty miles from Fort Apache. Faced with such overwhelming odds, the mystic had little choice but to submit. However, the presence of a strong force of soldiers within the reservation fanned inflammatory rumors that had been circulating the reservation, causing unrest even among the usually friendly White Mountain people. A large number of Indians followed the troops to their night's bivouac down the valley. Tensions increased as the cavalrymen began establishing camp. Suddenly and without warning, the warriors opened fire. Many of the formerly reliable scouts also turned their carbines on the soldiers. Captain Edmund C. Hentig and four enlisted men were cut down in the opening moments of the fight, as was Noch-ay-del-klinne. Carr and the others, surrounded and on the defensive for a few hours, managed to escape back to the post after dark. But the now-heated Apaches were not content to let the incident stop there; two days later they launched an almost unheard-of attack on Fort Apache itself. The garrison eventually drove off the assailants, but not before the troops suffered several additional casualties. Still worse, renegade elements of the Chiricahua and White Mountain tribes stampeded from San Carlos, once more striking terror throughout the territory as news spread that Apaches were on the loose heading south.[5]

The affair at Cibicu spurred the army to dispatch additional troops to the area in an effort to contain the renegades before matters got entirely out of hand. Willcox quickly moved his headquarters to Camp Thomas to be nearer the seat of events, at the same time summoning Captain William A. Rafferty with M Troop, Sixth Cavalry, and a scout company from Fort Bowie to join him there. Responding to Willcox's request for additional troops, Division of the Pacific commander Irvin McDowell ordered three troops of the First Cavalry and five companies of the Eighth Infantry to entrain for Arizona. Among the companies arriving from California was G Troop, First Cavalry, still commanded by the indefatigable Captain Reuben Bernard, who had been so diligent in his pursuit of Cochise a decade earlier. General Sherman himself mobilized Colonel Ranald Mackenzie's tough Fourth Cavalry, just completing an assignment to move the recently hostile Utes to a new reservation in Colorado, to take station in New Mexico and to cooperate with Willcox, regardless of department boundaries.[6]

But while railroads had reduced the time required to send reinforcements and supplies from distant posts, the wagon road conditions within Arizona negated much of that advantage. As one critical example, McDowell cited the main road leading to Fort Apache, isolated high in the mountains, which recent storms had washed out along steep canyon walls, making it impassable even for packmules. Therefore, it became necessary to dispatch both reinforcements and additional ammunition overland from posts in New Mexico.

Alarmed by increased military activity, the leaders of the disaffected Apaches—Juh, Geronimo, Nachez, and Chato—gathered seventy-four of their people and stole away from San Carlos bound for Mexico. Some of the other renegades already off the reservation, mainly White Mountain Apaches, were overawed by the military show of force and almost immediately surrendered. The more intransigent Chiricahua outlaws, however, continued toward Mexico. When they were reported to be along the line of the Southern Pacific, panicked railroad employees demanded to be relieved of their stations until the company could provide them with arms. The Apaches paused long enough to fight one rearguard action near Cedar Springs, then disappeared into Mexico to join the aging but still capable Nana in their old hideouts in the Sierra Madre.[7] The Mexican decision to prohibit United States troops from entering her territory remained in effect, therefore, the Apaches were relatively safe beyond the border, so long as they behaved themselves.

With the renegades beyond reach in Mexico, the situation quickly calmed down in southern Arizona. Several weeks passed and nothing more was seen of the Chiricahuas who had crossed the border. The White Mountain Apaches had all since returned to the reservation. By the middle of October, Mackenzie guardedly advised Willcox that, since there were no longer any hostile bands in Arizona, he was suspending active field operations. He authorized the borrowed reinforcements to return to their permanent stations, leaving only 1,186 men of the Sixth Cavalry and Twelfth Infantry to garrison all of Arizona Territory.[8]

Mackenzie may have been confident that the situation was under control, but early in the year rumors circulated that the renegades intended to cross into the United States for the purpose of forcing Loco's Warm Springs band to join them. Cavalry from Forts Bowie and Huachuca intensified patrols along the border for the next few months, in anticipation that Juh and Geronimo might return. A temporary cantonment, Camp Price, was established on the southern end of the Chiricahua Range as a more convenient base of operations.

Meantime, General Sherman's patience with the Apache situation was growing ever shorter. To underscore his resolve to settle it once and for all,

Loco, a principal chief of the Warm Springs Apaches, led a daring raid through southern Arizona in 1882. (Arizona Historical Society/Tucson, AHS Photo Number 895b)

Sherman, accompanied by Department Commander Willcox, made a personal tour of the territory during early spring to observe conditions first-hand. Sherman and his party arrived at Fort Bowie, where he conducted a brief inspection on March 31 before departing for Fort Grant on the following day.[9]

Sherman had stated in no uncertain terms that he wanted "this annual Apache stampede to end right now" and that he was prepared to send the entire U.S. Army to Arizona to accomplish that end if necessary.[10] Despite the general's determined stance, the renegade Apaches had other ideas. They needed reinforcements and there was only one place to recruit them. True to their stated intentions, a party led by Geronimo, Chato, and Naiche slipped past the border patrols during April and arrived at San Carlos a few days later. At sunrise on the morning of the 19th, they surrounded Loco's rancheria and with shouts of "Take them all!" and threats to shoot anyone who did not comply, the renegades quickly rounded up the entire band and herded them eastward along the hills bordering the Gila. When a detachment of reservation police, led by Albert D. Sterling, approached the deserted camp to investigate the disturbance, a rear guard left by Geronimo ambushed them, killing Sterling.[11]

Remarkably, Geronimo absconded with some 700 people, including 176 males considered to be of warrior age. Threatened with death if any attempted to turn back, Loco's band was compelled to go along. They soon reconciled themselves to the fact that they would be implicated in Sterling's murder, regardless of the circumstances.[12]

With Geronimo in the lead, Loco's band took a course generally east-southeast so as to skirt around Fort Thomas before crossing the Gila toward Stein's Peak. Willcox, immediately informed of the outbreak, once more requested reinforcements to come to the aid of his scattered forces. The first to arrive was a troop of the First Cavalry sent by rail from California, while a battalion of four troops of the Fourth Cavalry, under the command of Lieutenant Colonel George A. Forsyth, boarded a special train at Lepas, New Mexico, en route to Stein's Peak.[13] Backing his word to spare no effort, Sherman ordered the entire First Infantry to be transferred from Texas, and at the same time directed the Third Cavalry to move from the Department of the Platte to Arizona.

These movements nevertheless took time, and meanwhile the bronco Apaches were swiftly fleeing toward Mexico. However reluctant Loco's people may have been to leave the reservation initially, they lost no time in becoming willing accomplices in Geronimo's bloody rampage. The Apaches fell on unsuspecting ranchers and travelers, killing some thirty to fifty civilians along the way. An alarmed Governor F. A. Tritle complained that because the existing troops were so widely scattered the Indians were moving across the territory almost unimpeded. In an effort to assist, Tritle authorized the raising of a fifty-man company of civilian volunteers to take the field for the protection of the citizenry. Whether or not they were of any real value hardly mattered, their mere presence made good politics.[14]

Willcox telegraphed Captain William A. Rafferty, post commander at Fort Bowie, with news of the outbreak and the general course taken by the fugitives. Mounting all of the available men of M Troop and the Apache Scouts, Rafferty took the field to rendezvous with Captain Tullius C. Tupper's command, already marching toward the Stein's Peak range.

Forsyth and his battalion rode the cars as far as San Simon Station before disembarking in the early morning hours of April 22. Assuming the Indians would generally follow the Gila as far east as possible before diverging south toward the international border, Forsyth mounted his men and rode directly to Stein's Peak. From there, he scouted northward toward the river hoping to intercept the Apaches. Having seen the troops first and realizing there was little chance of evading them, the Apaches occupied a strong defensive position in Horseshoe Canyon, on the eastern flank of the Stein's Peak (or Peloncillo) range. The troops subsequently ran headlong into the Chiricahuas and engaged them in an indecisive skirmish lasting two and a half hours. Geronimo and Loco wanted to avoid a pitched fight, therefore, they used the high ground to their advantage by simply fading away among the ridges. Forsyth nonetheless had his nose bloodied with the loss of two soldiers and four scouts killed, and four men wounded. Unaware that he had just engaged the main party, he broke off the chase to march toward the Gila, where he still expected to encounter Loco's band.

The Apaches, meanwhile, circled through Doubtful Canyon and unexpectedly turned directly toward Fort Bowie. Slipping across the broad San Simon Valley at night, the band made camp in the foothills east of the Chiricahua Mountains between the post and the mining village of Galeyville. Although the Apaches maintained a close watch on the approaches from Fort Bowie, expecting all the while that troops would be sent out after them, nothing happened. In fact, the movements of the Apaches were so well veiled that Lieutenant W. S. Geary, left in charge of the garrison during Rafferty's absence, had no idea the Indians were in the vicinity. Nor could he have taken an offensive action had he known, since Rafferty had taken all the mounted troops, leaving Geary only an infantry company to occupy the post.[15]

Tupper and Rafferty, meanwhile, had joined forces to continue the search, though they were unaware of Forsyth's recent engagement. With Tupper in command by virtue of his seniority in grade, the battalion struck the trail of the hostiles and followed it southwesterly to the Chiricahua Range. By that time, however, Geronimo and Loco, the latter now fully committed to the venture because of his involvement in the Horseshoe Canyon fight, crossed the Animas Valley into New Mexico. From there, they would follow the familiar route along the Guadalupe Mountains into Mexico.

Tupper, now hot on the trail, closely pursued the Apaches into Chihuahua, catching up with them at a low mountain known as Sierra Media, about twenty-five miles south of Cloverdale, New Mexico, on the 27th. The Apaches, not expecting the Americans to cross the border, dropped their guard. The trap would have been complete had it not been for four Indians leaving camp just before·dawn and walking straight into the line of troops poised to charge the camp. Even though some of Tupper's men were still taking up positions on the far side of the camp, those already on the skirmish line were compelled to open fire or lose the advantage of surprise altogether. In the ensuing skirmish, the Apaches took shelter in the rocks and put up a determined resistance for several hours. The fight soon devolved into a stalemate because the troops lacked the strength to dislodge the Indians, yet the Apaches could not escape the cordon around their position. The standoff finally ended when Tupper, running low on ammunition, concluded to withdraw, leaving the renegades to their fate with the Mexicans.[16]

Had Tupper only known, Forsyth and his Fourth Cavalrymen were following the same trail, though not very vigorously by most accounts. When the two columns met and Tupper proposed combining forces to continue the pursuit, Forsyth demurred on the ground that, having only 450 men at his disposal, he needed still more to engage the Apaches with any hope of success. Tupper, barely able to conceal his frustration with Forsyth, later claimed that with only a hundred more men, he could have prevented the band from getting water and forced them to surrender at Sierra Media. A sarcastic Crook said of Forsyth's timidity, "A long column of troops makes a big show, but they don't catch Indians."[17]

The Americans may have failed to catch and defeat the Chiricahuas, but Tupper's determined pursuit served to push the Apaches into the clutches of a waiting Mexican force led by Lieutenant Colonel Lorenzo Garcia. Disorganized and off-guard as the result of their recent success against U.S. troops, the outlaw band was surprised by Garcia's infantrymen the very next day. In what was a disastrous fight for the Apaches; the Mexicans killed seventy-eight Indians and captured thirty-three. Most of the Apache losses were old men, women, and children. Most of the warriors escaped to the Sierra Madre— a factor that would prove telling in events to come.[18] Garcia subsequently contacted the American troops and ordered them to leave Mexican soil forthwith.

Another outbreak quelled, Rafferty and his men returned to Fort Bowie, where they had nothing more to occupy their time than to scout the area periodically for any signs that the Chiricahuas were attempting to reenter the country. Congressional concern over the Loco affair was manifested in the arrival of reinforcements throughout the Department of Arizona. The garrison at Fort Bowie nearly tripled in number when one troop of the Third Cavalry and one of the Sixth arrived during the summer. The additional mounted units enabled Captain Rafferty to extend his patrols all the way from the international border north to the Gila. The summer of 1882 also witnessed a renewal of cordial relations between Mexico and the United States, the effect of which was a mutual pledge to cooperate in defeating the Apaches. To the relief of army officers in southern Arizona and New Mexico, the two nations signed a formal accord on July 29 permitting the troops of either country to cross the border at will whenever they were in hot pursuit of Indians.[19]

If the army's successes in the field that spring were less than spectacular, the territorial volunteers compiled an even more dismal record. Reporting on the recent "campaign," a correspondent to the *Army and Navy Journal* wrote:

> The company of Rangers put in the field by the Pima County Board of Supervisors, and who left that hamlet with such a flourish of trumpets something less than two months ago, were mustered out of the service a few days since. Their expedition was a failure in every sense of the word. They report having killed about thirty-five squaws and children in Sonora, but that statement should be received with a liberal amount of salt. They returned to Tucson without their arms, they having encountered Gen. Reyes, the military commander of Sonora, who relieved them of their arms and virtually kicked their posteriors out of the State.[20]

The performance of the Tucson Volunteers did not mark the last use of militia forces in the Apache campaigns, but it did serve to point up their general ineffectiveness.

The outbreak of 1882 would have ended with the disappearance of the Chiricahuas into the vastness of the Sierra Madre had it not been for a later, yet significant, sideshow at the San Carlos Reservation in July. Disaffected elements among the reservation Indians banded together under the leadership of Natiotish, a White Mountain Apache, to murder Police Chief John L. Colvig, who had replaced Sterling, and three of his officers. Along with fifty-four followers, Natiotish left the reservation and raided into the Tonto Basin. Army Headquarters mobilized even more troops to crush this latest rebellion before it could build up steam. Fourteen companies converged on the area within a matter of hours. On July 17, six companies of the Third and Sixth Cavalries, supported by a force of Indian scouts, engaged the Apaches in an unusually conventional battle at Big Dry Wash (Chevelon's Fork). Attempting to draw the troops into an ambush, the Apaches took up defensive positions along the rim of a deep, narrow canyon. But seasoned guide Al Sieber detected the ploy and alerted Captain Adna R. Chaffee not to advance. Chaffee deployed some of his men along the opposite side of the canyon to engage the warriors, while other detachments crossed the canyon and fell on both flanks of the Apaches simultaneously. A score or more Apaches were killed in the attack, and nearly all the rest were wounded. The survivors hastened back to the reservation.

The Natiotish episode convinced Sherman that affairs in Arizona again required the strong hand and experience of George Crook. Wasting no time, Sherman expedited the orders even before Natiotish's outlaws were defeated, but unfinished business in the Department of the Platte delayed the new department commander's departure from Omaha until early September.

Upon his arrival in Arizona, Crook immediately noted the changes that had occurred in the territory since he had last seen it in 1875.

> We then had a frontier, and in Indian wars few suffered except the troops engaged. Now that has changed; we really have no frontier, and an immense amount of capital is invested, and cattle-raisers, prospectors, and farmers swarm where comparatively few years ago the foot of white men never trod . . . . People living in all parts of the United States are represented by numerous investments in the different industries, and all demand, with justice, that this Indian question shall be settled . . . .[21]

Crook went directly to San Carlos to try to determine for himself the causes of the frequent outbreaks. He, perhaps better than any other senior officer, appreciated the Apache character, especially the Apache desire for freedom and natural rejection of government controls. Meeting with the leaders on November 2, Crook was not surprised to find that they resented being huddled together near the agency. San Carlos was a dismal place situated on a hot, barren flat along the sandy bottomland of the usually dry Gila River, a misnomer in any language. The lack of ground suitable for farming, predictably, had made the Apaches totally dependent on the Indian Bureau. Many of their people were ill; many had already died from disease. To their credit, the frustrated Apaches expressed their desire to learn farming and to become self-sufficient if only the agency officials would permit them to choose their own places to live within the reservation.[22]

An underlying problem common to all Indians, Crook noted, was that their culture simply did not perceive the world in the white man's terms.

> They recognize at once the power which is sufficient to control and punish or protect them, and respect the individual holding this power,

but the abstract idea that this man merely represents the Government, and that his promises or actions or recommendations are liable to be disallowed by higher authority, they cannot understand.[23]

Crook further observed that, while he was not an apologist for the Apaches and admitted that "they are bad Indians, probably the very worst on the continent," they had been mistreated in many ways. Not the least of these was the sensational and often exaggerated newspaper accounts of their depredations, often followed by unwarranted attacks by civilians on their villages within the reservation. He recognized that the Indian side of the story was seldom, if ever, heard.

> Then when the outbreak does come public attention is turned to the Indians, their crimes and atrocities are alone condemned, while the persons whose injustice has driven them to this course escape scot-free and are the loudest in their denunciations.[24]

Nor was removal of the Apaches the answer in Crook's opinion, even though it was a popular idea among citizens throughout Arizona. Indeed, the Americans failed to recognize that they were in fact the intruders in Apacheria. Because they insisted on occupying Arizona, they demanded that the indigenous people be extracted. Their motives, not surprisingly, were as much to make a killing as to secure peace. Greedy whites were even then attempting to secure rich coal deposits in the southern part of the reservation; Mormons had appropriated Apache fields at Forestdale; and even their own agent was suspected of being involved in a scheme to acquire a silver mine discovered on Indian lands. Said Crook:

> The glibness with which people generally speak of moving them would indicate that all we have to do is to take them from their camps, as you would chickens from a roost, without reflecting that to attempt their removal would bring on the bloodiest Indian war this country has ever experienced. Besides this, where shall they be located? No other state or territory wants these Indians.[25]

The general was clearly still peeved over Howard's so-called treaty that had permitted the Chiricahuas to live in almost complete freedom along the international border and to raid the Mexicans with impunity, while being fed and cared for by the U.S. Government. The arrangement had been impractical from the outset, and Crook continued to blame Howard for much of the trouble that had transpired since Cochise's surrender. But he also recognized that the Chiricahuas could not be held accountable for past wrongs. "[T]o fight them now would be to endanger the life of every stockman and prospector within striking distance of their mountains, and would ruin many important interests in this Territory."[26] Crook concluded his council at San Carlos by promising several changes in reservation management. The Apaches would no longer have to submit to periodic counts; they would be allowed to live any place they chose within the reservation; they could travel about within the reservation without passes; and they would be on their own recognizance to police themselves. In return, they were expected to apply themselves to subsistence farming, keep the peace, and to stop making tizwin. Moreover, the San Carlos Agency and the subagency at Fort Apache were to be supervised by army officers backed by Crook's full confidence. Any whites attempting to exploit resources within the reservation were to be evicted.[27]

That accomplished, Crook thought the best chance for arriving at a peaceable resolution with the renegades was to communicate with them directly for the purpose of arranging a parley. Were he successful in doing so, another costly and potentially bloody campaign might be avoided. To avoid causing undue alarm, Crook organized a small party consisting of only two staff officers and a half-dozen reliable scouts, then rode to the border personally to await the outcome. Captain Emmet Crawford, meantime, stood by with three companies of scouts near Cloverdale in the event Crook needed support. To the general's disappointment, however, his emissaries failed to make contact with Juh or Geronimo, while heavy raiding continued in Chihuahua.[28]

Crook had no alternative but to prepare for the trouble that was sure to come. It was only a matter of time before the renegades began raiding north of the line. Relying on past successes, Crook organized packtrains to be headed by his trusted comrade, Thomas Moore, who had previously supervised his trains in Arizona and on both of his expeditions during the Great Sioux War. Scouts, who would act as interpreters and liaisons with the enlisted Indian scouts, included Al Sieber, Sam Bowman, and Archie McIntosh, a mixed-blood frontiersman who had worked with Crook in the Northwest as well as on the Apache campaign of 1872–73.

The army was still getting organized when Chato, a veteran warrior and one of the lesser leaders among the outlaw Chiricahuas, unexpectedly dashed into Arizona during March 1883 on a foray to collect a supply of ammunition for the main band. At the same time, Geronimo led another party into

General George Crook advocated using light, fast-moving columns supported by packtrains as the only effective means of countering the highly mobile Apaches. (Arizona Historical Society/Tucson, AHS Photo Number 51090)

Sonora to secure horses. Chato's raiders, numbering only twenty-six men, crossed the border southwest of Fort Huachuca on the 21st and immediately struck a charcoal camp at the edge of the adjacent mountains, killing four men. The marauders continued on a course almost due north, passing by the west side of the Whetstone Mountains, where they killed three more men at the Total Wreck Mine before crossing the San Pedro and the railroad near Benson. On the 23rd, Chato's warriors slew two men near Point of Mountain at the south end of the Galiuro Range, then fanned out in smaller groups to search for more sources of ammunition. The separate parties rode generally northeastward through the San Simon Valley north of Fort Bowie and across the Peloncillo Mountains to the Gila Valley, where they shot up the York Ranch, killing two men. Returning to the border via New Mexico, Chato happened upon Judge H. C. McComas, who was traveling with his wife and young son, Charlie, on the road from Silver City to Lordsburg. The Apaches murdered both parents, took the boy captive, and then made directly for their Sierra Madre sanctuary.[29]

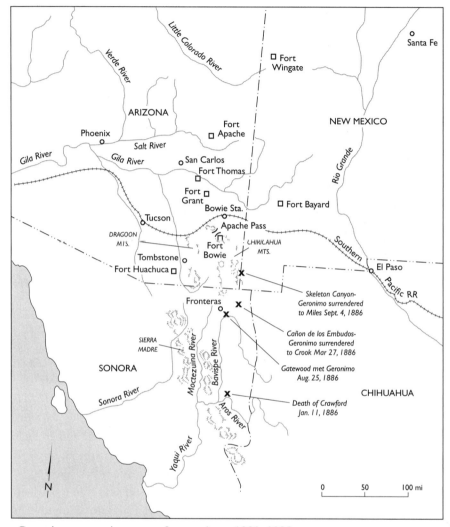

Geronimo campaign area of operations, 1881–1886

By the time troops from Fort Bowie and other stations could be alerted to the danger, the lightning-quick raid was over. Chato had proven too elusive for the cavalry to bother giving pursuit. On the other hand, Chato was disappointed that his men had scavenged precious little ammunition during their four-hundred-mile journey. Despite expectations that the renegades would return at any time, the episode caught the army off-guard, and scared the daylights out of people throughout the entire southern half of the territory.

It did, however, result in a significant benefit for Crook. One of Chato's raiders, Penaltishn, who came to be known to the whites as "Peaches" because of his unusual complexion, defected from the party and returned to San Carlos, where Lieutenant Britton Davis promptly arrested him. Peaches later made an invaluable contribution to Crook's efforts by offering to guide troops to the Chiricahua hideout in the Sierra Madre.[30]

Sherman, more frustrated than ever with the Apaches, ordered Crook to pursue and destroy the hostile bands, regardless of departmental or national boundaries. He likewise instructed the forces under Mackenzie's command in New Mexico to cooperate in every way possible. On April 2, Crook himself took the train to Willcox, where the troops and pack trains were then assembling. After briefly checking on preparations there, and hiring some civilian packers and a blacksmith at Fort Bowie, he made an important side trip to visit Mexican officials in Sonora and Chihuahua to ensure that they understood and concurred with his actions. Arriving back at Willcox, he proceeded on to Albuquerque to coordinate plans with Mackenzie.

By the end of the month, Crook had assembled his expedition at San Bernadino, a border ranch directly south of Fort Bowie, and was poised there to strike into Mexico. His column was composed of a company of the Sixth Cavalry and 193 Apache scouts led by Crook's trusted lieutenants, Emmet Crawford, Charles B. Gatewood, and J. O. Mackay. Bringing up the rear of the column was a packtrain of some 350 braying mules. Crook also took the precaution of picketing additional regular cavalry units at various points along the border to block the renegades should they attempt to cross into the United States. The Fourth Cavalry stood watch over southern New Mexico, while companies of the Third and Sixth Cavalries were posted across Arizona at Silver Creek, old Camp Rucker, and Calabasas. Rafferty's M Troop of the Sixth from Fort Bowie, in conjunction with a troop operating from Fort Huachuca, was to maintain patrols between those camps. The doughboys of Colonel "Pecos Bill" Shafter's First Infantry garrisoned the permanent posts and guarded strategic water holes to deny the renegades their use.

In only two weeks, Peaches put Crook on the trail left by Chato as he returned from his raid the previous month. The column followed it for several days until the signs became unmistakable. At that juncture, nearly two hundred miles south of the border, Crook corralled the packtrain under the guard of the regulars, and sent the seven companies of scouts forward on foot with three days' rations and a hundred rounds of ammunition for each man. Crawford found and surprised the rancheria halfway up a mountainside along the Bavispe River on the morning of May 15, 1883. In a fight lasting several hours, the scouts captured the village, killing nine Indians and taking five prisoners. The remainder evaporated into the craggy Sierra Madre.[31]

One of the captives, an adolescent girl, informed Crook that many of the Chiricahuas were tired of war and, in her opinion, could be induced to surrender. Crook was faced with the choice of either prosecuting a campaign with little chance of running the Apaches to ground, or working to secure their surrender. Favoring the latter, Crook released the girl to carry a message to the renegades, and two days later an influential headman, Chihuahua, appeared at Crook's camp. He informed Crook that the survivors of the band were thoroughly demoralized by the army's use of their kinsmen against them, and that most would willingly surrender to the Americans. He also described a young white captive closely resembling Charlie McComas. Satisfied that Crook could be trusted, most of the Apaches came in to surrender during the next few days. Among them were the leaders of the outbreak—Geronimo, Chato, Nachez, Loco, and Bonito, who all expressed their desire to return to San Carlos. But Crook was unwilling to forgive and forget so easily. He deemed them "bad Indians," and bluntly told them that he had not gone to all the trouble of chasing them down just to give them a chance to go on another rampage. To the astonishment of the Apaches, Crook candidly declared that he would prefer to wipe them out, and that Mexican soldiers were on the way to help him do just that. He therefore urged the Apaches to fight their way out, in order to give the troops an excuse for killing them. Geronimo, de facto leader of the hostile faction of the Chiricahuas since Juh's accidental death, considered the gravity of Crook's words for several more days, weighing whether or not the general was bluffing. In any event, the troops lacked the rations to feed themselves in addition to four hundred captives for very long. Growing ever more nervous at the prospect of Mexican troops arriving on the scene, Geronimo finally assented to do whatever Crook wanted, so long as the Chiricahuas could gather the remainder of their scattered people before returning to the United States.[32]

The column marched back to Arizona early in June, however, word had already reached the territorial press that only Loco and 325 Apaches, mostly Warm Springs people, were actually in custody. The public was furious to learn that Crook had allowed Geronimo, Chato, and some of the worst of the other leaders to delay coming in until later, after they had recovered the rest of their people. Worse yet, Crook had not disarmed any of the renegades, on the grounds that they needed to defend themselves from both the Mexicans and the citizens of Arizona.

Cavalry from Fort Bowie remained in the field during summer 1883, watching and waiting for Geronimo to cross the border. Captain Rafferty led a detachment to San Bernadino on July 10, purportedly to take charge of Indian stragglers coming into the United States, but failing to find any, he returned to the post a few days later. The following month, troops patrolled down the west side of the Chiricahua Mountains for the same purpose, but again found no signs of the Apaches. The fact that the area was ominously quiet caused many people in Arizona to denounce Crook's arrangement with Geronimo as a complete failure. The general was partially vindicated, however, when Nachez and seventy-nine Indians surrendered to Rafferty on October 23. It was probably not coincidental that the son of Cochise elected to bring his people to Fort Bowie and be escorted from there to San Carlos.[33] Chato and Mangus, son of Mangas Coloradas, surrendered during the following February, and, true to his word, Geronimo showed up at the border in March with the last eighty Chiricahuas and a herd of stolen Mexican cattle. By the spring of 1884, the prospects of peace in Arizona again seemed bright.[34]

That season also saw the transfer of the remainder of the Fourth Cavalry to the territory. In June, the assignment of one of those companies to Fort Bowie, along with Major Eugene Beaumont, necessitated a change of command. By that time all of the Chiricahuas were back on the reservation, thus freeing most of the troops to make improvements at the post. The facilities had changed little during the past several years because the cavalry had seen considerable field service and the infantry, usually only one company, was occupied with the normal garrison duties. However, with four companies at his disposal, and little scouting to perform, the energetic Beaumont set the men to work adding several amenities to the post, attaching porches to several buildings, constructing privies behind the officers' quarters, and erecting picket fences around the hospital and officers' quarters. Of added convenience were the four-hundred-gallon water tanks built to supply water for each barracks. Several of the adobe buildings were plastered to improve their exterior appearance and prevent erosion.[35]

Back at San Carlos, adjustment to the constraints of reservation life did not come easily for the restless Chiricahuas. Certain individuals among the recalcitrant factions, notably Kaytennae, continued to instigate trouble. Two rules particularly irritated the Apaches. The restriction against making tizwin made no sense to the Indians when they saw whites, army personnel included,

Group of officers at Fort Bowie, 1886. Major Eugene B. Beaumont, Fourth Cavalry, is seated second from left. (Arizona Historical Society/Tucson, AHS Photo Number 25609)

freely consuming liquor. Given the living conditions on the reservation, a tizwin drunk was one of the few outlets available to the men. And whites were repulsed at the Apache practice of wife beating and cutting off the nose of an unfaithful spouse. Indian men, conversely, considered such customs to be none of the white man's business. They had not promised to deny their culture when they surrendered. As a demonstration of their defiance, a large number of rebellious men staged a tizwin drunk, then dared Lieutenant Britton Davis, the agent at Fort Apache, to do anything about it. Davis, realizing he was at a disadvantage, referred the matter to Crook in hopes the Indians would meantime reconsider their actions. Unknown to Davis, however, his telegram was shelved at San Carlos when a hung-over Al Sieber, Crook's chief of scouts, advised Captain Francis E. Pierce that the incident was not serious and would quickly blow over.

When Crook failed to respond, as Davis had promised, Geronimo and young Mangus convinced Naiche, Chihuahua, and Nana that the army was scheming to punish them. Geronimo thereupon bolted from the reservation and headed for the Sierra Madre with forty-two warriors and ninety-two women and children. Chihuahua, meantime, split from the main group to lead a three-week foray through southern New Mexico before joining the others south of the border.[36] By this time Chato, having had enough of Crook's style of campaigning, was among Lieutenant Britton Davis's most trusted scouts. Loco and Bonito likewise refused to participate in the breakout.

Crook instantly deployed a net of troops over southeastern Arizona. While Lieutenants Gatewood and Davis took up the trail of the renegades with two troops of cavalry and a force of scouts from Fort Apache, other patrols were launched from Grant, Thomas, and Huachuca. Major Beaumont personally led a reconnaissance of two troops northeast from Fort Bowie, acting on intelligence that the Apaches were using the usual route from the Gila to Mexico via the Peloncillo and Guadalupe Mountains. After scouring the region to Stein's Pass and beyond all the way to the Gila Valley, Beaumont returned via Doubtful Canyon to double-check that favorite Apache pathway. Beaumont's efforts, like the others, were to no avail. The Apaches had once again demonstrated their adeptness at evading the troops by slipping through Crook's screen without a trace. While efforts focused on Chihuahua's band, Crook and his officers were unaware that Geronimo had already escaped into Mexico.[37]

Crook implemented a now familiar strategy by organizing two columns, composed mainly of Apache scouts, to pursue the renegades into the Sierra Madre. He quickly arranged for Captain Crawford to be recalled from Texas, where the Third Cavalry had been transferred a year previous, directing him to scout westward through New Mexico to rendezvous with Lieutenant Davis's force of scouts and packers at San Bernadino. A few days after Beaumont's return, Lieutenant Davis arrived at Apache Pass, where he laid over a day to rest and refit before continuing on toward the border. Later that same day, word reached Beaumont that the hostiles had been observed passing a nearby ranch. A detachment sent to investigate verified the truth of the report, whereupon a courier was dispatched to Davis with the information.[38]

Davis's movement through Fort Bowie signaled the beginning of one of the busiest periods in the history of the post. General Crook, always one to be at the seat of action, rode to Apache Pass with his staff on June 11 to establish his field headquarters for the coming campaign. During the next couple of weeks, Tom Moore's packtrain, along with another from San Carlos, paused at the fort on their way to San Bernadino. Following closely on their heels were recently enlisted companies of Indian scouts, part of two hundred authorized by Sherman, commanded by Lieutenant Charles B. Gatewood. Gatewood and his seventy-nine-man battalion of auxiliaries first searched eastward into the ranges of western New Mexico, to ensure that no renegades

The post trader's store is clearly evident in the lower right corner of this image taken during winter 1885–1886. The small building at the left, with a tent in front, is the guardhouse. (Arizona Historical Society/Tucson, AHS Photo Number 24725A)

were hiding there, then marched to Fort Bowie to rendezvous with a troop of the Fourth Cavalry and an additional battalion of one hundred scouts that had just arrived from San Carlos. Captain Wirt Davis, Fourth Cavalry, assumed overall command of the column.[39]

To the southeast of Fort Bowie, Crawford, with a troop of the Sixth Cavalry and a party of a dozen Mescalero scouts, intercepted Britton Davis near Guadalupe Canyon. Davis had just discovered the still-smoking ruins of a Fourth Cavalry camp that had been ransacked by Chihuahua's warriors. A sergeant and another man lay dead near the burned wagons and tents. The raiders were long gone, however, having captured a large quantity of ammunition, food, and other stores.[40]

Crook directed his two strike columns into Mexico, while along the border he posted cavalry at the usual strategic points to intercept the fugitive bands should they attempt to reenter the United States. Several companies of the Sixth Cavalry and the Tenth Infantry watched the New Mexico portion of the international line, while troops of the Fourth Cavalry from Forts Bowie, Huachuca, and elsewhere manned a picket line at water holes across Arizona, just north of the border. Each detachment was supplemented with five Indian scouts to conduct local reconnaissance. Taking every precaution at his disposal, Crook placed the Tenth Cavalry, only recently transferred from Texas, along

Typical cavalry troop in the field during the Geronimo campaign. Because of the rough terrain, supplies were transported by packmule. (Arizona Historical Society/Tucson, AHS Photo Number 51105)

a second line farther north to snare any of Geronimo's men who might infiltrate the first. Yet a third line of troops, mainly First Infantrymen, guarded the line of Southern Pacific Railroad.[41]

Crawford was first to strike the Apaches on June 23 when some of the scouts attacked a camp on the Bavispe River, deep in Mexico. The warriors were able to escape, but the scouts rounded up fifteen women and children. Crawford sent them under escort to San Bernadino, where they were met by a detachment from Fort Bowie that conducted them back to the post for safekeeping.[42] In late July, Wirt Davis and his column surprised another village, purportedly Geronimo's, near Nacori and in a brief engagement killed a woman and a youth. Just a few days later, on August 7, Davis's scouts again struck the same band, killing several Indians, one of them alleged to be a son of Geronimo. The scouts captured seven more Apache noncombatants, but the rest escaped and scattered into the mountains.

Even Crook became discouraged with the lack of substantive results, commenting that: "The Indians act differently than ever before, are split up in small bands and are constantly on the watch. Their trails are so scattered that it is almost impossible to follow them . . . . our scouts are practically compelled to cover the entire region, and cannot even venture to follow trails where they pass over prominent points for fear of their pursuit being discovered . . . ."[43]

Crawford picked up the trail of the Chiricahuas who had fled from Davis. Crawford did not attempt to follow it with the whole column because he had learned that the scouts usually were more successful when permitted to go out alone. He therefore placed Lieutenant Britton Davis in command of forty picked men, along with Al Sieber, Mickey Free, and Chato. Instructed by Crawford to follow Geronimo wherever he might go, Davis and his detachment undertook what became an epic journey down the east slope of the Sierra Madre, thence northward across Chihuahua. Since the Apaches were at liberty to steal fresh horses along the way, they soon outdistanced their pursuers and crossed into New Mexico. Davis and his men wound up, eventually, at El Paso in a destitute condition and from there returned to Arizona via rail. When young Lieutenant Davis, exhausted and frustrated, finally arrived back at Fort Bowie several weeks later, he immediately submitted his resignation from the army.[44]

Meanwhile, Geronimo appeared briefly in the vicinity of Guadalupe Canyon before vanishing back into Mexico. By October, Crook decided to call off the campaign and order the troops to return to Fort Bowie until he could revise his plans. In an effort to forestall the public censure that was sure to come, General Philip H. Sheridan, who had succeeded Sherman as commander of the army in November 1883, staunchly defended Crook's strategy.

The Apaches, conversely, never seemed to tire. In November 1885, just as the last of the scouts and the troops were coming in from the field, a warrior named Ulzana (also known as Josanie) led a party of only ten men on a swift raid into Arizona and across southern New Mexico. Covering twelve hundred miles in only a few days, and killing thirty-eight whites along the way, Ulzana lost but one man. The raid stunned both the army and the citizens. It could hardly have come at a worse time for Crook and Sheridan. The press, at the urging of business interests and a skeptical public, showed little understanding of the army's position and the conditions with which it had to contend. An embarrassed Sheridan felt compelled to meet with Crook personally in Arizona to sort things out. Sheridan had been convinced for some time that the only way to prevent further Apache outbreaks was to drive the tribe from the territory permanently. But Secretary of War William C. Endicott remained undecided, requesting Sheridan to report back to him with his observations.[45] The short, ruddy-complexioned general, who had overseen the enormous Division of the Missouri until Sherman's retirement two years earlier, arrived at Fort Bowie on November 29. With him were his aide and brother, Major Michael V. Sheridan, Inspector General Absalom Baird, and Colonel Luther P. Bradley, who commanded both the Thirteenth Infantry and the District of New Mexico. Sheridan spent the rest of that day and the evening at the post discussing the Indian situation with Crook. Aware that his superior did not favor the use of Indian scouts on the grounds that they were unreliable, Crook made certain that Crawford was on hand to speak in favor of Indian auxiliaries. Indeed, Sheridan was impressed with Crawford's testimony, and as an experienced officer, was reluctant to undermine the authority of his subordinates in the field. Also fortuitous was the arrival of a new contingent of one hundred White Mountain and Chiricahua scouts just three days prior to Sheridan's visit. The general was thus able to see for himself the appearance and discipline of the scouts. Although Sheridan remained concerned that Congress might reduce the army appropriation if it felt that mercenaries could handle the Indian situation better than regular troops, he conceded that Crook's methods were probably the best under the circumstances. He could continue to use the scouts for the present. It was also agreed that Bradley's district would be brought temporarily under the Department of Arizona to improve coordination of field operations. Nevertheless, he remained adamant in his conviction that the Apaches should be exiled to some place distant from their homeland. Sheridan and his party departed the next day to catch the train.

Having won the most crucial point, Crook immediately ordered Crawford to undertake another expedition into Mexico. The column assembled at Fort Bowie near year's end. Assisted by Lieutenants Marion P. Maus and Samson L. Faison of the First Infantry and William E. Shipp, Tenth Cavalry, Crawford led his new battalion out of Apache Pass on December 11. Couriers riding the ever-lengthening trail between Crawford's force and the post kept Crook apprised of events. With little to occupy his time except routine department communications, Crook the huntsman contented himself by hiking the mountainsides around Fort Bowie in search of foxes and deer.

Crawford succeeded in intercepting Ulzana's trail toward the outlaw sanctuary, but informed his commander that he saw no purpose in continuing after a fruitless pursuit of two weeks. Crook, meantime, spent the holidays patiently awaiting more positive news, while he ignored Sheridan's repeated requests to be updated on the situation. The close-lipped Crook would respond only when there was something worth reporting, until then anything he could devise to keep Sheridan off his back would only wind up as fodder for the newspapers.

The news was mixed when Lieutenant Maus showed up at Fort Bowie in mid-January to report that on the ninth the column had successfully attacked the main village deep in Sonora some two hundred miles south of the border. The unsuspecting Chiricahuas lost all of their supplies in the raid, after which Geronimo indicated that he wanted to discuss peace terms the next day. However, the negotiations were cut short when a force of Mexican irregulars arrived on the scene and began firing on Crawford's scouts. Crawford managed to get his own men to cease firing after about fifteen minutes, but when he and an interpreter approached the Mexican lines, a volley felled Crawford in plain view of both sides. Geronimo, no doubt, watched with great satisfaction as the Mexicans and Americans shot at each other, yet he did not leave. Deep in Mexican territory and outnumbered, Lieutenant Maus wisely withdrew, but not until the scouts had retaliated by killing or wounding most of the Mexican officers. He then reestablished contact with the broncos and was encouraged to learn that Geronimo was tired of fighting and wished to speak directly with Crook at some place near the international border. As assurance of their good faith, the Apaches turned over Nana and a number of others to Maus as hostages.[46]

As Maus turned on his back trail, Geronimo promised to meet Crook at Canyon de Los Embudos, about twelve miles below the border, after he had had time to round up his scattered people and collect caches of booty. Crook left Fort Bowie on March 23, after receiving word from Maus that Geronimo was nearing the border. In a meeting two days later, Crook tersely informed Geronimo that he no longer trusted him. Reminding Geronimo of his past lies and transgressions since the breakout, Crook warned, "If you stay out, I'll keep after you and kill the last one if it takes fifty years."[47] Geronimo may have realized that Crook was overreaching, yet the general's forthright manner and audacity impressed him. Further discussions led Crook to modify his stance somewhat by offering to accept Geronimo's surrender on the condition that the Chiricahuas would be sent to the East for two years. After that, they could return with their families to San Carlos. If they chose to continue fighting, on the other hand, Crook would be only too happy to accommodate them. On March 27 a conciliatory Geronimo said he and the others had discussed Crook's terms and they wanted no further trouble. They would surrender and accompany Crook to Arizona.

Photographer A. F. Randall's view captured Fort Bowie during the summer of 1886 at the height of the Geronimo campaign. Additional troops were being sheltered in tents on the parade ground. (Arizona Historical Society/Tucson, AHS Photo Number 25614)

While the Chiricahuas made ready to move, Crook rode ahead to Fort Bowie to dispatch the welcome news to Sheridan. Leaving behind Maus and the scouts to escort the prisoners, Crook and his staff returned to the post just in time to pay honors to the remains of Captain Crawford, recently escorted there from Mexico. On April 2, Crook, Post Commander Beaumont, and the other officers of the garrison solemnly assembled to witness the departure of Crawford's body. Two companies of the First Infantry accompanied the casket halfway to Bowie Station. Along the way, they were relieved by two companies of the Eighth Infantry that escorted the body to the railroad. Assembled at the station was an honor guard, appropriately composed of Crawford's Apache scouts, along with the officers and soldiers on duty at the supply camp. Bourke boarded the train to personally accompany the remains to Kearny, Nebraska, where Crawford's brother resided.[48]

The glow of Crook's success faded almost immediately when an unscrupulous trader near San Bernadino sold whiskey to the Chiricahuas just as they approached the border. Many of the Apaches, including Geronimo, became staggering drunk during the night. Tribollet, the trader, and his cohorts filled the Apaches with both liquor and lies about Crook's real intentions.[49] Fearful he had made a bad bargain, Geronimo and three dozen others, only twenty of them men, stole out of camp that night in a drizzling rain. Eighty Chiricahuas, among them Chihuahua, remained in the custody of the scouts, while Maus chased Geronimo for several days to no avail.

Crook had gambled and lost, for he had been well aware before entering Mexico that Sheridan and President Grover Cleveland insisted on an unconditional surrender. Moreover, Crook's decision to allow his "prisoners" to remain armed and under no restraint while being escorted to Arizona only made matters worse. Cleveland demanded that the Chiricahuas give up unconditionally, or be annihilated. Although Crook knew that he might be able to once again persuade the bronco Apaches to give up, he also knew that Sheridan was obligated to comply with the president's orders. At best, Crook's future in Arizona had been tenuous since the conference with his superior at Fort Bowie the previous fall, but only Sheridan's personal loyalty had saved him. Now his management of the campaign, if not his personal sense of integrity, was in direct conflict with higher command, including the White House. Crook therefore facilitated Sheridan's decision by requesting to be relieved from command of the department, an offer Sheridan promptly accepted.[50]

Sheridan, meantime, had already selected Crook's replacement. Colonel Nelson A. Miles, a Civil War veteran who had commanded the Fifth Infantry with considerable skill and energy for more than a decade during the plains wars, had been promoted to brigadier general in 1880. Not the least of his accomplishments was compelling the surrender of the famed Nez Perce, Chief Joseph, at the end of his epic bid for freedom in 1877. The Department of the Missouri may have been a prestigious command in army circles, but it was also a quiet one by that time. Miles's ability as an Indian fighter was exceeded only by his ambition. Determined to occupy the army's top command, Miles saw the Apache campaign as perhaps his last opportunity to distinguish himself. He lost no time in reporting to Fort Bowie, arriving there on April 10. He and Crook met to discuss the situation and formally transfer command two days later.[51]

The seventy-seven Chiricahuas who had come in with Maus, including Chihuahua, Nana and Ulzana, were retained at the post for a few days before being placed aboard the train at Bowie Station on April 7. Escorted by a detachment of the Fourth Cavalry, they were quickly whisked away to Florida, where they would be far removed from Geronimo's influence, and from aiding him should they be so inclined.

General Nelson A. Miles commanded the Department of Arizona after Crook was relieved in 1885. He somewhat warily accepted Geronimo's surrender at Skeleton Canyon in early September 1886. (Arizona Historical Society/ Tucson, AHS Photo Number 22235)

Miles himself had used Indian auxiliaries on the northern plains to good advantage, yet bending every effort to placate Sheridan, he adopted a more conventional strategy in Arizona. With the memory of the scout defection at Cibicu still fresh in mind, Miles chose to employ an overwhelming force of regulars to defeat conclusively the now tiny band of refractory Apaches under Geronimo and Nachez. Not unlike his predecessor, Miles assigned infantrymen to guard key water holes and mountain passes, as well as scout the ranges, since the rugged terrain often forced the cavalry to dismount anyway. Cavalry would instead be employed as "light scouting parties" to patrol the vast region along the Mexican border and the intervening plains between the mountain ranges. Miles also adopted new methods for locating and striking the renegades. He began by dividing the southern part of the territory into "districts of observation" interconnected by heliograph stations situated atop prominent mountain peaks. The network of stations, supplemented by the existing military telegraph system, would provide instantaneous signals as to the whereabouts of the hostiles whenever they attempted to

move through the country anywhere between central Arizona and the Rio
Grande. The heliograph stations, each manned by a half-dozen soldiers, along
with trained Signal Corpsmen, would preclude the necessity of patrolling
much of the region, thereby making more efficient use of the available
cavalry.[52] Miles determined to replace the scouts with small strike forces
consisting of officers and soldiers specially selected and physically qualified
for such duty. He further authorized troop commanders to dismount half
their men, selecting only the lightest and best riders to pursue the Indians
until they were caught or the detachments had exhausted themselves.
"Commanding officers," Miles ordered, "are expected to continue a pursuit
until capture, or until they are assured a fresh command is on the trail."
Leaving nothing to chance, he directed his troops to make certain that "every
cartridge will be rigidly accounted for, and when they are used in the field
the empty shells will be effectually destroyed" to prevent re-use by the hostiles.[53]

Within a month after taking command of the Department of Arizona,
Miles broached two questions that had been uppermost in the minds of
Arizona citizens. Why had the reservation Apaches, or the "captive" renegades
for that matter, never been disarmed? Crook, whom Miles accused of being
too lenient, had claimed that disarming an Apache was a breach of trust
implying his captor feared him. That argument had never sold well with
whites because, in fact, they *were* afraid of armed Apaches, and for good reason.
Miles, in concert with the sentiment of the region, also favored the permanent
removal of all Apaches from Arizona and their relocation in Indian Territory. Miles was keenly aware that President Cleveland, Secretary of the Interior
Lucius Q. C. Lamar, and Sheridan all opposed such action. Nevertheless,
the politically well-connected Miles pulled wires to arrange for a delegation
of those Warm Springs and Chiricahua leaders to visit Washington, D.C.,
for the purpose of making a direct plea to abandon San Carlos. In so doing,
Miles hoped that the Apaches would be appropriately overwhelmed with
American technology and progress, thus increasing their submissiveness to
the wishes of the government. In a trip that was rife with political intrigue
between the Miles and Crook loyalists, the Apaches eventually gained an
audience with the president, but no promises were forthcoming regarding
their future. In fact, no one in the government knew exactly what the
Apaches had been told and the issue became even more confused when the
delegation became separated, some of them going to Carlisle Barracks, Pennsylvania, and the rest to Fort Leavenworth, Kansas. Moreover, the factions represented by those leaders on the tour had been at peace since at least 1883,

therefore, they could not speak for some of the other bands at San Carlos, much less their renegade relatives in Mexico.

Back in Arizona, Miles named Captain Henry W. Lawton, Fourth Cavalry, to head a special detachment to track down Geronimo. Miles selected Lawton because of his brilliant record during the war. His splendid physique, character, and high attainments as an officer and commander peculiarly fitted him for one of the most difficult undertakings to which an officer could be assigned. He also possessed another vital element for success—the personal conviction that the Indians could be outmaneuvered, worn down, and subjugated.[54]

However, Geronimo struck terror in southern Arizona before Miles was ready. Crossing the border at the Santa Cruz on April 27, Geronimo and his men made what had become a classic style of raid down the valley. They first attacked the Peck Ranch, where they killed a mother and child, carried off another child, and held the father in custody for several hours before, in a most atypical act, turning him loose unharmed. The raid, which occurred farther west than the Apaches had operated in several years, caught the army entirely off-guard. Cavalry units were mobilized from all the posts in the region, including Fort Bowie, but Geronimo was moving too swiftly to be intercepted. A troop of the Tenth Cavalry, nevertheless, tracked the party for some two hundred miles before finally catching up with them at the Pinito Mountains, thirty miles into Sonora. Geronimo turned to engage briefly the pursuing black regulars, wounding one trooper, then rapidly outdistanced the troops as he rode toward the Sierra Madre.

Lawton, like so many others before, soon discovered that Indian campaigning in the Southwest was unlike service elsewhere. Setting out from Fort Huachuca on May 10 with thirty-five men of the Fourth Cavalry, twenty Eighth Infantry doughboys, a score of Indian guides, and hundred mules, he wore out his horses in only five days. Still, Lawton justified Miles's faith in him by continuing on the trail for nearly fourteen hundred miles. He gave up the dogged chase in June, no closer to catching Geronimo than when he had started.

After conferring with Miles at Calabasas early in July, Lawton reorganized and started once more for Sonora. This time he left his cavalry, as well as most of the officers, at a base camp before continuing on foot with a small detachment of handpicked men. Eventually, the fourteen survivors of Lawton's force, their shoes in shreds from hiking over sharp rocks, admitted defeat and limped back over the border. Dissention among the citizens began to grow once again, causing the politically astute Miles to realize that he could easily experience Crook's fate if he failed to produce positive results, and soon.

Lieutenant Charles B. Gatewood, Third Cavalry, was one of General Crook's most effective and trusted officers. (Arizona Historical Society/ Tucson, AHS Photo Number 19554)

During the time Lawton was in Mexico, Miles relocated his headquarters at Willcox to be more central to future operations. Consequently, Fort Bowie continued to be the focus of campaign activity throughout the summer of 1886. Lawton's dismal experience convinced Miles that Crook had not been so wrong after all in his use of Indian scouts, yet he was reluctant to concede that Apaches were superior to regulars at catching other Apaches. Although he continued to use some Apaches, he supplemented them with Pima and Yuma scouts. Both troops and scout detachments moved through the post during July, yet they failed to produce the success Miles craved. Only in August, when Geronimo was discovered near Fronteras did Miles feel that the end might be in sight. Word reached him at Fort Bowie that the Apaches were negotiating with the Mexicans, a turn of events that did not bode well for American interests. At this critical juncture, he unexpectedly wired Lieutenant Gatewood at Fort Apache for assistance. Gatewood's close association with the Apache scouts, and with Crook himself, made him an improbable candidate for a starring role in Miles's campaign, yet the new commander recognized that many of his predecessor's methods had been effective. Gatewood, as everyone knew, was the single best qualified officer in the army to carry out the delicate mission. George Wratten, said to know the Apache language and its dialects better than any other white man because of his close association with the Indians at San Carlos, later recorded that Geronimo "always had great faith in Lieutenant Gatewood, for he had never deceived him. He was the only man who could safely have gotten within gunshot of the old savage, and General Miles knew that when he sent him out."[55]

Gatewood chose two trusted scouts, Martine and Kayitah, both of whom had formerly been closely associated with the renegades and might prove to be valuable liaisons. The lanky Gatewood, whose prominent nose earned him the name "Beak" among the scouts, traveled to Fort Bowie to organize personally his little expedition. He selected Wratten, whom the Apaches also trusted implicitly, to serve as his interpreter. Tex Whaley went along as courier, and Frank Huston managed the small packtrain. Even though Miles preferred that Gatewood take an escort of twenty-five cavalrymen, the post commander claimed he had no men to spare. It was probably just as well, for Gatewood knew from experience that such a force could never get within reach of Geronimo. Riding hard and crossing the border south of Cloverdale, Gatewood and his party found Lawton's command on the Aros River, about 250 miles into Mexico, on August 3. Lawton related to Gatewood that, beyond finding one camp three weeks earlier, from which the occupants had escaped without a fight, he had seen no Apaches during his scout of several hundred miles. Gatewood's information that at least some of the Apaches were far to the northeast in the vicinity of Fronteras came as good news.

Marching through intermittent downpours, the combined command learned that two Apache women had contacted authorities at Fronteras, indicating that Geronimo wanted to talk peace. Geronimo, however, later stated that he was simply buying time to rest and find supplies, and had no intention of surrendering to the Mexicans.

Since Lawton's men were afoot, it was decided that Gatewood's mounted command would forge ahead for the last eighty miles in an effort to intercede. Arriving at Fronteras, Gatewood discovered that Mexican troops were planning to employ the old ruse of enticing the Apaches into town, getting them roaring drunk, then murdering them. Gatewood immediately left town on the pretense that he was rejoining Lawton, but circled around to pick up the trail left by the Indian women. Following it, and bearing a white flag for whatever protection it might provide, Gatewood approached near enough to Geronimo's camp in the Torres Mountains to send out Martine and Kayitah. Martine returned the next day to announce that they had spent the night in camp with the broncos and that Geronimo was willing to talk. The two scouts, among only a few that still enjoyed Geronimo's confidence, convinced him

Naiche and Geronimo at Fort Bowie following their surrender in September 1886. (Arizona Historical Society/Tucson, AHS Photo Number 19833)

that Gatewood was trustworthy, but he had detained Kayitah as insurance against a surprise attack by the troops. On August 24, "Beak" met with Geronimo on the Bavispe River, where he informed the Apache that Miles would accept his surrender unconditionally and that afterward he and the others in his band would be sent to Florida. The president would decide their ultimate fate. Gatewood emphasized that the only alternative was to fight it out, in which case U.S. troops would give them no rest. The wily Apache used a familiar response—he would surrender, but only so long as he could return to the reservation. Gatewood then played his trump card by informing Geronimo that such a condition was no longer possible. Even as they spoke, Gatewood told him, all of the Chiricahua and Warm Springs people at San Carlos were being sent off to Florida. There would no longer be any sanctuary north of the border, nor would there be any possibility of another outbreak if he should become disgruntled. Their families were gone, and now they were alone. That news visibly stunned Geronimo, and his mood changed almost immediately. Attempting to salvage a shred of dignity, the chief consented to surrender, but only to Miles, personally. Only then would he and his followers lay down their arms.

Gatewood sent word back to Miles at Willcox that a conference had been arranged at Skeleton Canyon, a short distance north of the border. But Miles himself came near scuttling the plan when he refused to meet with Geronimo, preferring instead that his loyal subordinate Lawton accept the surrender. As the skittish band of renegades, still armed and dangerous, approached the U.S. border, Miles fully expected them to bolt at any time. Were that to happen, he would suddenly find himself in the same predicament that had been Crook's downfall. Although Miles would willingly accept any and all laurels for defeating Geronimo, he was not about to place himself in a situation that might compromise his goal of commanding the army. Should there be any failure, Miles schemed to place the blame squarely on Gatewood, or Lawton for that matter. However, both officers continued to urge Miles to participate in the conference on the grounds that Geronimo would certainly flee back to Mexico if his one request was spurned. Geronimo even sent his brother to Fort Bowie as a personal guarantor of his sincerity. Miles, still wary, advanced only as far as the post to be nearer events as they unfolded, while placing himself beyond reproach if the surrender failed to materialize. Only when the renegades were north of the border, and the reservation Apaches were safely riding the rails toward Florida, did Miles finally consent to go to Skeleton Canyon. A troop of the Fourth Cavalry from Fort Bowie, led by Major Beaumont himself, served as his escort. The end came swiftly during a final council on September 4, 1886, in which Miles flatly repeated his terms, and Geronimo assented. It was done.[56]

Miles, accompanied by Geronimo, Naiche, three warriors, and a woman, returned to Fort Bowie the next day, arriving there shortly after dark. The general immediately ordered Major Beaumont to form a cordon of troops around the military reservation to prevent trigger-happy civilians from attacking the captives. Lawton arrived two days later with the other twenty-three renegades. Their brief stay at the post was uneventful, though Geronimo, freshly outfitted in white man's clothing and new boots, took the opportunity to strike a defiant pose along the parade ground for a local photographer, C. S. Fly. To avoid the possibility of any further trouble, or worse yet, another stampede, Miles had the Apaches disarmed, dismounted, and escorted out

Scene on Fort Bowie parade ground shortly after the arrival of the recently surrendered Chiricahuas, September 1886. (Arizona Historical Society/Tucson, AHS Photo Number 19520)

of the post on September 8 to catch a special train awaiting them at Bowie Station. The puzzled Apaches failed to comprehend the wry smiles among the soldiers as the Fourth Cavalry band played their old foes out of the post to the strains of "Auld Lang Syne." Miles and his staff departed the same day, punctuating an abrupt end to three hundred years of bloody warfare with the Apaches in Arizona.[57]

CHAPTER 10

It Seems like a Prison: Garrison Life

The second Fort Bowie that came into being during 1869–70 was typical of most frontier posts. It had no stockade; there were no loop-holed block-houses.[1] Never intended as a defensive work, the "fort" merely provided troops a base of operations from which they could patrol a vast geographical area while controlling the only reliable source of water in Apache Pass. The principal buildings were clustered immediately around the perimeter of an open parade ground, not unlike the central plaza of any Spanish-Mexican village in the American Southwest. The only feature distinguishing this isolated station as an army outpost was a huge national flag floating atop a white-washed flagstaff in the center of the parade ground, "proclaiming to all the presence of the soldier."[2]

The inhospitable terrain, only a small portion of which was suited to the construction of buildings, always imposed restrictions on the physical size of Fort Bowie, and thus limited the physical comforts that otherwise might have been afforded the residents. Compounding its retarded growth was the expectation throughout the army chain of command that the site might be abandoned at any time. In fact, a formal proposal to that effect was made in 1874, following the surrender of Cochise, when some in the army hierarchy concluded the post had no further military worth. The decision was deferred, however, and the outbreak of 1876 effectively put an end to the idea. At that, Fort Bowie continued to lead a tenuous existence prolonged only by successive Apache outbreaks during the 1880s.

Although field operations sometimes elevated the number of troops camped in the vicinity of the post, quarters and support facilities were designed for

Fort Bowie, circa 1887–1888. The post reflects the improvements executed by Major E. B. Beaumont, including the new post commander's house near the foot of Bowie Mountain (above and left of the flagstaff), an infantry barracks at the right upper corner of the parade ground, and adjacent to it, the recently constructed post headquarters. (Arizona Historical Society/Tucson, AHS Photo Number 1242)

two companies, usually cavalry, during most of the post–Civil War era. Only in 1883, as a result of increased Indian activity in the region, was an additional barracks constructed to house an infantry unit. Accordingly, the Fort Bowie garrison averaged 6 to 9 officers and about 150 men.

The number of army wives and children at Fort Bowie, consequently, was never large, but by 1870 the populace reflected a domestic presence. Mrs. Orsemus Boyd, who passed through the fort with her Eighth Cavalry husband during a change of station that year, related: "Camp Bowie, at which we remained three days, was nestled amid high mountains, and Indians often appeared on the bluffs above, from which they fired recklessly and sometimes effectively . . . . That little fort in the very heart of the mountain fastness sheltered a number of women and children."[3]

Of the six officers then at the post, four had their families with them. Included were those of Captains Dunn and Bernard, as well as First Lieutenants William H. Winters and Lawrence L. O'Connor. Census entries for the other two men, Captain Gerald Russell and Second Lieutenant Thomas F. Riley, failed to clarify their status, whether single, or married with wives away from the post. Regardless, the presence of such a high proportion of dependents speaks to the determination of many army wives to accompany their husbands, despite difficult living conditions. Compounding matters, quarters were assigned strictly according to rank, not family size or need. The higher an officer's grade, the more rooms he was allowed, regardless of marital status.

A shortage of officers' quarters was a chronic problem at Fort Bowie, a situation made even more acute when the garrison reached the three-company limit of the available barracks. Soon after Major Eugene B. Beaumont took command of the post during summer 1884, he complained to Department of Arizona Headquarters: "[In] quarters here, married officers and bachelors are crowded together so that there is no privacy."[4] He added that eight officers, some with families, were crowded into the four available houses. Beaumont sacrificed some of his own comfort and privacy to help alleviate the problem when he had the recently completed two-story commanding officer's quarters partitioned into two apartments. The Beaumonts occupied the west half of the house, while a junior officer resided in the east section.[5]

Army regulations of the era required that only single men be enlisted in the service. Nevertheless, soldiers were permitted to marry later, provided the company commander granted consent. Most captains, however, attempted to discourage their men from assuming the burden of a wife on a soldier's pay. Even in the 1870s and 1880s, a private's basic pay of $13 a month was a meager wage. Sergeants making $17 to $22 were in a somewhat more advantageous position to marry.

The army nevertheless refused to recognize soldiers' wives, even to the extent of denying them government quarters. The couple might be forced to occupy any available shack or other building on the fringes of the post, or even some habitation beyond the limits of the military reservation. The realities imposed by such an existence were gloomy indeed, especially if the company commander denied the soldier the privilege of residing out of quarters. Married men were granted no special consideration with regard to performing their normal share of company duty.[6]

In fact, the only women officially recognized by the army were company laundresses, and only because maintaining the soldiers' clothing was a military necessity that could not otherwise be provided at most stations in the West. Each company was allotted four laundresses who were rationed and housed at government expense. Like other personnel, they were also entitled to free medical care at post hospitals. Additionally, these washerwomen were permitted to charge by the piece for laundry services to supplement their living, the prices being established by a board of officers known as the post council of administration.[7]

Laundresses, not surprisingly, were always in high demand as wives and seldom remained single very long. The matrimonially inclined soldier could hardly overlook the advantages of marrying a woman on "Soapsuds Row," as the laundress quarters were commonly known. Physical appearance notwithstanding, such women possessed their own quarters, income, and rations— and soldier-husbands could escape communal life in barracks, while residing on the post. By combining rations and pay, a soldier's family could get by rather comfortably. When changes of station occurred, the army likewise stood the expense of moving laundresses to the new post. Any soldier's wife not already on the rolls lost no time in applying for the first vacancy.

Laundresses "had children of their own," one officer recalled, "plenty of them, and it was no rare sight to see the mother doing her share of the company washing, with a big soldier contentedly taking care of the children, sitting by the kitchen stove, or helping to hang out the clothes."[8] A total of twenty-nine children aged fifteen and under, of whom only five belonged to officers, lived at Fort Bowie in 1870.[9]

Quarters for laundresses at some posts were specially designed and constructed units—either individual cabins, or, more frequently, a row of

"Camp Merijildo." By the early 1890s, the stage station, shown here on the right, was being used as a laundress quarters. The few remaining structures of the first fort, also housing civilians and married soldiers, stand on the hill beyond. (Arizona Historical Society/Tucson, AHS Photo Number 44729)

modest one- or two-room apartments under a single roof. Occasionally, an unneeded barracks was partitioned into rooms for laundresses. In most instances, however, the mere location of laundress quarters on the fringes of a post reflected the social status of these women. At Fort Bowie, additional housing was always at a premium as a result of inadequate funding, and because space was so limited on the small plateau where the fort was situated. Hence, laundresses were housed initially at the abandoned First Fort, dubbed "Camp Merijildo"[10] Later, during the 1870s, the vacant privately owned mail station at the foot of the hill below the old post was utilized for that purpose. Five laundresses are known to have occupied the building in 1877.[11]

Although laundresses were in high demand at most military posts, the available evidence suggests that Fort Bowie may have been an exception to the norm. At a time when three companies were stationed at the post, and twelve laundresses were authorized, only seven were registered. Five of those women—Elizabeth Breen, Helen Driscoll, Bridget Flannery, Librada Rodney, and Rachel Stevens—were soldiers' wives, while Abrana Prudencia was married to a civilian employed as a domestic servant for one of the officers. Crescencia Carrillo was single, at least when the 1870 census was compiled. Interestingly, records indicate that Mrs. Rodney, Mrs. Prudencia, and Miss Carrillo were Hispanic natives of New Mexico.[12] It is impossible to know whether the latter two individuals were actually company laundresses, since there was nothing to prohibit women from working in the same capacity for officers or civilians at the post.

Although most laundresses were legitimately married and made the best homes that circumstances would allow, Congress decided in 1878 that they had become an expensive luxury, if not a social burden, and that they would be discontinued as an officially recognized auxiliary of the army. Only a few high-ranking officers defended laundresses by arguing that the mere presence of a few women had a certain ameliorating effect on an otherwise male society. The question was not so much whether soldiers could get along without laundry services, but whether the army could afford to sacrifice the beneficial social influences those women exerted on the troops.[13] Despite that reasoned argument, a general order promulgated that year tersely directed that "women will not be allowed to accompany troops as laundresses."[14]

The order nevertheless recognized the marital status of many laundresses by exempting married women until the end of their husbands' current enlistment. The edict did not prevent a married soldier from reenlisting, with permission, nor did it prohibit his wife from accompanying him from station to station so long as she was willing to be deprived of government quarters and other amenities formerly accorded laundresses. The order, in fact, did not abolish laundresses themselves, for laundry services were always a necessity, nor did it usurp the authority of post commanders to allow married soldiers to occupy quarters that were not needed for any military purpose. Congress merely severed the official relationship, and benefits, laundresses had enjoyed with the army. By the same stroke, post commanders acquired the prerogative of evicting troublesome washerwomen, whether married or single, from the military reservation, rather than having to deal with them through official channels.

The order apparently had a direct effect on the number of company laundresses at Fort Bowie. Just two years afterward, the census enumerator found only one woman, Mary B. Marringer, employed as a laundress. Mrs. Marringer's husband, the blacksmith in Company L, Sixth Cavalry, had been killed by lightning two years earlier on his way home from the post. Despite her loss, Mrs. Marringer remained with the army, probably as the only viable means of supporting her six children. By that time, however, two enterprising Chinese laundrymen, Ah Hee and Ah Low, had set up shop at the post to fill the void created by a lack of females. These immigrants likely came to the area as workmen on the recently completed Southern Pacific Railroad.[15]

Company laundresses were not the only women married to soldiers at frontier forts. Senior noncoms of the regimental and general staffs were frequently older career men who had married and reared families in the service. Post commanders saw to it, whenever possible, that these veteran soldiers were indulged with separate quarters of somewhat higher quality than those for married soldiers of the line. For many years, staff sergeants and their families at Camp Bowie had to endure two-room apartments crudely partitioned within the quartermaster and commissary warehouses, but after laundresses were no longer sanctioned, the old mail station was remodeled into three apartments for their use. In 1883, a special set of quarters was constructed for the noncommissioned staff, and at the end of the decade a separate house for the hospital steward was built adjacent to the new hospital. The wife of the hospital steward sometimes served as matron at the post hospital, but it would appear that the wives of other staff noncoms usually chose not to find employment, even though some had likely come from the laundress ranks. Befitting their elevated social status as wives of senior sergeants, these women considered themselves to be above the lowly class of common washerwomen. It is conceivable that some may have taken in laundry as a personal favor to neighboring bachelor sergeants, but in most instances the sergeants probably took their clothes to Soapsuds Row, as did other enlisted men.

The presence of families created a need for education at frontier army posts, but because dependents were officially invisible to the army, no funds were available in the army appropriation for the construction of schools, or for hiring teachers. Officers' wives frequently compensated for the lack of a post school by educating their children at home, but that advantage didn't extend to the children of less educated enlisted men and civilians at the post.

Late in 1877, the secretary of war convened a board of officers to examine the need for education in the army. The rate of illiteracy among the rank and file was found to be high, therefore, the committee concluded that the service might benefit by providing educational opportunities for the men, thereby producing more useful soldiers who would also be more capable citizens once they were discharged. Even though the board conceded that school attendance should remain voluntary, post commanders were to actively encourage their men to avail themselves of the opportunity. Not long afterward, the War Department authorized funds for constructing post schools, a reform that incidentally benefited the children of army families.[16]

When Army Headquarters surveyed the status of post schools a year later, Captain C. B. McLellan tersely asserted that Camp Bowie still lacked a school because there were no children currently at the post and none of the soldiers wanted to attend classes.[17] McLellan assured the adjutant general, however, that if any of the men expressed a desire for classes, he would establish a school at once. Apparently, there were no prospective pupils until the following summer when McLellan announced to the garrison that classes for enlisted men and children would commence on July 23, 1879. The school was established in Officers' Quarters no. 2, an unoccupied adobe house situated on the south side of the parade ground. Private George S. Allen, Sixth Cavalry, was assigned to duty as overseer for thirty-five cents a day extra pay. Children of both officers and enlisted men were invited to attend daytime classes, whereas evening sessions were conducted strictly for soldiers. It is not known how long this first school remained in operation, but certainly less than two years. Department headquarters approved plans for a school building to be erected at Fort Bowie that same year, but a subsequent shortage of funds forced the curtailment of those plans.

By spring 1881, McLellan had reopened the school, this time in the library room. The schedule of classes was much the same, with children attending during the day, the soldiers in the evening after retreat parade. An enlisted man was again granted extra duty pay to serve as teacher. However, the school term was short-lived. McLellan was forced to curtail classes on July 1 when the men detailed as teachers were ordered to rejoin their companies for field service chasing marauding Apaches. McLellan further declared there was no one left on post qualified to assume the job during their absence.[18] Classes reconvened in March 1882, but lasted only three months before being suspended "owing to the nonattendance of any enlisted men."[19]

Finding teachers proved equally difficult even in quiet times because many soldiers possessing the requisite skills preferred to do only military duty; teaching school was beneath their dignity as soldiers. In some instances, the children made life doubly unpleasant for the teacher by playing pranks and otherwise disrupting class. When a soldier tired of the job, a sure way to be relieved was to show up drunk.[20]

The general reform movement that began in the United States Army in the latter part of the nineteenth century was reflected in *Army Regulations* of 1881. The revised regulations provided further guidelines for education at military posts by making school attendance compulsory for the children of all enlisted men, as well as urging that officers' children attend as well. Those officers opting to educate their children at home were admonished to keep them from playing on or otherwise making any noise around the parade ground. Classes were supposed to be conducted from 9:30 until noon, and from 1:00 to 3:00 in the afternoon, but the Fort Bowie school sometimes operated for only two and a half hours daily, excepting Saturdays. In the event of absences, the commanding officer's orderly, acting as truant officer, was sent to the quarters of any enrolled children to request that they be sent to school, or to receive from a parent an excuse for a child's nonattendance.[21]

The post school at Fort Bowie continued to operate intermittently throughout the 1880s and early 1890s. Major Eugene B. Beaumont, commanding Fort Bowie in 1887, reported during one intermission: "There is no school room at the post, no children for pupils and, unless enlisted men are compelled to attend, a school is useless."[22] The lack of attendance may have been a residual effect from the law abolishing laundresses. As early as 1883, the secretary of war observed: "Indeed, since the passage of the law substantially abolishing 'camp women' the number of soldiers' children has largely diminished, so that there is no urgent call for such schools."[23] During those times when school was in session, the curriculum included basic subjects such as arithmetic, American history, grammar, spelling, reading, geography, and writing, and by 1891, algebra, geometry, and trigonometry had been added.[24]

Despite Beaumont's dismal commentary, the department quartermaster authorized construction of a twenty-five by fifty-foot frame structure on the west perimeter of the parade ground, adjacent to the old hospital, in 1888. The interior of the school building was a single large room also suitable for courts-martial and religious services, suggesting that the building may have been justified for its multiple-use potential.[25]

An established schedule of bugle calls regulated garrison life for almost everyone on the post, including dependents and civilian employees. The guardhouse clock was the official timepiece, and the post bugler (sometimes called the orderly bugler) assigned to the guard was responsible for sounding the calls according to a prescribed schedule. A typical day at Fort Bowie is reflected in the following order of service calls published in 1883:

1st Call for Reveille	5:40 AM
Reveille	5:45 AM
Assembly	5:47 AM
Stable Call	Immediately thereafter

Mess Call (Breakfast)	6:30 AM
Fatigue	7:00 AM
Sick Call	7:30 AM
1st Call for Guard Mount	8:00 AM
Assembly for Guard Details	8:10 AM
Adjutant's Call & Guard Mount	8:13 AM
Orderly Call	11:00 AM
Recall from Fatigue	11:30 AM
Mess Call (Dinner)	12:00 Noon
Fatigue	1:00 PM
Recall from Fatigue	4:30 PM
Stable Call	5:00 PM
1st Call for Retreat	5 minutes before sunset
Assembly	5 minutes after 1st Call
Retreat	As soon as roll has been called and Cos. at parade rest.
School Call	Following Retreat
1st Call for Tattoo	8:25 PM
Tattoo	8:30 PM
Taps	9:00 PM

****

1st Call, Sunday Morning Inspection 7:45 AM
To Arms 8:00 AM[26]

Although the routine varied little, weekends were somewhat more relaxed for most of the men. Cavalrymen performed the usual stable duty, of course, but all other enlisted men, except those on guard, devoted Saturday morning to thoroughly cleaning their quarters. Bunks and lockers were stacked, floors were scrubbed, lamps and windows cleaned, and the entire barracks was generally placed in good order. During winter, the men cleaned out and reblackened the large cast-iron heaters. Some of the men bathed in the afternoon, then lined up at the company barber shop for a weekly shave and perhaps a haircut.[27] There were no officially recognized barbers, but at least one man in every company possessed, or acquired, enough barbering skills to provide the service. Afterward, soldiers visited the bar at the Post Trader's Store (and later the post canteen) and generally loafed about the fort enjoying a respite from the usual tedium of garrison duties. They were, however, required to attend evening parade.

Cavalrymen groomed their horses on the picket line twice daily. (Fort Bowie Photo Album, Paper, 1858-1894, Museum of American West Collection, Autry National Center)

Sunday morning was usually reserved for an open-locker barracks inspection conducted by the company commander, although weekly inspections at Fort Bowie were being scheduled on Saturday mornings in 1890 to leave the men completely free on Sundays. Formal religion accounted for little of the frontier regulars' time. Fort Bowie, like most posts, rarely had a post chaplain in residence. Members of the garrison desiring religious services sometimes held informal prayer meetings at the adjutant's office or at the post school. More formal worship services relied on infrequent visits by itinerate ministers or chaplains from neighboring posts. Reverend Charles H. Cook, for example, spent nearly two weeks at the post as the guest of one of the officers. During that time, he preached at least one service daily, rotating among the company quarters and gatherings of officers and their families. Cook should not have been surprised at the dismal turnout for a sermon titled "Ten Virgins" that he delivered to K Company, Third Cavalry. However, a subsequent presentation was well received by the audience he encountered at the guardhouse. The reverend reported with considerable satisfaction that the ten prisoners, along with members of the guard, responded with "good singing and attention." He may not have taken into account, however, that under the circumstances, he had the most captive of audiences.[28]

Not until 1891 was a regular chaplain assigned to Fort Bowie to provide religious guidance for the garrison and oversee the school. Reverend John D. Parker, stationed at Fort Robinson, Nebraska, received orders to report to Fort Bowie on January 10. Despite the more healthful climate in Arizona, the newly appointed chaplain was immediately afflicted with "gastric catarrh and nervous prostration." The surgeon confined Parker to his quarters for the next seven months, and eventually declared that he was "incapacitated for further service." Meantime, the post had been slated for abandonment, thus bringing to a close an extraordinarily dismal record for religion and formal education at Fort Bowie.[29]

The Sabbath was otherwise reserved for rest and relaxation. Some of the literate men took advantage of the post library to catch up on national news or to spend a few leisurely hours reading for self-improvement. In addition to a few hundred books, the library stocked periodicals such as *Harper's Monthly, Century Magazine, Frank Leslie's Illustrated, the Army and Navy Journal*, and *Forest and Stream*. Newspapers included the *San Francisco Chronicle, St. Louis Globe-Democrat, New York Herald, Baltimore Sun*, and the *Chicago Sunday Times*. The residents of Fort Bowie may have been geographically isolated, but they were by no means intellectually disconnected from the world.[30]

Sunday was also a day for baseball games among the post nines, or even competitions with teams from neighboring posts or towns. These events were eagerly anticipated and were well attended by the entire garrison. Other times, the men probably engaged in games of horseshoes among themselves and resident civilians, with many onlookers cheering and placing sidebets on their favorites.

The unofficial caste system in the army dictated that officers and enlisted men live within defined, segregated societies, and except for routine official contacts, that line was seldom crossed. Officers and their families, consequently, relied to a great extent on their own resourcefulness and the tight-knit community of the post for leisure activities. With time on his hands, Fort Bowie surgeon Joseph P. Widney amused himself by "shooting a lot of fat worthless cats that are about the buildings. The butcher dresses their skins for me."[31] He failed to record what use he had for the skins.

Many surviving personal accounts of frontier service suggest that reading and writing were the two most common pastimes along officers' row. Officers usually possessed some degree of higher education; many were West Point graduates. It was a rare officer who did not build at least a modest personal library consisting of works on military and technical subjects, history, philosophy,

Troops of the Fourth Cavalry at retreat dress parade, Fort Bowie 1886. Clearly visible is the sharply sloping parade ground, rising twenty-five feet from north to south. (Arizona Historical Society/Tucson, AHS Photo Number 25613)

As Fort Bowie matured, recreational facilities eventually included a tennis court for the officers and their families. (Fort Bowie Photo Album, Paper, 1858–1894, Museum of American West Collection, Autry National Center)

and the classics. Dr. Widney probably spoke for many in the officer corps, especially at remote stations like Camp Bowie, when he wrote, "The books help to render the time endurable."[32] Officers commonly subscribed to hometown or national newspapers to keep abreast of national and world events. Wives, too, spent much of their spare time reading, as well as corresponding with relatives in the East.

The women of officers' row filled their days with a variety of pursuits designed, consciously or unconsciously, to combat boredom. Visiting was always popular, though human nature and the confines of the garrison often created cliques among the families, leading to malicious gossip and discord. At many posts, the ranks held by officer-husbands determined the social pecking order among the women, often to a more pronounced degree than among the officers themselves.

Despite the divisions that sometimes occurred between households, wives frequently gathered to join in artwork and handcrafts, music, and discussion of literary works. Whist and other parlor games were also popular among both wives and couples, as was sharing stereopticon slides by lamplight. During the 1870s, officers and their ladies at Camp Bowie engaged in croquet matches at a court laid out at one edge of the parade ground. In the years just before the post was abandoned, a visiting correspondent reported that "lawn tennis, minus the lawn, is the outdoor diversion for ladies, officers, and children and at present the crisp mountain air enables one to play for hours without sensible fatigue."[33]

Discipline in the Regular Army was rigid, especially on the western frontier where primitive conditions and isolation contributed to aberrant behavior. Nevertheless, the army expected officers to comport themselves as gentlemen, even on the frontier, by imposing a strict code of conduct conforming to the social standards of the Victorian era.[34] Despite its best efforts to preserve those protocol traditions in the West, however, boredom and the confines of a small post frequently led to abuses of acceptable social conduct. Although limited flirting was condoned, even between officer's wives and bachelor officers, married women were considered to be "untouchable to the surrounding masculine society," as one historian has described the phenomenon. The army could not afford any breach of the code for fear it would undermine the whole social, if not organizational, structure.[35] Nevertheless, human nature sometimes defied the code. In those instances, the army dealt unsympathetically with offenders by using the catchall charge of "conduct unbecoming an officer and gentleman," as expressed in the sixty-first Article of War.

A particularly scandalous episode disrupted the serenity of Fort Bowie in 1877 when Second Lieutenant Duane Merritt Greene was accused of seducing the wife of the post surgeon, S. A. Freeman. Greene, a bachelor, arranged to take his meals at the Freeman home, a not uncommon practice at frontier posts where cooks and servants often were at a premium. But during times when the doctor was absent in the field, others noticed that Greene began paying close attention to Mrs. Freeman, becoming her "constant companion" over a three-month period. The relationship, turned intimate, quickly became common knowledge and was "condemned as being improper by nearly every person serving at the post." When Doctor Freeman learned of the torrid affair upon his return home, he immediately confronted Greene with the accusation, based on his wife's own confession that the two had been having sexual intercourse. Greene not only flippantly dismissed the allegation, he had the audacity to routinely show up for a tension-charged dinner at the Freeman quarters a few hours later.

That very afternoon, Greene and Mrs. Freeman openly flaunted their relationship by appearing together at the billiard room in the Post Trader's Store, and later at the croquet ground. An enraged Freeman stormed from the hospital to confront Greene in the midst of his croquet game, before an audience of several other officers and ladies of the garrison. But even that metaphorical douse of cold water failed to cool the ardor of the amorous couple. When Freeman returned home later that day, he was astonished to discover his wife and the lieutenant locked in the bedroom "for the purpose of committing adultery."[36]

The situation had reached such sordid proportions by that time that post commander William M. Wallace could no longer ignore what had become the talk of the garrison. Compelled to take official action against Greene, he drafted charges and specifications under the catch-all article "conduct unbecoming an officer and gentleman," but he stopped short of placing him under arrest. Enlisted men may have been expected to succumb to their baser instincts with the disreputable women at local "whiskey ranches," but an officer openly engaging in sexual liaisons flagrantly violated social mores, even by frontier standards. Not only was it bad form, it set an example for enlisted men that might undermine discipline. The lieutenant, realizing his prospects for a bright career were dimming by the minute, hastily offered a compromise. If the commanding officer agreed not to file charges, Greene would tender his resignation, effective in six months; meantime, he would take a leave of absence. The army was only too happy to accept Greene's offer, and quickly sweep the seamy affair under the official carpet. Meanwhile, the notorious Mrs. Freeman accompanied her husband to Fort Yuma, perhaps to maintain her economic security in an age when women without men were accorded few opportunities for self-sufficiency. The excitement over, life at Fort Bowie soon returned to its normal state of dreary solitude.

Photographs taken at Fort Bowie indicate that officers, their wives, and other family members took pleasure rides on horseback or by buggy into the surrounding area to view the natural beauty. Siphon Canyon, with its comparatively cool shaded areas and unusual rock formations, was a favorite picnic destination.[37] In the years following Apache removal, large parties sometimes ventured to Pinery Canyon and other scenic spots in the Chiricahua Mountains for extended outings. Dr. Widney recorded that he and other officers passed the time by forming group outings to climb nearby Helen's Dome and Bowie Mountain to observe the surrounding country from those vantage points.[38] Hunting for deer, wild turkeys, quail, and occasionally bear in the mountains surrounding the post was also popular with many officers stationed at Apache Pass, including General George Crook.

The completion of the Southern Pacific Railroad in 1880 connected Fort Bowie with the outside world as never before. With Bowie Station only a

Officers and ladies frequently turned to horseback riding as a favorite pastime. (Fort Bowie Photo Album, Paper, 1858–1894, Museum of American West Collection, Autry National Center)

short distance away, mail delivery became faster and more reliable. A new town, Willcox, quickly sprang up along the tracks where they intersected the military road to Fort Grant. The railroad encouraged some officers and ladies at Fort Bowie to make more elaborate excursions. In 1890, one group arranged with friends at Fort Grant to rendezvous with them at Willcox, where a circus was performing. Easy access to the railroad also facilitated trips to more distant places, exemplified when Lieutenant and Mrs. Charles G. Lyman took the cars for a holiday in El Paso.[39] Such trips would have been considered out of the question just a few years earlier.

On some occasions, the residents of officers' row were inspired to plan rather extravagant undertakings as diversions from the normal humdrum. In January 1890, the officers and ladies arranged an evening ball "that proved to be an enjoyable affair."[40] A special event of that nature called for serving refreshments, developing and printing a program, making gowns or digging out finery from the bottoms of trunks, decorating a hall, and arranging for musicians when a regimental band was not available. Anticipation was half the fun. Even the presence of only a dozen officers, resplendent in glittering dress uniforms, augmented by ladies bedecked in colorful, if somewhat outdated, gowns allowed the participants to escape temporarily from an otherwise dreary existence.

Weddings within the officer corps were major social events; enlisted personnel, of course, were excluded from the guest list. Although several weddings must have taken place at the post during its active years, only two became a matter of record, and both occurred within the same family. Major Eugene B. Beaumont's family included two daughters, Natalie and Hortense, both of whom were married in the imposing two-story frame commander's quarters that loomed on the south side of the parade ground. Natalie's wedding took place on the evening of April 23, 1885, though some of the more distant guests had begun arriving at the post two days earlier to get an early start on the festivities. On the night of the event, "The parlors were elegantly decorated with evergreens and choice flowers appropriate to the glad occasion," the *Arizona Daily Citizen* reported.[41] More than twenty people were in attendance, including Hortense and her fiancé, Lieutenant Charles P. Elliott. A visiting civilian minister hired for the occasion performed the ceremony.

Three months after Geronimo's surrender and his brief appearance at Fort Bowie in fall 1886, the younger Beaumont daughter was married in the same house. It, too, was a formal affair, with all the officers present arrayed in full-dress uniform. Conveniently, the Fourth Cavalry band was stationed at the post at that time to provide accompaniment for the ceremony, and "the assembled guests indulged in a few dances, and about midnight supper was served, shortly after which the merry party separated with cordial greetings to the newly married couple."[42] The next morning the couple took the train from Bowie Station to California to begin an extended honeymoon.

Whether Fort Bowie supported the Order of Free Masons or other fraternal organizations has not been documented, though such societies were fairly common among officers and soldiers elsewhere on the frontier. The post did, however, host a group calling itself "The Bowie Social Clan." Although the exact purpose of this club was not defined, its name implies an informal group that may have held its twice-weekly meetings in the officers' clubroom at the Post Trader's Store. A notice published in the *Army and Navy Journal* assured any visiting officers from other posts they would be "warmly welcomed."[43] Copious amounts of "ceremonial" libations probably contributed in no small measure to the warmth and camaraderie of Clan meetings.

A party of officers, wives, and children picnicking in the Chiricahua Mountains. (Fort Bowie Photo Album, Paper, 1858-1894, Museum of American West Collection, Autry National Center)

Of a more official nature were post lyceums, instituted in the Department of Arizona during 1891. Apparently, the department commander felt that his line officers were becoming lethargic in their duties and were in need of professional stimulation. The first session was conducted at Fort Bowie on November 10, 1891, and sessions continued twice a week thereafter. Each officer present at the post took his turn to prepare and deliver a lecture concerning some aspect of an assigned topic, such as guard duty, minor tactics, or military law. Following the presentation, the assembled officers discussed and debated fine points of the topic for the benefit of all. Lyceums continued on a regular schedule until the post was abandoned in 1894.[44]

Closely associated with the garrison family was the post trader, a civilian licensed to operate a general mercantile store on the military reservation. The secretary of war appointed the merchants from a list of applicants, a system that invited the use of political influence and, at times, encouraged graft. Sidney R. DeLong, a trained civil engineer and veteran of the California Column, promptly gained employment with the Tucson freighting firm of Tully, Ochoa, & Company after the war. The multitalented DeLong also

Officers conducting a lyceum session on porch at Fort Bowie, circa 1893. (Fort Bowie Photo Album, Paper, 1858–1894, Museum of American West Collection, Autry National Center)

Sidney DeLong came to the territory as a soldier in the California Column. Remaining in Arizona after the Civil War, he invested in mining, published a newspaper, served as mayor of Tucson, and was post trader at Fort Bowie for many years. (Arizona Historical Society/Tucson, AHS Photo Number 23787)

became editor of the *Weekly Arizonian* and was elected mayor of Tucson in 1871 and again in 1872. His experience in managing the post trader's store at Camp Crittenden, not to mention his own prior military service, provided him the experience to take over Tully and Ochoa's operation at Fort Bowie beginning in 1869. Besides being the only source of a wide variety of commercial goods in the area, the trader operated the soldiers' bar, along with a billiard room for officers.[45] DeLong, additionally, held the position of postmaster during his tenure, with his store doubling as the post office. Thus, the trader's establishment was the unchallenged social center at the post, as recounted by a visitor in 1870:

> Our first and only night at Bowie was passed with pleasure and profit to ourself [*sic*], and we presume our fellow-travelers passed it likewise. We visited the post trader's establishment—and bearded lion of the tribe of DeLong in his den, but, instead of scalping us, he attempted to drown us with champagne—which, of course, he found impossible.[46]

The enterprising DeLong expanded his operation to include a hotel at Fort Bowie during the 1880s. He probably adapted the old mail station to that purpose, since that was the only other privately owned building on the post. The station contained seven rooms, plus a kitchen, though the record

Post trader's store, also containing an officers' club room and the enlisted men's bar, was the social center of Fort Bowie. It burned while being used as the canteen. (Arizona Historical Society/Tucson, AHS Photo Number 44749)

is not clear how many may have been designated as guest accommodations. Mrs. Maggie Nevins managed the hotel for DeLong in 1885. Later it was operated by Miss Emma Peterson.[47]

The army made no official effort to provide off-duty amusements for either officers or enlisted men; consequently, boredom was a significant morale factor throughout the era. Its effects created continuing, serious disciplinary problems for the service. The regulars became legendary for their rough ways and hard drinking, though that generalization cannot be applied universally to all men who served in the ranks during the Indian Wars. Still, isolation and the availability of liquor caused many men to turn to vices they otherwise might have avoided had more wholesome pastimes been available. Statistics compiled during the 1880s, which probably included only cases exhibiting the most acute symptoms, revealed that one in every twenty-five men suffered from the effects of alcoholism.[48]

The most readily available source of liquor at most posts, including Camp Bowie, was the soldiers' bar at De Long's establishment. There the men could drink and play pool or cards. Now and then a musically talented man may have played a squeeze-box, guitar, or harmonica for the enjoyment of the others. The place may have boasted a piano, though it is not known if DeLong went to the expense of purchasing one.

DeLong also maintained a clubroom and a billiard room for officers apart from a bar intended exclusively for the enlisted men. These rooms, occupying the south section of the store building, were a physical manifestation of the army's caste system segregating the officers from soldiers. Bachelors as well as married officers frequented the place throughout the day and evening hours. So long as an officer had no required duty to perform, such as being officer of the day or serving as a member of garrison court martial, he was at liberty to visit the clubroom whenever he chose. Since the club was the social center of the post, it was an unspoken expectation that an officer frequent the place on a regular basis to keep up relationships and stay current on army gossip. There the officers could play cards, drink, smoke cigars, and those so inclined might join in songs recalling the Civil War or West Point days.

That the patrons became raucous at times was evidenced by a directive from the post commander in 1878 restricting use of the billiard room to evenings from 5:30 P. M. until tattoo, and closing it on Sundays. Lieutenant Clark, in charge of the post at that time, admonished the garrison: "The simple reminder of the proximity of the quarters of Mr. DeLong's family, will be sufficient to secure freedom from all boisterousness and loud talking in the Billiard Room while this indulgence lasts. . . . Entrance to and exit from the Billiard room will be made by the south door."[49]

Alcoholism was as prevalent among commissioned officers, if not more so, as among enlisted men simply because officers had easier access to liquor and were better able to afford it. Moreover, they had more free time on their hands, since day-to-day management of companies usually fell to the first sergeants. Drinking problems, however, were ignored unless they hampered an officer's performance, or he embarrassed the service by becoming publicly inebriated on duty. Second Lieutenant Robert D. Walsh, for example, was officially reprimanded by the post commander at Fort Bowie for his "intemperate habits." The post commander later concluded that Walsh had overcome the problem, until the lieutenant appeared "at the pay table while his troop was being paid . . . in an intoxicated condition." The commander thereupon took immediate action by placing the lieutenant under arrest and removing him from command of his troop.[50]

Drinking often led to fistfights and outright brawls among the enlisted men. Prior to the advent of bottled beer, whiskey was an especially notorious catalyst of violence when men of volatile temperament overindulged. Noting the effect alcohol was having on discipline in the Department of Arizona during 1871, Colonel George Stoneman issued an order prohibiting the sale of intoxicating liquors on all military posts under his jurisdiction. Soldiers being soldiers, some evaded the order by going off-post to "whiskey ranches" that invariably sprang up just outside the military reservations.[51] Just two months after Stoneman's order took effect, the *Arizona Citizen* observed: "At nearly every post in Arizona whiskey is bought by the Gal[lon] and carried on the Post by the men. We have reliable sources, that the troops are more dissipated than before the order."[52]

Just how long the unpopular order remained in effect is not known, but it must have been quietly rescinded when Lieutenant Colonel George Crook succeeded Stoneman as department commander later that year. The sale of whiskey at military posts posed a continuing problem. Captain Samuel S. Sumner, commanding Camp Bowie in 1874, found it necessary to restrict DeLong from selling liquor to soldiers and laundresses, except by the glass, presumably because they had been purchasing it in bulk quantities at the store and consuming it elsewhere.[53]

Fort Bowie suffered from isolation throughout its active life. According to one soldier, "There was no entertainment."[54] Sixth Cavalryman S. W. Grant vividly remembered the isolation during the time he was stationed at the post in 1876: "There were no ranches within a radius of twenty miles and if we wanted any fun we had to go about twenty miles [*sic*] to Camp Grant where they had a dance hall and a saloon just off the reservation. Or we sometimes went to Hooker's ranch. We consequently spent most of our money with the post trader, for, of course, a soldier had to spend his money somewhere."[55]

Prior to the arrival of the railroad, the only village established in the immediate vicinity was Dos Cabezas, a mining camp approximately twelve miles northwest of the post that sprang up as the result of a modest gold strike at the base of the mountains. Although it never amounted to much, the camp boasted a stage station and several saloons providing liquor and prostitutes to the miners. Soldiers occasionally secured passes to frequent the village, simply because it provided the nearest diversion to the dull routine of the post.[56]

Other settlements eventually appeared along the railroad. Bowie Station, established thirteen miles north as a water stop on the Southern Pacific, remained small despite the erection of a hotel, a "club house," and cattle pens. Although visitors bound for Fort Bowie often detrained there, Bowie Station never evolved as a recreational attraction for soldiers. Willcox, on the other hand, was considered the "closest real town . . . . soldiers spent

Willcox, Arizona, served as a principal recreational outlet for troops from both Fort Bowie and Fort Grant, making for much rowdy behavior that sometimes turned deadly. (Arizona Historical Society/Tucson, AHS Photo Number 48669)

their money there and were quite welcome," according to a former Fourth Cavalry trooper.[57] Sixth Cavalryman Anton Mazzanovich described Willcox in 1881 as "a typical wild and woolly frontier burg." He recalled that the Norton & Stewart Store contained a combination saloon and gambling joint where cowboys and soldiers played poker and faro. Also in the town were a "Mexican monte layout," a railroad depot, and a dance hall "going full blast." At that time, and no doubt on other occasions when troops were in the field, an infantry bivouac stood near the tracks to guard arriving supplies. "Everybody toted a gun," according to Mazzanovich. "One's dress would not have been complete without the old reliable .44 or .45 frontier Colt swung at the hip."[58] The volatile combination of free-flowing liquor and armed men almost always led to violence, as when one Fort Bowie soldier murdered another at Willcox in 1882.[59]

On another occasion, the temptations in Willcox overcame the better sense of three noncommissioned officers who violated orders not to leave their camp just outside town. Sergeants James Radigan and Joseph C. Byrd, along with Corporal John Kelly, all belonging to M Troop, Third Cavalry, went into Willcox on the night of November 21, 1883. When Captain William A. Rafferty discovered the men drinking in a saloon after midnight, he immediately ordered them back to camp. In a drunken act of disobedience, the men ignored Rafferty's instructions, forcing him to send yet another noncom into town to reiterate the order. The offenders were later tried and found guilty of breaching military discipline, but the post commander, none other than Captain Rafferty, was uncommonly lenient in view of the men's past good records. Instead of being reduced to the ranks and confined at hard labor, as the court recommended, the captain commuted the sentences to a mere fine of one month's pay for each man.[60]

Since post traders were not prohibited from keeping whiskey for sale to authorized persons, abuses were bound to happen. On one occasion in 1883, Captain Leo O. Parker, temporarily commanding Fort Bowie, saw a soldier "about half drunk going from the bar room towards the commissary store house, he had a bottle up to his mouth and appeared to be drinking. He then threw the bottle on the stones."[61] When Parker asked the clerk, Jack Dunn, if he had sold a bottle to the man, Dunn denied having done so. Parker nevertheless reminded the clerk of Captain Rafferty's order that liquor was not to be sold by the bottle. A few days later, Dunn, who would later become a founder of Bisbee, Arizona, sold two bottles of whiskey to a sergeant sent in from the field to obtain supplies for his company. Parker immediately informed the clerk that he would be fired for defying orders, but allowed Dunn to keep the store open until DeLong could return to replace him.[62]

The post trader's store continued to be the focus of recreation for the garrison, but by the late 1870s competitors sometimes encroached on DeLong's monopoly. The threat posed by Apaches had discouraged illicit dives from being established in the area until after the much-feared chief's capitulation in 1872. Likewise, the army's efforts to keep the Indians distanced from liquor further prevented such businesses from taking root until the Chiricahuas were removed to the San Carlos Reservation four years later. But the prediction that whiskey ranches would spring up outside the military reservation was realized only too soon. One early resident said, "Beyond that particular six mile square was a kind of a 'No Man's Land,' where [was] established every kind of joint imaginable to lure the dollars away from the soldiers. . . . [The bars] were peopled by some pretty tough hombres."[63]

In 1877 two entrepreneurs, George Atkins and Roscoe Bryant, started a ranch "within a stone's throw" of the post. Captain William M. Wallace informed the pair that he was aware they were

maintaining abandoned women, and keeping intoxicating liquor for
no other purpose than to trade with the men of this garrison. The
presence of such a place is necessarily subversive of Military discipline. I shall therefore use every means in my power to break it up. In
furtherance of such action I have directed the Post Trader not to sell
anything to any person who shall have anything to do with the place
in question, and have ordered that citizens not in Government
employ are prohibited from coming or remaining upon the Military
reservation of this Post without permission of the Commdg Officer,
and upon committal of the second offense the party offending will be
placed in confinement in the Post Guard House.[64]

The proprietors, blatantly ignoring Wallace's warning, continued their activities until early August, when Wallace ordered Second Lieutenant John A.
Rucker to evict the unsavory occupants. He took the further precaution of
posting a three-man guard at the saloon to prevent the former residents
from reoccupying it. On the surface, Wallace's action appeared to be aimed
at eradicating the problem, yet his stipulation that the Atkins crowd be
removed "to a point one mile distant from this post in a northeasterly direction" suggests an ulterior motive. Practical-minded commanding officers
sometimes chose to tolerate prostitution on or near military posts as a means
of managing tensions among the men and to maintain morale. Wallace's
decision to condone the Atkins dive, rather than use his authority to eradicate it, indicates that he was more concerned with keeping the operation at
a respectable distance from the fort than with altogether eliminating access
to prostitutes.[65]

Just how many such establishments were in the vicinity of the post has not
been determined, but in 1888 an unspecified number of houses of prostitution were operating in the vicinity of Goodwin Canyon, about two and one-half
miles northwest of the fort. At the same time, at least two other disreputable places, one operated by James Barrack, the other by Mrs. Ada Miller,
were doing a thriving business three miles north along the road to Bowie
Station. Those two saloons, known collectively as the "Hog Ranch," stood
on opposite sides of the road, just outside the boundary of the military
reservation. Barrack ran a saloon and gambling den, while Mrs. Miller augmented rot gut whiskey with a few prostitutes.[66] Barrack's establishment was
particularly troublesome, and on at least one occasion he harbored an army
deserter in his cellar. Both places apparently were well patronized by the

garrison, because in 1893 the surgeon urged "that moral suasion be exerted upon proprietors of the 'hog ranch' to induce them to send off the diseased wenches" to counteract an upsurge of venereal disease among the troops.[67] Not surprisingly, his suggestion went unheeded.

On the eve of the closure of the fort in 1894, the post adjutant requested local rancher Thomas Whitehead to identify a soldier who came to his homestead on Sunday, probably on a sexual lark, "with one of the hog ranch women, a woman of bad character . . . such actions are perfectly disgraceful."[68] Considering that neither the soldier nor the rancher was within the military reservation at the time of the alleged visit, Whitehead probably ignored the demand. At one point, the commanding officer attempted to eradicate the Hog Ranch by cutting off its water supply. When Major Noyes learned that government freighters coming from Bowie Station were delivering water to the saloons, he threatened to bar them from the reservation if the practice continued. He went even further by posting guards over the three reliable springs within the reservation to deny Hog Ranch inhabitants access to water.[69] Despite these efforts, the "ranches" were finally put out of business only by the army's exodus from Fort Bowie.

"All men need an outlet in the way of comradeship and society," wrote one veteran officer, "and if they can not get it in a good and legitimate way, they will seek it in a bad and illegitimate direction."[70] The combined effects of curtailing liquor sales and the consequent proliferation of hog ranches resulted in a grass-roots effort within the army to find a more wholesome alternative. In the mid-1880s troops at Fort Sidney, Nebraska, established a trial "canteen" modeled after similar clubs in the British Army. The men themselves operated the facility, under the supervision of an officer appointed by the post commander. Initially, canteens offered light meals of coffee and sandwiches, along with snacks such as pickles, crackers, and sausages at reasonably affordable prices, since most of the items were purchased at cost from the post commissary. Later, beer—at a nickel a glass—and wine were added to the fare. The men could also indulge themselves with newspapers and magazines, table games, and billiards. The concept proved both beneficial to the men and profitable. Excess proceeds, managed by a council of enlisted men, were used to improve the canteen itself, provide the attendants a nominal wage, and make distributions to the units of the garrison as supplements for their company funds. Within two years, several other posts created canteens as word of the concept and its successes spread throughout the service.[71]

The post canteen was seriously damaged when it caught fire in 1893. Here soldiers fight the fire after most of the contents had been removed. (Arizona Historical Society/Tucson, AHS Photo Number 44750)

Predictably, post traders objected to canteens on the grounds they infringed on their exclusive right to dispense beer and wine on military reservations. And, if soldiers were spending their off-duty hours at the canteen, it meant they would be spending less time, and money, at the trader's establishment. The system, unauthorized initially, was challenged in 1888, probably as a result of congressional lobbying by the traders, when the Treasury Department ruled that chewing and smoking tobaccos, as well as cigars, procured from the Subsistence Department could not be resold to the men through canteens. Likewise, beer, wine, and tobacco sold at those clubs were subject to federal tax under Internal Revenue laws. A short time later, Secretary of War William C. Endicott, bending to political pressure, prohibited canteens from selling alcoholic beverages altogether, a maneuver calculated to lure soldiers back to the traders' saloons. In truth, he had no choice because the traders had the law on their side.[72]

Despite these hurdles, the canteen concept caught on and became immensely popular with the rank and file. There was an undeniably rough element that would frequent hog ranches in any event, yet most soldiers were content simply to have a decent place to relax, sip coffee, and visit with their comrades.

Many post and company commanders, recognizing the beneficial effects of canteens in reducing disciplinary problems, were vehemently opposed to the secretary's stance favoring post traders. They argued, convincingly, that eliminating beer and wine from the canteens would only induce good soldiers to return to the vile whiskey ranches, thus increasing drunkenness, injuries or even deaths, and absences without leave. Moreover, post traders were notorious for gouging the enlisted men with high prices and some in the army thought the service would benefit by abolishing traderships. "Certainly," opined one soldier, "they are not needed and should not be allowed where there is a town—even a small one—near the post."[73] The War Department subsequently surveyed officers throughout the army for their opinions on the two systems. Many officers selfishly preferred to retain traders' stores simply because they would have no other recreational facility.[74] However, it was pointed out that officers could be granted government-subsidized clubs of their own, corresponding to the canteens. Regardless of dissenting votes, there was an overwhelming preference for canteens, and early in 1889 President Grover Cleveland directed the secretary to publish regulations for the establishment and management of the clubs.[75] Although the sale of hard liquor was forbidden at canteens, in accordance with law, the secretary rescinded the policy restricting beer and wine. Inebriation, however, was not condoned and bartenders at canteens were charged with refusing to serve anyone who appeared intoxicated.

Later that year, the army adopted a policy lifting the protective sanctions enjoyed by sutlers and post traders for so long. No longer were they accorded the exclusive right to sell common necessities to the soldiers. Canteens were permitted to sell not only alcoholic refreshments and food but other staples as well—at cost. It spelled financial doom for DeLong and other traders because they simply could not compete with a nonprofit enterprise sanctioned by the government.

DeLong, in fact, had foreseen the coming dilemma when the creation of post canteens appeared imminent. Nevertheless, Henry E. Noyes, the post commander, came to the trader's defense by protesting the abolishment of the store on the basis of Fort Bowie's isolation. Noyes argued to higher authority that, even though many of the articles kept for sale by the trader could be purchased cheaper at a canteen, the latter could never offer the variety of goods stocked by DeLong. Noyes further explained that the store served not only the garrison but the growing number of civilians settling in the area as well.[76] Although the department commander might have agreed that the trader could stock more goods, civilian dependency on the store was hardly relevant. In fact, civilian use of the saloon only contributed to the army's problems. The store, therefore, was to be closed and a canteen started. But Noyes feared that in the interim the absence of any recreational facility "would bring a colony of whiskey ranches, with their usual compliment of prostitutes, gamblers, etc. to the borders of the reserve, exposing enlisted men to a temptation too strong for many of them to resist, with the usual results; as well as to venereal disease, etc."[77] All things considered, it seemed reasonable for the army to allow DeLong to continue operating his business until a canteen could be started.

Barely a month later, on February 3, 1890, Troops C and H, Fourth Cavalry, founded the first canteen at Fort Bowie. According to the regulations governing such establishments, the post commander had authority to make available a government building that was not otherwise needed, but the furnishings were to be purchased by the companies from the proceeds of the business. The erection of a new hospital on the south side of the post happened to coincide with the need for a building to house the canteen, thus for several months a portion of the old hospital was devoted to that purpose.[78] The canteen proved a huge success. At the end of June, the council proudly reported total receipts of $508.30 for the month, and discounting the price of fixtures, stock, and other expenditures, the business realized a net profit of $93.81.[79]

Drinking may have been the dominant recreational activity at Camp Bowie, but it was by no means the only way that soldiers occupied their spare time. Some of the more creative men organized amateur theatricals to combat boredom. When Reverend Cook visited the post on his way to the Pima Indian Reservation in December 1870, he discovered the men planning "an exhibition, etc. tonight—kind of theater."[80] A month later, they again staged the "Bowie Varieties." According to the *Arizona Daily Citizen*, "The boys in blue at C[amp] Bowie are a jovial set, judging from a programme of songs, dances, and laughable farces received and which were performed Jan. 18."[81] Such improvised entertainment broke the monotony for the players, who devoted their spare time to preparing for the event, and for the spectators, who had something to anticipate for days or even weeks in advance.

Officially recognized holidays and other special occasions afforded eagerly awaited departures from the normal garrison schedule for all residents. Independence Day, the most patriotic of all, was observed by the firing of a cannon salute either at reveille or noon, the shots corresponding to the number of states in the Union at the time. The troops looked forward to the holiday with great anticipation, if for no other reason than the post commander's suspension of all unnecessary work and duty for the day. At most forts a program of events included children's games and various contests for the soldiers, such as foot races, wrestling, and horse races. A baseball game was traditional, as was a special meal in each company mess.[82] No record has been found regarding Christmas activities at Fort Bowie, but it may be assumed that the garrison performed only essential military duties on that day. Along officers' row, it was a time for calling on other residents, each visit being an occasion for imbibing whiskey-laden eggnog and other beverages.

In common with that of other frontier posts, the populace of Fort Bowie included a number of civilian employees in addition to military families. Included were guides, interpreters, teamsters, herders, and clerks, as well as blacksmiths and other skilled artisans—all employed by the Quartermaster Department. Fort Bowie at one time even boasted a civilian Prussian baker, an exceptional circumstance probably created by the lack of any soldiers with the necessary skills. Civilian employees were quartered in some of the old buildings at "Camp Merejildo." However, by the mid-1880s those structures were no longer habitable. Major Beaumont secured funds to construct a new five-room house near the Bowie Station Road, a short distance from the old mail station. By 1889, after the rapid decline in Indian activity and a corresponding reduction in the size of the garrison, only the post blacksmith lived in the house. A year later, the post engineer, a civilian charged with maintaining and operating the steam-powered water system, also occupied one of the apartments in the building.[83]

Medical facilities at Fort Bowie were similar to those found at other southwestern posts. The first hospital at Fort Bowie was a crude adobe structure situated atop the hill a short distance north of the quartermaster corral. Major Charles McCormick, medical director for the Department of California, described it: "The hospital consists of one log house containing 3 beds, and one wall tent with two beds. There have been 13 cases under treatment between July 1, and December 31, 1866, with an average command of 115. It is perfectly healthy. For a camp I do not think this can be considered 'bad.'"[84]

When the post was relocated to its new site in 1869, a large quartermaster storehouse was one of the first structures erected, near the northwest corner of the parade ground. By summer 1870, however, the supplies were moved into another structure and the building converted to a hospital containing rooms for an eight-bed ward, plus steward's quarters, dispensary, office, and kitchen. The structure, intended only to serve the purpose temporarily, suffered from a leaking roof for years. A series of repairs failed to remedy the problem, and in 1880 an inspector pronounced the Fort Bowie hospital to be "the poorest in the Department, in regard to its adaptability of the building."[85] By the next year, the wooden floors in several of the rooms needed to be replaced. Major Beaumont declared the building both unsafe and unfit for housing the sick. Moreover, it was situated between the new headquarters and the quartermaster-commissary storehouse, probably the most active and noisiest place on the post. Nevertheless, the old hospital continued in use for several more years.[86]

Beaumont's pleas for a new hospital failed to elicit a response until the Quartermaster Department eventually approved funds in 1887. The prevailing thought that Fort Bowie might be abandoned at any time cast doubt as to whether the new hospital would actually be constructed. In the absence of a decision by Army Headquarters, work proceeded on the hospital during 1888 and 1889. When completed, the large adobe building contained all of the features considered necessary for a medical facility of the day, including offices for both the surgeon and the steward, dispensary, a twenty-four by fifty-foot ward, bathroom, dining room, kitchen, pantry, and living quarters for the cook and hospital attendant. A new three-room house for the hospital steward was conveniently located adjacent to the hospital. The building repre-sented an unprecedented luxury for the steward, since he had previously resided in a spare room in the old hospital, and later in an apartment in the noncommissioned staff officers' quarters at the north end of the post.[87]

Most frontier post hospitals were staffed by two professionals, a surgeon and a hospital steward, augmented by a few soldiers and civilians from the garrison to perform menial tasks. The surgeon, described by critics as only good for "treating clap and confining laundresses," was answerable only to the post commander and to the medical director at Department of Arizona Headquarters.[88] Doctors appointed to the Regular Army initially were paid as first lieutenants of cavalry, and were titled assistant surgeons.

Acting assistant surgeons, sometimes termed contract physicians, wore the uniform of their rank and were to be shown the respect accorded other commissioned officers. When soldiers at Fort Bowie got the notion that the doctor was not a legitimate officer, Captain William A. Rafferty reminded them of the surgeon's status in no uncertain terms. He circulated a memo: "The commanding officer has learned with surprise that some enlisted men of this Post are so ignorant of their duties as soldiers as not to be aware that

Post hospital (left) with adjacent hospital steward's quarters. (Fort Bowie Photo Album, Paper, 1858–1894, Museum of American West Collection, Autry National Center)

the regulations of the Army Par. 2286, require them to show to acting assistant surgeons the same respect and Military courtesy as to commissioned officers."[89]

The surgeon's chief assistant was the hospital steward, an enlisted man and member of the noncommissioned staff of the post. One steward, appointed from the ranks, or recruited directly from civilian life, was authorized for each garrison. In either instance the recommending officer had to ensure that the candidate was "temperate, honest, and in every way reliable, as well as sufficiently intelligent, and skilled in pharmacy, for the proper discharge of the responsible duties likely to be devolved upon him."[90] Although most stewards met those standards, there were exceptions. The steward serving at Camp Bowie in 1867, for instance, was a twenty-year army veteran described as "a strange man. Is a regular graduate of one of the best medical schools of England, is Irish by birth—but with the national failing for liquor, has thrown away his life."[91] Such a well-qualified and "kind-hearted old man," as the surgeon characterized him, nevertheless was quite an asset to the hospital. On another occasion in 1876, Hospital Steward Third-class

Louis Dahl became so intoxicated on duty that he neglected the patients and cursed the surgeon. In most instances, however, stewards were considered to be "excellent men, pharmacists, record keepers, property men, and general managers and wardmasters."[92]

The steward's medical duties included both filling prescriptions and extracting teeth, since the army had no regular dentists during the Indian Wars. A surgeon witnessing their work remembered the crude methods employed, though he seemed more concerned with his own annoyance than the patient's agony. "Observing their operations, I felt convinced that the ancient barbers did better work. . . . To see a steward shutting his eyes when he pulled, and listen for the expected crunch or snap of a crushed or broken molar . . . got on my nerves."[93] Traveling dentists sometimes visited military posts in the West, such as a Dr. Timberlake, who stopped at Camp Bowie during June 1874. Their services, nevertheless, were as uncertain as they were infrequent, thus the garrison was usually at the mercy of the steward for dental care.[94]

Prior to the creation of the Hospital Corps in 1887, stewards represented the only enlisted personnel assigned to the Medical Department. Consequently, surgeons relied exclusively on soldiers detailed from line companies to serve as hospital attendants. Serving as a nurse, known derogatorily as a "bedpan pusher," was not popular with the men. Besides disposing of waste, nurses were required to change bedding, give sponge baths, feed feeble men who were unable to eat in the hospital mess, police the hospital and the surrounding grounds, and, at times, sit up at night to monitor the condition of seriously ill men. The only advantage for those detailed was that they were excused from all other duty. "Very naturally," one surgeon wrote, "the company commanders were not anxious to see their best men detached from their organizations, and we generally were supplied with the worst they had and on them we had to depend for the nursing service, working and policing of our hospitals."[95] The difficulty in obtaining reliable men for hospital duty is reflected in the frustration expressed by Acting Assistant Surgeon Widney:

> My hospital cook, who is a kind of half-witted fellow, got some liquor in camp Saturday, and of course the result was he lost what little sense he had. I had to send him to the guard house and have him punished. . . . Between a crazy cook and a crazy patient it was rather too much. It is the craziest country I ever saw. Shall deem myself fortunate if I get out of it with sound wits left.[96]

Party of hunters from Fort Bowie, including an Oriental man, probably an officer's cook. (Fort Bowie Photo Album, Paper, 1858–1894, Museum of American
West Collection, Autry National Center)

From time to time, a hospital matron would be hired from among the
civilians at the post. The matron, usually the wife of a soldier or of the steward
himself, did the hospital laundry and assisted the surgeon on those relatively
rare occasions when females were admitted for treatment, usually childbirth.
Although matrons were by definition women, rare exceptions occurred at
Fort Bowie in 1881 and again in 1888 when Chinese men were hired in that
capacity, probably because women were at a premium.[97]

Beyond the treatment of patients, the surgeon occupied much of his time
with the issues relating to sanitation and food. He was constantly watchful

for unhealthful practices and conditions, paying particular attention to the toilets and the areas behind the company kitchens. Most privies, or sinks as the army called them, at Camp Bowie were simply earthen pits lined with adobe bricks. One or more sinks were located behind each barracks, as well as near the corrals, hospital, guardhouse, and other major buildings. Adobe or frame enclosures provided a degree of privacy for the users. Liquid waste either evaporated or leached into the soil, while dehydrated solid waste accumulated in the vaults. Details of soldiers, usually prisoners, refreshed the sinks periodically by shoveling in a layer of new soil, sometimes mixed with lime, over the excrement. When a pit became filled, it was covered with earth and a new one dug nearby.

Common sense should have dictated the placement of sinks, but in the nineteenth century it did not always. In 1885, the surgeon reported that a pit privy for a Third Cavalry saddler's quarters was not only full but was located "within a few feet of a gulch down which water runs in the rainy season. This stream runs into the water supply for animals at this post and close to the supply for men."[98] The surgeon wisely recommended that it be moved to another gulch, one that did not drain into the water supply. A few years earlier, when the surgeon suspected that Apache Spring might be the source of several cases of severe diarrhea, a detail assigned to dredge it out discovered "an accumulation of refuse matter such as tin cans, piece of blankets, raw hide, etc."[99] Those insoluble materials were suggestive of other pollutants that might have already decomposed in the drinking water.

The construction of a water system at Fort Bowie in the mid-1880s allowed the installation of "water closets" in the officers' quarters. The system operated by means of a steam-powered pump that forced water from Bear Spring, three-quarters of a mile to the east, to stone reservoirs above the post. Water flowed by gravity through iron distribution pipes to the various buildings. Nevertheless, drainage problems arose and it became necessary to install pipes to improve waste disposal. Not until the early 1890s were the troops accorded urinals flushed by running water, resulting in a significant improvement in sanitation. By the time the post was abandoned, all of the officers' quarters and the hospital boasted the unprecedented convenience of overhead flush toilets.[100]

At the opposite end of the spectrum, the surgeon attempted to preserve the military efficiency of the garrison by encouraging healthful habits among the men. Foremost among those was bathing. Even though most company commanders urged their men to bathe weekly, many men resisted because regular bathing was the exception among working-class Americans in the nineteenth century. Complicating the problem was the lack of bathing facilities at Camp Bowie. The post surgeon reported in 1878 that "there are not at present, nor is it believed there ever have been, any bathing facilities at this Post."[101] The men were thus on their own to make use of either Apache Spring or Bear Spring, neither of which was very convenient. A surgeon's request for tin bathtubs in 1885 was effectively denied when he was informed that such items had to be purchased from an existing account for building repairs that was already insufficient for those purposes.[102] Continuing efforts by the surgeons eventually resulted in the installation of bathtubs at each barracks and the hospital. Officers' houses were supplied with one tub each connected to hot water boilers in the kitchens. The surgeon proudly announced in 1893 that even though regulations did not require the men to bathe, most of them were taking advantage of the facilities.[103]

Perhaps the most important aspect of the surgeon's job, after treating the sick and injured, was trying to ensure that the soldiers were provided with adequate and nutritious food. A lack of fresh vegetables was a persistent problem at almost every post in the West, and frequently was the cause of scurvy outbreaks among soldiers. Limitations imposed by distance and transportation prevented central procurement of fresh produce by the Subsistence Department, therefore the army was compelled to rely on local sources of supply, at least in those regions where farming was practicable. The introduction of desiccated mixed vegetables, dried while fresh and formed into blocks under great pressure, provided the troops a marginal substitute, but the concoction was never very palatable or popular with the men.

The shortage of vegetables was more acute at Camp Bowie than at many stations because the high elevation, lack of water, and rocky soil prevented crops from being raised successfully within at least thirty miles of the post. Dr. Widney nonetheless came up with a creative alternative in 1867 when he introduced the troops to traditional Apache mescal, a dish prepared by slowly baking the bulbous root of the agave plant in a covered pit. "I intend to have it cooked regularly for the men," he wrote. "Think it will prevent scurvy from which they have suffered very much every winter before. . . . It will, to say the least, be a pleasant addition to their fare."[104] Whether the soldiers shared Widney's enthusiasm for mescal was not recorded.

In March 1869, a detachment of eight men under the command of Captain Homer J. Ripley marched to a budding agricultural settlement near the crossing of the San Pedro River to establish a post garden. Ripley's detachment remained there only a few days to complete the tilling and planting before returning to the post, leaving one man behind to tend the crops. The effort apparently failed during the first season, or it became too dangerous for gardeners to remain on San Pedro in the face of Apache raiding, because by December the post surgeon reported that the health of the men was beginning to suffer for want of vegetables.

The post commander purchased large quantities of onions, turnips, and beets at Silver City, New Mexico, in 1878.[105] The following summer the post commander sent his commissary officer, First Lieutenant William H. Winters, all the way to Mesilla on the Rio Grande to procure a supply of vegetables for the garrison. Although those measures served the needs of Fort Bowie for some months afterward, they did not pose a practical long-term solution. The next season, troops planted a garden at Ciénaga San Simon, a fairly dependable source of water about thirty miles northeast of the post. But, within only four months, the new garden also failed and was abandoned.[106]

Thereafter, the Fort Bowie garrison relied primarily on canned vegetables and fruits provided by the Subsistence Department, although the post purchased some produce from local farmers during the 1880s and the troops renewed their efforts to cultivate a garden from time to time.[107] Certainly, the completion of the Southern Pacific Railroad across Arizona opened the possibility of obtaining fresh vegetables from the Santa Cruz Valley, and perhaps even as far away as California.

The cradle-to-grave nature of the post surgeon's duties called for him to attend births, as well as act as coroner and undertaker. Some expectant mothers in the garrison went to the hospital to deliver, while others preferred to remain at their quarters. The hospital matron or some other experienced midwife on the post usually assisted with the delivery. No detailed record of births at Fort Bowie has been discovered, but preliminary research has identified at least fifteen children born at the post, two to civilian parents and the remainder to military personnel.[108]

Sudden death was commonplace on the frontier. Disease claimed the most lives, but the Fort Bowie cemetery contained an inordinate number of soldiers and civilians killed in violent encounters, either among themselves, or, more frequently, with Apaches. Although post burial registers vary somewhat, an 1883 record lists at least seventeen persons out of a total of sixty-one as "Killed by Apache Indians."[109] A number of others were unidentified or died from unknown causes, creating the possibility that an even higher percentage of deaths might be attributed to violence.

Fort Bowie cemetery as it appeared in 1886. The cemetery, started with the burial of California Volunteers killed in action in 1862, eventually contained the graves of several dozen soldiers and civilians, many of them killed by Indians in the vicinity of the post. (Arizona Historical Society/Tucson, AHS Photo Number 25610)

Officers accounted for a disproportionate number of deaths at Fort Bowie. Two commanding officers died in service at the post. First Lieutenant John C. Carroll was among those killed in action with Indians during the particularly turbulent years immediately after the Civil War. Major Eugene W. Crittenden, Fifth Cavalry, died of a sudden and severe heart attack in 1874 at age forty-three. In a related case, the wife of Post Commander W. M. McLellan died and was buried in the post cemetery. Mrs. George Macomber suffered particularly tragic losses when her two-year old son died in September 1868, followed just a year later by her husband, a lieutenant in the Thirty-second Infantry, who was killed accidentally while stacking hay. Two other young Sixth Cavalry lieutenants, J. A. Rucker and Austin Henely, died in a double drowning accident near Camp Supply at the southern end of the Chiricahua Mountains. The camp would later be renamed in honor of Rucker.

A military funeral was a simple and somber ceremony that began at the post. The procession was formed with the band or field musicians in the lead, followed by an escort composed of a specific number of men according to the rank of the deceased. Next came the clergy and the surgeon, just ahead of the coffin and six pallbearers. Arrayed in a column behind the remains were the mourners of the garrison, led by the soldier's company when the funeral was for an enlisted man. Any civilians who wished to attend brought up the rear.[110] An army wife described what happened once the procession reached the cemetery and the coffin was placed over the open grave.

> The adjutant of the battalion read the burial service, [the escort then fired three volleys] and the trumpeters stepped to the edge of the graves and sounded taps, which echoed sad and melancholy far over those parched and arid lands. My eyes filled with tears, for one of the soldiers was from our own company, and had been kind to me.[111]

The procession then reformed and marched back to the post to the strains of the "The Girl I Left Behind Me," or some other lively tune calculated to lift the spirits of the men.

Only a small proportion of frontier regulars found army life desirable enough to serve more than one enlistment. A few made a career of the army, but for most, especially those that had enlisted to experience the glamour of being a soldier, one five-year enlistment was ample time to convince them that civilian life was preferable. The realities of frontier army life with its rigid discipline, perpetual routine, isolation, and oppressive boredom, caused many men to desert before their terms expired. Those who stayed nonetheless looked forward to enlistment's end. Former Second Cavalryman Reginald A. Bradley undoubtedly summed up the feelings of many soldiers when he revealed years later: "I had come to New Mexico and Arizona to see what the wild, empty country of the Southwest was like, and by the time we left Fort Bowie, I had seen all I cared to."[112]

CHAPTER 11

The Whole Problem Is Changed: The Final Years

Both the army and the citizens of southern Arizona Territory breathed a sigh of relief with the exodus of the Central Chiricahuas and their Warm Springs relatives. By fall 1886, some three to four hundred Apaches had been relocated in what was to them the inhospitable environment of the southeastern United States. Only six tribes—the Mojave, Yuma, San Carlos, White Mountain, and Tonto Apaches—remained on the reservations and they were reported to be peaceful and prosperous following the departure of the more volatile Chiricahuas.[1]

The prominence that Fort Bowie experienced during the Sierra Madre and the Geronimo Campaigns, not to mention visits by such notables as Generals Sherman, Sheridan, Crook, and Miles, influenced the Quartermaster Department to provide additional funds for some of the improvements Major Beaumont had envisioned upon his arrival in 1884. An imposing, if not garish-looking, commanding officer's quarters, which Beaumont criticized for having "a great amount of useless ornamentation and . . . an absurd plan," had been completed at the south end of the parade ground in 1885. Nevertheless, by the time Beaumont took charge of Fort Bowie, work on the house was too far along for major changes to be made in its design. The bakery situated along the east side of the parade was never adequate for its intended job, a fact that became even more pronounced when the garrison swelled to over three hundred enlisted men at the height of the Geronimo campaign. During 1886 a new and larger bake house was constructed off the northwest corner of the parade, alongside the track of the old overland road. The old bakery, which had experienced a fire shortly

The elaborate 1884 commanding officer's quarters, described by Major E. B. Beaumont as having "a great amount of useless ornamentation and of an absurd plan." (Fort Bowie Photo Album, Paper, 1858–1894, Museum of American West Collection, Autry National Center)

before its replacement, was converted for use as a tailor shop where soldiers and officers could have uniforms fitted or specially made. Constructed some six hundred feet west of the new bakery, across the road, was a duplex quarters for two of the senior noncoms, the post ordnance sergeant, and the post quartermaster sergeant. The hospital steward, also a member of the post noncommissioned staff, was quartered in the former overland mail station at the foot of the hill. A sure indication that Fort Bowie was not the primitive station it once had been was the addition of a building in 1887 housing a steam engine and ice machine. Besides its use for operating the ice machine, the engine powered a large circular saw and pumped water for a system of water distribution pipes and hydrants throughout the post. Other amenities included a bathhouse for the cavalry and a library, where members of the garrison could read the latest newspapers and borrow books purchased through a post fund for that purpose.[2]

As military activity in Arizona subsided dramatically in the wake of Geronimo's final surrender, the army immediately scaled down its operations by discharging over four hundred Indian scouts and transferring the Eighth

Row of officers' quarters along the east side of the parade ground. Note the steep grade, necessitating the terraced arrangement. (Arizona Historical Society/Tucson, AHS Photo Number 25608)

Infantry to the Department of the Platte. The First Infantry was likewise sent to California, while other troops temporarily on duty in the territory returned to Texas. Consequently, the costs for supporting the troops in Arizona were reduced by $1 million within a year, a bittersweet pill for the territorial economy that had so long depended on the military as a mainstay of its economy. The department was expanded to include the southern portion of California, below the thirty-fifth parallel, with the headquarters moved from Prescott to Los Angeles, and New Mexico was once again made a district within the Department of Arizona.[3]

Although the last of the Apache wars had temporarily retarded the economic progress of the territory, Governor C. Meyer Zulick soon announced that the removal "has already had a beneficial effect on our industries."[4] National economic conditions had depressed the prices of precious metals from what they had been a few years previous, yet Zulick credited his territory with the annual production of over $6 million in silver, gold, copper, and other minerals. The proliferation of railroads finally made it possible to have ores crushed, assayed, and purchased at Tucson and at other points within Arizona, thus enhancing the profitability of mining. The governor also continued to extol the territory's temperate climate and its benefits to livestock grazing. Referring to the disastrous winter of 1886–87 on the northern plains, Zulick proclaimed that cattle raising "has thrived in Arizona while thousands of cattle in other and less favored localities have perished from cold, hunger, and thirst. . . . it has grown to such proportions that it is now one of the leading, most important, and flourishing industries of the Territory."[5] The numerous small cattle ranches that had sprung up in the vicinity of Fort Bowie testified to Zulick's statement.[6] Despite the governor's exaggerated claim that ninety thousand people inhabited the territory in 1887, a figure more than double the number at the beginning of the decade, the official census taken three years later revealed that the population increase, though substantial, was closer to twenty thousand.[7]

With the remaining Apaches on the reservations at San Carlos and White Mountain indisposed to create trouble, southern Arizona was suddenly a tamer place than it had ever been. Nevertheless, the ever-energetic Miles, reluctant to allow his troops to sink into the lethargy of garrison routine, saw the recent campaigns as the impetus for a new type of training. Conventional garrison duties were necessary, Miles reasoned, but they were merely preparatory to field service.

> While the principal object of stationing troops as at present in this department is to hold under surveillance and restraint the thousands of turbulent and well-armed Indians living on the various reservations, and to give prompt and effective protection to the scattered settlements, it is the duty of the military, even while enjoying a condition of perfect peace, to be at all times in condition to render the most effective service, and to make themselves thoroughly familiar with every section of the country in which, at some future time, they may have to campaign.[8]

Although Miles had never been the outspoken advocate for the use of scouts that Crook was, he nevertheless witnessed their value in the recent campaign. Still, he considered regular troops to be superior in general. Guides, in Miles's opinion, wasted more time than they saved, and they made the army entirely dependent on their services. On the other hand, if the troops could be trained to become intimately familiar with the regions surrounding their posts, the cavalry could get along without guides and scouts and could plan their own strategies. Miles was of the opinion that the principal advantage the Indians had over the army was that they had been raised as subsistence hunters, trained to move rapidly over familiar ground, observing their enemy, without being seen. Betraying a racial prejudice, the general expressed his view that "Possessing more intelligence, the same art can be acquired with careful practice by white men with almost, if not quite, equal success."[9]

Miles put his theory into practice by publishing a general order on August 20, 1887, directing that all the troops in the department were to consider themselves on field duty. Commanding officers were enjoined to school their men in all practical aspects of field service, at the same time suspending most conventional drills and nonessential duties at posts. Additionally, they were to establish outposts at key points and set up a communications network similar to the one Miles had used in the recent campaign. Even though the heliograph system had been dismantled shortly after Geronimo surrendered, Miles ordered it to be reestablished. All troops were to become intimately familiar with their operational areas.

Miles went a step further by designing practical field exercises that would be instructive as well as competitive. A "raiding party" would be designated at one post and charged with the objective of capturing another fort, provided they were able to evade patrols from the opposing forces sent out expressly to intercept them. The purpose of the exercise was to encourage initiative and ingenuity among the officers, while conditioning the troops and forcing them to familiarize themselves with the country. Miles did, however, establish certain rules for the maneuvers and authorized referees from the opposing side to accompany the raiders. If the aggressors were caught before they reached their objective, they were to go to the nearest post, where the commander would report his capture directly to Miles. Another detachment would then be ordered out to resume the exercise. Conversely, if the raiding party succeeded in capturing its objective, the men were granted a respite of ten days with no duty at that post before returning to their home station. A victory was credited when the aggressor force was able to approach within one thousand yards of the flagstaff without being detected. All of the troops were to take the field in ultralight marching order, leaving behind sabers, revolvers, superfluous horse equipment, and anything else that might compromise speed and endurance.[10]

Miles's maneuvers spanned a period of three months during fall 1887 and involved most of the troops in the southern districts of Arizona and New Mexico. The exercises were moderately effective in providing both officers and troops with realistic field experience against a semi-conventional foe. Progressive as such training was, Miles surely knew that the Apaches followed no rules and, having been conditioned to the local environment from childhood, possessed unsurpassed physical endurance and ability to cross vast distances over terrain that defied regular troops. The raids led by Chato and Ulzana bore mute testimony to their stamina and cunning.

So-called guard gate spanning the interval between the granary and the subsis-
tence storehouse, considered to be the main entrance to Fort Bowie. (Fort
Bowie Photo Album, Paper, 1858–1894, Museum of American West Collection,
Autry National Center)

Nevertheless, of ten practice forays conducted by the cavalry, five resulted
in the raiders being overtaken and captured, while on the other occasions
the raiders eluded their pursuers only to be ambushed by defenders lying
in wait at the posts.

Second Lieutenant Carter P. Johnson, a former enlisted man who had
obtained a commission in 1876, led one "raid" that particularly impressed
Miles. Leaving Fort Grant with a party of Tenth Cavalrymen, Johnson was
expected to march directly for Fort Lowell. However, he struck out northwest,
marching at night, then utterly vanished for three weeks. When the patrols
had given up trying to find him, Johnson came out of hiding, circled west
through Tucson and proceeded southeast to threaten Fort Huachuca. Then,
he feinted west again, decoying the commanding officer there to send out
patrols in the wrong direction, while he and his twenty-one "buffalo soldiers"
suddenly countermarched cross-country to surprise and capture Fort Bowie
at 12 o'clock noon on October 31. Johnson had slipped through all of the
post's defenses, much to the chagrin of the Ninth Infantrymen manning
picket posts on the surrounding hills and the troopers of the Fourth Cavalry
patrolling the various approaches to the fort. In accordance with the rules,

Johnson's detachment enjoyed a ten-day furlough before continuing their sortie. Just after leaving Fort Bowie, the shrewd lieutenant again did the unexpected by infiltrating the defenses of Fort Huachuca and capturing its six-company garrison. [11]

Despite their benefits, the innovative field exercises inaugurated by Miles were cancelled after he left the department late in 1888. The rounding up of the last organized band of free-roaming hostile Indians in the United States made it clear to the army that Indian campaigning was a thing of the past. In the late 1880s, the army inaugurated "camps of instruction" in which the scattered elements of regiments were brought together, sometimes for the first time since the Civil War, for training in battalion and regimental tactics. The renewed emphasis on conventional warfare reflected the dawn of a renaissance that was to eventually transform the army from the constabulary role it had assumed into a force for national defense.

With the old renegade bands broken up and living a continent away, it seemed highly unlikely that U.S. troops would again have to contend with a significant Apache outbreak. However, an incident at San Carlos in spring 1887 had rekindled old fears among the populace of Arizona. One of Crook's formerly loyal scouts, known among whites as the Apache Kid, or simply as the Kid, joined in a tizwin drunk on the reservation and, in a stupor, recalled an old grudge against another Apache living on Arivaipa Creek. The explosive combination of smoldering animosities and tizwin influenced the Kid, four other scouts, and some friends to ride to the man's house and murder him. On their return to the reservation, they found Captain Francis E. Pierce, the agent, awaiting them. Pierce had them arrested, but as the prisoners were being placed in the guardhouse, someone opened fire, severely wounding renowned guide Al Sieber standing nearby.

Later that month, the Kid and his cohorts were tried by court-martial, found guilty and sentenced to life imprisonment at Fort Leavenworth. The outlaws were still being held in the guardhouse at San Carlos several months later when word came that they were to be confined at the federal prison on Alcatraz Island in San Francisco Bay, rather than at Fort Leavenworth. They were there only a few months before Secretary of War William C. Endicott had the judge advocate general's department review their cases, found that the evidence did not support the court's findings, and remitted the balance of the sentences. Their dishonorable discharges from the army stood, however.

The story might have ended there had it not been for a legal twist of fate when the Supreme Court rendered a decision in April 1889 freeing reservation

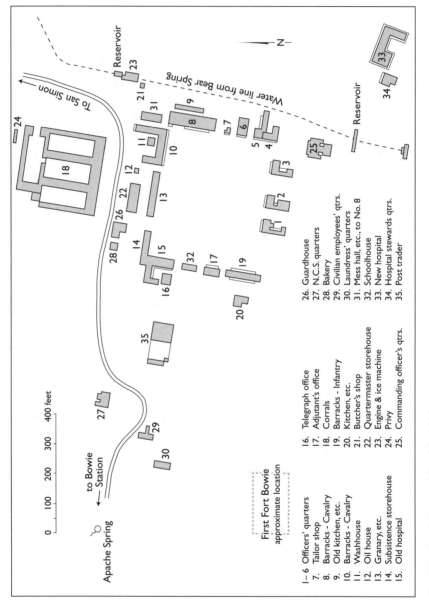

0   100   200   300   400 feet

Apache Spring

to Bowie
Station

First Fort Bowie
approximate location

1-6 Officers' quarters
7.   Tailor shop
8.   Barracks - Cavalry
9.   Old kitchen, etc.
10. Barracks - Cavalry
11. Washhouse
12. Oil house
13. Granary, etc.
14. Subsistence storehouse
15. Old hospital

16. Telegraph office
17. Adjutant's office
18. Corrals
19. Barracks - Infantry
20. Kitchen, etc.
21. Butcher's shop
22. Quartermaster storehouse
23. Engine & ice machine
24. Privy
25. Commanding officer's qtrs.

26. Guardhouse
27. N.C.S. quarters
28. Bakery
29. Civilian employees' qtrs.
30. Laundress' quarters
31. Mess hall, etc., to No. 8
32. Schoolhouse
33. New hospital
34. Hospital stewards qtrs.
35. Post trader

To San Simon

Reservoir

Water line from Bear Spring

Reservoir

N

Fort Bowie, Arizona, May 20, 1889

Apache Kid (top row, second from right) and companions, 1888. (Arizona Historical Society/Tucson, AHS Photo Number 4542)

Indians sentenced by the regular Federal District Courts of Arizona. The ruling effectively nullified the Kid's first trial, thus exposing him to indictment and retrial by a territorial grand jury. Arizonans were never known to be lenient when it came to Apaches, so it came as no surprise when the Kid was found guilty a second time and ordered to spend seven years in the hell-hole known as Yuma Prison. But on November 2, as Sheriff Glenn Reynolds and his deputy were escorting the prisoners through the Pinal Mountains southwest of Globe, the Kid and the others saw their chance to escape. They swiftly overwhelmed and murdered Reynolds before dashing off into the wilderness.[12]

The Apache Kid's escape marked the beginning of an Arizona legend. The territorial newspapers were only too happy to sound the alarm of another Apache outbreak, even if it involved only a few individuals. Indian scouts and regular troops were immediately dispatched from Forts Grant and Apache in an attempt to recapture the Kid, but they found no trace of him. Colonel Benjamin H. Grierson, who succeeded Miles in November 1889 shortly after the Kid's disappearance, took a lesson from his predecessor by directing that some seventy-five of the outlaw's relatives and other sympathizers be removed from the reservation to deprive the Kid and his gang of any aid.

A guard escorted the Indians to Fort Union, New Mexico, where they were held for several months until that post was abandoned.[13]

Meantime, three of the fugitives were killed, leaving only the Kid and three companions of the original party on the loose. Grierson kept units in the field, chasing them from mountain range to mountain range, in a relentless endeavor to deny them rest and supplies. Although the Apache Kid's escapades were less serious than the press made them out to be, his notoriety provided a convenient scapegoat for almost every unexplained murder in southeastern Arizona. When Robert Hardie, a Tombstone resident, was ambushed and killed near Rucker Canyon in spring 1890, the citizens of that mining community petitioned the president with a familiar plea to provide more protection for the region. Grierson, ever a master of dry wit, remarked: "It appeared from that remarkable manifesto that the lives of all the people of Arizona were endangered by murderous, bloodthirsty Apaches."[14] First Lieutenant Hugh J. McGrath and forty men of C Troop, Fourth Cavalry, rode out of Fort Bowie on May 27 to search the surrounding area, but found no signs of Indians. Sonoran troops likewise threw out a screen of cavalry just south of the border, but they too saw nothing of the outlaws. Hardie's body, strangely enough, lay where it fell for two days before friends recovered the remains and took them to Tombstone. A subsequent examination disclosed that not only was the body free of mutilation, it remained fully clothed with money and other items still in the pockets. The single bullet hole in Hardie's corpse further suggested that someone other than Indians had waylaid him.[15]

Hardie's murder was just one of many attempts to create an "Indian scare" in the vicinity of Fort Bowie. Soon afterward a rancher named Reynolds, living near Rucker Canyon, added to the excitement by claiming that Indians had attempted to steal his horses. However, his conflicting statements convinced Lieutenant Fuller, who had been sent to investigate the incident, that the rancher had fabricated the story. Another report of cattle having been killed by Indians near old Camp Crittenden also proved to be false. Grierson covered himself by directing the commanding officers at Forts Bowie and Huachuca to patrol the border area, though he confided that the rumors were "entirely groundless, gotten up by malicious persons bent upon their favorite scheme of calling upon the Government for assistance, with the design of having the country occupied by troops so they can be better able to dispose of their products at high rates."[16]

It was the same old game the residents of southern Arizona had played for years. The resurgence of attempts to justify a military presence in the

Reflecting changing times, four Apache regulars of Company I, Tenth Infantry, pose at their quarters, Fort Bowie. (Fort Bowie Photo Album, Paper, 1858–1894, Museum of American West Collection, Autry National Center)

region was doubtless sparked by recent reports that the army might abandon several posts in the territory. It was something, in fact, that had been considered for several years. As early as 1882, Sherman had expressed his concern with the proliferation of army posts across the West:

> For a hundred years we have been sweeping across the continent with a skirmish line, building a post here and another there, to be abandoned next year for another line, and so on. Now we are across, and have railroads everywhere, so that the whole problem is changed; and I advise the honorable Secretary of War to go to Congress with a plan that will approximate permanency, instead of as heretofore meeting specific temporary wants by special appropriations, often in the interest of private parties.[17]

The recent growth of the railroad, Sherman observed, simplified military logistics. Moreover, the Indians had been subjugated, and unbroken white settlement across the trans-Mississippi had so blurred the frontier that a line could no longer be defined. Looking to the future needs of the nation, Sherman advocated a reduction in the number of forts and the consolidation of troops near cities where supply and transportation would be facilitated. He even submitted a long list of those posts he considered to be obsolete for military purposes—Fort Bowie among them.[18] Two years later, the secretary of war responded by setting the consolidation into motion, directing that those excess posts be turned over to the Interior Department for final disposition.[19] The Apache campaigns of the mid-1880s intervened just in time to prevent Fort Bowie and other Arizona posts from being axed, but by 1889 Grierson, too, saw no further need to maintain garrisons at Grant, Lowell, Verde, McDowell, Thomas, and Mojave. He reasoned that all of those posts were old and in poor repair; any further expense on them could not be justified.

> The frontier on the plains has almost disappeared by reason of the operations of the army which opened the way for the building of railroads and made possible the grand invasion of the people, all plainly indicate that the time has come when a large number of posts now occupied by troops can with safety and propriety be abandoned as a matter of economy and means of improving the discipline and efficiency of the Army.[20]

Yet Grierson exempted the post at Apache Pass because

> All past experience shows that during the Indian troubles Fort Bowie has been the center of operations, and its importance must necessarily continue in view of its situation in the mountain range through or near which the Indians are apt to travel in going into or returning from Mexico.[21]

Neither could he ignore the fact that the army had spent $15,000 on building repairs and improvements at Fort Bowie during the past year. Included among those improvements were a new hospital, a schoolhouse, an ammunition magazine, and a gun shed to protect the few artillery pieces from exposure to the elements. An annex a short distance from the hospital served as quarters for the hospital steward, replacing the more distant old mail station that had been adapted previously for that purpose.

The condition of the barracks was a perennial problem at Fort Bowie. During the height of the Apache campaigns of the 1880s, the quarters were woefully insufficient for the number of troops stationed at the post. Many times elements of the garrison were obligated to live in tents on the parade ground. Beaumont's repeated attempts to justify the erection of additional

Fort Bowie as it appeared just prior to its abandonment in 1894. (Arizona Historical Society/Tucson, AHS Photo Number 100,797)

quarters for the men had been singularly unsuccessful. The capture of Geronimo subsequently caused a reduction in the size of the garrison, a situation that effectively undermined Beamont's argument to build additional housing. The barracks, nevertheless, had fallen into disrepair by that time and had always suffered from inadequate ventilation. The infantry barracks, in fact, was never finished and had no ceiling. Summer heat and overcrowding drove many of the men to sleep outdoors or in other nearby buildings.[22]

Major Beaumont was able to justify funds to improve the water system with larger diameter pipe that would transport an increased volume of water from Bear Spring to the post. Additional water was required to supply the bathhouses that had been constructed for the men, as well as the trees Beaumont had had planted around the officers' quarters.

A post canteen, where the enlisted men could buy beer, sandwiches, and other light foods during their off-duty time also was added in 1890. The canteen was intended to provide a more wholesome recreational facility than the several "whiskey ranches" that had sprung up just beyond the limits of the military reservation.[23]

Fort Bowie, however, had not assumed the staid existence of many other western forts whose importance had waned. Aside from the modest amenities added during the late 1880s, among them a tennis court, it remained a rawboned, desolate post with little appeal for the men stationed there. One trooper of the Fourth Cavalry, a unit that had been relegated to the post for the previous six years, probably spoke for many of his comrades upon learning that they were at last being transferred to California and Washington Territory in June 1890: "We were not sorry to leave isolated, dry, lonely Fort Bowie; to march to the railroad lines and take the cars for a change of station more to the liking of the restless young men of C Troop, 4th Cavalry."[24]

Despite the abandonment of several other posts in the territory during 1890 and 1891, Fort Bowie managed to justify its existence because of continuing, albeit minor, incidents of violence in the region.[25] On several occasions, Second Cavalry detachments were sent out to investigate rumors that hostile Indians had been seen in the area between the international border and the southern extremity of the Chiricahua Mountains. None of those reports were found to have much, if any, foundation, though the army could not ignore that a few holdout renegades probably still lurked in the Sierra Madre. However, most of the sightings were actually Mexican bandits and other lawless elements frequenting the area, or simply were the product of the overactive imaginations of residents anxious to keep army payrolls in the territory.[26] As late as 1891, the department commander described Fort Bowie as being "well situated for the work required of it. . . . the quarters for officers and enlisted men are set upon the sides of the hills, leaving the small parade ground a severe slope. The drill ground is a mile and a half from the post."[27]

The Apache Kid continued to menace the region from time to time, though the phantom outlaw's reputation had grown considerably larger than reality. For the most part, he remained in the mountains bordering the White Mountain Reservation, but the citizens of Arizona were ever ready to believe that he was ranging all over the southern portion of the territory. Although the Kid probably did murder an Apache woman on the reservation, along with a young boy near Florence in May 1892, his connection with other crimes in the region was less certain. Two white men were murdered south of Separ, New Mexico, in August, and teamster Florentine Monger was shot from ambush near Moore's Ranch, south of Fort Bowie, two months later. About the same time, a Mr. Daniels was killed near Pinery Canyon. Cavalry patrols dutifully responded to cries of "hostile Apaches" being on the loose, yet no evidence was found linking those deaths to Indians.[28]

Citizens loudly censured the army for not taking sufficient action to stop the Kid's activities, but Captain Lewis Johnson, the agent at San Carlos, doubted "whether anything but chance, accident, or treachery will effect his capture," despite the best efforts of the troops and the Indian Police. Johnson got to the heart of the matter with the reminder that "this man, though Indian by race is in reality a fugitive from civil justice and not a so-called 'renegade,' he having, while under sentence of imprisonment en route to the Territorial prison at Yuma, escaped with other Indian convicts from a sheriff and deputy."[29]

The army simply absolved itself of any responsibility by taking the position that the Apache Kid was not a military problem, which indeed he was not; rather, he was a matter for civil authorities. The territorial government subsequently placed a $5,000 reward on the Kid, dead or alive, though it was never claimed.[30]

By 1892, the army could hardly justify the expense of maintaining a garrison at Fort Bowie. Department commander Alexander McDowell McCook expressed the obvious when he wrote: "During the times of peace now enjoyed by the Territory of Arizona, Bowie as a military post ceases to be of such military importance, and could be abandoned when proper shelter can be made for its garrison at other posts in the department."[31] No action was taken on his suggestion, however, probably because of the persistent, though false, rumors of Indian raids in the area. Although the army was aware that a few renegade Chiricahuas remained in Mexico, McCook was of the opinion that the continued occupation of Fort Bowie, one of only nine posts left in the territory, would have no effect on the situation one way or the other. In his annual report for 1893, he recommended that the garrison be withdrawn by the end of November.

While the *Denver Post* heralded McCook's position with great enthusiasm, he failed to take into account the proclivity of Arizona's citizens to suckle the government nipple. The general's letter successfully made its way up the chain of command all the way to the desk of Acting Secretary of War L. A. Grant, who said he would approve closing the post so long as there were no serious objections. But Arizona Governor L. C. Hughes did object. Coincidentally, the governor was in Washington at the very time the recommendation reached Grant's office. Hughes lodged a protest the very next day, using the now threadbare argument that Fort Bowie was situated on the trail the Apaches traditionally used in their movements between San Carlos and Mexico. Ignoring the reality that the Chiricahuas had been banished from Arizona six years earlier, he could not resist adding that the post was adjacent to the old Cochise stronghold in the Dragoon Mountains, though anyone familiar with the area knew that its use as an Indian hideout had long since passed. Were the troops withdrawn from the post, Hughes contended, the Apache Kid would face no opposition in moving freely through the country. Grant, who accepted Hughes's response at face value, apparently failed to realize that the governor's concern was based on the exaggerated threat posed by a solitary outlaw, who just happened to be an Indian. What the governor knew full well, but did not reveal, was that the Kid was the responsibility of his very own territorial government![32]

McCook was not content to allow the fate of Fort Bowie be settled so easily. On October 21 he countered the governor's comments, informing his superiors that no reports concerning the Apache Kid had been received during the previous six months, and in view of that the post should be abandoned immediately. But the issue had gotten into the political arena and it seemed expedient for the secretary of war to drop the matter, for the moment anyway. The adjutant general telegraphed McCook on November 2 that the secretary was suspending any immediate action on his recommendation.[33]

Governor Hughes and the citizens of southeastern Arizona were keenly aware that another of their golden geese was in grave danger of extinction.

View looking northeast across the parade ground, circa 1893. Note the thriving trees, street lamp, and fire hydrant, unheard-of amenities at Fort Bowie in earlier years. (Fort Bowie Photo Album, Paper, 1858–1894, Museum of American West Collection, Autry National Center)

As soon as he arrived back at Prescott, Hughes instigated a torrent of petitions and affidavits from residents enumerating supposed Indian depredations in the vicinity of the fort.[34] McCook, however, was just as determined to rid the army of what he viewed as just another expensive asset that had no compensating value. The Kid, he stated, had not committed any depredations during the past sixteen months, and he had it on reliable authority that the Kid had been living in the Sierra Madre during that period. Dismissing the letters submitted by the Arizonans, McCook repeated his desire to abandon the place, adding candidly that "Fort Bowie has been a hospice for the people of that district of Arizona; the medical officers and hospital have been much in demand."[35] General of the Army John M. Schofield, admitting that McCook was probably correct, nevertheless bowed to political pressures by cautioning that it would cost little to keep the troops there awhile longer in order to appease the governor.

Ironically, the final demise of Fort Bowie hung on the very factor that had led to its establishment a quarter of a century earlier—water. When Apache Spring became threatened with pollution from waste and sewage from the post in 1884, Major Beaumont had designed and installed a system to convey water from somewhat more distant Bear Spring instead. The same drought that decimated the cattle industry in southeastern Arizona during the early 1890s also impacted Fort Bowie. By that time, the increased size of the garrison, and the need for better fire protection, demanded a more ample water supply, but by 1890 even the output from Bear Spring was diminishing. Post commanders were forced to impose conservation measures on the garrison, including the curtailment of irrigating lawns and trees, and restricting bathing. Within another year, the troops had to resort to hauling water in wagons from Apache Spring, but because of the danger of pollution, all drinking water from that source had to be boiled. Unexpectedly heavy rains during late summer and fall 1893 temporarily replenished the stone reservoirs that Beaumont had constructed years earlier, yet they had little effect in rejuvenating the two major springs. Several months later, Major Thomas McGregor notified McCook that if water could not be found, the post would have to be abandoned whether the citizens liked it or not. The plainspoken McGregor scoffed that, "the politicians of Arizona don't want the Post abandoned, because they could not longer sell hay to it at $100 a ton."[36] Only too aware of political realities, and Schofield's position on the matter, McCook directed McGregor to bend every effort to secure water. So, following the old adage about desperate times calling for desperate measures, McGregor had some of his men lay a charge of blasting powder in the rocks near Bear Spring in hope of jarring something loose. The resulting explosion, according to one witness, "blew the bottom out of a mountain, finding water quite as surprisingly as Moses did."[37]

By late summer 1894, the secretary of war could no longer justify the retention of Fort Bowie as an active post, public opposition notwithstanding. The outlawry occurring in the region by that time was a civil matter not requiring military involvement, nor in fact was it legal for the army to act in the capacity of a posse comitatus. Convinced that the interests of the people of Arizona had been served to every extent possible, Army Headquarters issued orders in September transferring the remaining two troops of the Second Cavalry from Fort Bowie to Fort Logan, Colorado, just south of Denver.[38]

On October 17, without any fanfare, the last troops of the garrison prepared to march out of the pass to board a train at Bowie Station. In that dusty column, appropriately, were nine women and children, the last of scores of army dependents who had endured the hardships and deprivations of frontier life to be with their soldier-husbands at Apache Pass. Sadly, this was not a routine change of station, when some would stay behind and

Troop of the Second Cavalry marching out of Fort Bowie in the early 1890s. The rambling post trader's store, viewed from the rear, dominates the background. (Arizona Historical Society/Tucson, AHS Photo Number 70127)

newcomers would soon arrive to perpetuate the regularity of garrison life. As that last cavalcade was forming to leave the post, visiting novelist Owen Wister observed that even then the finality of the event was not fully comprehended by some:

> Remember the last morning when the troops left, Mrs. Fowler watering her chrysanthemums that hereafter would have no mistress. Also the appealing looks of pet dogs begging not to be left behind. Also the gradual dismay of cows, cats, and all domestic animals that were left behind . . . . [39]

A trumpet sounding "forward' for the last time, the troops were soon over the rim and out of sight. With that final exodus, free-roaming Chiricahua Apaches and the blue-coated soldiers who had come to conquer them passed into history and became the stuff of legend. And Apache Pass, for the first time in more than three decades, lay deserted. No more would it echo with the beating of Apache drums, the braying of mail-coach mules, or the shrill strains of cavalry trumpets. Once again, only the gurgling of Apache Spring intruded on the stillness.

Fort Bowie represented the quintessential frontier army post. Tucked high in the scenic Chiricahua Mountain range, it remained a primitive, isolated station throughout its military occupancy. Yet, its contributions were disproportionately significant to its small size. For three decades, the Fort Bowie garrison stood watch over Apache Pass, which, ironically, had been the scene of the infamous Bascom Affair that set the stage for hostilities between the Americans and the Chiricahua Apaches thereafter. The pass was also the scene of a most uncharacteristic pitched battle between the Apaches and U.S. troops to control the spring, an event that prompted the establishment of Fort Bowie at that location.

Nevertheless, the Chiricahuas demonstrated time and again that the soldiers did not particularly intimidate them, as they audaciously attacked mail carriers, coaches, travelers, and the soldiers themselves, sometimes within sight of the garrison. The proliferation of headboards in the post cemetery bearing the inscription "Killed by Indians" was mute testimony to Fort Bowie's status as a "combat" post. Although a similar claim might be made for other forts in the West, no other remained within the immediate zone of conflict for so long as did Fort Bowie.

The influence exerted by Fort Bowie eventually extended over a broad region of southeastern Arizona. It was first and foremost a cavalry post, with elements of seven of the army's ten regiments serving there at one time or another. Troops from its garrison patrolled a vast area of southeastern Arizona, in a seemingly vain attempt to thwart Apache raiding back and forth across the international border. That war of attrition, frustrating by its very nature, nevertheless exacted an irreversible toll on the Apaches, convincing them either to live on reservations or to seek refuge in the remoteness of the Sierra Madre in Mexico. At the same time, the presence of Fort Bowie gradually encouraged white settlement in the region, attracting ranchers to the immediate vicinity of the post and farmers to the San Simon and San Pedro valleys. The completion of the long-anticipated southern transcontinental railroad to the Pacific, facilitated in no small measure by troops in southern Arizona, accelerated economic development of the territory on a broad scale. At last, the heavy machinery necessary for profitable mining could be brought in, while cattle and agricultural produce could be exported to market. Moreover, by facilitating the mobility of troops and supplies, the railroad became an irresistible factor in bringing an end to free-roaming Indian life. Fort Bowie's situation near the line of the Southern Pacific, combined with its key position in the heart of the Chiricahua domain, made the post a natural choice as the base of operations for major expeditions launched by General George Crook and his successor, Nelson A. Miles, in the finale of Apache resistance. Fittingly, both of the legendary Chiricahua leaders, Cochise and later Geronimo, surrendered near Fort Bowie in 1872 and 1886, respectively. Indeed, Fort Bowie witnessed the last active campaigning against previously unconquered Indians within U.S. territory, thus ending the Indian Wars.

Epilogue

Following the departure of the garrison, First Lieutenant Herbert H. Sargent and a handful of soldiers lingered behind for a few days to complete the shipping or disposal of a vast amount of property that had accumulated at the fort during the army's occupancy. Shortly thereafter, a civilian caretaker was appointed, ostensibly to prevent trespassing and civilian looting of the deserted buildings, though the buildings were ravaged nonetheless. The military reservation was transferred to the General Land Office of the Department of the Interior on November 14, 1894, pending final disposition of the property. The lands were eventually sold at public auction on June 20, 1911, for an average price of $1.77 per acre and were thereafter used for grazing cattle.[1]

In 1964, influenced largely by the research and recommendations of National Park Service historian Robert M. Utley, Congress recognized the historical significance of Fort Bowie by establishing it as a unit of the National Park System. Regrettably, the lumber in the buildings had long since been salvaged by local residents, exposing the adobe walls to the elements and causing most of the structures to erode into shapeless mounds of earth. Nevertheless, the natural surroundings at Fort Bowie National Historic Site are little changed from their appearance during historical times and the ruins contribute in no small measure to the ghostliness of the scene. It is a contemplative place—one of the few publicly accessible frontier forts where, with little imagination, visitors can mentally transport themselves back to that bygone era, for it is still remote, wild, and lonely.

Fort Bowie Commanding Officers

Maj. Theodore A. Coult, California Volunteers, July–August 1862

Capt. Hugh L. Hinds, Fifth California Infantry, September–December 1862

lst Lt. John F. Qualey, Fifth California Infantry, January–April 1863

Capt. Thomas T. Tidball, Fifth California Infantry, May 1863–January 1864

1st Lt. Benjamin F. Bayley, Fifth California Infantry, February 1864

Capt. Thomas T. Tidball, Fifth California Infantry, March–April 1864

1st Lt. Benjamin F. Bayley, Fifth California Infantry, May 1864

Capt. Thomas T. Tidball, Fifth California Infantry, June 1864

Capt. Nicolas Quintana, First New Mexico Infantry, July 1864

Capt. Thomas T. Tidball, Fifth California Infantry, August 1864

Capt. N. Quintana, First New Mexico Infantry, September–December 1864

Lt. Col. Clarence E. Bennett, First. California Cavalry, January–April 1865

2nd Lt. Thomas Caghlan, First New Mexico Infantry, May–June 1865

Capt. John L. Merriam, First California Cavalry, July 1865

Maj. James Gorman, First California Cavalry, August 1865–March 1866

1st Lt. James Mann, First New Mexico Infantry, April 1866

Capt. William H. Brown, Fourteenth U.S. Infantry, May 1866

Capt. Jonathan B. Hager, Fourteenth U.S. Infantry, June–July 1866

1st Lt. George L. Choisy, Fourteenth U.S. Infantry, August–September 1866

2nd Lt. John R. Eschenberg, Fourteenth U.S. Infantry, October 1866– April 1867

1st Lt. John C. Carroll, Thirty-second U.S. Infantry, May–Oct. 1867 (KIA 11/5/67)

1st Lt. Robert Pollock, Thirty-second U.S. Infantry, November 1867– January 1868

Capt. Homer J. Ripley, Thirty-second U.S. Infantry, February–August 1868

1st Lt. George Macomber, Thirty-second U.S. Infantry, September 1868

Capt. Homer J. Ripley, Thirty-second U.S. Infantry, October 1868–June 1869

Capt. Reuben F. Bernard, First U.S. Cavalry, July–August 1869

Capt. Thomas S. Dunn, Twenty-first U.S. Infantry, September 1869–July 1870

Capt. Reuben F. Bernard, First U.S. Cavalry, August 1870–February 1871

Maj. Andrew W. Evans, Third U.S. Cavalry, March–September 1871

Capt. Harry M. Smith, Twenty-first U.S. Infantry, October 1871- March 1872

Capt. Joseph T. Haskell, Twenty-third U.S. Infantry, April–June 1872

Capt. Samuel S. Sumner, Fifth U.S. Cavalry, July 1872

2nd Lt. Henry C. Johnson, Twenty-third U.S. Infantry, August 1872

Capt. Samuel S. Sumner, Fifth U.S. Cavalry, September 1872–September 1873

Maj. Eugene W. Crittenden, Fifth U.S. Cavalry, October 1873–February 1874

Capt. Samuel S. Sumner, Fifth U.S. Cavalry, March 1874

Capt. Joseph T. Haskell, Twenty-third U.S. Infantry, April 1874

Capt. Samuel S. Sumner, Fifth U.S. Cavalry, May–June 1874

Major Eugene W. Crittenden, Twenty-third U.S. Infantry, July 1874

Capt. Samuel S. Sumner, Fifth U.S. Cavalry, August 1874–March 1875

1st Lt. Calpraith P. Rodgers, Fifth U.S. Cavalry, April–June 1875

1st Lt. William M. Wallace, Sixth U.S. Cavalry, July–September 1875

Capt. Curwen B. McLellan, Sixth U.S. Cavalry, November 1875–March 1877

1st Lt. William M. Wallace, Sixth U.S. Cavalry, April 1877–March 1878

Capt. Curwen B. McLellan, Sixth U.S. Cavalry, April–September 1878

Capt. Daniel Madden, Sixth U.S. Cavalry, October–November 1878

Capt. Curwen B. McLellan, Sixth U.S. Cavalry, December 1878–April 1879

Capt. Daniel Madden, Sixth U.S. Cavalry, May 1879

Capt. Curwen B. McLellan, Sixth U.S. Cavalry, June–July 1879

2nd Lt. Timothy A. Touey, Sixth U.S. Cavalry, August 1879

Maj. Daniel Perry, Sixth U.S. Cavalry, September–December 1879

1st Lt. Louis A. Craig, Sixth U.S. Cavalry, January 1880

Capt. Curwen B. McLellan, Sixth U.S. Cavalry, February 1880

Maj. Daniel Perry, Sixth U.S. Cavalry, March–April 1880

Capt. Daniel Madden, Sixth U.S. Cavalry, May–June 1880

Capt. Curwen B. McLellan, Sixth U.S. Cavalry, July–September 1880

1st Lt. Louis A. Craig, Sixth U.S. Cavalry, October 1880

Capt. Curwen B. McLellan, Sixth U.S. Cavalry, November 1880–June 1881

Capt. William A. Rafferty, Sixth U.S. Cavalry, July–August 1881

Capt. David J. Craigie, Twelfth U.S. Infantry, September 1881

Capt. Reuben F. Bernard, First U.S. Cavalry, October 1881

Maj. George B. Sanford, First U.S. Cavalry, November–December 1881

Capt. Moses Harris, First U.S. Cavalry, January 1882

Capt. William A. Rafferty, Sixth U.S. Cavalry, February–March 1882

1st Lt. William L. Geary, Twelfth U.S. Infantry, April–May 1882

Capt. William A. Rafferty, Sixth U.S. Cavalry, June 1882–June 1883

1st Lt. George K. Hunter, Third U.S. Cavalry, July–August 1883

Capt. Leopold O. Parker, First U.S. Infantry, September–October 1883

Capt. William A. Rafferty, Sixth U.S. Cavalry, November 1883

1st Lt. George K. Hunter, Third U.S. Cavalry, December 1883

Capt. William A. Rafferty, Sixth U.S. Cavalry, January 1884

Maj. Daniel Perry, Sixth U.S. Cavalry, February–May 1884

Maj. Eugene B. Beaumont, Fourth U.S. Cavalry, June 1884–February 1885

Capt. William A. Thompson, Fourth U.S. Cavalry, March 1885

Maj. Eugene B. Beaumont, Fourth U.S. Cavalry, April–October 1885

Capt. Matthew Markland, First U.S. Infantry, November–December 1885

Maj. Eugene B. Beaumont, Fourth U.S. Cavalry, January–June 1886

Capt. Theodore A. Baldwin, Tenth U.S. Cavalry, July 1886

Capt. Folliot A. Whitney, Eighth U.S. Infantry, August 1886

Maj. Eugene B. Beaumont, Fourth Cavalry, September–November 1886

Capt. William A. Thompson, Fourth U.S. Cavalry, December 1886

Capt. Otho W. Budd, Fourth U.S. Cavalry, January 1887

Maj. Eugene B. Beaumont, Fourth U.S. Cavalry, February–March 1887

Capt. Otho W. Budd, Fourth U.S. Cavalry, April 1887

Maj. Eugene B. Beaumont, Fourth U.S. Cavalry, May–November 1887

Capt. Alfred Morton, Ninth U.S. Infantry, December 1887–January 1888

Maj. Eugene B. Beaumont, Fourth U.S. Cavalry, February–April 1888

Capt. Alfred Morton, Ninth U.S. Infantry, May 1888

Maj. Eugene B. Beaumont, Fourth U.S. Cavalry, June–November 1888

Maj. Henry E. Noyes, Fourth U.S. Cavalry, December 1888–August 1889

1st Lt. William Black, Twenty-fourth U.S. Infantry, September 1889

Maj. Henry E. Noyes, Fourth U.S. Cavalry, October 1889–May 1890

Maj. Thomas McGregor, Second U.S. Cavalry, June 1890–April 1891

Capt. Daniel C. Person, Second U.S. Cavalry, May 1891

Maj. Thomas McGregor, Second U.S. Cavalry, June 1891–April 1892

Capt. James N. Allison, Second U.S. Cavalry, May–June 1892

Maj. Thomas McGregor, Second U.S. Cavalry, July–October 1892

Capt. William C. Rawolle, Second U.S. Cavalry, November 1892

Maj. Thomas McGregor, Second U.S. Cavalry, December 1892–April 1893

Capt. William C. Rawolle, Second U.S. Cavalry, May 1893

Maj. Thomas McGregor, Second U.S. Cavalry, June–December 1893

Units Stationed at Fort Bowie

First California Cavalry 1864–66
Fifth California Infantry 1862–64
First New Mexico Infantry 1864–66

First U.S. Cavalry 1869-71; 1881–82
Second U.S. Cavalry 1890–94
Third U.S. Cavalry 1870–71
Fourth U.S. Cavalry 1884–90
Fifth U.S. Cavalry 1872–75
Sixth U.S. Cavalry 1875–85
Eighth U.S. Cavalry 1869–70

First U.S. Infantry 1882–86
Eighth U.S. Infantry 1886
Ninth U.S. Infantry 1887–88
Tenth U.S. Infantry 1892–93
Twelfth U.S. Infantry 1881–82
Fourteenth U.S. Infantry 1866–67
Twenty-first U.S. Infantry 1869–72
Twenty-third U.S. Infantry 1872–74
Twenty-fourth U.S. Infantry 1891–92
Thirty-second U.S. Infantry 1867–69

Notes

INTRODUCTION

1. El Puerto del Dado, translated, meant a passageway through which one took a chance, or gamble, because of its reputation for danger. It was known by this name to Spanish soldiers at least as early as 1766. See Utley, *Clash of Cultures*, p. 17; and Hafen, *Mountain Men*, IX, p. 233.

2. Ancestors of the nomadic Apaches probably originated in the western part of Canada, but over time southward migration brought them to the Great Plains, and eventually to the Southwest. The Apaches, never numbering more than about six thousand individuals collectively during historical times, were classed in two major subdivisions, Eastern and Western. The former included those traditionally residing east of the Rio Grande—Lipan, Kiowa-Apache, and Jicarilla, while the Western included the Navajo (though of a distinct culture), Mescalero, Western Apache, and Chiricahua tribes. The Chiricahuas were composed of three principal bands: Northern, Southern, and Central, with the Chiricahuas themselves distinguishing yet a fourth band, the Bedonkohes. Sweeney, *Cochise*, pp. 3–7; Angie Debo, *Geronimo:*, pp. 9, 12–13.

3. The question of annexing Texas had been a topic of political debate in the U.S. since 1843. When the Senate failed to ratify a treaty proposed to achieve that end, President John Tyler followed up by submitting a joint resolution, requiring only a simple majority in both houses of Congress. The House and Senate compromised on the resolution, passing it just days prior to Tyler's leaving office. However, the decision to annex Texas was only one source of friction between the U.S. and Mexico. Despite agreement reached between the two nations in 1843, Mexico had defaulted on payments of financial damage claims submitted by American citizens having financial interests in Mexico. Moreover, the boundaries of the Texas Republic were disputed by both sides, a factor that prompted the U.S. to encourage the Texans to occupy the disputed territory lying between the Nueces River and the Rio Grande. Bauer, *Mexican War*, pp. 5–13.

4. After learning that hostilities between the U.S. and Mexico had commenced, Commodore John D. Sloat took it upon himself to capture Monterey, fearing that if he delayed, the British would use the opportunity to take it for themselves. Frémont, acting independently, fell in with American rebels and simultaneously occupied the capital. Neither of the actions was officially authorized

by higher U.S.authority and Frémont's declaration that California had been conquered proved premature. When Kearny arrived to occupy California in December, he encountered a force of loyal Californians near San Pascual. Although the Californians bested the U.S.Dragoons, they retreated in the face of late-arriving artillery, leaving the field in Kearny's possession. Sporadic fighting continued until opposing forces were finally defeated and the province declared to be in U.S.hands in early 1847. Ibid., pp. 165–69, 186–92.

5. One of the guides, Joaquin Antoine Jacques Leroux, is said to have spent several months each year during the 1830s trapping the country between Taos and California. A native of St. Louis, the French-Spanish Leroux became a naturalized citizen of Mexico to facilitate free passage into the country west of the Rio Grande. When Kearny conquered New Mexico and declared its inhabitants to be U.S. citizens, Leroux made an easy transition. Cooke promptly hired him as his chief guide for his expedition. Leroux's biography is recounted in Hafen, *Mountain Men*, IV, pp. 173–83; see also IX, p. 234, for his involvement with David E. Jackson's 1831 trek across Arizona. The map of Cooke's march is reproduced in the back flyleaf of Ricketts, *Mormon Battalion*. A cryptic legend, attributed to Leroux, for the area west of his route appears to be conjectural, yet it precisely plots a route through what is obviously Apache Pass. It may have been that Leroux recalled nothing remarkable about the journey across the San Simon flats, but Apache Pass undoubtedly left an impression on him.

6. New Mexico Territory initially included what we know today as the states of New Mexico and Arizona. However, the terms of the Treaty of Guadalupe–Hidalgo specified a southern boundary along the Gila River. Sheridan, *Arizona*, pp. 52–53.

7. Statistics for 1852 list California's total population as 255,122, of which 171,841 were white and 1,678 were black. The majority of the 54,803 "foreign residents" probably were Mexicans. DeBow, *Statistical View*, p. 394.

8. Weller, an astute politician, conceded to pressure that the proposed roads be termed "military roads," knowing that the Republican-controlled House of Representatives would raise objections to Secretary of War Davis having control over the expenditures. As Weller predicted, the House moved to transfer the projects to the Interior Department, which the senator wanted all along. Pro-southern interests, headed by William Smith of Virginia, managed to amend the legislation to authorize an additional $200,000 for the construction of a road from El Paso to Fort Yuma, essentially following Parke's railroad survey, to augment the central route. The measure passed the Senate on February 14, 1857, and was signed into law by President Franklin Pierce shortly thereafter. Jackson, *Wagon Roads West*, pp. 161–62, 164, 172–74. The El Paso–Fort Yuma contract was let to James B. Leach, who hired three hundred men and organized them into six fifty-man crews to work on different segments simultaneously. The nature of the road work was improvement on the already existing route, not new construction. The secretary of the interior stipulated that no heavy grading or bridging was to be done. Most of the labor was by hand, supplemented by mule teams, and consisted of removal of brush, large rocks, and other obstacles,

grading steep banks, and minor rerouting, all of which was for the purpose of better adapting the roads to wagon traffic. An interesting account of the Leach contract is related in Jackson, pp. 218–32.

9. Parke, *Reports of Explorations*, VII, p. 149.

10. Ibid., pp. 303–304.

11. *Annual Report of the Postmaster General*, 1858, p. 86 (hereafter cited as *ARPG* with respective year).

12. Ibid., p. 1000.

13. Ibid., pp. 1000–1001.

14. Ibid., p. 996.

15. The northern terminus was actually fixed at Tipton, Missouri, because rail service had been abolished from St. Louis to that point by the time mail coaches began running in 1858. The junction of the two routes initially was to be Little Rock, but the contractors requested that it be changed to Preston, Texas. The Butterfield schedule, as finalized, excluded both points to run via Ft. Smith, Arkansas and Sherman, Texas. Winther, *Transportation Frontier*, 49–50; Nevin, *The Expressmen*, p. 33; The total distance from St. Louis to San Francisco, via the Oxbow, was officially 2,795 miles. But the first 160 miles, from St. Louis to Tipton, Missouri, was served by a railroad. *ARPG*, 1859, p. 743.

16. Politics entered heavily into the decision for the Oxbow Route. Clearly, congressional intent was to permit the contractor to chose his own route, so long as he delivered to San Francisco on a twenty-five-day schedule. James Birch entered a proposal for service over the exact route later stipulated by Postmaster Brown, except that it would have only one terminal, in Memphis. Brown violated congressional directions by taking it upon himself to change the terms to two termini, further specifying that they would be St. Louis and Memphis, the latter his hometown. This maneuver excluded all the bidders, and gave Brown the latitude to assign the contract to Butterfield. Austerman, *Sharps Rifles and Spanish Mules*, pp. 88–90; *ARPG*, 1858, pp. 86, 988.

17. William G. Fargo had served as a messenger for Henry Wells's express service in New York during the mid-1840s. That relationship led to an 1850 merger of three companies in which Butterfield, Wells, and Fargo each had part ownership, thus creating the American Express Company. Wells became president of the new enterprise, and Fargo was appointed treasurer. In 1852, Wells and Fargo expanded their growing empire by entering into another joint venture to provide express service, by steamship via Panama, to California. The firm also entered into the banking business, thus securing their foothold in California. Eight years later, Butterfield partnered with Fargo to bid successfully on the transcontinental overland mail contract to the Pacific Coast. However, when the company's board of directors ousted Butterfield on grounds of mismanagement in 1860, Wells, Fargo & Company created a financial empire by stepping in to assume operational control of the mail line by virtue of Fargo's significant financial interests. Consequently, Wells, Fargo & Co. controlled both sea and land communications with the nation's west coast. Theobald and Theobald, *Wells Fargo in Arizona Territory*, pp. 1–3.

18. Everything went comparatively well on the San Antonio–San Diego route, until Birch was reported lost at sea during a trip to New York in October 1857. During the next few months the business continued to operate under its own momentum, but Birch's partners, Isaiah C. Woods and George H. Giddings, realized that the company would have to be reorganized if it were to survive. Therefore, in March 1858, Giddings, formerly a San Antonio businessman and partner in a mail contract to Santa Fe, arranged to purchase both Birch's and Wood's interests in the San Diego route. Ibid., pp. 120–21.

19. Way did not record a single station between El Paso and Tucson, and the company facility at the latter point was primitive. "There is no tavern or other accommodation here for travelers, and I [was] obliged to roll myself in my blanket and sleep either in the street or in the corral, as the station house had no windows or floor and was too close and warm. The corral is where they keep their horses and mules, but I slept very comfortably as the ground was made soft by manure." Duffen (ed.), "Overland via 'Jackass Mail' in 1858" 157. The above quotation is found on 160–61 .

20. Lieutenant Sylvester Mowry, who as a civilian later operated the Mowry Mine near Tubac, recorded thirteen permanent water stations in the 244 miles lying between El Paso and San Pedro Crossing. He additionally noted the existence of five other water holes "where a supply is found most of the year," giving an average of about nineteen miles between reliable water sources, or only thirteen miles including the seasonal ones. This and much other reliable information was provided in a printed "Letter of Lieutenant Mowry, U.S.A. to the U.S.Mail Contractors, Upon the Overland Mail Route to California," September 20, 1857. Small Collections, Arizona Historical Society.

21. Winther, "Southern Overland Mail": 96–97.

22. Tevis, *Arizona in the '50s*, p. 93. Additional information about the location and appearance of the station are found in "The Butterfield State Station and the Chiricahua Indian Agency: An Investigation of Their Locations in Apache Pass" and "The Apache Pass Stage Station: A Reassessment of Its Location," both in the Fort Bowie NHS files, and in Greene, "Historic Structure Report," pp. 285–90.

23. Nevin, *Expressmen*, p. 33. Butterfield staff consisted of station agents, who oversaw the operations, employees, stock, and company property at each location; drivers, and on-board conductors, whose job it was to protect the mail and look after the passengers. The route was subdivided into six divisions, each managed by a superintendent. "Special Instructions to Conductors, Agents, Drivers, and Employees." Butterfield Overland Mail Company. Copy in Fort Bowie NHS files.

CHAPTER 1: THE ARMY MEETS COCHISE

1. Goetzmann, *Army Exploration in American West*, pp. 195–97.

2. The Military Department of New Mexico, headquartered at Santa Fe, included that portion of today's Arizona lying east of 110 degrees longitude.

Thus, in a practical sense, Tucson and the Santa Cruz Valley marked the western boundary of that department. Thian, *Military Geography*, pp. 79, 86.

3. Frazer, *Forts and Supplies*, pp. 119–21.

4. Frazer, *Forts of the West*, pp. 6–7.

5. Bonneville proceeded as far west as Tubac and Tucson, the extent of his administrative jurisdiction. The report is published in Walker, "Bonneville's Report,": 343–62.

6. Ibid.: 358.

7. The report, prepared by Captain John W. Davidson, and concurred in by Major Enoch Steen, Lieutenants Benjamin F. Davis and Richard S. C. Lord, is cited in Walker, "Bonneville's Report": 357n52.

8. Ibid.: 357.

9. Sweeney, *Cochise*, p. 119.

10. The quotation is attributed to James H. Tevis, Arizona pioneer and Butterfield Overland Mail Company station keeper at Apache Pass in 1858–59. Sweeney, *Cochise*, p. 118.

11. In addition to two daughters, Cochise fathered two sons by his first wife, Taza in the early 1840s, and Nachez (or Naiche) in about 1856. Taza, being the eldest, was groomed to eventually assume his father's position as chief of the Chiricahuas. Ibid., p. 142.

12. It should be noted that Steck, unlike some Indian agents, supported a strong military presence in southeastern Arizona. His report included an endorsement on Bonneville's recommendation for a new post at Lucero Spring, near the overland mail route. He further suggested that at least six companies of troops were needed to keep peace in the region. See *Annual Report of the Commissioner of Indian Affairs*, 1859, p. 347 (hereafter cited as *ARCIA* with year). In assessing Cochise's motives for avoiding conflict with the Anglos, Edwin R. Sweeney offers two influences—the strengthening of Mexican military garrisons just south of the border, thus increasing the risks of raiding there, and the proliferation of Americans in southern Arizona, which changed the balance of power against the Apaches. Sweeney, *Cochise*, p. 119.

13. Cochise married Mangas Coloradas's daughter, Dos-teh-seh, in about 1840. She remained his principal wife thereafter, bearing both of his sons. Mangas, like Cochise, was of large physical stature, reportedly standing six feet four inches tall and weighing approximately 250 pounds. The Warm Springs Apaches, also known as Mimbres, Copper Mines, and Mogollons, composed the eastern band of the Chiricahuas. They were closely related, culturally, linguistically, and through intermarriage, to the central Chiricahuas. Sweeney, *Cochise*, pp. 4–5, 44–45, 132–33.

14. Apache agent Michael Steck estimated that the Chiricahuas numbered approximately 150 adult warriors, plus 500 women and children in 1858. *ARCIA*, 1859, p. 346.

15. Much of the foregoing has been synthesized from the detailed biographical treatment of Cochise found in Sweeney, *Cochise*, pp. 133–41.

16. *Sacramento Daily Union*, March 4, 1861. Copy in files at Fort Bowie National Historic Site.

17. Felix Martinez was the son of one Tellez and Jesus Martinez. Following Tellez's death, his widow, Jesus, became Ward's common-law wife in 1859. Jesus lived with Ward until his death in 1867. Although both John Ward and Jesus Martinez went to their graves believing that the boy had been killed, he indeed survived. It seems probable that Felix was taken by White Mountain (also called Coyotero) Apaches and remained with them at least for a period of months when he was given to another Indian family. The boy was raised among this clan and eventually became known as Mickey Free, later becoming an army scout and interpreter during the 1870s and 1880s. Much controversy and misinformation has surrounded Free. Perhaps the most thorough and reliable biographical treatment is provided by Allan Radbourne, in "Salvador or Martinez: The Parentage and Origins of Mickey Free," *The Brand Book*, pp. 20–45. See also, Radbourne, "Naming of Mickey Free": 341–36.

18. Heitman, *Historical Register*, I, p. 197; Schoenberger, "Lieutenant George N. Bascom at Apache Pass,": 85 argues that Bascom, at the age of twenty-five, was not as young and inexperienced as some writers have characterized him.

19. Return for January 1861, Post Returns, Fort Buchanan, A. T., 1859–1862, microfilm copy at Main Library, University of Arizona.

20. Sweeney, *Cochise*, p. 148.

21. A complete roster of these men, as well as the detachments that arrived later at Apache Pass, is recorded in a letter from Charles K. Mills to Jan Ryan, June 30, 1991, Fort Bowie NHS files.

22. Fort McLane, also known as Fort Floyd, Fort McLean, Camp Wheeler, and Camp Webster, was situated along the Mimbres River, some fifteen miles from the Santa Rita Copper Mines, and approximately thirty-eight miles northwest of present-day Deming, New Mexico. It was established on September 16, 1860. Hart, *Tour Guide to Old Western Forts*, p. 130; Frazer, *Forts of the West*, p. 100.

23. The exact site of Bascom's camp has been debated for many years, with all of the traditionally accepted possibilities lying in Siphon Canyon. Larry L. Ludwig, "An Archeological Survey of Possible Bascom Affair Sites," MS, 1993, Fort Bowie NHS files; Sweeney, *Cochise*, p. 149. All previous secondary descriptions, notably Russell, "Chief Cochise vs. Lieutenant Bascom," and Utley, "Bascom Affair," are derived from William S. Oury, "A True History of the Outbreak of the Noted Apache Chieftain Cachise in the Year 1861," typescript at University of Arizona Library, copy on file at Fort Bowie NHS. Oury's account, originally appearing as a serial in the *(Tucson) Arizona Star* beginning June 28, 1877, stated, "Lieut. Bascom . . . marched down the canyon [past the station] about three-quarters of a mile and struck camp." Despite being an early account of the Bascom Affair, it must be remembered that Oury, a Butterfield employee in Tucson, did not arrive at Apache Pass until eleven days after the opening events, thus he did not personally see Bascom's first camp. See Sweeney, *Cochise*, pp. 143, 161–63. The author has relied on the accounts left by Daniel Robinson, formerly a

sergeant in the Seventh Infantry, who was present at the 1861 event. See Daniel Robinson, "Apache Affairs in 1861," typescript, Daniel Robinson Papers, Library, Fort Laramie National Historic Site, and Robinson, "A Narrative of Events Pertaining to C, F, and H Companies of the Seventh Infantry while Serving in New Mexico and Arizona from October 1860, to April 1862," MS, ibid. An edited version of the former appeared as "The Affair at Apache Pass" in *Sports Afield*: 79–83, but it lacks many of the pertinent details included in the draft manuscript. To date, Robinson's is the only eyewitness account discovered that specifically locates the site of Bascom's meeting with Cochise. Unfortunately for historians, the two versions differ on a key point. Robinson in "Apache Affairs" states that Bascom's company "pitched their tents on the plateau east of the station." In "Narrative of Events," he located the camp "about 200 yards *west* of the station" (italics added). Based on extant terrain features and logical proximity to Apache Spring, the author has concluded that the east site more closely corresponds with Robinson's description. For an annotated treatment of Robinson's account, see McChristian and Ludwig, "Eyewitness to the Bascom Affair": 277–300.

24. The names of the Butterfield employees are found in Oury, "True History of the Outbreak." Walsh, spelled "Welch" in some accounts, is absent from some narratives. However, as general agent for the Butterfield Overland Mail in the Tucson district, Oury was in a position to know the men employed at Apache Pass Station. The error probably originated in "The Murder of James Wallace," *Arizonian*, February 9, 1861, reproduced in *The Butterfield Overland Mail across Arizona*, p. 23.

25. Robinson later described these women as "two squaws . . . one old and haggard, the other young and rather good looking for an Indian—mother and daughter I thought. . . . They belonged to Cochise's camp about a mile away; the oldest was part Mexican, and the other a Mexican that had been stolen by the Apaches when a child; having grown up among them, she was considered as much of an Apache as any of them, and was known by the name of Juanita." See Robinson, "Apache Affairs."

26. Sweeney, *Cochise*, p. 150.

27. Robinson, "Apache Affairs."

28. It should be noted that Robinson used the term "dinner" to indicate the noon meal, not the evening meal, as is common usage today. The army in the nineteenth century designated the three daily meals as breakfast, dinner, and supper. This detail becomes important in determining the chronology of events in the Bascom Affair. Sweeney, for instance, misconstrues the time of Bascom's first meeting with Cochise as being in the evening, whereas it actually occurred in the afternoon. Sweeney, *Cochise*, p. 150.

29. Like many other aspects of the Bascom Affair, there is almost no agreement as to exactly how many Apaches were in the party. Bascom himself recorded that he "captured six Indians." Later in the same report, he stated that he hung six warriors, three of whom were Coyoteros captured by Surgeon B. J. Irwin near Ewell's Station, and that he turned over to the guard at Fort Buchanan a

woman and two boys. Bascom to Morrison, February 25, 1861, in Sacks, "New Evidence": 266–67; Oury recorded that the party consisted of "Cochise accompanied by three bucks, a squaw, and a boy . . . ." See Oury, "True History of the Outbreak." Sergeant Robinson recalled that six dismounted Apaches came to the camp. But, in the same account, he contradicted himself by stating, "Two of them were captured, and two others made their escape, one killed." It may be that he included only the adult males in his figure of six. See Robinson, "Narrative of Events." Nelson Davis, who arrived with the westbound stage on February 6, 1861, gave the number of hostages as eight—six men, a woman, and a boy. Nelson J. Davis to Charles Hosory [?], Washington, D.C., August 20, 1894, typescript in files at Fort Bowie NHS (hereafter cited as Davis account). According to Surgeon Irwin, it was he who later suggested executing six of the hostages, "man for man," in reprisal for the six whites killed. He offered the three warriors he had captured, and Bascom consented to hanging "three of the hostages taken by him," suggesting there were others, probably the woman and two children. See Irwin, "Fight at Apache Pass." The author has concluded that the initial party included Cochise, his brother Coyunturo, three other warriors, a woman, and two boys. During the event, Cochise escaped and one warrior was killed, thus leaving three men, a woman, and two boys in Bascom's custody, which agrees with his report. It is interesting to note that Irwin, who was not present at the early phase of the Bascom Affair, verified that one Apache male hostage was shot and killed, but places that occurrence on February 4, when Bascom's talk with Cochise broke down. According to Irwin, it was then that the Apache hostages attempted to escape, which seems unlikely.

30. Although Bascom claimed in his official report that he allowed Cochise to leave on the condition that he would return with the boy in ten days, the lieutenant obviously had arranged for his men to be in position to capture the Apache party. Bascom's report to his commanding officer, as well as most of the other relevant primary documents, is quoted in Sacks, "New Evidence."

31. The details of this incident vary from one account to another. The author has relied heavily on eyewitness recollections provided in Robinson, "Apache Affairs," combined with his, "Narrative of Events." See also the evaluation of sources in Sweeney, *Cochise*, pp. 150–51.

32. Robinson, "Apache Affairs."

33. Ibid.

34. Ibid. Conversely, Bascom indicated in his report that he did not actually speak with Cochise. Rather, "when about one hundred and fifty yards from the house, I began to suspect from their actions that all was not right and refused to go further." Sacks, "New Evidence," p. 266. It can be speculated that the presence of Francisco indicated Cochise's intent to negotiate an exchange, because the Coyoteros probably had possession of Felix Martinez.

35. Of this incident, Bascom stated only that "they paid no attention to my orders but went into the ravine where the Indians were, and were immediately seized by them." Sacks, "New Evidence," p. 266. No other eyewitness accounts are

available at the time of this writing to corroborate Robinson's narrative, although Irwin mentioned that, "Wallace and his companions . . . incautiously mingled with Cochese's [*sic*] party." Irwin, "Fight at Apache Pass."

36. Details of the encounter vary somewhat among the respective accounts. See Robinson, "Apache Affairs"; "Murder of James Wallace"; "The Apaches' Attack on the Overland Mail," *Alta California*, February 19, 1861, reproduced in *The Butterfield Mail across Arizona*, p. 24.

37. Bascom's description of this event is in Sacks, "New Evidence," p. 266. Another myth associated with the Bascom Affair is the alleged confrontation between Bascom and Sergeant Reuben F. Bernard, First Dragoons. Russell contended that Bernard argued vehemently with Bascom when the lieutenant rejected Cochise's offer. The story goes that Bernard was later court-martialed for his insubordination, though historians failed to find a copy of the proceedings and assumed that it had either been destroyed or lay hidden in the depths of the National Archives. Truth is, the whole tale was spurious because Bernard's company did not arrive at Apache Pass until February 14, eight days after Bascom's meeting with Cochise. See Russell, "Cochise vs. Bascom." Sacks was the first to challenge the story and was on the right trail in "New Evidence," p. 273. The regimental return for February 1861 records that Company D, to which Bernard belonged, left Fort Breckinridge on February 10 "on a scout against Apache Indians." Regimental Returns, First Dragoons, 1846–1861, Returns of Regular Army Regiments, Cavalry, Records of the Adjutant General's Office, RG 94, National Archives, microfilm copy at AHS.

38. Robinson related that Bascom sent a sergeant with a detail of soldiers down the canyon to meet and escort the stage to the station. His version indicates that the detachment discovered and removed the barricade on Tuesday night, then returned to the station before dawn on Wednesday. This does not agree with the traditional chronology of events, but neither can his sequence be entirely dismissed. The sergeant noted that a lady aboard the stage appeared "the least daunted of any of her fellow passengers." Robinson, "Apache Affairs."

39. Some accounts refer to only two captives being taken from the wagon train. One author, basing his information on early Arizona histories, gave their names as Jordan and Lyons. See Russell, "Cochise vs. Bascom," repeated in Utley, "Bascom Affair," p. 64. Bascom himself identified the three men by the names used herein. Sacks, "New Evidence," pp. 266–67. A contemporary newspaper account, probably based on a February 14 interview with A. B. Culver, who had just come from Apache Pass, reported that eight Mexicans were burned and three other men, two Americans and a "half-breed Cherokee," were captured. See *Sacramento Union*, March 4, 1861. Relying on a February 9, 1861, article in the *Tucson Arizonian*, the author believes that only two of the men had been tortured; the rest lay dead, probably shot or lanced on and near the road. Robinson speculated that the wagons belonged to a Mexican train that had passed by the station, headed west, on February 3. However, in that scenario, the train would have been miles beyond the reaches of the pass by the time trouble began. It is

also reasonable to assume that Cochise would not have waited to offer the three additional white men had he captured them earlier. Robinson, "Apache Affairs."

40. "Apaches' Attack." The number of people aboard the stage varied with the telling, but nine seems to be the most credible. Those that can be accounted for by name were: driver King Lyon, conductor Nelson J. Davis, First Lieutenant John Rogers Cooke, W. S. Grant (supply contractor to Fort Buchanan); William Buckley, superintendent of the Tucson–El Paso Division of the Butterfield Mail, *Arizonian*, February 9, 1861. Nelson J. Davis account. The author finds no foundation for a persistent legend that Cochise's warriors damaged the bridge spanning what is known today as Willow Gulch. According to William S. Oury, Superintendent Buckley took the lines of the team and drove the stage hell-bent toward the station. Reaching the partially destroyed bridge, but being unable to stop, Buckley supposedly lashed the team ahead and the coach was successfully dragged across the span on its axles. Oury, who did not arrive at Apache Pass until a few days later, apparently concocted this dramatic fabrication, embellishing the role of his old supervisor for the sake of making a good story, when his account was published in the *Arizona Star*, June 28, 1877. It should be noted that, despite the appearance of the tale in numerous publications since that time, the only source for it is Oury himself. No other witness mentioned anything about skidding the coach across a damaged bridge, something that should have been a vivid recollection to all had it happened. The author's version, therefore, is based on the testimony of Nelson J. Davis, the conductor aboard the stage who actually drove it on to Apache Pass Station after Lyon was wounded. Supporting evidence is taken from A. B. Culver's report to *Arizonian*, February 9, 1861. Culver, a Butterfield employee who had arrived on the stage from Mesilla that afternoon, was present at the station when the Tucson coach arrived and therefore heard of the night's events directly from the participants.

41. Robinson suggested that several men were sent out from the station at different times, but Surgeon Irwin recalled that only one soldier slipped out with the message to Fort Buchanan. See Robinson, "Apache Affairs;" Irwin, "Fight at Apache Pass." This is corroborated by Oury, "True History of the Outbreak." A thorough analysis of the event, which suffers only in the respect that Robinson's unpublished accounts had not been discovered at the time it was written, determined that several soldiers carried out the mission. Mills, "Incident at Apache Pass," p. 100.

42. Robinson, indulging in a bit of self-aggrandizement in "Apache Affairs," places himself in charge of the detail, but Bascom, the more reliable source, recorded that First Sergeant Huber commanded the herd guard.

43. The stone breastworks still present today on Overlook Ridge, and often attributed to the 1862 Battle of Apache Pass, probably were constructed by Seventh Infantrymen during the Bascom Affair. Personal communication with park ranger Larry Ludwig, Fort Bowie NHS, August 30, 2000.

44. Both Robinson and Buckley reported that the westbound stage arrived during this skirmish, rather than on Wednesday, February 6, 1861. Robinson,

"Apache Affairs"; "Apaches' Attack." Nevertheless, the author has elected to use the traditional arrival date, based on the account in the February 9, 1861, issue of the *Arizonian*. The information in that article was provided to the newspaper by A. B. Culver, who was conductor on that very coach and is therefore considered to be the better source.

45. "Murder of James Wallace."

46. The men comprising Irwin's detachment are identified in a letter from Mills to Ryan, June 30, 1991. However, Irwin's report specifically cites four men, Corporal Faber and Privates Leiter, Saliot, and Christy, whom Mills places with Sergeant Robinson's wagon train escort. Irwin to Chapin, February 25, 1861, in Sacks, "New Evidence," p. 264.

47. Irwin, "Fight at Apache Pass"; Irwin to Chapin in Sacks, "New Evidence," p. 264. For his actions in the Apache Pass affair, Irwin was awarded the Medal of Honor shortly before his retirement in 1894. Heitman, *Historical Register*, I, p. 564.

48. Oury, "True History of the Outbreak."

CHAPTER 2: THE MARCH OF THE CALIFORNIA COLUMN

1. Winther, "Southern Overland Mail and Stagecoach Line": 105–106.

2. Gidding's contract was modified on February 4, 1860, to eliminate his service from Yuma to San Diego because it duplicated the service Butterfield provided. Giddings was favored with the San Antonio–Los Angeles route as the result of his earlier business relationship with Blair. Blair, previously a politically well-connected attorney, had served as a lobbyist in Washington for Giddings. Austerman, *Sharps Rifles and Spanish Mules*, pp. 155, 160–61.

3. Stein's Peak was christened by Major Enoch Steen, commanding a battalion of the First Dragoons that camped there en route to occupy Tucson in 1856. A cartographer preparing a map in 1859 misspelled his name as "Stein," an error that was never corrected, though the pronunciation has remained Steen. See "An Historic Chronology of Doubtful Canyon and Stein's Pass," Fort Bowie National Historic Site historical files. The distinctive conical mountain, near the east entrance to Doubtful Canyon, or Stein's Pass, is situated near the Arizona–New Mexico state line, approximately ten miles north of Interstate 10.

4. Ibid., pp. 168–69. The quotation, attributed to William S. Oury, is found in Thrapp, *Conquest of Apacheria*, p. 19.

5. Austerman, *Sharps Rifles and Spanish Mules*, pp. 169–71; J. Jones to William S. Grant, May 4, 1861, roll 13, M1120, microfilm collections, Arizona Historical Society, copy in Fort Bowie NHS files.

6. Heitman, *Historical Register*, I, p. 886.

7. For an authoritative study of the Sibley campaign, see Alberts, *Battle of Glorieta*. Much of the foregoing treatment of events leading to Sibley's invasion has been drawn from Colton, *Civil War in the Western Territories*, pp. 3–32. and Utley, *Frontiersmen in Blue*, pp. 211–30.

8. When President Lincoln learned of Lynde's cowardly conduct, he personally ordered him to be dropped from the army's rolls. He was subsequently,

but briefly, reinstated for purposes of retirement in 1866. *General Orders No. 102*, Adjutant General's Office, November 25, 1861; Heitman, *Historical Register*, I, p. 649.

9. Baylor's, and later Sibley's, arrival at El Paso confirmed for Colonel Canby that the Confederate invasion would follow the Rio Grande, not the Pecos River, which was another possible avenue from Texas into the territory. Accordingly, Canby abandoned the eastern posts to concentrate his forces at Fort Craig. See Alberts, *Battle of Glorieta*, p. 13.

10. This company, comprising 105 men recruited in the Mesilla Valley, became known as the "Arizona Rangers." Thompson, *Henry Hopkins Sibley*, p. 241.

11. George Giddings, standing in for his deceased brother, received a contract to deliver mail biweekly between San Antonio and San Diego for the Confederate postmaster general on August 28, 1861. The contract, backdated to April 1, was to run through June 30, 1865. Austerman, *Sharps Rifles and Spanish Mules*, p. 181.

12. Hunt, *Major General James Henry Carlton*, pp. 33–42, 47–54, 57, 85–92, 113, 165–67, 171–93; Heitman, *Historical Register*, I, p. 282.

13. Heitman, *Historical Register*, I, p. 1062.

14. That many of the California Volunteers officers took the officer caste to extremes, is recounted in George Hand, *Civil War in Apacheland*, pp. 70–71, 77–78, 85–86. Hand's account also records the intensive drilling experienced by the California Volunteers. On January 23, 1863, for instance, the First Infantry was subjected to an inspection by Major Henry D. Wallen, of the Seventh Infantry, a West Point graduate and officer with twenty-three years' experience. Hand noted, "We went through the co[mpany] drill. Being the ranking co. we set the pattern and performed our part so well as to surprise the regular officers." Ibid., p. 100.

15. It should be noted that since Texas was Confederate territory, the U.S. Mail had to be routed from Missouri down the Santa Fe Trail via Bent's Fort and Santa Fe, thence south along the ancient Camino Real to Fort Thorn, where it intersected the former Butterfield Overland Road to San Diego. Carleton to Drum, May 24, 1862, in Orton, *Record of California Men*, p. 51; Austerman, *Sharps Rifles and Spanish Mules*, p. 196.

16. Pettis, *California Column*, p. 8; James M. McNulty, "Extracts from a Report on the March of the Column from California, from Fort Yuma to the Rio Grande, during the Summer of 1862," in Barnes, *Medical and Surgical History of the War of the Rebellion*, p. 347 (hereafter cited as "McNulty report").

17. Orton, *Record of California Men*, pp. 42–43; Colton, *Civil War in the Western Territories*, pp. 14–18.

18. Calloway's battalion was composed of his own Company I, First Infantry CV, a detachment of Company A, First Cavalry CV, and a detachment of Company K, First Infantry CV, serving as crews for two mountain howitzers. Orton, *Record of California Men*, p. 47.

19. Accounts of the fight at Picacho Pass are found in Colton, *Civil War in the Western Territories*, p. 104; Pettis, *California Column*, pp. 9–10; and Orton, *Record of California Men*, p. 47.

20. Hand, *Civil War in Apacheland*, p. 78.

21. Shinn's Light Battery A, Third Artillery, comprised four guns—two Model 1841 twelve-pounder mountain howitzers and two Model 1841 six-pounder bronze field guns. Carlton to Canby, May 3, 1862, *Record of California Men*, p. 48.

22. *War of the Rebellion: A Compilation of the Official Records*, Ser. I, vol. 50, pt. 1, p. 142 (hereafter cited as *O. R.* with respective volume and part).

23. Jones was captured by secessionists near Picacho, six miles above Mesilla and taken before Colonel William Steele, C.S.A., in command of a rear guard force left there by Sibley. Steele imprisoned Jones, but the plucky messenger managed to get word to Canby anyway, which in turn caused Steele to abandon the territory. Carleton's report of the affair, rendered on July 22, 1862, can be found in Orton, *Record of California Men*, p. 57. See also Eyre to Cutler, July 8, 1862, pp. 60–61, ibid. Jones's statement is in *O. R.*, 50: 1, pp. 119–20. A second contemporary account is in *Sacramento Union*, August 14, 1862, copy in Hayden Collection, Arizona Historical Society. Jones, incidentally, was the same man who had given chase to the Apache war party that ran off stock from the San Simon station prior to the war.

CHAPTER 3: A SHARP LITTLE CONTEST: THE BATTLE OF APACHE PASS

1. Orton, *Record of California Men*, p. 52.

2. The so-called Arizona bill (HR 357) was passed by the House on May 8, 1862, but languished in the Senate for nine months. President Abraham Lincoln signed the legislation February 24, 1863. Sacks, "Creation of the Territory of Arizona": 122–25, 133–34. This article presents a fine synthesis of the events and political process leading to territorial status. Carleton's proclamation is found in *O. R.*, vol. 50, pt. 1, pp. 96–97.

3. Orton, *Record of California Men*, p. 52.

4. Carleton's march itinerary was a carefully calculated risk. On the one hand, the water sources would not accommodate the entire column at any one time. The wells needed time to replenish themselves and even where there were natural springs, such as at Apache Pass, the rate of flow was so limited that it would cost many hours to water all of the animals and to refill the water wagons. A detailed account of these procedures is found in "Column from California," *Army and Navy Journal*, March 28, 1868, p. 503.

5. *O. R.*, 50: 1, p. 98.

6. Ibid., p. 121.

7. Anonymous, "Diary of the March to the Rio Grande," *Alta California*, August 4, 1862 copy contained in Bancroft's "Scraps," p. 82, Arizona Historical Foundation.

8. Ibid., p. 82. The "hill and rising ground" probably described the prominent hill located approximately three-fourths of a mile southwest of Apache Spring, the rising ground meaning the area south of the post cemetery.

9. Orton, *Record of California Men*, p. 59.

10. "Scraps," p. 82; Pemmican is an emergency food that originated among North American Indians. It consists of lean meat pounded into a paste and mixed with fat and berries to form cakes that can easily be transported in all kinds of weather.

11. *O. R.*, 50: 1, pp. 122, 131; "Scraps," p. 83. The anonymous correspondent who wrote of this event stated that Eyre ordered the herders to take the horses farther up the head of Siphon Canyon, where the grazing was better. Six soldiers, it was claimed, took it upon themselves to check out Corporal Brown's story by conducting a search of the area. They claimed to have found Keith's body only thirty yards from the site of Eyre's meeting with Cochise. It seems unlikely that the events occurred in exactly the way they were presented in the *Alta California* article. The writer was critical of Eyre's conduct, and may have skewed the sequence of events to reflect badly on the officer. See "Scraps," pp. 82, 83. For another account critical of Eyre, see *Sacramento Union*, August 18, 1862; the author has chosen to accept Eyre's version of the encounter on the basis that it seems unlikely that he would have deliberately falsified an official report when his statements could have been contested by other officers of the command.

12. The soldiers' graves had been "torn up by Apaches and headboards split" by the time other elements of the California Column passed by a short time later. *Sacramento Union*, August 18, 1862.

13. The quotation is found in "Scraps," p. 193. See also *O. R.*, 50: 1, p. 122, and *Sacramento Union*, August 18, 1862.

14. Orton, *Record of California Men*, p. 60.

15. The last contingent of four hundred Texans, under Colonel William Steele, withdrew from Fort Fillmore on July 8, 1862, just four days after Eyre and the First California Cavalry arrived at the Rio Grande. The Confederates, low on supplies, were forced to forage in the local area, acquiring subsistence from a hostile populace. Steele remained at Fort Bliss and Franklin, Texas, only briefly before retiring on the long trail back to San Antonio. Colton, *Civil War in the Western Territories*, p. 113.

16. For reasons that are not clear, Eyre did not send word back to Carleton about the encounter at Apache Pass until after his (Eyre's) arrival at Fort Thorn on July 6, 1862. That report did not reach Carleton until July 21, six days after the Battle of Apache Pass. Orton, *Record of California Men*, p. 58.

17. Carleton's General Orders No. 10, detailing the order of march for the column is found in *O. R.*, 50:1, pp. 90–91. A useful table listing the components of each battalion and respective unit strengths is in pt. 2, pp. 24–25.

18. Carleton stockpiled thirty days' rations and twenty-five thousand pounds of corn at San Simon for Eyre's command. As it happened, Eyre did not return to Arizona. Learning that Colonel William Steele's Texans were fleeing down the Rio Grande, he immediately gave chase, but was ordered by Colonel John M. Chivington, the district commander, to halt at Las Cruces to await further instructions. Eyre, clearly peeved, felt that he lost a golden opportunity to capture the

last of the Confederates in that region. Elements of Eyre's command eventually proceeded down the Overland Road as far as Fort Davis, Texas, where his men raised the national colors to reclaim the post for the U.S. late in August. *O. R.*, vol. 50, pt. 1, pp. 127–28; Greene, "Historic Resource Study: Fort Davis National Historic Site," pp. 30–31.

19. Company E, First Infantry CV, was organized in August 1861 as the "Washington Rifles." Its members were recruited entirely from Sacramento. Thomas L. Roberts was commissioned captain on August 26 and served in that capacity until mustered out with the company on September 13, 1864, at Los Pinos, New Mexico. He afterwards pursued private business interests in Santa Fe, where he died of natural causes just four years later. Thrapp, *Encyclopedia*, vol. 3, pp. 1227–28. Roberts's command was comprised initially of seventy-two men of Co. E, First Infantry C V; twenty-four men of Co. B, Second Cavalry CV; the "Jackass Battery," twenty men; and a detachment of ten men belonging to Co. H, First Infantry C. *O. R.*, 50: 1, p. 130.

20. *O. R.*, 50:2, pp. 10–11. The so-called Jackass Battery, which was to play a significant role in the events at Apache Pass, was formed early in 1862 while the California Column wintered at Fort Yuma. According to Julius C. Hall, a member of the battery, two twelve-pounder mountain howitzers were detached from First Lieutenant John B. Shinn's Light Battery A, Third U.S. Artillery, the only Regular Army unit assigned to the Carleton's brigade. The ten-man crews for each gun were selected from among the infantry and were trained by Shinn's regulars, which probably accounts for the proficiency the volunteers demonstrated at the Battle of Apache Pass. The so-called battery, technically only a section (two guns), was placed under the command of Lieutenant Jeremiah Phelen, who remained with the ad hoc unit until sometime prior to the march from Tucson, when he was replaced by Lieutenant William A. Thompson; Hall remembered three howitzers, but that is contradicted by other reliable accounts. See Hall, "In the Wild West." A cavalry officer correctly recalled only two guns—see Cremony, *Life among the Apaches*, p. 160—as did Hazen, in "Notes of Marches," p. 45. Another member of the California Column indirectly verified that the two mountain howitzers were taken from Shinn's Battery (a full battery comprised six guns) when he recorded that "A battery of 4 pieces of the 3rd U.S. Artillery commanded by Lt. Shinn to day passed through" and elsewhere mentioned the "small battery of 2 mountain howitzers." See Thomas Akers Diary, University of Arizona Library. The detachments, each commanded by a chief of piece (sergeant), consisted of a gunner and three crew members, plus two ammunition carriers. A driver was assigned to care for each of the three mules: a shaft mule to either draw or carry the tube, a carriage mule, and an ammunition mule. The detachment for each gun thus totaled ten men. See *Manual for Light Artillery*, pp. 2–3. An outline history of Battery A, Third U.S. Artillery, is contained in Rodenbough, *Army of the United States: Historical Sketches*, p. 345. Shinn, incidentally, was breveted major in 1865 for arduous and meritorious service in recognition of his performance during the California Column's march to the Rio Grande. *Historical Register*, I, p. 883.

21. *O. R.*, 50:2, pp. 8, 10–11; ibid, pt. 1, pp. 128–29; Hazen, "Notes on Marches," p. 46.

22. Roberts mentioned taking the water tank wagon, while another member of the California Column recorded that he had "three company wagons." One of those was probably the tank, the other two being standard six-mule army wagons. Cremony's command consisted of sixteen cavalrymen and twelve infantrymen detached from E Company; *O. R.*, 50:1, p. 131; "Vedette's Letters from the California Column for Texas, under Gen. Carleton," *Alta California*, August 16, 1862, in Bancroft's "Scraps," p. 195. (hereafter cited as "Vedette's Letters").

23. Hazen, "Notes on Marches," p. 45; Andrew Ryan, *News from Fort Craig, New Mexico, 1863: Civil War Letters of Andrew Ryan, with the First California Volunteers*, p. 34. The detail comprised a sergeant, three privates, and two civilians. See Teal, "Soldier in the California Column": 40.

24. Cremony, *Life among the Apaches*, p. 161; Sweeney, *Cochise*, pp. 198–99.

25. Captain Cremony later stated that the Indians were firing at ranges of only thirty to eighty yards from the road—in *Life among the Apaches*, p. 161. In the author's view, the scene of the action afforded ample cover in both rocks and brush. The Apaches, concealed on the eastern slope of the hill, probably allowed most of the column to pass by before opening an enfilading fire from the rear on both sides.

26. Spherical case shot was an antipersonnel round consisting of a cast-iron shell filled with approximately eighty-two .69-caliber lead musket balls. Melted sulphur was added to solidify the balls within the hollow shell. Afterwards, a cylindrical cavity bored through the center of the mass was filled with a one-ounce bursting charge of black powder. An adjustable time fuse, made of wood or rolled paper and marked off into seconds, was inserted into a metal or wood plug in the iron shell. Estimating the range and cutting the fuse accordingly permitted the shell to be fired and exploded on, or preferably above, enemy positions at varying distances. Aerial bursts over personnel were the most effective. The maximum range of the twelve-pound mountain howitzer loaded with this type of ammunition was approximately eight hundred yards. *Ordnance Manual*, pp. 280–81, 386; *Report of the Board on Behalf of Executive Departments at the International Exposition Held at Philadelphia, PA., 1876*, p. 693.

27. Hazen, "Notes of Marches," p. 45.

28. One soldier claimed that O'Brian's body was stripped of all clothing and the head and feet were cut off. "Vedette's Letters," pp. 195–96. Another stated that the Indians "succeeded in dragging off O'Brian's body." He added that the corpse was discovered two miles away. See Albert J. Fountain, "Old Time Reminiscences," *Rio Grande Republican*, January 2, 1891. Although Sergeant George Hand was not present, others later told him that "the Indians shot him, and literally cut him to pieces before the boys could get back to him." Hand, *Civil War in Apacheland*, p. 64.

29. A company was composed of two platoons of no particular number of men. In nineteenth-century usage, a platoon was simply half a company, regardless of

its size. The term "skirmishers" described a tactical deployment wherein soldiers were maneuvered into an extended rank, or open order, five yards between files. In conventional nineteenth century battle, skirmishers preceded the main line of battle by some distance to clear the way and protect the advance. By making initial contact with the enemy, skirmishers forced the enemy to expose his position, particularly in wooded or broken terrain. The deployment was also used for small-unit actions and against unconventional foes, when close-order formations were not appropriate. It relied on individual initiative, taking advantage of terrain, and individual marksmanship, rather than mass fire. Consequently, skirmish order became the standard formation used for fighting Indians in the West. Jamieson, *Crossing the Deadly Ground*, pp. 44, 104–105; Albert Jennings Fountain, a world adventurer in his youth, later settled in California and entered the newspaper business. On the eve of the Civil War, he studied law and made an unsuccessful attempt to pass the bar examination. In August 1861, he was appointed lieutenant of Company E, First Infantry CV. He afterwards led an interesting life as a political figure, lawyer, and military figure in Texas and New Mexico. At one point, he was appointed as legal counsel for William H. Bonnie, aka Billy the Kid. Fountain and his young son disappeared under mysterious circumstances following a controversial trial in 1896. Thrapp, *Encyclopedia*, vol. 1, pp. 512–13.

30. *O. R.*, 50: 1, p. 131.

31. The California Volunteer Infantry was armed with the .58-caliber Model 1855 Springfield rifled musket. A state-of-the-art weapon in its day, the Springfield fired a five-hundred-grain hollow-base bullet with a muzzle velocity of 950 feet per second. It was accurate enough to put ten consecutive shots into an eleven-inch bulls-eye at three hundred yards, and could reliably hit a man on horseback at twice that range. A well-trained soldier could fire an average of three shots per minute, under ideal conditions. At the Battle of Apache Pass, the steep terrain occupied by the Apaches would have forced the troops to fire uphill, thereby reducing the musket's effective range. "Summary Statements of Quarterly Returns of Ordnance and Ordnance Stores On Hand in Regular and Volunteer Army Organizations for the Quarter Ending December 31, 1864"; Fuller, *Rifled Musket*, p. 5; Butler, *United States Firearms*, pp. 86–87; Garavaglia and Worman, *Firearms of the American West*, pp. 160–65.

32. "Vedette's Letters," p. 197.

33. Changing the angle of the howitzer trail allowed the breech to be depressed beyond the normal limits of the elevation screw, but it placed greater stress on the carriage when the guns were fired. The stock trails of both guns were cracked as a result. Thompson afterwards sent one of his gunners back to Tucson with one of the damaged carriages where it could be repaired by a competent blacksmith. *O. R.*, 50: 2, pp. 26–27.

34. This heroic incident, not noted by Roberts in his official report, was recounted by Mitchell's company commander. Cremony, *Life among the Apaches*, p. 163.

35. Fountain, "Old Time Reminiscences."

36. Ibid.

37. Ibid.

38. Teal, "Soldier in the California Column": p. 41 (hereafter cited as "Teal Diary").

39. Ibid.; both the First and Second Cavalry CV were armed with the .52–caliber breech-loading Sharps carbine. In all probability, those issued from Benicia Arsenal to the volunteers were a mixture of Models 1852, 1853, and 1855. All of these were quite similar, varying only in priming systems and other small details. The carbine fired a cartridge consisting of a conical bullet and attached powder charge in a linen case. Separate copper primers were used, either placed on the cone manually, or by an automatic feed system. Each cavalryman also carried a percussion Model 1851 Colt Navy revolver, caliber .36, and a saber. "Summary Statements of Quarterly Returns Ordnance and Ordnance Stores on Hand in the Cavalry Regiments in the Service of the United States during the Third Quarter Ending Sept. 30, 1863," microfilm publication no. 1281, National Archives and Records Administration; Garavaglia and Worman, *Firearms of the American West*, pp. 136–38, 184, 193, 240–41.

40. This is a synthesis of several published accounts of Teal's fight, including "Teal Diary"; *O. R.*, 50:1, p. 133; "Vedette Letters"; Cremony, *Life among the Apaches*, p. 161; and . Fountain, "Old Time Reminiscences," as repeated in "Battle of Apache Pass," *Arizona Cavalcade*, pp. 31–32. An early reference to the wounding of Mangas Colorados is in Dunn, *Massacres of the Mountains*, p. 332, originally published in 1886. This account relies on statements by John Cremony, a less than reliable source, but another author points out that Apache legend, as told to Eve Ball, supports the story that Mangas was wounded and taken to Janos, Chihuahua, for medical treatment. Sweeney, *Cochise*, p. 201.

41. Cremony, *Life among the Apaches*, p. 166.

42. Fountain, "Battle of Apache Pass," p. 34. A Minie ball was the hollow-based bullet used in the .58-caliber Springfield rifled musket. Widely credited to French army Captain Claude Minie, the bullet actually adopted by the U.S. Army was designed by James H. Burton, an employee at Harpers Ferry Arsenal. Whereas Minie's bullet relied on an iron cup wedge in the base to expand the bullet to engage the rifled bore, Burton's simpler bullet employed only the hollow base itself, expanded by the gas of the powder charge, to accomplish the same thing. An excellent discussion on the bullet is in Garavaglia and Worman, *Firearms of the American West*, pp. 157–60.

43. Betzinez, *I Fought with Geronimo*, p. 42; Ball, *In the Days of Victorio*, p. 47; *O. R.*, 50:1, p. 128.

44. Hand, *Civil War in Apacheland*, pp. 111–12.

45. Cremony, *Life among the Apaches*, p. 167.

46. *O. R.*, 50:1, pp. 129, 131; "Teal Diary," p. 42.

47. *O. R.*, 50:1, p. 132.

48. There is little consensus among the available accounts relating to this incident. Captain Roberts, who discovered the remains on July 17 approximately three miles from the mouth of the canyon, reported finding four—"three bodies a short distance from the left-hand side of the road, and stiller farther to the left another body." He further stated that his surgeon identified them as Indians, two wearing government shoes.The author considers Roberts's official report to be the most credible, though he failed to offer any opinion as to who the individuals might have been or how they were killed. See *O. R.*, 50:1, p. 132. Cremony accompanied Roberts's column and apparently saw the bodies, though he did not record the number. His account of the supposed circumstances was written six years after the event, apparently relying on the hearsay of persons who recalled a party of miners having been attacked: *Life among the Apaches*, pp. 174–75. Lending credence to Cremony's version of the story is that Lieutenant Colonel Eyre reported meeting a party of thirty Mexican miners near Cow Springs on July 1 en route from Pinos Altos to Sonora. Lieutenant Colonel E. E. Eyre to Lieutenant Benjamin C. Cuter, AAG, July 6, 1862, *O. R.*, 50: 1, p. 123. A soldier under Roberts's command stated a short time after the incident that they found "the bodies of nine Apaches perforated with ball holes and evidently killed in a running fight with some parties to the writer unknown." *Alta California*, August 16, 1862 (Bancroft, "Scraps," p. 196). Another member of the California Column, who passed that way in August, noted finding "a fresh grave, where the bones of 8 men were deposited by General Carlton." *Sacramento Union*, October 18, 1862. Yet another witness, writing of the event in 1908, remembered finding "the bodies of thirteen white men" three miles east of the pass. See Fountain, "Battle of Apache Pass," p. 35. One authority surmises that the initials on the holster may have been those of Sergeant William Wheeling, the courier killed in that vicinity on June 18. The large bloodstain nearby indeed could have accounted for the killing site of either Wheeling or the Hispanic courier. Roberts and his men were unaware of that incident at the time. Personal communication with Larry Ludwig, Fort Bowie NHS, August 30, 2000. That two of the dead men wore army shoes, according to Roberts, may indeed suggest the bodies of Wheeling and his Mexican companion, while the others, identified by Dr. McKee as Indians, could have been Apache casualties, though it is unlikely those bodies would have been left behind. However, a trooper in Eyre's command wrote to a friend: "They killed two of our express men in the same place [camp where the night attack occurred] just a few days before." *Alta California*, August 16, 1862 (Bancroft, "Scraps," p. 193).

49. A ciénaga, on the usually dry San Simon River thirteen miles south of the station, provided a reliable source of good water. A cut-off departed from the main stage route six miles north of Apache Pass and went along the base of the mountains directly to the cienega. From that point it connected with the Butterfield Overland Mail Road at the station. This somewhat longer route was used by trains plying the road, but Roberts failed to take it. Although he explored

the bed of the San Simon for six or seven miles above the station, he simply did not go far enough to discover the ciénaga. Eyre had camped at the ciénaga, though he too took the longer route via San Simon Station, then south along the river bed. *O. R.*, 50:1, pp. 122, 132.

50. *O. R.*, 50:1, pp. 132–34; "Teal Diary." The route Cremony followed around the Dos Cabezas was in use, at least occasionally, prior to 1857. In that year, Second Lieutenant H. W. Freedly, Third Infantry, conducted a train from Fort Thorn to Calabasas via the main Butterfield road, but noted that "there is a road which passes down the river and around the northern point of the Dos Cabezas and joining the main road again at Nugent's Spring. This road is said to be better than the main road as it avoids the playa and the pass in the mountains, it however is not so direct nor so well watered." Freedly to Major D. S. Miles, June 10, 1875, Letters Received, R.G. 393, NA. Copy in Fort Bowie NHS files.

51. Roberts' quote is in *O. R.*, 50:1, p. 128; Eyre's statement is taken from Orton, *Record of California Men*, p. 61.

CHAPTER 4: THE POST AT APACHE PASS

1. The directive establishing Fort Bowie was contained in *General Orders No. 12*, Headquarters, Column from California, July 27, 1862. Surgeon David Wooster was assigned as the first post surgeon, as noted in *O. R.*, 50: 2, pp. 40–41.There were seventy-two men on duty with Company G, Fifth California, at the time it garrisoned at Fort Bowie: Post Returns, Fort Bowie, July 1862, Returns from United States Military Posts, 1800–1916, Records of the Adjutant General's Office, RG 94, microfilm publication M617, roll 129 (hereafter cited as Post Returns with date). Colonel George Washington Bowie, a Maryland native, had served as an infantry officer in the regular army during the Mexican War and was awarded brevet rank as major for his actions at Contreras and Churabusco. Prior to the Civil War, he practiced law in California, according to Heitman, *Historical Register*, 1, p. 234. One enlisted man characterized Bowie as "the only man (officer) of the 5th Reg. worthy of notice. He is a gentleman, a lawyer, but not soldier. He thinks a great deal of the men but can never make soldiers of any body of men—discipline is in want." See Hand, *Civil War in Apacheland*, p. 78. This author believes Carleton probably selected the Fifth to garrison Fort Bowie in order to preserve the integrity of his own First California Infantry. Carleton knew that the remaining companies of the Fifth would be marching east from California during coming months, therefore it made sense to detach the companies of that regiment.

2. *G. O. No. 12*, July 27, 1862, Headquarters Column from California, *O. R.*, 50:2, p. 41.

3. From the outset, Fort Bowie was supplied from depots at Tucson, Fort Yuma, and even as far away as San Francisco. This basic system of logistics would remain in place for as long as the post was active, although the advent of the Southern Pacific Railroad eventually replaced overland supply by wagon. Author's note.

4. When the battalion under Captain E. B. Willis approached Apache Pass on July 29, the troops were unaware that Carleton had garrisoned the spring. At the entrance, three miles west, Willis deployed his two companies of infantry in skirmish order on either side of the road, with Shinn's battery forming the advance guard. Arriving at the station, Willis's men were pleasantly surprised to find Company G already guarding the area. "Diary of Corporal Alexander Grayson Bowman, Company B, Fifth Regiment, California Volunteers, October 18 1861–February 22, 1865." Copy in files at Fort Bowie NHS.

5. Carleton to Fergusson, August 3, 1862 in *O. R.*, 50:2, p. 47.

6. Carleton to Lt. Col. Richard C. Drum, ibid., pt. 1, pp. 100, 123; *Sacramento Union*, October 18 and November 6, 1862. A minor gold rush to Pinos Altos occurred in 1860, attracting miners from both California and the Mesilla area. The exodus of the U.S.Army from New Mexico Territory in 1861 left the district open to Apache raids, a situation taken advantage of by both Cochise and Mangas Coloradas. See Paul, *Mining Frontiers of the Far West*, pp. 156–57; Sweeney, *Cochise*, pp. 178–81.

7. Coult indicated just how primitive Fort Bowie was when he requested lumber for fabricating office furniture, carpenter's tools, and horseshoeing equipment. Coult to Lt. Benjamin C. Cutler, August 9, 1862, *O. R.*, 50:1, p. 135.

8. Coult to Cutler, August 1, 1862, included with Post Returns, August 1862.

9. Coult to Cutler, August 9, 1862, *O. R.*, 50:1, pp. 134–35.

10. Ibid.

11. Post Return to August 10, 1862; *O. R.*, 50:2, 73–74.

12. Greene, "Historic Structures Report," p. 25. Much of the discussion to follow in this narrative relies on Greene's detailed structural history of the post.

13. The cavalry detachments did not make up a part of the regular garrison, since their presence was temporary and related solely to the mission of protecting the mail riders. Post Returns, August–November 1862.

14. *General Orders No. 11*, Column from California, July 21, 1861, in *O. R.*, 50:1, p. 92.

15. This realignment was authorized on November 9, 1861. Thian, *Military Geography*, p. 87. According to *G. O. No. 29*, AGO., troops crossing department boundaries remained under the command of the general under whose orders they were operating. The troops were to be withdrawn as soon as their position came under the control of the proper department commander. *O. R.*, 50:1, p. 99.

16. Ibid., p. 79; Carleton to Drum, September 20, 1862, *O. R.*, 50:2, p. 100; *G. O. 85*, Dept. of New Mexico, ibid., pt. 1, p. 145.

17. Carleton to Major David Fergusson, August 3, 1862, in *O. R.*, 50:2, p. 47. Coult proposed to Colonel West, commanding the District of Arizona, that supply and troops rotations at Fort Bowie would be facilitated by assigning the post to the District of Western Arizona, headquartered at Tucson. Apparently, this administrative change was approved in October 1862. See Murray, "History of Fort Bowie," p. 80. The description of Mesilla was provided by an anonymous California soldier writing to the *Sacramento Union*, February 27, 1863.

18. The District of Western Arizona remained an administrative unit of the Department of the Pacific until the end of 1862. In December, Wright notified Carleton that, since the California Column had left the Department of the Pacific when it took up stations in New Mexico, Carleton was being relieved of the District of Western Arizona. That did not sit well with Carleton, and the district was soon made a part of the Department of New Mexico. *O. R.*, 50:2, p. 271; Wright to Carleton, December 19, 1862, ibid., p. 255. The District of Arizona was defined in General Orders no. 20, September 5, 1862, ibid., pt. 1, p. 115. The realignment was effected by *G. O. No. 13*, AGO, January 14, 1863 according to Thian, *Military Geography*, p. 79.

19. Coult to Lieutenant W. A. Thompson, October 2, 1862, *O. R.*, 50:2, pp. 145–46.

20. In making his request for meat, Hinds was careful to specify "anything but pemmican." Hinds to Coult, October 7, 1862, Miscellaneous Reports Fort Bowie records, Arizona Historical Society. Typescript copy in Fort Bowie NHS files.

21. Carleton to West, October 21, 1862, *O. R.*, 50:2, p. 189.

22. Murray, "History of Fort Bowie," p. 80.

23. Greene, "Historic Structure Report," pp. 27–27.

24. Hinds to Coult, October 7, 1862, Misc. Reports, Fort Bowie records, AHS.

25. Ibid.; Post Returns, October 1862.

26. Hinds to Coult, October 7, 1862, Misc. Reports Fort Bowie records, AHS.

27. Coult to Lieutenant W. L. Rynerson, December 30, 1862 in *O.R.*, 50:2, p. 269–70

28. Coult to Lieutenant Colonel Richard C. Drum, December 31, 1862, ibid., p. 270.

29. Wright to Carleton, December 19, 1862, ibid., p. 255. Wright deemed it "important to secure both Arizona and Mesilla from being again overrun by the rebel hordes that a respectable force should occupy those districts, another object I have in view is to keep an eye on the neighboring States of the Mexican Republic, where most of the disaffected from this State go." *O. R.* 50:2, p. 350.

30. Sweeney, *Cochise*, p. 204.

31. California troops from Fort West struck the Mimbres Apaches soon after Mangas's death, dealing them a serious defeat in March. A second column operating in that area early in 1864 probably wiped them out. See Utley, *Frontiersmen in Blue*, pp. 251–52; Thrapp, *Conquest of Apacheria*, pp. 20–23.

32. Mesilla was abandoned as district headquarters in favor of Hart's Mill, Texas by virtue of *G. O. No. 5*, District of Arizona, March 14, 1863, in *O. R.*, 50:2, pp. 351–52. West's decision may have been influenced by undesirable social conditions in the larger town of Mesilla, or a desire to be near the Mexican town of El Paso, the better to monitor any Confederate activities occurring there. Too, old Fort Bliss afforded facilities not available in Mesilla, even though it was approximately fifty miles farther from Tucson.

33. Ibid.

34. The system of one company in turn relieving another at stations west-to-east across Arizona was perpetuated as the Fifth California Infantry crossed the territory to take station in New Mexico. Consequently, Company G, the founders of Fort Bowie, left in December 1862. It was relieved by Company E, which remained until April, at which time Company K arrived. That company, one of the longest tenured of the volunteers, served at Fort Bowie until September 1864. Post Returns.

35. Harrover to West, April 25, 1863, *O. R.*, 50:1, p. 213. This skirmish is also recounted, though incorrectly dated "1864," in Orton, *Records of California Men*, pp. 670, 698.

36. *G. O. No. 8*, May 12, 1863, Headquarters Tucson, *O. R.*, 50:2, pp. 431–32.

37. Sweeney, *Cochise*, pp. 210–12.

38. Ibid., 212–13.

39. Ibid., 213–14; Post Returns, July 1863.

40. Yager to Captain C. R. Wellman, August 22, 1863, in *O. R.*, 50:1, p. 232.

41. Kuhl to Wellman, September 1, 1863, in ibid.

42. Report of Captain J. H. Whitlock, September 12, 1863, ibid., p. 242.

43. For example, Mexican cavalry wiped out Susopa's camp near Janos in November 1863, killing twenty-one Apaches and capturing seven others. Sweeney, *Cochise*, p. 216.

44. Debate over granting Arizona territorial status raged almost without intermission after Lincoln's election in 1860. Although the slavery issue initially delayed action, that became a moot point after the California Column reoccupied the area two years later. Advocates of the measure argued that Arizona was rich in gold and silver and would contribute significantly to the national treasury. A territorial government was needed, they claimed, to help bring law and order to the region, thereby allowing economic development of the territory. Those opposed to admitting Arizona submitted that with only about six thousand residents (some claimed no more than one thousand), Arizona hardly warranted the expenditure of the $50,000 necessary to establish the territory. Other critics opined that would-be office seekers were putting personal interests over those of the territory. Nevertheless, the House of Representatives passed the legislation on May 8, 1862. The Senate, however, launched into a round of new debates that resulted in the tabling of the bill until the next session of Congress. It was not taken up again until February 1863. Some in the Senate thought that the creation of new territories in the West should be deferred until the Civil War ended, but supporters continued to beat the drum of Arizona's undeveloped riches, a point that gained favor in the face of increasing wartime expenses. Opposition quickly dissolved as Democrats joined Republicans to vote in favor of the bill. For a thorough discussion of this topic, see Sacks, "Creation of the Territory of Arizona," pt. 2: 109–48.

45. Carleton to Colonel George W. Bowie, April 15, 1864, *O.R.*, 50:2, p. 820.

46. Ibid.

47. Utley, *Frontiersmen in Blue*, p. 257.

48. Rigg's report is found in *O.R.*, 50:1, pp. 360–70.

49. Charles and Jacqueline Meketa, *One Blanket and Ten Days' Rations*, pp. vii, 3, 7–9. In January 1865, Lieutenant Colonel Clarence E. Bennett was sent from Tucson to take charge of new construction at Fort Bowie. By virtue of his rank, he became the temporary post commander until May. Thus, Company A was burdened with construction duties, though Bennett reported that "There are only about men enough for two guards in addition to cut and haul fuel and hay and haul water. Escort duty and other work about the post makes duty very hard on this garrison, and, in addition, to expect them to build a post is truly a great expectation" (quoted in Meketa, p. 17). See also Post Returns, July 1864–May 1865. Later inspections would reveal that little, if anything, was accomplished toward new construction during this period.

50. Sweeney, *Cochise*, 218–20.

51. Davis claimed to have killed forty-nine Indians and captured sixteen in this fight. His troops destroyed the camp. The complete report is published in Davis to Cutler, June 5, 1864, *O. R.*, 50:2, pp. 869–72.

52. Ibid., p. 259.

53. Bosque Redondo was a desolate area on the Pecos River in eastern New Mexico. Carleton had displaced the Navajos and Mescaleros there primarily because of its isolation from their homeland, and the homelands of their relatives still at war. Fort Sumner stood watch over the captives. A brief account of this episode is in Utley, *Frontiersmen in Blue*, 236–39. For a more comprehensive treatment, see Gerald Thompson, *The Army and the Navajo: The Bosque Redondo Reservation Experiment 1863–1868*.

54. Sweeney, *Cochise*, pp. 223–24.

55. The foregoing is drawn in part from Sweeney, *Cochise*, pp. 226–30, with some details taken from the Report of Lieutenant Colonel Clarence E. Bennett, February 25, 1865 in *O. R.*, 50:1, p. 401. See also the Report of Captain John L. Merriam, February 22, 1865, ibid. It should be noted that Bennett's report included the remark that "the mail is not considered safe the way it is now carried by one man." This implied that a change had occurred in the express system since Carleton initiated it two years earlier.

56. Report of Lieutenant Colonel Clarence E. Bennett, July 6, 1865, *O. R.*, 50:1, pp. 415–19.

57. Ibid.

58. Report of Lieutenant Colonel Clarence E. Bennett, July 21, 1865, ibid., pp. 421–23. When Bennett sent back a six-man detachment to Fort Bowie, they were ambushed southwest of present-day Willcox on July 13. One soldier was killed and two were wounded. Although they were forced to abandon their wagon, the men escaped to arrive at the fort the next day. Sweeney, *Cochise*, p. 233.

59. Ibid.

60. The lumber camp consisted of only the most primitive equipment. In lieu of a steam-powered saw, the men labored in saw pits. This crude method of making lumber called for a log to be placed lengthwise over a pit more than

head-deep. One man standing over the pit operated one end of a two-man saw, while another man handled the lower end. The two men, working in tandem, cut the logs into dimensioned lumber. As can be imagined, it was slow, difficult work. *Special Orders No. 29*, Fort Bowie, July 11, 1865; Greene, "Historic Structures Report," p. 32.

61. Ibid., pp. 32–33.

62. Post Returns, November 1865; Sweeney, *Cochise*, pp. 237–39.

63. Fort Mason had been established on August 21, 1865, to replace the old post at Tubac. The new fort was built thirteen miles south of Tubac along the Santa Cruz River at Calabasas. The site was selected by and named after Brigadier General John S. Mason. The post, never more than a temporary cantonment, was abandoned in 1866. Frazer, *Forts of the West*, p. 11.

CHAPTER 5: NEITHER LIFE NOR PROPERTY IS SECURE IN ARIZONA

1. Fort Bowie was changed to Camp Bowie at least by January 1867. However, *General Orders No. 2*, Headquarters, Division of the Pacific, April 5, 1879, restored it to Fort Bowie. Abandoned Reservation File, Records of the General Land Office, RG 49. Copies on file at Fort Bowie NHS.

2. Bradford, *Battles and Leaders of the Civil War*, p. 27.

3. Thian, *Military Geography*, pp. 76, 80, 99; Utley, *Frontier Regulars*, pp. 169–70.

4. Report of Inspection of Fort Bowie, A. T., Brigadier General Charles A. Whittier, March 1, 1866, Records of the Office of the Inspector General, RG 159, National Archives. Copy at Fort Bowie National Historic Site. (hereafter cited as Whittier inspection report).

5. Ibid.

6. Rodenbough, *Army of the United States*, pp. 602–5; Post Returns, May 1866.

7. The claimants were given as Byrnes, [Tom] Wallace, Dodson, Harris, and [John] Anderson, the post sutler. *Prescott Arizona Miner*, March 14, 1866. Members of the California volunteers discovered mineral bearing deposits as early as 1863 and 1864. Sidney R. Delong to Colonel E. B. Beaumont, October 17, 1885, Letters Received, Fort Bowie, A. T.

8. Stevens, "Colonel John Finkle Stone": 74.

9. Ibid.

10. Austerman, *Sharps Rifles and Spanish Mules*, p. 198

11. John and Lillian Theobald, *Arizona Territory Post Offices*, p. 38; "Memorial by the Arizona Territorial Legislature to Establish Mail Routes in the Territory," (no. 25), *House Executive Documents*, 39th Cong., 2d sess., serial 1302.

12. Report of inspection of posts in Arizona, July 15, 1867, *House Executive Documents*, no. 1, 40th Cong., 2d sess., serial 1327, p. 83. Later in 1867, the Santa Fe Stage Company, coupled with the Tomlinson & Company U.S. Mail Line, established service from Santa Fe to Los Angeles, including a circuitous route taking in Prescott, Tucson, and Fort Yuma. At that time, forts and settlements

south and east of Tucson had no dependable service. Theobald and Theobald, *Wells Fargo in Arizona Territory*, p. 24.

13. Greene, "Historic Structure Report," pp. 265–66.

14. Sweeney, *Cochise*, p. 292; Bell, *New Tracks in North America*, II, p. 42. Tri-weekly service between Tucson and Mesilla (route no. 17,408) was inaugurated in September 1867. Annual Report of the Postmaster General, *House Misc. Documents.*, 4, serial 1369; Theobold, *Arizona Territory Post Offices*, p. 39; Sloane, *Butterfield Mail*, p. 10; Billings, *Circular no. 4: Report on Barracks*, p. 472. George Hand recorded that in 1866–67 he and Tom Wallace owned a two-thirds share of the mail contract ($26,000 per year) between Tucson and Mesilla. The contractor for the entire route to San Diego was veteran frontiersman John Jones, Carleton's special express rider who had narrowly escaped death at the hands of the Apaches in 1862. Hand accused Jones of unfair dealings and thus terminated their partnership. *Civil War in Apacheland*, p. 176; Theobald and Theobald, *Wells Fargo in Arizona Territory*, pp. 24–25. The partnership of Cook & Shaw held the main contract for mail service between Santa Fe and El Paso. *Santa Fe Gazette*, June 20, 1868.

15. *San Francisco American Flag*, April 26, 1867, based on dispatches from Mesilla dated March 5 and from Santa Fe on April 5; *New York Herald*, April 22, 1867, from a dispatch of March 18. Copies of the articles are in the Hayden Collection, Arizona Historical Society, Tucson.

16. As the result of an act of Congress passed on July 28, 1866, the nine three-battalion infantry regiments were reorganized, each battalion becoming a new, small regiment of ten companies. Accordingly, the Third Battalion, Fourteenth Infantry, to which Company E at Camp Bowie belonged, was redesignated as the Thirty-second Infantry. This change is reflected in the February 1867 Post Return. Although it might be mistaken for a change of station, Company E simply became Company G. See Rodenbough, *Army of the United States*, p. 605; Ganoe, *History of the United States Army*, pp. 306–307.

17. Whittier inspection report.

18. The Union Pacific Railway Eastern Division (not to be confused with the Union Pacific Railroad building across Nebraska, Wyoming, and Utah) sponsored two survey parties to examine possible transcontinental routes south of the Gila River. According to Bell, one was led by a Mr. Runk; the other, to which Bell belonged, by L. H. Eicholtz. Each team was composed of twenty-five engineers, plus cooks, teamsters, guides, and a thirty-man cavalry escort. Bell, *New Tracks in North America*, II, pp. 44–45. Eicholtz's journal of the expedition, which provides a brief second-hand reference to Camp Bowie and the Carroll incident, is in the collections of the Colorado Historical Society, Denver.

19. Hunter, "Early Days in Arizona": 105. Bell, perhaps succumbing to a fit of Victorian romanticism to embellish his story, gave Carroll's age as eighteen, "and [he] looked even younger, for his hair was very fair, and he had not the least tinge of whisker on his smooth cheeks." Actually, Carroll had been in the army since 1861, initially as a first sergeant in the Fourteenth Kentucky Infan-

try. He rose to the rank of captain by the end of the war. Carroll was mustered out in January 1865, but was appointed as a second lieutenant in the Regular Army in February 1866. The cemetery record gives his age as twenty-three, which may be correct. Bell, *New Tracks in North America*, II, p. 46; Heitman, *Historical Register*, I, p. 286; Appendix C, "Report of Interments at Fort Bowie, A. T., March 22, 1883," in Greene, "Historic Structure Report," p. 321.

20. This account of Carroll's death relies largely on Bell, *New Tracks in North America*, II, pp. 280–85. The "record of events" states that Carroll was killed "within $3^1/_2$ miles of the post." Post Returns, November 1867.

21. Green, "Historic Structure Report," p. 41

22. Ibid., p. 42.

23. Ibid., p. 99; "Description of Post," Medical History, Fort Bowie.

24. For further information relating to the development of the Model 1866 Springfield rifle, see McChristian, *U.S. Army in the West*, pp. 30–32; Garavaglia and Worman, *Firearms of the American West*, pp. 12–15.

25. Widney to Miss L. N. Widney, May 13, 1868, Joseph P. Widney Letters, Gustave Schneider Collection, Arizona Historical Society (hereafter cited as Widney Letters).

26. Ripley to Wright, May 13, 1868, Letters Sent, Fort Bowie, RG 393, microfilm copy at Fort Bowie NHS; *Santa Fe New Mexican*, June 23, 1868; Widney to Miss L. N. Widney, May 13, 1868, Widney Letters. Another account of the skirmish is recorded in "Letter from Camp Bowie," *Santa Fe New Mexican*, June 23, 1868.

27. Surgeon Widney was of the opinion that the Apaches, after the skirmish of May 13, were "loathe to leave with so little profit." Widney to Miss L. N. Widney, May 20, 1868, Widney Letters.

28. Hubbard to Ripley, June 3, 1868, Letters Received, Fort Bowie, RG 393, National Archives, microfilm copy at Fort Bowie NHS; Ripley to Acting Assistant Adjutant General, Sub-district of Tucson, June 3, 1868, ibid.; Post Return, Fort Bowie, May 1868. The incident was also recorded in *Santa Fe Gazette*, June 13 and June 20, 1868, and *Santa Fe New Mexican*, June 16, 1868.

29. Ibid.; biographical sketch of Joseph Pomeroy Widney (publisher unknown: no date) in Gustave Schneider Collection, Arizona Historical Society.

30. *Santa Fe New Mexican*, July 21, 1868; *Santa Fe Gazette*, August 1, 1868.

31. By late fall, Cochise made his presence known far to the north in what was traditionally the home of his old allies, the White Mountain Apaches. The Chiricahuas happened upon a trading party from Zuni and immediately relieved them of all their goods and animals, and even their clothes. The whites were indeed fortunate that one Apache recognized their leader as a former friend. The seven men were set free, stark naked, to make their way back to Zuni. Sweeney, *Cochise*, pp. 259–60.

32. Ganoe, *History of the U.S. Army*, p. 309.

33. "Report of the Commanding General," *Annual Report of the Secretary of War*, 1868, pp. 46–47.

34. Greene, "Historic Structures Report," pp. 42, 47.

CHAPTER 6: CAPTURE AND ROOT OUT THE APACHE

1. (Tubac) *Weekly Arizonian,* January 31, 1869.

2. Greene, "Historic Structures Report," pp. 48–49 For a contemporary description of Fort Bowie, see Inspection Report, Camp Bowie, A.T., Lieutenant Colonel Roger Jones to Brevet Major General James B. Fry, April 28, 1869, copy at Arizona Historical Society.

3. Young, *Western Mining,* p. 144; Paul, *Mining Frontiers,* p. 158; Keane and Rogge, *Gold and Silver Mining in Arizona,* pp. 44–45. Freighting in southern Arizona during this time is discussed in Walker, "Wagon Freighting in Arizona": 192–93.

4. "Report of the Secretary of War," *House Executive Documents,* 40th Cong., 3d Sess., No. 1, p. 47 (hereafter cited as *ARSW* with year). Halleck was widely respected in the army for his intelligence, having graduated third in his class at West Point. Like most top ranking graduates, Halleck chose the Engineers. For two years during the Civil War, he commanded the Union Army. Heitman, *Historical Register,* 1, p. 491.

5. Halleck requested that he be assigned one or two additional regiments of infantry especially for service in Arizona. He also called for the enlistment of two hundred more Indian scouts in Arizona to augment the two hundred already authorized in the Division of the Pacific. Ibid., p. 48.

6. Valputic and Longfellow, "Fight at Chiricahua Pass": 370. Estevan Ochoa grew up in a freighting family that operated between Chihuahua and Independence during the heyday of the Santa Fe Trail. He went into business for himself during the 1840s in Mesilla, and owned a flour mill in Las Cruces. Ochoa later moved his headquarters to Tubac, where he had ready access to contracts with the U.S. Army. In 1868, he again relocated to Tucson, where by the 1870s he headed the largest freighting firm in Arizona. Albrecht, "Estevan Ochoa": 35–40.

7. Report of Major General E. O. C. Ord, September 21, 1869 in *ARSW,* 1869, p.124 (hereafter cited as Ord report); Walker, *The Statistics of the Population of the United States, Ninth Census,* I, p. 12; Thian, *Military Geography,* p. 54.

8. Sweeney, *Cochise,* pp. 262–64.

9. Ord report, p. 121. Edward Otho Cresap Ord was an 1839 graduate of the U.S. Military Academy. During the first two decades of his career, he served in the Third U.S. Artillery, becoming a brigadier general of volunteers at the beginning of the Civil War. He was breveted several times for gallant and meritorious service in combat, rising to the rank of major general by the end of the war. Heitman, *Historical Register,* 1, p. 759.

10. Reuben F. Bernard biographical file, Hayden Collection, Arizona Historical Society.

11. Bernard to Lieutenant W. H. Winters, February 9, 1869, William Carey Brown Papers, University of Colorado (hereafter cited as Brown Papers).

12. Bernard to Winter, March 23, 1869, ibid.; Post Returns, March 1869.

13. The name "Camp Merijilda" derived from the post guide, Merijilda Grijalva, whose services had been so valuable to the California Volunteers. Greene, "Historic Stuctures Report," p. 51.

14. Medical History, Fort Bowie, May and July 1869, Records of the Surgeon General's Office, RG 112, NA (hereafter cited as Medical History with respective month and year).

15. Post Returns, June and July 1869.

16. *Weekly Arizonian*, July 17, 1869; "Col. John Finkle Stone and the Apache Pass Mining Company," *Arizona Historical Review.* 75.

17. Post Returns, August 1869.

18. Ganoe, *History of the United States Army*, pp. 324–25; Rodenbough, *Army of the United States*, p. 675. Colonel George Stoneman, commanding the Twenty-first Infantry, thus inherited command of the District of Arizona per *G. O. no. 1*, District of Arizona, August 16, 1869. See also *G. O. No. 31*, Dept. of California, May 12, 1869; Post Returns, August 1869.

19. "Diary Kept by Sarah Keener While Crossing the Plains in Covered Wagon From Texas to California 1869," typescript copy at Fort Bowie NHS (hereafter cited as Keener Diary).

20. Stone apparently had never held commissioned rank, but had been a member of Brig. Gen. Albert Sidney Johnston's Utah Expedition in 1857–58. Afterwards, he resided in Denver and, later still, New Mexico. He served as a deputy U.S.marshal there until 1867, when he was appointed a deputy customs collector in Tucson. See "Colonel Stone and the Apache Pass Mining Company," pp. 74–75; *Weekly Arizonian*, July 3 and September 4, 1869. Sarah Keener observed on September 8: "They are preparing a gold mine here which is said to be very rich. Have the machinery all on the ground," Keener Diary. First Lieutenant George Macomber, who arrived at Camp Bowie with Company D, Twenty-first Infantry in August 1869, became a shareholder in the Apache Pass Mine. However, Macomber was killed in a haying accident on September 19. Stone's death the following month brought an end to the ill-fated venture. Post Returns, September 1869; Greene, "Historic Structures Report," p. 299. A year later, a visitor to the post reported that "the quartz mill . . . presented a very poverty stricken appearance. There being no covering over the machinery, stamps, dies, engine, etc., were badly rusted, and the whole concern was fast becoming worthless." See J. H. Marion, *Notes On Travel*, p. 34. A Mr. Hopkins reportedly acquired Stone's interest in the mine in January 1870, after which a Mr. Arnold from California bought the entire business for $125,000. *Weekly Arizonian*, January 29, 1870; ibid., March 5, 1870.

21. This account is a summary of information found in the issues of the *Weekly Arizonian*, previously cited, as well as Post Returns, October 1869; Medical History, October 1869; Valputic and Longfellow, "Fight at Apache Pass," 374–75; and M. P. Johnson biographical file, Arizona Historical Society. Presumably, the bodies of those killed on the stage were brought to Camp Bowie for burial, although an 1883 burial register available to the author listed only Colonel Stone. There were, however, several "unknown" burials listed adjacent to Stone's name, which may account for the others. "Report of Interments at Fort Bowie, A. T. March 22, 1883," Appendix C, in Greene, "Historic Structures Report," pp. 321–22.

22. Bernard to Dunn, October 10, 1869, Brown Papers. Winters was cut from the same cloth as his superior, Captain Bernard. He had risen from the ranks, twice, to become a commissioned officer. On the second occasion, he had started his enlistment as a private, and was promoted consecutively to corporal, sergeant, and second lieutenant within the First Cavalry. Heitman, *Historical Register*, 1, p. 1051.

23. Post Returns, October 1869; Bernard to Dunn, October 10, 1869, Brown Papers; Medical History, October 1869.

24. Captain Bernard later recommended all of the participants in this fire fight for the Medal of Honor. Bernard to Colonel John P. Sherburne, December 20, 1869, Brown Papers.

25. Bernard to Devin, October 22, 1869, ibid.

26. Private Edwin Elwood, Troop G, Eighth Cavalry, was shot through the right breast and Private Charles H. Ward suffered a broken leg. These statistics, as well as the quotation, are from Bernard's letter, ibid.

27. Regardless, none of the wounded men died under Tidemann's care; Dorr was post surgeon at Camp Crittenden at the time of these events, but had preceeded Dr. Tidemann at Camp Bowie. Valputic and Longfellow, "Fight at Chiricahua Pass," p. 378 and 378n.31.

28. Lafferty, who had been a member the California Volunteer Cavalry from 1864 to 1866, continued his army career with the Eighth Cavalry. He attained the permanent rank of captain in 1876, but because he had been a lieutenant at the time of his heroic actions, his brevet was based on the lower grade. Lafferty died in 1899. Heitman, *Historical Register*, 1, p. 611.

29. Surgeon Dorr's account of his fight is found in Valputic and Longfellow, "Fight at Chiricahua Pass": 376–77.

30. Bernard to Devin, November 2, 1869, Brown Papers.

31. Ibid., November 14, 1869, ibid.

32. Ibid.

33. Post Returns, January 1870; Sweeney, *Cochise*, pp. 278–79.

34. Post Returns, February 1870.

35. Bernard, commanding Camp Bowie, must have had information suggesting that Cochise was north of the post because scouting detachments were sent to Mt. Graham on two occasions during February and early March. Post Returns, February and March 1870.

36. Heitman, *Historical Register*, 1, p. 853; Rodenbough, *Army of the United States*, pp. 199–204.

37. Post Returns, March 1870.

38. Marion, *Notes On Travel*, pp. 6–9; Utley, *Frontier Regulars*, p. 192. The Department of Arizona embraced all of that territory, as well as that part of California lying south of a line extending from the northwest corner of Arizona to Point Conception. Thian, *Military Geography*, p. 52.

39. Greene, "Historic Structures Report," pp. 51–52. The new corrals were not completed until October 15. Medical History, October 1870.

40. Post Returns, August 1870; Medical History, September 1870.

41. Sweeney, *Cochise*, p. 281.

42. Ibid., p. 284.

43. Ibid., pp. 281–86; Post Returns, November 1870.

44. Post Returns, December 1870 and January 1871; Medical History, January 1871.

45. Post Returns, March 1871. *Weekly Arizonian*, April 1, 1871; Elements of the Eighth Cavalry operating from Fort Bayard, N.Mex. also trailed a war party to the Chiricahua Mountains and attacked their rancheria approximately thirty miles south of Camp Bowie on February 12. These were probably the same Indians who had stolen stock around Silver City. *Las Cruces Borderer*, April 27, 1871; Sweeney, *Cochise*, p. 305. Not all of the depredations in the region could be blamed on Cochise, however. During March, prior to his departure from the Gila River country, a rancher, L. B. Wooster, was killed near Tubac and a woman was kidnapped. Earlier incidents included the murder of the mail rider between Tucson and Tubac and the slaying of another man just three miles outside Tucson in January. Thrapp, *Conquest of Apacheria*, p. 85.

46. Following the theft of stock at Silver City, Captain William C. Kelly and a small detachment of the Eighth Cavalry joined forces with seven skilled civilians to track the raiders to the mountains some thirty miles south of Camp Bowie. Kelly struck the rancheria on February 12, scattering the occupants, and destroying the camp of seventeen wickiups. Numerous items were found in the camp that implicated the Apaches in several depredations dating back to 1868. In a second incident at nearly the same time, thirty civilians led by noted Indian fighter John Bullard trailed horse thieves from Cochise's band from Fort Bayard around the Mogollon Mountains and attacked them on February 24. Sweeney, *Cochise*, pp. 305–7.

47. A man named McKenzie apparently was killed first, on April 13, prompting five others to give chase. Cochise turned on his pursuers, killing Chapin, Long, and Unter. Another man, Lopez, was slightly wounded and the fifth man, Borques, escaped unharmed. *Las Cruces Borderer*, April 27, 1871; May 4, 1871.

48. Ibid., May 4, 1871. The commanding officer at Camp Bowie began posting five-man infantry picket guards at Ciénaga San Simon and Sulphur Springs, two traditional trouble spots, in February 1871. These were in addition to the long-standing detachment maintained at San Pedro Crossing. The guard detachments continued in force until June 1872. Post Returns, June 1872.

49. Post Returns, April 1871. On this way home, Lieutenant Colonel Escalante (identified by Sweeney as Colonel Elias) attacked and wiped out a family rancheria of ten Apaches in the southern Chiricahua Mountains. Sweeney, *Cochise*, p. 314.

50. Cushing was the brother of the famed Alonzo H. Cushing, who was killed while commanding his battery in the center of Pickett's Charge at the Battle of Gettysburg. Rodenbough, *Army of the United States*, p. 205; Post Returns, May 1871; Sweeney, *Cochise*, p. 313.

51. A legend persists that while Jeffords was engaged in carrying the mail east of Tucson, he gained Cochise's respect by entering his camp alone and unarmed to negotiate a truce to protect his express riders. See Angie Debo, *Geronimo*, p. 76. However, this has been contested as an apocryphal story, probably conjured up by Jeffords himself many years later. Sweeney, *Cochise*, pp. 292–96. For further details relating to Jefford's appointment as emissary from Pope and the meeting itself, see Sweeney, pp. 309, 315.

52. This force of irregulars, possessed of a lynch-mob mentality, was organized to retaliate for Apache raids in the Santa Cruz Valley. On April 28, 1871, they fell on an unsuspecting camp at the Camp Grant reservation, killing all but a few of the inhabitants. Of 128 bodies found on the grizzly scene, only 8 were men. It remains one of the most disgraceful events in Arizona history. An official report of the affair is found in Colyer, *Peace with the Apaches*, pp. 31–33. See also Thrapp, *Conquest of Apacheria*, pp. 87–90.

53. Post Returns, June 1871.

CHAPTER 7: WE WILL MAKE PEACE

1. Fritz, *Movement for Indian Assimilation*, p. 71.

2. Ibid., 70–78. In a landmark reversal of previous Indian policy, Congress abolished the concept of "domestic dependent nations." Although previous treaties were to be honored, no new treaties would be negotiated with Indian tribes, a measure that was to have serious implications in the resolution of future conflicts, including that with Geronimo. Utley, *Indian Frontier*, pp. 129–40, Wooster, *Military and United States Indian Policy*, pp. 10–11.

3. Thrapp, *Conquest of Apacheria*, pp. 83–94.

4. Crook did not seek, nor even want, the position as commander of the Department of Arizona. After being relieved of the command of the Department of Columbia in 1870, he enjoyed comfortable duty in San Francisco as a member of a "benzene board" to evaluate the fitness of excess officers. When Major General George H. Thomas, commanding the Division of the Pacific, had queried Crook about such an assignment a few years earlier, he declined for the reason that he was tired of Indian campaigning, which entailed arduous duty without compensation. After Major General J. M. Schofield replaced Thomas in 1870, he made Crook a similar proposition, which met with the same response. Crook professed to be uncomfortable with the whole situation, made worse by the fact that the appointment initially was only a temporary one. Invited to dine with the Stonemans at Wilmington on his way to Arizona, Crook related that he "had to accept out of politeness, but never passed through such an ordeal. Mrs. Stoneman, while trying to be polite, could not help showing in every action that she would like to tear me to pieces. . . . if only she knew how I hated to go to Arizona, she might feel differently." Crook, *Autobiography*, pp. 159–62.

5. Bourke, *On the Border with Crook*, p. 137; Robinson, *General Crook and the Western Frontier*, p. 110.

6. Post Returns, July 1871; Crook, *Autobiography*, p. 176. A quotation from Crook's report substantiating his intention to focus his efforts on Cochise is quoted in Sweeney, *Cochise*, p. 319.

7. Crook, *Autobiography*, p. 164.

8. Medical History, July 1871. A brief account of this skirmish is related in Rodenbough, *Army of the United States*, p. 676. Private Jeremiah Henessy was so severely wounded in this fight that he was sent to San Francisco and given a medical discharge the following spring. Ibid., April 1872. Private Charles W. Harris was killed in the skirmish. The wounded were: Privates Joseph Bossard, Jeremiah Hennesy, and John Williams. Return of the Twenty-first Infantry, July 1871, Returns of Regular Army Infantry Regiments, June 1821–December 1916.

9. Farley spent five months in the post hospital, but finally recovered and returned to duty. He took his discharge on March 1, 1872, having had enough of Indian fighting. Farley, "Early Day Indian Fighting"; Post Returns, July 1871; Medical History, July 1871; *Arizona Citizen*, July 29, 1871.

10. Before leaving Arizona, however, Cochise personally organized one last raid to secure more horses to support the trip to New Mexico. On September 4, 1871, twenty-five Chiricahuas dressed as Papago Indians audaciously rode across the parade ground at Camp Crittenden, then proceeded to drive off several dozen horses and mules under guard nearby. Other Chiricahuas stole eighty head of horses near Fronteras at about the same time. Sweeney, *Cochise*, pp. 323–24.

11. Crook, *Autobiography*, p. 167.

12. Colyer's lengthy and detailed report, including copies of his correspondence to and from the Indian Bureau and the War Department, provides an interesting perspective on the Apache situation at the time. The quotation is found on p. 9. of *Peace with the Apaches*.

13. Ibid., p. 168.

14. Post Returns, October 1871; Medical History, October 1871; *Arizona Citizen*, November 11, 1871. Post trader Sidney R. DeLong was one of the sources crediting Cochise with the raid. In a dispatch dated October 27, DeLong flatly stated: "Cachise [*sic*] is not now upon the reserve at Canada Alamosa." *Las Cruces Borderer*, November 8, 1871. Sweeney, in *Cochise* (pp. 326–27), concludes that the raid was perpetrated by Juh and his Southern Chiricahuas operating from Mexico. The exact date of the raid varies among accounts, however, this author relies on Russell's report, which fixes it as October 20. Russell to Captain H. M. Smith, October 27, 1871, Letters Received, Fort Bowie, A. T., RG 393, National Archives; supplemental details are found in Barney, *Tales of Apache Warfare*, p. 22.

15. Russell to Smith, October 27, 1871, ibid. A retelling of the fight by Russell to a friend is in *Las Cruces Borderer*, November 8, 1871.

16. Crook, *Autobiography*, p. 168.

17. It should be noted that no Indian depredations occurred within the patrol area of Camp Bowie during the months of November and December

1871, probably because of the normal decline in Apache operations with the onset of winter, and because Cochise remained near Canada Alamosa. Post Returns, November and December 1871.

18. Sweeney, *Cochise*, pp. 332–33.

19. *Weekly Arizona Miner*, February 10, 1872.

20. Ibid., Medical History, January 1872; Smith to AAG, Dept. of Arizona, January 25, 1872, Letters Sent, RG 393; ibid., January 30, 1872. A mail driver coming through from Las Cruces a few days later reported an attempted attack on a supply train near Ralston, New Mexico. The train had previously passed through Fort Bowie. *Arizona Citizen*, February 3, 1872; Post Returns, February 1872.

21. Medical History, February 1872.

22. Crook, *Autobiography*, p. 169. An example of Howard's religious fervor was related by Lieutenant Royal E. Whitman. When Howard approached a delegation of Apache leaders at Camp Grant in 1872, Howard suddenly knelt and began to pray aloud. "In two minutes there wasn't an Indian to be seen. They scattered just like partridges when they see a hawk," Whitman recalled. Thrapp, *Conquest of Apacheria*, p. 110.

23. ARCIA, 1872, p. 148.

24. Ibid., 154.

25. Ibid., 168–69.

26. A copy of Howard's letter to Crook, in which he dropped his opposition to field operations, is reprinted in the 1872 ARCIA, p. 169. Lest the intent of the Peace Policy be subverted, Howard subsequently impressed upon Crook the necessity for all the army officers in the territory to understand that the objective was to place the Indians on the reservations, and keep them there, for the benefit of all concerned. Ibid., p. 171.

27. Ibid., 155.

28. Ibid., 158.

29. Sweeney, *Cochise*, p. 342.

30. Post Returns, May 1872. The attack occurred on May 4: *Las Cruces Borderer*, May 15, 1872. When Abrahams failed to show up at Camp Bowie by the morning of May 6, Sergeant Merzetti and ten privates of Troop D, Fifth Cavalry, were sent to investigate. Medical History, May 1872.

31. Sweeney, *Cochise*, pp. 341–45; Post Returns, August 1872. A detachment was also sent to the San Pedro Valley to protect settlers there. Post Returns, June 1872.

32. Thrapp, *Conquest of Apacheria*, pp. 115–16. This event is also recounted in Serven, "Military Posts on Sonoita Creek": 45.

33. Ibid., pp. 113–18.

34. Medical History, August 1872; September 1872.;

35. Ibid., September 1872; Howard, *My Life*, 186–89. Howard's roster differs slightly. Since Howard wrote his memoirs many years later, Sladen's record of the individuals comprising the party is probably more accurate. In addition to Howard and himself, Sladen named Jacob May, whom he called their "interpreter,

guide, philosopher, and friend"; Bloomfield, the German driver; Stone the cook; two Apache guides, Chie and Ponce; and Streeter, a packer hired at Canada Alamosa. See Sladen, *Making Peace*, pp. 35–36, 87.

36. Sladen further noted that their movements could have been detected for twenty-four hours before they reached Cochise's camp and that Cochise later boasted that his people could see troops leaving Camp Bowie as soon as they came out of Apache Pass. See *Making Peace*, p. 75. Howard mentioned that a detachment of soldiers from the post was posted at Sulphur Springs Station (also known by that time as Rodgers' Ranch). Having few provisions left by that time, the soldiers shared their rations with the general and his party. Howard, *My Life*, p. 198.

37. Ibid., p. 203.

38. Ibid., p. 205.

39. The quotation is from Howard, *My Life*, p. 220; The foregoing synthesis of the meetings between Howard and Cochise is drawn from Howard's autobiography, pp. 196–221; "Account of Gen'l. Howard's Mission to the Apaches and Navajos," reprinted from *Washington Daily Morning News*, November 10, 1872; *ARCIA*, 1872, pp. 148–58; Medical History, October 1872. Sweeney, *Making Peace* provides an extremely detailed first-hand narrative of the event.

40. As a result of establishing a special Chiricahua reservation, Howard recommended that the "feeding stations' at Camp McDowell, Date Creek, and Beal Spring be abolished, and that the San Carlos Reservation boundary be reduced by eliminating that portion below the Gila. *ARCIA*, 1872, 175–77.

41. *ARCIA*, 1873, p. 291.

CHAPTER 8: THIS SEDENTARY LIFE

1. Schmidt, *General George Crook*, pp. 213–14.

2. Cramer, "Tom Jeffords": 266–67; Frederick G. Hughes Papers, Arizona Historical Society. Copies of selected documents filed at Fort Bowie NHS.

3. Medical History, February 1873.

4. Ibid., March 1873.

5. *ARCIA*, 1872, pp. 80–81.

6. The potential for shipping freight to Guaymas, on the Sonoran coast of the Gulf of California, thence by wagon to Tucson, had not been forgotten. However diplomatic problems and thefts saw it tried for only a short time. Colonel D. B. Sackett to Inspector General R. B. Marcy, June 30, 1873, Records of the Inspector General's Office, RG 159, copy in files, Fort Bowie NHS; Walker, "Wagon Freighting in Arizona": 199–200.

7. Post Returns, April 1873; p. 11.

8. Annual Report of the Secretary of War, I, *House Executive Documents*, 43d Cong., 1st sess., 1874, no. 270 (serial 1615).

9. After the Civil War, a cattle trail was established from near Fort Concho, Texas, up the Concho River to its headwaters, thence southwest to the Horsehead

Crossing of the Pecos, near present-day Pecos, Texas. It then followed that stream northward to Pope's Well, where it divided, one branch continuing westward along the old military trail to intersect with the stage road at El Paso. Wagoner, "Overstocking of the Ranges": 23–24; Dale, *Range Cattle Industry*, p. 51.

10. Sacket to Marcy, June 30, 1873, RG 159.

11. Crook to Assistant Adjutant General, Division of the Pacific, July 7, 1873, Letters Sent, Department of Arizona, RG 393.

12. Crook to AG, U.S.A., December 8, 1873, ibid. Not to be overlooked was the self-righteous Howard's eagerness to conclude a peace with the infamous Cochise. It is this author's conclusion that Howard, who had little experience with western tribes up to that time, displayed considerable naivete in dealing with Cochise. Howard's actions, and his obvious inattention to details, leave the impression that he was more concerned with bolstering his own reputation by proclaiming a peace than with concluding a realistic, durable agreement that considered all of the affected parties. Jeffords, too, was accused of being culpable. Crook leveled sharp criticism at Jeffords for his close relationship with Cochise. "Such an acquaintance, made and continued during the course of hostilities . . . will militate strongly against Gen. Howard's endorsement of this Agent and do much to strengthen the conviction now freely entertained in New Mexico, Arizona, Sonora, and along the Pacific, that the Cochise reserve is not the Utopia its friends describe it to be. The general rule is that the only white men who can maintain friendly relations with hostile Indians are those engaged in the illicit traffic whereby the Indians are furnished the means to carry on their warfare." Ibid. Jeffords's treatment by the territorial press is treated by C. L. Sonnichsen in "Tom Jeffords and the Editors": 117–30.

13. Jeffords to Commissioner of Indian Affairs Edward P. Smith, May 31, 1874, Records of the New Mexico Superintendency, RG 75, copy in Fort Bowie NHS files. Apache raiding in Sonora is examined by Sweeney in *Cochise*, pp. 374–86. The extent of the raids in Mexico is suggested by newspaper accounts that claimed over one hundred persons were killed, in addition to large numbers of livestock stolen. Sackett to Marcy, June 30, 1873, RG 159.

14. Crook posted no less than eleven companies of cavalry and one of infantry at new Camp Grant during January 1873. See Robinson, *Diaries of John Gregory Bourke*, I, p. 62 (hereafter cited as *Bourke Diaries*), Camp Bowie, conversely, had a garrison of only 138 men at that time for the purpose of "policing" the Chiricahua Reservation. Crook, still distrustful, wanted a strong force within easy striking distance of the reservation in the likely event of trouble, yet distant enough to cause Cochise no alarm. For further insight on Crook's motives, see also Bourke, *On the Border with Crook*, p. 236.

15. The complete transcript of this conference is found in Robinson, *Bourke Diaries*, I, pp. 468–70. Bourke made a quick trip alone to Camp Bowie, arriving there on January 31 and returning to Sulphur Springs on February 2. He did not clarify the exact purpose of that visit, but it was probably in the nature of a courtesy call to make the post commander, Samuel Sumner, aware that Department

Headquarters staff were in the vicinity and to advise him of their business with Cochise. Ibid., p. 63; Post Returns, January 1873.

16. Crook to AAG, Division of the Pacific, July 7, 1873, RG 393.

17. Jeffords reported that he was experiencing shortages of clothing supplies, causing some of the young men to threaten that they would secure clothing and blankets "elsewhere, that is, by raiding." Cochise intervened to assist Jeffords in quelling those threats. *ARCIA*, 1874, p. 287.

18. Ibid., p. 288; Sweeney, *Cochise*, p. 387.

19. Ibid., p. 288.

20. Ibid.

21. Sweeney, *Cochise*, p. 397. A contemporary account of the burial of Cochise was published in *Army and Navy Journal*, July 11, 1874, p. 758 (hereafter cited as *ANJ*).

22. *ARCIA*, 1874, p. 288.

23. *ARSW*, 1875, p. 57. Even the press seemed to be satisfied that the Chiricahuas at Apache Pass had been behaving themselves. It was reported that during October and November "nearly all the Chiricahuas were camped within shot distance of the post and visited it almost every day. It would have been impossible for them to have been raiding anywhere at that time." *Arizona Citizen*, December 26, 1874.

24. *ARCIA*, 1875, p. 209.

25. Ibid. The machinery at the old mine had been removed several years earlier. By 1875, the building was in a dilapidated condition. Jeffords requested $1,000 to move the supplies to Apache Pass, as well as take down, move, and reerect the log buildings then at Pinery Canyon. Greene, "Historic Structures Report," pp. 288–89.

26. *ARCIA*, 1875, p. 209.

27. *ARCIA*, 1876, p. 3.

28. W. W. Belknap to Secretary of the Interior, September 21, 1874, Fort Bowie, A. T., Consolidated Correspondence File, Report of Colonel James A. Hardee, inspector general, June 28, 1875, ibid.

29. *ARCIA*, 1876, pp. 3–4. A former post commander at Fort Bowie wrote of Rogers's character: "I never heard of M. Rogers owning any cattle or doing anything else but sell whiskey to soldiers and keeping a little forage for the overland mail animals." Endorsement by Major A. W. Evans, March 6, 1872, Letters Received, Fort Bowie, A. T., RG 393.

30. *ARCIA*, 1876, pp. 3–4; *ARSW*, 1876, p. 98.

31. Post Returns, April 1876. Austin Henely was a native of Ireland who immigrated to America and enlisted in the Regular Army in 1864. After serving a three-year enlistment in the infantry, Henely secured an appointment to the U.S. Military Academy in 1868. He graduated four years later and was assigned to the Sixth Cavalry. Heitman, *Historical Register*, 1, p. 523.

32. *Arizona Citizen*, September 30, 1876. A typescript copy of the article is in the Hayden Collection, Arizona Historical Society.

33. *ARCIA*, 1876, pp. 3–4. Hughes recorded that one of those killed was a friendly Apache. Hughes to his wife, June 5, 1876, Frederick G. Hughes Papers, Arizona Historical Society.

34. Kautz to AAG, Divivision of the Pacific, June 30, 1876, Letters Received, Fort Bowie; *ARCIA*, 1876, pp. 10–11; *ARSW*, 1876, p. 102.

35. Although Taza had sworn as recently as June 3 that he would die before moving to San Carlos, the department commander observed a dramatic change in the chief's attitude immediately after the June 4 shootout. Telegrams. Kautz to AAG, Divivision of the Pacific, June 3 and 6, 1876, Letters Received, Fort Bowie.

36. *ARCIA*, 1876, p. 3–4. Pi-hon-se-nay must have made a remarkable recovery because he escaped, taking two men and three women with him en route to San Carlos. He was later identified as one of the renegade leaders and was discovered hiding out on the Warm Springs reservation the following month. ARCIA, 1877, pp. 20–21; *Arizona Citizen*, June 24, 1876; July 22, 1876. Agent Clum's account of the Chiricahua removal and subsequent events is in "Fighting Geronimo": 36–41.

37. *ARSW*, 1876, p. 98; ibid., 1877, p.135; Martin to AAG, Dept. of Arizona, July 29, 1876, Letters Received, Fort Bowie.

38. Kautz to McLellan, July 29, 1876, LR, Fort Bowie.

39. *ARSW*, 1877, pp. 134–36, *Arizona Citizen*, January 6 and 20, 1877. When Rucker found and attacked a rancheria in the southwest corner of New Mexico on January 9, killing ten Apaches and capturing Geronimo's nephew, Apaches already at San Carlos became angry and bolted south of the Gila. H. B. Burton to Dr. Sanford, February 3, 1877, H G. Burton File, Arizona Historical Society.

40. *ARCIA*, 1877, pp. 20–21. In an attempt to stem the raids through the San Pedro and Sonoita valleys into Mexico, Kautz established Camp Huachuca on the northeast end of the mountains by the same name on February 12, 1877. It replaced Camp Crittenden, abandoned in 1873 after peace was established with Cochise. Huachuca was given permanent status in 1878 and was redesignated as a fort in 1882. *ARSW*, 1877, p. 137; Frazer, *Forts of the West*, pp. 9–10.

41. Post Returns, February-May 1877.

42. *ARCIA, 1877*, pp. 20–21. For a detailed account of the roundup at Ojo Caliente, see John P. Clum to Anton Mazzanovich, November 21, 1877, Anton Mazzanovich Papers, Arizona Historical Society.

43. The quotation is found in *Army and Navy Journal*, October 13, 1877. A transcontinental Western Union telegraph line had been extended from Denver south to Santa Fe, where it connected with the military system. Western Union had already made plans to build down the Rio Grande to connect with the military line at El Paso. That line across Texas made a junction with the existing Western Union line from New Orleans to San Antonio. *ANJ*, July 14, 1877; *Arizona Citizen*, February 10, 1877; ARSW, 1877, p. 148. The first telegraph line was less than perfect, having been constructed "with materials at hand, and not generally the best . . . ." Still, it was a far cry from the days when expressmen had to hand-carry urgent military messages from one post to another. To keep

the line in good order, it was recommended that communications districts be established, with a sergeant of the Signal Corps responsible for each. The entire system in the department would be under the supervision of a signal officer. *ARSW*, 1878, p. 195.

44. Friendly Indians reported in April that forty-three renegades were in the Chiricahua Mountains, while reinforcements left the reservation at Tularosa to join them. *Silver City Herald*, April 12, 1877.

45. Sidney R. DeLong, the post trader, informed the newspapers that Apaches had stolen two horses from the Wood Brothers corral within the limits of the fort, and two more from Jeffords's corral. Tracks discovered later indicated that the raiders had been within fifty yards of officers' quarters. *Arizona Citizen*, April 14, 1877; Tait was killed on May 29. A biased dispatch authored by Roscoe L. Bryant, alleged to have been a participant in the events, criticized West for withdrawing in the face of only four or five Apaches. However, the editor later retracted the disparaging remarks and upheld West's reputation as an officer. *Arizona Citizen*, June 9, 1877; June 16, 1877. The size of the raiding party, initially reported by the scouts as numbering thirty-five or forty men, was later revised down to only six. Captain W. M. Wallace to AAG, Dept. of Arizona, May 30, 1877; LS, Fort Bowie; June 11, 1877, ibid.

46. Wallace to AAG, Dept. of Arizona, June 9, 1877; ibid., June 4, 1877, LS, Fort Bowie.

47. *ARSW*, 1877, p. 137. The dispatch was written by Henry Alihugh, who was in all probability the telegraph operator at Fort Bowie. *Arizona Citizen*, June 2, 1877.

48. Arizona Governor John P. Hoyt notified the army in June that troops from both countries were no longer permitted to cross the border in pursuit of Indians. Since friendly relations continued in the border regions, the Mexican government's decision apparently was prompted by internal considerations, rather than anything the U.S. had done. *ARSW*, 1878, pp. 193–94.

49. *ARSW*, 1878, p. 193.

50. *ARSW*, 1877, p. 140.

51. For further discussion of this situation, see ibid.

52. *ARSW*, 1878, p. 193.

53. Debo, *Geronimo*, p. 119.

54. The army lost two promising and energetic young officers, Austin Henely and John A. Rucker, in a dual drowning accident in White River near the south end of the Chiricahua Mountains on July 11, 1878. Henely got into trouble when he attempted to cross the river during a violent thunderstorm. His friend Rucker tried to save him, but both men drowned. Their bodies were returned to Fort Bowie and buried in the post cemetery on July 13. Post Returns, July 1878; Medical History, July 1878. Today the place is known as Rucker Canyon. Alexander, *Arizona Frontier Military Place Names*, p. 102.

55. *ARSW*, 1878, p. 195; Sacket to Marcy, June 30, 1873, RG 159.

56. McDowell also recommended that the military telegraph line from San Diego to Maracopaville be taken down, since it duplicated the commercial Western

Union line that was keeping apace of the railroad. The salvaged materials, he suggested, could be used to construct a network of connecting lines among the forts that did not yet have the telegraph. *ARSW*, 1879, p. 132.

57. *Arizona Weekly Star*, October 27, 1881. A one-year contract for mail delivery between Willcox and Fort Bowie was awarded to A. E. Boone, Washington, D.C., beginning July 1, 1882. Delivery was to be three times weekly. Coaches were to leave Willcox at 9:00 A.M. on Monday, Wednesday, and Friday. Returns from the fort were on Tuesday, Thursday, and Saturday, departing at 7:00 A.M. and arriving at Willcox at 4:00 P.M. Annual Report of the Postmaster General, *House Ex. Doc.*, 47th Cong., 2d sess., (2111) no. 93, p. 1146.

58. Myrick, "Railroads of Southern Arizona": 155–70, provides a useful overview of this topic.

59. *Arizona Weekly Star*, October 27, 1881.

60. *ARSW*, 1880, p. 207; *Geronimo: His Own Story*, pp. 104–106; Debo, *Geronimo*, pp. 120–22.

61. *ARSW*, 1880, pp. 216, 219.

62. A sure indication that Fort Bowie was no longer so isolated was the encroachment of "persons of questionable character" on lands near the post. The problem was serious enough by 1877 that the post commander, W. M. Wallace, officially notified civilian squatters to stay beyond the one-mile limit of the military reservation. At the same time, he requested that the reserve be expanded to include thirty-six square miles in order that the saloons and brothels would be less attractive to the garrison. Wallace also justified the expansion on the post's need to guarantee grazing lands for army stock. The president approved the request on November 27, 1877. Wallace to AAG, Dept. of Arizona, June 20, 1877; *Post Orders No. 88*, June 22, 1877; Secretary of War George W. McCrary to President Rutherford B. Hayes, November 24, 1877. Copies in Fort Bowie files.

63. The Department of Arizona Headquarters recommended in October 1878 that all posts in the department be officially redesignated as "forts." Colonel Orlando B. Willcox to AG, U.S.A., October 10, 1878, Communications Sent, August 24, 1871–December 31, 1886, Department of Arizona, RG 133, NA, copy in files, Fort Bowie NHS; *General Orders No. 2*, April 5, 1879, Division of the Pacific, RG 94, NA.

CHAPTER 9: TO END THIS ANNUAL APACHE STAMPEDE RIGHT NOW

1. "Report of the Acting Governor of Arizona," *ARSI*, 1881, 930.

2. A sure sign that the territory was changing was the existence of eleven schools in Cochise County alone. Ibid., 1883, p. 505. By 1887, the population of Arizona Territory was estimated at about ninety thousand. ibid., 1887, p. 753.

3. Ibid., 1881, p. 917.

4. *House Executive Documents*, 47th Cong., 1st sess., nos. 58, 188. The request was denied, thus forcing the citizens of Cochise County to raise $5,600 to organize and equip a company of volunteers for the purpose of ridding the region of outlaws. "Governor's Report," *ARSI*, 1883, p. 514.

5. Those killed at Cibicu Creek and the Fort Apache defense included Hentig, seven privates of Troop D and one private of Troop E, Sixth Cavalry, and two privates of the Twelfth Infantry. A contemporary account of the fight is in the *Army and Navy Journal*, September 10, 1881: 124. For a first-hand account, see Thomas Cruse, "The Fight at the Cibicu, and Nock-ay-del-Klinne, Apache Medicine Man," *Winners of the West*. A thorough secondary description is found in Thrapp, *Conquest of Apacheria*, pp. 217–30. Although Willcox attempted to charge Carr with responsibility for allowing the Cibicu affair to get out of hand, Generals Sherman and McDowell were of the opinion that Willcox had lacked good judgment by allowing himself to be maneuvered into using troops to execute a police action. Robert M. Utley, *Frontier Regulars*, pp. 372–74.

6. Such was Sherman's confidence in Mackenzie that he placed the colonel in command of all forces in the field for the duration of the emergency. *ARSW*, 1881, p. 139–41. Bernard's troop was again stationed at Fort Bowie for about a month during October and November 1881. Post Returns, October and November 1881.

7. See *ANJ*, September 10, 1881: 124; Utley, *Frontier Regulars*, pp. 374–75. Major George B. Sanford's report of the action at Cedar Spring on October 2 is published in *ARSW*, 1881, pp. 146–47.

8. *ARSW*, 1882, p. 147; *House Ex. Doc.*, 47th Cong., 1st sess., (serial 2031), no. 193.

9. *ARSW*, 1882, p. 147. Camp Price was named for Lieutenant Colonel William R. Price, Sixth Cavalry, who died on December 30, 1881, of disease contracted in the field. Ibid., pp. 151–52. Post Returns, March and April 1882; Medical History, March 1882.

10. *ARSW*, 1881, p. 144.

11. Betzinez, *I Fought with Geronimo*, p. 56; *ARSW*, 1882, pp. 147–48; Utley, *Indian Frontier of the American West*, p. 197.

12. Betzinez, *I Fought with Geronimo*, p. 56.

13. Forsyth had gained a reputation for being the hero of the Battle of Beecher's Island on the Republican River in 1868. He was afterwards appointed as aide-de-camp to Lieutenant General Sheridan, commanding the Division of the Missouri, serving in that capacity from 1869 to 1881. Heitman, *Historical Register*, 1, p. 430. A full account of the Loco outbreak is presented in Vandenberg, "Forsyth and the 1882 Loco Outbreak Campaign" 174–95. For Forsyth's own account of the affair, see *Thrilling Days in Army Life*, pp. 79–121.

14. "Governor's Report," *ARSI*, 1883, p. 512. Estimates of the numbers of whites killed vary according to sources. See Utley, *Frontier Regulars*, p. 375, and Vandenberg, "Loco Outbreak": 181.

15. Post Returns, April 1882; Medical History, April 1882.

16. Thrapp, *Conquest of Apacheria*, pp. 228–36; Vandenberg, "Loco Outbreak": 188–91. Thrapp claims that the troops killed fourteen warriors in the Tupper fight, while a contemporary source gave the losses, supposedly based on the later testimony of prisoners, as seven in that engagement, and thirteen at Horseshoe

Canyon. See *ANJ*, May 6, 1882: 918. Betzinez, *I Fought with Geronimo*, pp. 68–69, also recounts this fight, stating that only one woman was killed. One Fort Bowie soldier, Private William W. Goldrick, Troop H, Sixth Cavalry, was killed in the fight. At the time of his death, Goldrick, a thirty-one-year-old native of Maine, was nearing the end of his second enlistment. Post Returns, April 1882; Registers of Enlistments in the United States Army, Regular Army Cavalry Roll 38, p. 303, entry 114, Records of the Adjutant General's Office, RG 94, National Archives.

17. Thrapp, *Conquest of Apacheria*, p. 236.

18. Telegram, Mackenzie to McDowell, April 30, 1882, published in *ANJ*, May 6, 1882: 918; *ARSW*, 1882, pp. 148–50.

19. Post Returns, May–July 1882.

20. *ANJ*, July 15, 1882: 165. Having to pass through hostile territory without arms posed a real problem for the volunteers. They overcame the disadvantage by cutting a stick for each man that he carried across his saddle to resemble a rifle. The ruse worked and the company returned to Tucson unharmed. Thrapp, *Conquest of Apacheria*, pp. 252–53.

21. *ARSW*, 1883: 165.

22. Further details concerning Crook's meeting with the San Carlos Apaches can be found in *ARSW*, 1883, pp. 163–67.

23. Ibid., p. 164.

24. Ibid., p. 165–66.

25. Ibid., 169; Bourke, *On the Border with Crook*, p. 441.

26. Ibid., p. 166.

27. An official summary of Crook's council with the Apaches is in Bourke, p. 172–73.

28. Utley, *Frontier Regulars*, p. 378; Davis, *Truth about Geronimo*, p. 55.

29. Crook's official summary of Chato's raid is found in *ARSW*, 1883, pp. 161–62. Charlie McComas, kidnapped at the time his parents were killed, was never found. Thrapp, *Conquest of Apacheria*, p. 270.

30. As soon the army became aware of Chato's entry into the U.S., Crook telegraphed the commanding officer at Fort Bowie to scout thoroughly the Chiricahua Mountains and to watch the San Simon and Sulphur Spring valleys for any sign of movement. Simultaneously, he directed troops at Camp Thomas to proceed toward Nogales. Two more companies moved from Camp Grant to White River, while cavalry and Indian scouts from Fort Huachuca scoured the San Pedro Valley. Crawford and his scouts were instructed to move north from Cloverdale to the Stein's Peak range, keeping an eye on the Animas Valley at the same time. Miraculously, Chato managed to avoid all of these forces so effectively that they never sighted his party during the entire episode. Ibid., 162–63.

31. Ibid., p. 175; *ANJ*, June 16, 1883: 1043; Bourke, *On the Border*, p. 453.

32. In addition to the sources previously cited, John G. Bourke's personal narrative of the 1883 campaign was published as *An Apache Campaign in the Sierra Madre*.

33. Troops from Fort Bowie escorted at least four more parties of Apaches to San Carlos between November 1883 and May 1884. Post Returns, July–December 1883 and January–May 1884.

34. Britton Davis's entertaining account of his adventure escorting Geronimo and his stolen cattle to the reservation, with much of the story centering on Sulphur Springs, near Fort Bowie, is found in *The Truth about Geronimo*, pp. 84–101.

35. Greene, "Historic Structure Report," pp. 58–59.

36. Chihuahua went eastward along the north side of the Gila, but then paused to reconsider his actions. Concluding that Geronimo and Mangus had lied to him about the threat, he decided to hide out until the excitement had passed. Once the army took Geronimo's trail toward Mexico, he would lead his people back to San Carlos and surrender. The plan was foiled, however, when Lieutenant Davis and his scouts discovered and followed Chihuahua's trail, forcing his band to flee into New Mexico and eventually rejoin Geronimo. Had it not been for that unfortunately coincidence, Geronimo's force would have been reduced by some eighty persons. Thrapp, *Conquest of Apacheria*, pp. 315–18.

37. Post Returns, May 1885.

38. Ibid., June 1885.

39. Davis's column was supported by two packtrains—one consisting of 52 mules under the command of Lieutenant James S. Pettit, First Infantry, and another of 110 mules. Post Returns, June 1885.

40. Eight men belonging to Troop D had been left in charge of supply camp, while Captain Allen P. Hatfield, Assistant Surgeon Leonard Wood, and Captain Henry W. Lawton, with a company of scouts from Fort Huachuca, scouted the vicinity. The men killed in the attack were Sergeant Peter Munich, Private Dezo Vislavki, and Saddler John H. Niehouse. Davis, *Truth about Geronimo*, p. 153; Thrapp, *Conquest of Apacheria*, pp. 424–25; Post Returns, June 1885.

41. Crook's troop dispositions are detailed in Post Returns, pp. 326–27. G Troop, Fourth Cavalry, was sent from Fort Bowie to set up camp at old Camp Rucker at the southern end of the Chiricahua Mountains on July 12. Fort Bowie also supported the campaign logistically by sending supplies to a camp established on the border at Lang's Ranch, New Mexico. Post Returns, July 1885.

42. Four of the captives were retained at the border by Second Lieutenant Hugh J. McGrath for unknown reasons, while the remaining eleven were brought to Fort Bowie by Lieutenant Robert Hanna. Ibid.

43. Thrapp, *Conquest of Apacheria*, p. 331.

44. Davis, in *Truth about Geronimo*, pp. 176–95, recounts the harrowing tale in which the detachment only narrowly escaped from Mexico.

45. Hutton, *Phil Sheridan*, p. 364.

46. *ARSW*, 1886, p. 9.

47. The Crook-Geronimo conference is detailed by Captain Bourke, an eyewitness, in *On the Border*, pp. 474–76.

48. Ibid., p. 481–82. The town of Crawford, Nebraska, just beyond the boundary of Fort Robinson, was named for the deceased officer. Crawford had previously served with distinction at that post. Buecker, *Fort Robinson*, p. 44.

49. Thrapp, *Conquest of Apacheria*, pp. 346–47, argues that Tribolett's presence may have been much more than coincidental. He suggests that the whiskey trader may have been part of the "Tucson Ring," whose financial interests

would not have been served by an Apache surrender. Cunningham, "Blame the Bootlegger."

50. Hutton, *Phil Sheridan*, pp. 364–65.

51. The exact date of Miles's arrival, April 10, is noted in Post Returns, April 1886, although his own report in *ARSW*, 1886, p. 165, states that he assumed command of the Department of Arizona two days later. Wooster, *Nelson A. Miles*, p. 145, gives the date as April 11, which seems reasonable and coincides with Schmitt, *General George Crook*, p. 266.

52. For further information relative to the heliograph and its use during the Geronimo Campaign, consult Bruno J. Rolak, "General Miles's Mirrors": 145–60, and Robbins, "Some Reflections on the Heliograph": 24–31. An interesting first-hand narrative by one of the enlisted Signal Corpsmen is Neifert, "Trailing Geronimo by Heliograph." Two stations were located at Fort Bowie, one atop Bowie Mountain, the other at the post itself. The official report was rendered by Second Lieutenant A. M. Fuller—see "Heliograph Report" in *ARSW*, 1887.

53. Miles wanted to ensure that the Apaches did not reclaim fired cartridge cases and reload them, which was relatively easy to do with commercial reloading tools. The complete *Field Order No. 7* is found in *ARSW*, 1886, p. 166.

54. Ibid., p. 167.

55. Wratten, "George Wratten: Friend of the Apaches," *Geronimo and the End of the Apache Wars*, p. 98. As a youth, Wratten clerked in the general store at San Carlos, which afforded him the opportunity to learn the difficult Apache language and to become closely acquainted with the Chiricahuas. Wratten modestly credited Gatewood with being the only man who could approach the renegades, though he himself was also in that exclusive class. His fascinating story is presented on pp. 91–124.

56. Miles's own version of the surrender are in his autobiography, *Personal Recollections*, 2, pp. 519–28. See also, Wooster, *Nelson A. Miles*, pp. 148–53; Utley, *Frontier Regulars*, pp. 388–90; Bourke, *On the Border*, p. 484; Post Returns, August–September 1886; Medical History, August–September 1886.

57. Miles, *Personal Recollections*, 2, p. 527–28.

CHAPTER 10: IT SEEMS LIKE A PRISON: GARRISON LIFE

1. The first Fort Bowie, established in 1862 following the Battle of Apache Pass, indeed featured atypical stone breastworks around the perimeter. Such defensive works were considered a prudent precaution as a result of the boldness and tenacity demonstrated by the Apaches during the pitched battle to control the nearby spring. If the California Volunteers, who first occupied the place, had been more familiar with Apache tactics and habits, they might have saved themselves the trouble of building breastworks. Like most western Indian tribes, the Apaches were loath to attack fixed positions, rather, they favored hit-and-run raids primarily for the purpose of acquiring stock and booty, at the least risk to themselves.

This chapter focuses on garrison life at the second Fort Bowie because of the near absence of personal accounts from that early period of occupation, and because the second fort was inhabited by Regular Army troops who typified the frontier experience.

2. Forsyth, *Story of the Soldier*, p. 103. Forsyth provides a graphic description of the typical frontier fort, which could have been Fort Bowie as well as a host of other posts.

3. Boyd, *Cavalry Life in Tent and Field*, p. 156.

4. Major E. B. Beaumont to Assistant Adjutant General, Department of Arizona, August 2, 1884, Letters Sent, Fort Bowie, Group 393.

5. Greene, "Historic Structures Report," pp. 184–85.

6. Stallard, *Glittering Misery*, pp. 54–55.

7. *Army Regulations*, 1863, pp. 24, 35, 246.

8. Forsyth, *Story of the Soldier*, p. 133.

9. *Federal Census—Territory of New Mexico and Territory of Arizona*, pp. 49–50 (compendium hereinafter cited as *Federal Census* with year of particular record).

10. "Camp Merijildo" honored Merijildo Grijalva, who was captured as a boy by the Apaches in 1849. Following his escape a decade later, he began scouting for the army, working in that capacity at Fort Bowie during the Civil War and intermittently for many years thereafter. Edwin R. Sweeney, *Cochise*, pp. 61, 84.

11. Greene, "Historic Structures Report," p. 199.

12. The census made no distinction between whites and Hispanics, but it did segregate blacks. Interestingly, no blacks, either male or female, resided at Fort Bowie at that time. *Federal Census*, 1870, pp. 133–38.

13. The thesis of women as a mitigating influence on soldiers is developed by Cynthia A. Wood, "Army Laundresses and American Civilization on the Western Frontier," an essay delivered at the Arizona History Convention, April 27, 2001. Copy provided to the author.

14. *Regulations of the Army of the United States and General Orders in Force February 17, 1881.* p. 20.

15. Medical History, August 1878; "1880 Census, Arizona Territory, Camp Bowie (Pima Co.)," June 13,1880, microfilm collections, Arizona Historical Society (hereinafter cited as "1880 Census"). Ah Hang, a Chinese cook, also worked at the post, but his employer was not identified. Ibid.

16. Foner, *The United States Soldier between Two Wars*, pp. 25–26.

17. Captain C. B. McLellan to Adjutant General, U.S.A., December 26, 1878, Letters Sent, Fort Bowie.

18. *Circular.* Fort Bowie, April 30, 1881; *Orders No. 65*, Fort Bowie, June 1, 1881, ibid.; *Orders No. 76,* July 1, 1881, ibid. See Orders and Circulars, Fort Bowie, RG 393, copies in research files at Fort Bowie NHS.

19. *Orders No. 61*, Fort Bowie, June 2, 1882.

20. Stallard, *Glittering Misery*, pp. 94, 98.

21. Ibid., 94–95; *Orders No. 158*, Fort Bowie, October 27, 1884.

22. Greene, "Historic Structures Report," p. 203.

23. *Annual Report of the Secretary of War*, 1883, p. 45.

24. *Circular No. 3*, Fort Bowie, July 22, 1879; *Orders No. 97*, Fort Bowie, July 23, 1879.; Captain Thomas MacGregor to AG, USA, June 21, 1891, LS, Fort Bowie.

25. Ibid., p. 204.

26. *Orders No. 43*, Fort Bowie, April 9, 1883. *Orders No. 73*, June 30, 1890, represents a somewhat abbreviated schedule preferred by the post commander at that time. It corresponds with the recollections of ex-Fourth Cavalryman Reginald Bradley. See Reginald A. Bradley interview by Don Rickey, Jr., January 9–10, 1968, Bradley biographical file, Arizona Historical Society (hereafter cited as Bradley interview). The schedule of service calls was adjusted seasonally to take full advantage of the available daylight hours.

27. A Saturday bath and once-a-week shave were common among working-class men in the United States during the late nineteenth century. Rather than being exceptional, army life simply reflected the norm for the majority of the civilian populace. Author's note.

28. "Day Book of Reverend Chas. H. Cook of Chicago, Illinois," Charles H. Cook Papers, Arizona Historical Society (hereafter cited as Cook Papers).

29. Captain Thomas MacGregor to AG, June 21, 1891, LS, Fort Bowie.

30. Captain W. A. Rafferty to quartermaster general, May 6, 1883, LS, Fort Bowie.

31. J. P. Widney to Sister (Bell Widney), December 4, 1867, Widney Letters, Gustave Schneider Collection, Arizona Historical Society (hereafter cited as Widney Letters).

32. J. P. Widney to Mother (Mrs. A. Widney), December 15, 1867, ibid.

33. *Army and Navy Journal*, January 27, 1894: 378.

34. In apparent contrast to the strict standards of the Victorian era, flirting was considered socially acceptable, if not expected. Not only did it occur among married persons, but between married women and bachelor officers. However, it was to be rigidly controlled, with neither party crossing the imaginary line of propriety. Officers were governed by a "knightly idealism," as one historian has described it, while wives made "queenly responses rather than clandestine love affairs." Men, consequently, had to tread very carefully in this realm to be socially accepted, yet above reproach. The custom is discussed more thoroughly in Knight, *Life and Manners*, pp. 142–43.

35. Anne M. Butler, *Daughters of Joy*, p. 128.

36. Charge and Specifications preferred against 2nd Lieut. D. M. Greene, 6th Cavalry," Duane Merritt Greene ACP File, Records of the Adjutant General's Office, RG 94, NA.

37. Major E. Major E. B. Beaumont to AAG, Dept. of Arizona, October 28, 1887, LS, Fort Bowie.

38. Widney to Bell Widney, October 23, 1867, Widney Letters; ibid., January 1, 1868.

39. *ANJ*, November 29, 1890: 225.

40. *Arizona Daily Star*, January 19, 1890.

41. *Arizona Daily Citizen*, April 25, 1885.

42. *ANJ*, January 8, 1887: 471.

43. *ANJ*, November 29, 1890: 225.

44. Captain Thomas McGregor to AAG, Dept. of Arizona, April 1, 1892, LS, Fort Bowie.

45. Ibid., pp 215–18; "1880 Census"; Kane, "An Honorable and Upright Man": 297–99.

46. Marion, *Notes on Travel*, p. 36.

47. *Orders No. 138*, Fort Bowie, October 10, 1885; "Register of Guests, Fort Bowie Hotel," copy in research files, Fort Bowie NHS. Emma Peterson later married ex-soldier Neil Erickson after he took his discharge following the Geronimo Campaign. They established a homestead south of Fort Bowie near the mouth of Bonita Canyon, from which they sold farm produce to the post commissary. Faraway Ranch Collection, Erickson records, Western Archeological Center, Tucson.

48. An official report published by the secretary of war noted that forty-one out of every one thousand soldiers were hospitalized for alcoholism. This ratio, however, was not reflected among the four regiments comprised of black men. To their credit, those units evidenced only five and one-half alcoholics per one thousand men. Rickey, *Forty Miles*, pp. 156–59.

49. *Circular No. 5*, Fort Bowie, September 3, 1878, RG 393.

50. Major Henry E. Noyes to AAG, Dept. of Arizona, May 16, 1890, LS, Fort Bowie.

51. *Arizona Citizen*, March 25, 1871.

52. *Arizona Daily Citizen*, May 20, 1871. Other evidence suggests that the statement in the *Citizen* may have been a biased exaggeration. The Medical Department reported no cases of alcoholism at Fort Bowie during the years 1871–72, indicating that Stoneman's order had a beneficial effect on the men, though it probably did nothing for the profits made by liquor distributors in the territory. In 1872–73, there were eight cases of alcoholism recorded. Billings, *Circular No. 8*, p. 534.

53. *Special Orders No. 33*, Fort Bowie, May 12, 1874.

54. Interview with Reginald A. Bradley by Don Rickey, Jr., January 9–10, 1968, Bradley interview.

55. Camp Grant was actually about sixty miles from Fort Bowie. Grant, "The Story of S. W. Grant," Hayden Biographical File, Arizona Historical Society.

56. Ibid. *Arizona Daily Citizen*, December 16, 1876.

57. Early descriptions of Bowie Station are in *Arizona Weekly Star*, October 27, 1881, and *Arizona Daily Citizen*, February 9, 1882. The quotation is from Bradley interview.

58. Mazzanovich, *Trailing Geronimo*, pp. 192–93.

59. *Orders No. 171*, Fort Bowie, November 23, 1882, directed a witness to the affair, Sergeant F. H. Schoning, to appear at the trial being held in Tombstone.

60. *Orders No. 151*, Fort Bowie, December 10, 1883, ibid.

61. Captain L. O. Parker to Sidney DeLong, November 9, 1883, LS, Fort Bowie.

62. It would appear that Fort Bowie was not in compliance with *G. O. No. 24*, AGO, series 1881, RG 94, in that the post commander authorized whiskey to be sold by the drink to enlisted men, but not by the bottle. Ibid.

63. Personal reminiscences of Dan R. Williamson, October 9, 1926, Dan Williamson Collection, Arizona Historical Society.

64. Captain W. M. Wallace to George Atkins, Roscoe Bryant, and others, June 22, 1877, LS, Fort Bowie. When Wallace later discovered that DeLong had indeed violated the order by doing business with the hog ranch residents, he immediately closed the store for an undetermined period of time. *Orders No. 114*, Fort Bowie, August 12, 1877.

65. Wallace to Lieutenant John A. Rucker, August 6, 1877, LS, Fort Bowie. Army attitudes toward sexual conduct are discussed in Butler, *Daughters of Joy*, p. 145.

66. James Barrack was killed in a gunfight with Mathew "Deadshot" Moss near the Hog Ranch on January 4, 1888. Apparently, Barrack was romantically involved with his neighbor, Ada Miller. When he became convinced that Moss was competing with him for Miller's attentions, he went gunning for Moss. The two met at J. C. Anderson's mining camp, located about three-fourths of a mile from the saloons. Barrack opened fire first, but Moss lived up to his nickname by shooting Barrack dead. "Records of coroner's jury in the case of the death of James Barrack," January 5, 1888, Cochise County, Arizona Territory. Transcripts in research files at Fort Bowie NHS.

67. Major Thomas McGregor to W. Shillum, U.S.deputy marshal, October 8, 1892, L S, Fort Bowie; Medical History, December 1893.

68. McGregor to Shillum, October 8, 1892, LS, Fort Bowie; First Lieutenant H. H. Sargent to Thomas Whitehead, June 3, 1894, ibid.

69. *Orders No. 68*, Fort Bowie, July 28, 1889; Second Lieutenant John M. Neall to post quartermaster, August 1, 1889, LS, Fort Bowie.

70. Forsyth, *Story of the Soldier*, p. 136.

71. Foner, *Between Two Wars*, pp. 92–93.

72. *Circular No. 9*, AGO, November 6, 1888. Decisions relating to canteens are discussed in *ANJ*, December 22, 1888: 321.

73. *ANJ*, July 2, 1887: 971. Another soldier recommending that traders ought to be abolished was of the opinion that "the Commissary and Quartermaster Departments ought to furnish everything the soldier really needs. The post canteen should furnish the beer and nothing else; should be simply a place where the men can go and get a glass of beer. Each company should have its own amusement room, supplied with a billiard table, etc., and be allowed to sell cigars, tobacco, etc. If the billiard tables, cigars, etc. are kept at the same place as the beer, the canteen become[s] a loafing place, and the men are just as liable to be absent from their duties and quarters, as if they went to the post trader or to a town or village." *ANJ*, March 23, 1889: 597.

74. Ibid., August 10, 1889: 1029.

75. *GO no. 75*, AGO, September 27, 1889, RG 94.

76. Noyes's letter is quoted in Greene, "Historic Structures Report," p. 219.

77. Major Henry E. Noyes to AAG, Dept. of Arizona, January 6, 1890, LS, Fort Bowie.

78. Noyes to AG, April 9, 1890, ibid.

79. Major Thomas McGregor to AG, July 6, 1890, ibid.

80. Cook Papers.

81. *Arizona Daily Citizen*, February 4, 1871.

82. Typical of the directives regarding Independence Day observances are *Orders No. 87*, July 3, 1885, and *Orders No. 82*, July 3, 1886. George Washington's birthday and Thanksgiving Day were also observed at Camp Bowie by suspending all labor and nonessential duties. No salutes or other ceremonies were conducted on those occasions, so the men probably celebrated by indulging in beer and other refreshments.

83. Officers at Camp Bowie employed both men and women as household servants and cooks. Some were Caucasians, but by 1880 the work force also included Hispanics and a few Orientals. Single females, regardless of physical attributes, proved difficult to retain because lonely soldiers invariably began courting them, whereupon the servants eventually resigned to marry their soldier-suitors. *Federal Census*, 1870; "1880 Census"; Stallard, *Glittering Misery*, p. 30.

84. Brigadier General Irvin McDowell to Major Roger Jones, August 5, 1867, appended to "Report of Inspection of Camp Bowie, May 22, 1867," copy in Fort Bowie file, AHS at Arizona Historical Society.

85. Greene, "Historic Structure Report," p. 135.

86. A wing extending at right angles from the west face of the Hospital was added in 1874 to serve as a dining hall. Ibid. pp. 131–33.

87. Ibid., pp. 207–14.

88. Ashburn, *History of the Medical Department*, p. 127.

89. *Orders No. 81*, Fort Bowie, July 5, 1882.

90. *Army Regulations*, 1861, p. 361.

91. Widney to Mrs. A. Widney, December 15, 1867, Widney Letters.

92. *Orders No. 108*, Fort Bowie, December 7, 1876; Ashburn, *History of the Medical Department*, p. 117. Easy access to medicinal brandy was frequently the downfall of hospital stewards. Author's note.

93. Ashburn, *History of the Medical Department*, pp. 108–09.

94. Medical History, Fort Bowie, June 1894.

95. Ashburn, *History of the Medical Department*, p. 117.

96. Widney to Mrs. A. Widney, December 15, 1867, Widney Letters. Hospital cooks usually were better qualified for the job than other men because of the special requirements of the patients. However, that was no assurance that the individuals liked the duty, as exemplified in the case of Private Louis Warren, First Infantry, who became so drunk that he could not perform his duties. Some men committed such acts intentionally to get relieved from an onerous job. *Orders No. 44*, Fort Bowie, April 10, 1883.

97. Lee Moon was hired per *Orders No. 49*, Fort Bowie, April 30, 1881. In the foregoing order, Moon is referred to as a nurse, but in a subsequent document relieving him of duty, his title is given as matron, which is probably correct. *Orders No. 129*, Fort Bowie, October 14, 1881. Two other Chinese men, Lee Sing and Wong Sing, subsequently were employed as matrons. *Orders No. 144*, Fort Bowie, October 22, 1885; *Orders No. 61*, Fort Bowie, July 1, 1888.

98. Medical History, Fort Bowie, January 1885.

99. Ibid., July 1878.

100. The topic of sanitation at Fort Bowie is treated more thoroughly in Greene, "Historic Structure Report," pp. 239–42.

101. The surgeon made an issue of this deficiency because even the hospital lacked a bathroom. To alleviate the problem, he recommended erecting a simple screen, hinged to one wall in the dining room to afford basic privacy. Medical History, July 1878.

102. Major E. B. Beaumont to Quartermaster General, August 22, 1885, LS, Fort Bowie.

103. Medical History, June 1893.

104. Widney to Bell Widney, November 20, 1867, and January 28, 1868, Widney Letters.

105. *Orders No. 135*, Fort Bowie, November 13, 1878.

106. Medical History, July 1868; Post Returns, Fort Bowie, March 1869; Medical History, March 1869, December 1869, August 1870, March 1871, July 1871.

107. Beaumont to AAG, Dept. of Arizona, February 12, 1885, LS, Fort Bowie; "Report of Inspection of Fort Bowie, A. T.," RG 159, NA. Copy in research files at Fort Bowie NHS.

108. "Fort Bowie Births," a tabulation in process by Park Ranger Larry Ludwig. Copy in research files at Fort Bowie NHS.

109. "Record of Deceased Officers and Soldiers at Fort Bowie, Arizona Territory," Consolidated Correspondence File, RG 92, NA. Copy in research files at Fort Bowie NHS.

110. Upton, *Infantry Tactics*, pp. 376–79.

111. Summerhayes, *Vanished Arizona*, pp. 36–37.

112. Bradley interview.

CHAPTER 11: THE WHOLE PROBLEM IS CHANGED: THE FINAL YEARS

1. Mangus, son of the famed Mangas Coloradas, had fled from San Carlos along with Geronimo and the others. However, once in Mexico, the bands had split up and at the time that Captain Lawton reached the extent of his expedition, Mangus was still farther south in Chihuahua. Thus, when Lawton turned north toward Fronteras with Crawford to seek out Geronimo with Miles's peace offer, Mangus was left behind. Nothing more was heard of him and his whereabouts were a mystery to U.S.authorities. Eventually, in October 1887, he returned to Arizona, via the Black Range and Mogollon Mountains of New Mexico. After

a hard chase, he and his band of only two warriors, two boys old enough to bear arms, three women, and five children were captured by elements of the Tenth Cavalry. Their exile to Florida marked the final curtain for the free-roaming renegade Apaches. *ARSW*, 1887, p. 158; Thrapp, *Conquest of Apacheria*, pp. 330, 366.

2. Greene, "Historic Structures Report," pp. 61–65.

3. *ARSW*, 1887, p. 158.

4. "Governor's Report," *ARSI*, 1886, p. 917; see also *ARCIA*, 1886, p. XLI.

5. "Governor's Report," *ARSI*, 1887, p. 756. By the end of the decade, Arizona was to experience its own hard lessons about stock growing. Serious range deterioration was evident by 1889 and within two years overgrazing had destroyed much of the formerly lush grassland in the southern part of the territory. The very climate that made it possible to graze cattle year-around also contributed to abuses of the land before ranchers realized that the range would support only limited numbers of animals, and the grasses needed time to recuperate. Overgrazing led to the incursion of mesquite, an exotic, fast-spreading shrub that choked out the grasses. Arizona experienced a severe drought in 1891, during which thousands of cattle (721,000 were on the tax rolls at that time and probably represented only half the actual number in the territory) died the following spring. Only when the rains failed to come during the summer of 1892 did ranchers realize just how serious the problem had become. Losses averaged 50 to 75 percent before thousands of head were transferred to ranges in Texas, California, Kansas, Indian Territory, Nevada, and even Oregon. The drought persisted until July 1893, but by that time many of those who had speculated in cattle had been ruined financially, both by conditions in Arizona and the nationwide depression known as the Panic of 1893. The stock growers who survived learned to calculate carrying capacities of their ranges, developed alternative water sources such as wells with windmill pumps, and to specialize in calves and yearlings, thus reducing the impacts on ranges. J. J. Wagoner, "Overstocking of the Ranges": 23–26.

6. Inspection Report, Fort Bowie, July 3, 1889, Records of the Inspector General's Office, RG 159.

7. Ibid. The 1880 census recorded Arizona's population as 40,040, while a decade later it stood at 59,020. Pima County, which originally included Fort Bowie, had a population of 17,006 in 1880. Cochise County, which had been created by the time the 1890 census was taken, embraced 6,938 persons, while the remainder of Pima County had 12,673. Porter, *Compendium of the Eleventh Census: 1890*, 1, p. 8 (hereafter cited as 1890 Census).

8. *ARSW*, 1888, p. 126.

9. Ibid.

10. Ibid., pp. 125–26.

11. Johnson's remarkable feat is related in Miles, *Personal Recollections*, 2, p. 541–43. When Miles was selected to head the Division of the Missouri, he was replaced on November 24, 1888, by Colonel Benjamin H. Grierson, who had been the sole commander of the Tenth Cavalry since its organization in 1866.

Wooster, *Nelson A. Miles*, pp. 174–75; Leckie and Leckie, *Unlikely Warriors*, pp. 299–300. During September and October 1889, twelve troops of cavalry and four companies of infantry, plus a Hospital Corps detachment assembled near Fort Grant for a conventional "camp of instruction," which included training in field maneuvers, heliograph signaling, field hospital duty, attack and defense of convoys, as well as the usual company and battalion drills. *ARSW*, 1890, p. 163. A heliograph system, replacing the one dismantled at the end of the Geronimo Campaign, was established across southern New Mexico and Arizona during the fall of 1889. Messages could be flashed over a minimum of two thousand miles between the connecting stations. *ARSW*, 1890, pp. 166–67. In addition to the station on Bowie Mountain, troops from Fort Bowie manned a heliograph at Rucker Canyon. Post Returns, June and July 1890.

12. For an authoritative account of the Apache Kid episode, see Wharfield, "Apache Kid": 37–46.

13. *ARCIA*, 1890, p. 11; *ARSW*, 1890, pp. 167–68.

14. *ARSW*, 1890, p. 171.

15. Ibid., Post Returns, May 1890.

16. *ARSW*, 1890, p. 175. A cook employed by a ranch in the Animas Mountains was "shot, roasted, and tortured to death" in April 1889. The crime, initially blamed on the Kid, was later traced to three Mexicans.

17. *ARSW*, 1882, p. 10.

18. Ibid., p. 11. Not so widely published was the government's concern over labor unrest in metropolitan areas. Besides the reasons cited in the text, General Sheridan wanted to post federal troops where they could readily be called up to quell such disputes. They were, in fact, used in that role on a few occasions in Chicago and elsewhere. Hutton, *Phil Sheridan and His Army*, p. 351.

19. *G.O. No. 72*, AGO, July 5, 1884, stipulated that abandoned posts would be considered for adaptation as Indian schools, and failing that, they would be sold to the public.

20. Ibid., 1889, p. 188.

21. Ibid., p. 189.

22. Greene, "Historic Structures Report," pp. 104–5, 116, 158–60.

23. Ibid., pp. 64–66; Major Henry E. Noyes to AAG, Dept. of Arizona, January 6, 1890, Letters Sent, Fort Bowie, RG 393, NA.

24. The Fourth and Second Cavalry Regiments exchanged departments in response to *G. O. No. 5*, Division of the Pacific, May 19, 1890, *ARSW*, 1890, p. 172; Reginald A. Bradley interview, Arizona Historical Society.

25. *ARSW*, 1891, p. 124; Frazer, *Forts of the West*, pp. 10–14.

26. The Post Returns indicate numerous scouts along the Mexican border and as far southeast as Guadalupe Canyon. Although some the alleged murders were attributed to parties other than Indians or were outright fabrications, Private Frederick Meyers was mysteriously murdered near the camp at San Bernadino on or about July 7, 1891. The extent and nature of these mostly abortive patrols can be found in the Post Returns for the period June 1890 through October

1891. It is interesting to note that most of the Fort Bowie garrison marched to the train station on April 21, 1891, to render honors to President Benjamin Harrison, who paused there during a western tour. Ibid., April 1891.

27. *ARSW*, 1891, p. 256. The parade ground was entirely unsuited for mounted drill, therefore a field was laid out on the flats below in the San Simon Valley. Bradley interview.

28. An interesting sidelight to these events was the use of Indian regulars as trackers. These Apaches were part of an army experiment lasting from 1890 to 1894 to assimilate Indians into white society. The plan called for Indians to be enlisted for full five-year terms, during which time they would be trained, uniformed, and employed like other regular troops, rather than enlisted simply as scouts for short periods. Special segregated Indian companies, I and K for the infantry, L and M for the cavalry, were created within several regiments by consolidating the white troops. White officers specially selected for their qualifications commanded the Indian companies. Company I, Tenth Infantry, was stationed at Fort Bowie from September 1892 until March 1893. The experiment ultimately was terminated because many officers, including Crook and Sheridan, did not support the concept. See Dunlay, *Wolves for the Blue Soldiers*, pp. 195–97; Post Returns, September 1892–March 1893.

29. *ARSW*, 1892, p. 130; ibid., 1893, p. 139; Post Returns, October 1892.

30. Over the years, sightings of the Apache Kid were reported in the Ash Flat area, the Santa Catalina Mountains near Tucson, the Tombstone vicinity, and as far south as the old haunts in the Sierra Madre. The last reliable report placed him at the Guadalupe Mountains of New Mexico in 1924. Wharfield, "Apache Kid": 46. It is believed that the Kid sometimes joined forces with Masse, a member of Geronimo's band who had escaped from the prisoner train on its way east in 1886. Additionally, the army was aware that a party of five Chiricahuas, who had not come in with Geronimo, remained at large in Mexico. *ARSW*, 1891, p. 260.

31. Ibid., 1892, p. 126.

32. *Denver Post*, September 23, 1893; Governor L. C. Hughes to Secretary of the Interior Hoke Smith, September 28, 1893, Fort Bowie Reservation File, RG 92; Endorsement, Major General John M. Schofield, September 15, 1893, ibid.; Assistant Secretary of the Interior to Governor L. C. Hughes, September 29, 1893, ibid.

33. Endorsement, McCook, October 21, 1893, ibid.; telegram, Adjutant General to McCook, November 2, 1893, ibid.

34. Cochise County, which had been carved from Pima County in 1881, boasted over seven thousand inhabitants by the early 1890s. Numerous persons, both businessmen and employees, relied on military contracts to supply the post with beef, wood, hay, and other essentials. *1890 Census*, p. 8.

35. McCook's informant was none other than Britton Davis, former officer and trusted associate of General Crook. After leaving the army subsequent to the Sierra Madre Campaign, Davis found employment managing American cattle and mining interests in Chihuahua. Accordingly, he was in a good position to

know the whereabouts of the Apaches. McCook to Adjutant General, March 7, 1894, Reservation File. The very property Davis managed was adjacent to the Sierra Madre. Davis, *Truth About Geronimo*, p. 194. Incidentally, frontier army doctors had a long tradition of ministering to civilians, even though army regulations did not sanction the practice. In sparsely settled regions like southern Arizona, post surgeons could hardly turn away seriously ill or injured citizens who were willing to pay nominal fees for treatment.

36. Owen Wister, *Owen Wister Out West*, p. 202.

37. Wister was a bystander when the spring was blasted open on May 14, 1894. Ibid.

38. Fort Logan was established in 1887 as part of the army's program to abandon most of the old frontier posts and to concentrate troops at metropolitan areas where they could be more easily and economically supplied. Frazer, *Forts of the West*, p. 39.

39. First Lieutenant Herbert H. Sargent was in charge of the small detail that remained at the post for a short time to supervise the packing of stores and equipment. Originally in Owen Wister, "Stray Notes on the Abandonment of Fort Bowie, October 17, 1894," Owen Wister Collection, Arizona Historical Society, and previously quoted in Greene, "Historic Structures Report," pp. 306–7. The cemetery, surrounded by its picket fence, remained undisturbed for another year until a contractor was sent to disinter the remains of the military personnel and remove them to the national cemetery at the Presidio of San Francisco. Ibid., p. 278.

EPILOGUE

1. Post Returns, October 1894; Murray, "History of Fort Bowie," p. 303n.; *Annual Report of the Quartermaster General*, p. 76; *Reports of the Department of the Interior for the Fiscal Year Ended June 30, 1911: Administrative Reports*, 1, p. 118.

Bibliography

ARCHIVAL MATERIALS

Arizona Historical Foundation, Hayden Library, Tempe.
    Herbert H. Bancroft, "Scraps," a collection of California newspaper articles
        relating to Fort Bowie and other Arizona topics.
    Henry Martyn Robert Papers, Sachs Collection.
Arizona Historical Society Library, Tucson.
    Edward Arhelger biographical file
    E. B. Beaumont Collection
    Reuban F. Bernard biographical file
    John G. Bourke Diaries (microfilm)
    Reginald A. Bradley interviews
    H. G. Burton biographical file
    Charles H. Cook Papers
    Natalie Beaumont Forsyth Papers
    Fort Bowie records
    Charles B. Gatewood Collection
    James Benton Glover Papers
    Hayden Collection
    Frederick G. Hughes biographical file
    M. P. Johnson biographical file
    Anton Mazzanovich Papers
    Microfilm Collections. MC 12–Misc. Reports, Fort Bowie records.
    Charles Morton Papers
    John A. Rockfellow Papers
    Charles D. Roberts biographical file
    Gustave Schneider Collection
        Joseph P. Widney Letters
    Small Collections
    Wardwell Letters
    Dan Williamson Collection
    Owen Wister Collection
    Arthur Woodward Collection

Arizona Historical Society. Fort Lowell Museum, Tucson.
    Mills, Charles K. "Incident at Apache Pass: The Bascom Affair and Its After-
        math." Undated typescript.
California State Library, Sacramento.
    Records of the California Volunteers.
Colorado Historical Society Library, Denver.
    William A. Bell Papers.
National Archives (Main), Washington, D.C.
    Record Group 49, Records of the General Land Office:
        Military Reservation File–Fort Bowie, A. T.
    Record Group 75. Records of the Bureau of Indian Affairs
    Record Group 92, Records of the Office of the Quartermaster General
        Consolidated Correspondence File, Fort Bowie, A. T.
    Record Group 94, Records of the Adjutant General's Office:
        Post Returns, Fort Bowie, A. T. 1862–1894
        Registers of Enlistments in the United States Army, 1798–1914
    Record Group 98, Records of U.S. Army Continental Commands
        Department of the Missouri Correspondence
        Department of New Mexico Correspondence
        Department of the Pacific Correspondence
    Record Group 112, Records of the Surgeon General's Office
        Post Medical History, Fort Bowie, A. T., 1877–1894
    Record Group 133, Records of the Department of Arizona
    Record Group 156, Records of the Office of the Chief of
    Ordnance:
        Quarterly Summary Statements of Ordnance and Ordnance Stores in the
        Hands of Troops, 1863–1876
    Record Group 159, Records of the Office of the Inspector General
        Inspection reports, Fort Bowie, A. T.
    Record Group 393, Fort Bowie records:
        Letters Received, 1869–1879
        Letters Sent, 1873–1894
        Miscellaneous Correspondence 1877–1879
        Orders, 1874–1894
National Park Service. Fort Bowie National Historic Site: historical files; Fort
Davis National Historic Site, Fanny Dunbar Corbusier recollections; Fort
Laramie National Historic Site, Daniel Robinson Papers; Western Archeologi-
cal Center Library, Tucson, Faraway Ranch Collection (Neil Erickson records),
Fort Bowie file.
University of Arizona Library, Special Collections, Tucson.
    Thomas Akers Diary
    Fort Bowie Records
    Frank A. Schilling Collection

University of Colorado Western Historical Collections, Norlin Library, Boulder.
  William Carey Brown Papers
  John K. Houston Papers, Boulder.
U.S. Army Military History Institute. Order of Indian Wars Collection. Carlisle, Pennsylvania.
  Reuben F. Bernard Papers
  John Redington Papers

U.S. GOVERNMENT PUBLICATIONS

U.S. Congress, House Executive Documents:
  33d Cong., 2d sess., 1857, Serial 797.
  33d Cong., 2d sess., 1855, Serial 801.
  35th Cong., 1st sess., 1858, Serial 921.
  35th Cong., 2d sess., 1859, Serial 977.
  35th Cong., 2d sess., 1859, Serial 1008
  36th Cong., 1st sess., 1860, Serial 1025.
  39th Cong., 2d sess., 1868, Serial 1302.
  40th Cong., 2d sess., 1868, Serial 1324.
  40th Cong., 3d sess., 1868, Serial 1367.
  41st Cong., 2d sess., 1869, Serial 1411.
  41st. Cong., 2d sess., 1870, Serial 1412.
  41st. Cong., 3d sess., 1870, Serial 1446.
  42d Cong., 2d sess., 1871, Serial 1503.
  42d Cong., 3d sess., 1872, Serial 1558.
  43d Cong., 1st sess., 1873, Serial 1597.
  43d Cong., 1st sess., 1874, Serial 1615.
  43d Cong., 2d sess., 1875, Serial 1635.
  44th Cong., 2d sess., 1876, Serial 1742.
  45th Cong., 2d sess., 1877, Serial 1794.
  45th Cong., 2d sess., 1877, Serial 1802.
  45th Cong., 3d sess., 1878, Serial 1843.
  46th Cong., 2d sess., 1879, Serial 1903.
  46th Cong., 2d sess., 1879, Serial 1911.
  46th Cong., 3d sess., 1880, Serial 1952.
  47th Cong., 1st sess., 1881, Serial 2010.
  47th Cong., 1st sess., 1881, Serial 2018.
  47th Cong., 1st sess., 1881, Serial 2027.
  47th Cong., 1st sess., 1881, Serial 2030.
  47th Cong., 1st sess., 1881, Serial 2031.
  47th Cong., 2d sess., 1882, Serial 2091.
  47th Cong., 2d sess., 1883, Serial 2111.
  48th Cong., 1st sess., 1883, Serial 2182.
  48th Cong., 1st sess., 1883, Serial 2191.

48th Cong., 2d sess., 1884, Serial 2277.
48th Cong., 2d sess., 1884, Serial 2287.
49th Cong., 1st sess., 1885, Serial 2369.
49th Cong., 1st sess., 1885, Serial 2379.
49th Cong., 2d sess., 1885, Serial 2449.
49th Cong., 2d sess., 1886, Serial 2461.
49th Cong., 2d sess., 1886, Serial 2468.
50th Cong., 1st sess., 1887, Serial 2533.
50th Cong., 1st sess., 1887, Serial 2541.
50th Cong., 2d sess., 1888, Serial 2628.
51st Cong., 1st sess., 1889, Serial 2715.
51st Cong., 2d sess., 1890, Serial 2831.
52d Cong., 1st sess., 1892, Serial 2921.
52d Cong., 2d sess., 1892, Serial 3077.
52d Cong., 2d sess., 1892, Serial 3084.
52d Cong., 2d sess., 1893, Serial 3198.
53d. Cong., 2d sess., 1893, Serial 3206.
53d. Cong., 3d sess., 1894, Serial 3295.

Annual Reports of the Commissioner of Indian Affairs to the Secretary of the Interior. Washington, D. C.: GPO, for the years 1859, 1860, 1868, 1872–1893.

Annual Reports of the Postmaster General. Washington, D.C.: GPO, for the years 1858–1861, 1867, 1868.

Annual Report of the Quartermaster General of the Army to the Secretary of War for the Fiscal Year Ended June 30, 1895. Washington, D.C.: GPO, 1895.

Annual Reports of the Secretary of War. Washington, D.C.: GPO, 1867–1894.

Barnes, Joseph K. *The Medical and Surgical History of the War of the Rebellion (1861-65).* 6 volumes. Washington, D.C.: GPO, 1870.

Colyer, Vincent. *Peace with the Apaches of New Mexico and Arizona.* Washington, D.C.: GPO, 1872.

DeBow, J. D. B. *Statistical View of the United States.* Washington, D.C.: Beverley Tucker, 1854.

Federal Census—Territory of New Mexico and Territory of Arizona. Washington, D.C.: GPO, 1965.

Heitman, Francis B. *Historical Register and Dictionary of the United States Army from Its Organization, September 29, 1789 to March 2, 1903.* Washington, D.C.: GPO, 1903.

Ordnance Manual. Philadelphia: J. B. Lippincott and Co., 1861.

Parke, John G. *Report of Explorations for That Portion of a Railway Route, Near the Thirty-second Parallel of Latitude, Lying Between Dona Ana, On the Rio Grande, and Pimas Villages, on the Gila.* Special printing of House Executive Document No. 129. [GPO], c.1855.

Porter, Robert P. *Compendium of the Eleventh Census: 1890.* Part I. Washington, D. C.: GPO, 1892.

Register of Officers and Agents, Civil, Military, and Naval in the Service of the United States. Washington, D.C.: GPO, 1870, 1872, 1877.

Regulations of the Army of the United States and General Orders in Force on the 17th of February, 1881. Washington, D.C.: GPO, 1881.

Report of the Board on Behalf of United States Executive Departments at the International Exhibition held at Philadelphia, PA, 1876. 2 vols. Washington, D.C.: GPO, 1884.

Reports of the Department of the Interior for the Fiscal Year Ended June 30 1911: Administrative Reports. 2 vols. Washington, D.C.: GPO, 1912.

Report of the Board on Behalf of United States Executive Departments at the International Exhibition Held at Philadelphia, PA, 1876. 2 vols. Washington, D.C.: GPO, 1884.

The War of the Rebellion: A Compilation of the Official Records of the Union and Confederate Armies. Series I, 53 vols. Washington, D.C.: GPO, 1880–97.

Walker, Francis A. *The Statistics of the Population of the United States, Embracing the Tables of Race, Nationality, Sex, Selected Ages, and Occupations.* Washington, D.C.: GPO, 1872.

Walker, Francis A., and Charles W. Seaton. *Compendium of the Tenth Census (June 1, 1880) Compiled Pursuant to an Act of Congress Approved August 7, 1882.* Washington, D. C.: GPO, 1885.

NATIONAL PARK SERVICE SPECIAL REPORTS

Greene, Jerome A. "Historic Structure Report, Historical Data Section, Fort Bowie: Its Physical Evolution, 1862–1894, Fort Bowie National Historic Site, Arizona." Denver: National Park Service, July 1980.

———. "Historic Resource Study: Fort Davis National Historic Site," Denver: National Park Service, November 1986.

Kelly, Roger E. "Talking Mirrors at Fort Bowie: Military Heliograph Communication in the Southwest." Flagstaff: Northern Arizona University for the National Park Service, January 1967.

Robbins, John. "Historic Structures Report, Ruins Stabilization Architectural Data: Fort Bowie National Historic Site, Cochise County, Arizona." Denver: National Park Service, September 1983.

Sheire, James W. "Historic Structures Report, Part II, Historic Structures Report." Washington, D. C.: National Park Service, August 1968.

Utley, Robert M. "Historical Report on Fort Bowie, Arizona." Santa Fe: National Park Service, January 1967.

BOOKS

Account of Gen'l Howard's Mission to the Apaches and Navajos. Washington, D.C.: Washington Daily Morning Chronicle, 1872.

Alberts, Don E. *The Battle of Glorieta: Union Victory in the West.* College Station: Texas A&M University Press, 1998.

Alexander, David V. *Arizona Frontier Military Place Names 1846–1912.* Las Cruces, N. Mex.: Yucca Tree Press, 1998.

Altshuler, Constance Wynn. *Cavalry Yellow and Infantry Blue: Army Officers in Arizona between 1851 and 1886.* Tucson: Arizona Historical Society, 1991.

——. *Chains of Command: Arizona and the Army, 1856–1875.* Tucson: Arizona Historical Society, 1981.

——. *Starting with Defiance: Nineteenth-Century Arizona Military Posts.* Tucson: Arizona Historical Society, 1983.

——. *Chains of Command: Arizona and the Army, 1856–1875.* Tucson: Arizona Historical Society, 1981.

Arizona Cavalcade: The Turbulent Times. Edited by Joseph Miller. New York: Hastings House, 1962.

Ashburn, P. M. *A History of the Medical Department of the United States Army.* Cambridge, Mass.: Houghton Mifflin Co., 1929.

Austerman, Wayne R. *Sharps Rifles and Spanish Mules: The San Antonio–El Paso Mail, 1851–1881.* College Station: Texas A&M University Press, 1985.

Ball, Eve. *In the Days of Victorio: Recollections of a Warm Springs Apache.* Tucson: University of Arizona Press, 1970.

Barney, James M. *Tales of Apache Warfare, 1874–1885.* Private printing, 1933.

Battles and Leaders of the Civil War: Being for the Most Part Contributions by Union and Confederate Officers. Edited by Ned Bradford. New York: Penguin Books, 1956.

Bauer, K. Jack. *The Mexican War, 1846–1848.* New York: Macmillan Publishing Co., 1974.

Beck, Warren A., and Ynez D. Haase. *Historical Atlas of the American West.* Norman: University of Oklahoma Press, 1989.

Bell, William A. *New Tracks in North America: A Journal and Adventure Whilst Engaged in the Survey for a Southern Railroad to the Pacific Ocean During 1867–8.* 2 vols. London: Chapman and Hall, 1869.

Betzinez, Jason. *I Fought with Geronimo.* 1959, Reprint, Lincoln.: University of Nebraska Press, 1987.

Billings, John S. *Circular No. 4, Report on Barracks and Hospitals with Descriptions of Military Posts.* Reprint, New York: Sol Lewis, 1974.

——. *Circular No. 8, Report on Hygiene of the United States Army with Descriptions of Military Posts.* Reprint, New York: Sol Lewis, 1974.

Bourke, John G. *An Apache Campaign in the Sierra Madre.* New York: Charles Scribner's Sons, 1958.

——. *The Diaries of John Gregory Bourke.* Vol. 1. Edited by Charles M. Robinson III. Denton: University of North Texas Press, 2003.

——. *General Crook in the Indian Country: A Scout with the Buffalo Soldiers.* Reprint. Palmer Lake, Colo.: Filter Press, 1974.

——. *On the Border with Crook.* 1891. Reprint, Chicago: Rio Grande Press, 1962.

Boyd, Mrs Orsemus B. *Cavalry Life in Tent and Field.* New York: J. Selwin Tait & Sons, 1894.

Buecker, Thomas R. *Fort Robinson and the American West, 1874–1899.* Lincoln: Nebraska Historical Society, 1999.

Butler, Anne M. *Daughters of Joy, Sisters of Misery: Prostitutes in the American West, 1865–90.* Urbana: University of Illinois Press, 1987.

Butler, David F. *United States Firearms: The First Century, 1776–1875.* New York, N.Y.: Winchester Press, 1971.

Clarke, Dwight L. *Stephen Watts Kearny: Soldier of the West.* Norman: University of Oklahoma Press, 1961.

Clendenen, Clarence C. *Blood on the Border: The United States Army and the Mexican Regulars.* London: Macmillan Co., 1969.

Collins, Charles. *An Apache Nightmare.* Norman: University of Oklahoma Press, 1999.

———. *The Great Escape: The Apache Outbreak of 1881.* Tucson: Westernlore Press, 1994.

Colton, Ray C. *The Civil War in the Western Territories: Arizona, New Mexico, and Utah.* Norman: University of Oklahoma Press, 1959.

Conkling, Roscoe P. and Margaret B. *The Butterfield Overland Mail, 1857–1869: Its Organization and Operation over the Southern Route to 1861, Subsequently over the Central Route to 1866, and under Wells, Fargo and Company in 1869.* Glendale, Calif.: Arthur Clark Co., 1947.

Corbusier, William T. *Verde to San Carlos.* Tucson, Ariz.: Dale Stuart King, 1968.

Cremony, John C. *Life among the Apaches.* 1868. Reprint, Lincoln: University of Nebraska Press, 1983.

Dale, Edward Everett. *The Range Cattle Industry: Ranching on the Great Plains from 1865 to 1925.* Norman: University of Oklahoma Press, 1960.

Davis, Britton. *The Truth about Geronimo.* Lincoln: Bison Books, 1976.

Debo, Angie. *Geronimo: The Man, His Time, His Place.* Norman: University of Oklahoma Press, 1976.

Deibert, Ralph C. *A History of the Third United States Cavalry.* No publisher (probably Third Cavalry). n.d.

De Montraval, Peter R. *A Hero to His Fighting Men: Nelson A. Miles, 1839–1925.*

DeVoto, Bernard. *The Year of Decision 1846.* Boston: Little, Brown and Co., 1943.

Dunlay, Thomas W. *Wolves for the Blue Soldiers: Indian Scouts and Auxiliaries with the United States Army, 1860–90.* Lincoln: University of Nebraska Press, 1982.

Dunn, J. P., Jr. *Massacres of the Mountains: A History of the Indian Wars of the Far West , 1815–1875.* 1886. Reprint, New York: Archer House, Inc., n.d.

Eales, Anne Bruner. *Army Wives on the American Frontier: Living by the Bugles.* Boulder. Colo.: Johnson Books, 1996.

Eccleston, Robert. *Overland to California: Diary of Robert Eccleston on the Southwestern Trail , 1849.* Berkeley: University of California Press, 1950.

Faastad, Ben. *Man of the West: Reminiscences of George Washington Oaks, 1840–1917.* Edited by Arthur Woodward. Tucson: Arizona Pioneers Society, 1956.

Faulk, Odie B. *The Geronimo Campaign.* New York: Oxford Press, 1993.

Finch, Boyd L. *Confederate Pathway to the Pacific: Major Sherod Hunter and Arizona Territory, C. S. A.* Tucson: Arizona Historical Society, 1996.

Foner, Jack D. *The United States Soldier between Two Wars: Army Life and Reforms, 1865–1898.* New York: Humanities Press, 1970.

Fountain, Albert J. "The Battle of Apache Pass," *Arizona Cavalcade: The Turbulent Times.* Edited by Joseph Miller. New York: Hastings House, 1962.

Forsyth, George A. *The Story of the Soldier.* New York: D. Appleton & Co., 1900.

———. *Thrilling Days in Army Life.* 1900. Reprint, Lincoln: University of Nebraska Press, 1994.

Frazer, Robert W. *Forts and Supplies: The Role of the Army in the Economy of the Southwest, 1846–1861.* 1972. Reprint, Albuquerque: University of New Mexico Press, 1983.

———. *Forts of the West: Military Forts and Presidios and Posts Commonly Called Forts West of the Mississippi river to 1898.* Norman: University of Oklahoma Press, 1977.

———. *Mansfield on the Condition of the Western Forts, 1853–54.* Norman: Univeristy of Oklahoma Press, 1963.

Frémont's Fourth Expedition: A Documentary Account of the Disaster of 1848-1849 with Diaries, Letters, and Reports by Participants in the Tragedy. Edited by LeRoy R. and Ann W. Hafen. 15 vols. Glendale, Calif.: Arthur Clark Co., 1960.

Fritz, Henry E. *The Movement for Indian Assimilation, 1860–1890.* Philadelphia: University of Pennsylvania Press, 1963.

Fuller, Claud E., *The Rifled Musket.* Harrisburg, Pa.: Stackpole Books, 1958.

Ganoe, William Addleman. *The History of the United States Army.* Ashton, Md.: Eric Lundberg, 1964.

Garavaglia, Louis A. and Charles G. Worman, *Firearms of the American West, 1803–1865.* Niwot: University of Colorado Press, 1998.

Goetzmann, William H. *Army Exploration in the American West, 1803–1863.* New Haven: Yale University Press, 1959.

Geronimo and the End of the Apache Wars. Edited by C. L. Sonnichsen. Tucson: Arizona Historical Society, 1987.

Geronimo: His Own Story. New York: Penguin Books, 1996.

Granger, Byrd Howell. *Arizona's Names (X Marks the Spot).* Tucson: Falconer Publishing Co., 1983.

Greene, A. C. *900 Miles on the Butterfield Trail.* Denton, Texas: University of North Texas Press, 1994.

Greene, Jerome A. *The Crawford Affair: International Implications of the Geronimo Campaign.* Reprinted from *Journal of the West,* vol. 11, no. 1 (January 1972): 143–153.

Griffen, William B. *Apaches at War and Peace: The Janos Presidio, 1758–1858.* Norman: University of Oklahoma Press, 1998.

Haley, James L. *Apaches: A History and Culture Portrait.* Garden City, N.Y.: Doubleday & Co., 1981.

Hand, George. *The Civil War in Apacheland: Sergeant George Hand's Diary, California, Arizona, West Texas, New Mexico, 1861–1864.* Edited by Neil C. Carmony. Silver City, N. Mex.: High Lonesome Books, 1996.

Handbook of American Indians North of Mexico. Edited by Frederick Webb Hodge. 2 vols. 1907, 1910. Reprint, New York: Pageant Books, 1959.

Hart, Herbert M. *Tour Guide to Old Western Forts.* Boulder, Colo.: Pruett Publishing Co., 1980.

Heap, Gwinn Harris. *Central Route to the Pacific.* Edited by LeRoy R. and Ann W. Hafen. The Far West and the Rockies Historical Series. 15 vols. Glendale, Calif.: Arthur Clark Co., 1957.

Hein, O. L. *Memories of Long Ago.* New York: G. P. Putnam's Sons, 1925.

Horn, Tom. *Life of Tom Horn: Government Scout and Interpreter.* Norman: University of Oklahoma Press, 1964.

Howard, O. O. *My Life and Experiences among Our Hostile Indians.* Hartford, Conn.: A. D. Worthington & Co., 1907.

Hunt, Aurora. *The Army of the Pacific.* Glendale, Calif.: Arthur Clark Co., 1951
———. *Major General James Henry Carlton, 1814–1873: Western Frontier Dragoon.* Glendale, Calif.: Arthur H. Clark Co., 1958.

Hutton, Paul Andrew. *Phil Sheridan and His Army.* Lincoln: University of Nebraska Press, 1985.

Jackson, W. Turrentine. *Wagon Roads West: A Study of Federal Road Surveys and Construction in the Trans-Mississippi West, 1846–1869.* 1952. Reprint, New Haven: Yale University Press, 1965.

Jamieson, Perry D. *Crossing the Deadly Ground: United States Army Tactics, 1865–1899.* Tuscaloosa: University of Alabama Press, 1994.

Johnson, Virginia Weisel. *The Unregimented General: A Biography of Nelson A. Miles.* Boston: Houghton Mifflin Co., 1962.

Keane, Melissa, and A. E. Rogge. *Gold and Silver Mining in Arizona, 1848–1945: A Context for Historic Preservation Planning.* Phoenix: Dames & Moore Intermountain Cultural Resource Services, 1992.

King, James T. *War Eagle: A Life of General Eugene A. Carr.* Lincoln: University of Nebraska Press, 1963.

Knight, Oliver. *Life and Manners in the Frontier Army.* Norman: University of Oklahoma Press, 1978.

Leckie, William H., and Shirley A. Leckie. *Unlikely Warriors: General Benjamin H. Grierson and His Family.* Norman: University of Oklahoma Press, 1984.

Lummis, Charles F. *General Crook and the Apache Wars.* Flagstaff, Ariz.: Northland Press, 1966.

McChristian, Douglas C. *The U.S. Army in the West, 1870–1880: Uniforms, Weapons, and Equipment.* Norman: University of Oklahoma Press, 1995.

Making Peace with Cochise: The 1872 Journal of Captain Joseph Alton Sladen. Edited by Edwin R. Sweeney. Norman: University of Oklahoma Press, 1997.

Marion, John H. *Notes On Travel Through the Territory of Arizona, Being An Account of the Trip Made by General George Stoneman and Others in the Autumn of 1870.* Edited by Donald M. Powell. Tucson: University of Arizona Press, 1965.

Manual for Light Artillery, 1863. Reprint, Staten Island, N.Y.: Jacques Noel Jacobsen, Jr., 1968.

Meketa, Charles, and Jacqueline Meketa. *One Blanket and Ten Days Rations: New Mexico Volunteers in Arizona, 1864–1866.* Globe, Ariz.: Southwest Parks and Monuments Association, 1980.

Miles, Nelson A. *Personal Recollections and Observations of General Nelson A. Miles.* 1896. Reprint, 2 vols. Lincoln: University of Nebraska Press, 1992.

Miller, Darlis A. *The California Column in New Mexico.* Albuquerque: University of New Mexico Press, 1982.

————. *Soldiers and Settlers: Military Supply in the Southwest, 1861–1885.* Norman: University of Oklahoma Press, 1989.

Moore, Yndia. *The Butterfield Mail Across Arizona: together with a chronological outline of the history of transportation and communication in Arizona, in commemoration of the centennial of the arrival of the first Butterfield mail pouches carried across the eastern border of what is now Arizona at Stein's Pass on October 1, 1858.* Tucson: Arizona Pioneers' Society, 1958.

Moorehead, Max L. *The Apache Frontier: Jacobo Ugarte and Spanish-Indian Relations in Northern New Spain, 1769–1791.* Norman: University of Oklahoma Press, 1968.

The Mountain Men and the Fur Trade of the Far West. Edited by LeRoy R. and Ann W. Hafen. 9 vols. Glendale, Calif.: Arthur H. Clark Co., 1965.

Myrick, David F. *Railroads of Arizona.* 2 vols. Berkeley: Howell-North Books, 1975.

Nevin, David. *The Expressmen.* The Old West series. New York: Time-Life Books, 1974.

Nevins, Allan. *Frémont: Pathmaker of the West.* New York: Longmans, Green & Co., 1955.

News of the Plains and Rockies, 1803–1865. Compiled by David A. White. 8 vols. Spokane, Wash.: Arthur Clarke Co., 1998.

Nye, W. S. *Carbine and Lance: The Story of Old Fort Sill.* Norman: University of Oklahoma Press, 1943.

Oaks, George Washington. *Man of the West: Reminiscences of George Washington Oaks, 1840–1917.* Edited by Arthur L. Woodward. Tucson: Arizona Pioneers' Historical Society, 1956.

Ogle, Ralph Hedrick. *Federal Control of the Western Apaches: 1848–1886.* Albuquerque: University of New Mexico Press, 1940.

Oliva, Leo E. *Soldiers on the Santa Fe Trail.* Norman: University of Oklahoma Press, 1967.

Ormsby, Waterman L. *The Butterfield Overland Mail.* Edited by Lyle H. Wright and Joephine M. Bynum. San Marino, Calif.: Huntington Library, 1998.

Orton, Richard H. *Records of California Men in the War of the Rebellion, 1861–1867.* Sacramento: State Printing Office, 1890.

The Papers of the Order of Indian Wars. Fort Collins, Colo.: Old Army Press, 1975.

Parker, James. *The Old Army: Memories, 1872–1918.* Philadelphia: Dorrance & Co., 1929.

Paul, Rodman Wilson. *Mining Frontiers of the Far West, 1848–1880.* New York: Holt, Rinehart and Winston, 1963.

Pettis, George H. *The California Column.* New Mexico Historical Society Publication No. 11. Santa Fe: New Mexican Printing Co., 1908.

Pierce, Michael D. *The Most Promising Young Officer: A Life of Ranald Slidell Mackenzie.* Norman: University of Oklahoma Press, 1993.

Porter, Joseph C. *Paper Medicine Man: John Gregory Bourke and His American West.* Norman: University of Oklahoma Press, 1986.

Porter, Robert P. *Compendium of the Eleventh Census: 1890.* Part I. Washington, D.C.: 1892.

Radbourne, Allan. "Salvador or Martinez: The Parentage and Origin of Mickey Free." In *The Brand Book,* edited by Francis B. Taunton. London: English Westerner's Society, 1972.

Ricketts, Norma Baldwin. *The Mormon Battalion: U.S. Army in the West, 1846–1848.* Logan: Utah State University Press, 1996.

Rickey, Don, Jr. *Forty Miles a Day on Beans and Hay: The Enlisted Soldier Fighting the Indian Wars.* Norman: University of Oklahoma Press, 1963.

Robinson, Charles M., III, *General Crook and the Western Frontier.* Norman: University of Oklahoma Press, 2001.

Rockfellow, John A. *Log of an Arizona Trail Blazer.* Tucson: Arizona Silhouettes, 1955.

Rodenbough, Theodore. *The Army of the United States: Historical Sketches of Staff and Line with Portraits of Generals-in-Chief.* New York: Argonaut Press, 1966.

Roe, Frances M. A. *Army Letters from an Officer's Wife.* 1909. Reprint, Lincoln: University of Nebraska Press, 1981.

Russell, Don. *One Hundred and Three Fights and Scrimmages: The Story of General Reuben F. Bernard.* Washington, D.C.: United States Cavalry Association, 1936.

Ryan, Andrew. *News From Fort Craig New Mexico, 1863: Civil War Letters of Andrew Ryan with the First California Volunteers.* Edited by Ernest Machand. Santa Fe, New Mexico: Stagecoach Press, 1966.

Schmitt, Martin. *General George Crook: His Autobiography.* Norman: University of Oklahoma Press, 1960.

Scott, Hugh Lennox. *Some Memories of a Soldier.* New York: Century Co., 1928.

Sheridan, Thomas E. *Arizona: A History.* Tucson: University of Arizona Press, 1995.

Simmons, Marc. *Massacre on the Lordsburg Road: A Tragedy of the Apache Wars.* College Station: Texas A&M University Presss, 1997.

Sladen, Joseph Alton. *Making Peace with Cochise: The 1872 Journal of Captain Joseph Alton Sladen.* Edited by Edwin R. Sweeney. Norman: University of Oklahoma Press, 1997.

Sonnichsen, C. L., ed. *Geronimo and the End of the Apache Wars: Commemorating the Centennial of the Surrender of Naiche and Geronimo, September 4, 1886.* Tucson: Arizona Historical Society, 1987.

Stallard, Patricia Y. *Glittering Misery: Dependents of the Indian-Fighting Army.* Norman: University of Oklahoma Press, 1999.

Summerhayes, Martha. *Vanished Arizona: Recollections of My Army Life.* Chicago: Lakeside Press, 1939.

Sweeney, Edwin R. *Mangus Coloradas, Chief of the Chiricahua Apaches.* Norman: University of Oklahoma Press, 1998.

———. *Cochise: Chiricahua Apache Chief.* Norman: University of Oklahoma Press, 1991.

Tevis, James H. *Arizona in the '50s.* Albuquerque: University of New Mexico Press, 1954.

Theobald, John and Theobald, Lillian. *Arizona Territory Post Offices and Postmasters.* Phoenix: Arizona Historical Foundation, 1961.

———. *Wells Fargo in Arizona Territory.* Tempe: Arizona Historical Foundation, 1978.

Thian, Raphael P., comp. *Notes Illustrating the Military Geography of the United States 1813–1880.* Reprint. Austin: University of Texas Press, 1979.

Thomas, David Hurst, Jay Miller, Richard White, Peter Nabokov, and Philip J. Deloria. *The Native Americans: An Illustrated History.* Atlanta,: Turner Publishing, 1993.

Thompson, Gerald. *The Army and the Navajo: The Bosque Redondo Reservation Experiment, 1863–1868.* Tucson: University of Arizona Press, 1982.

Thompson, Jerry. *Henry Hopkins Sibley: Confederate General of the West.* Natchitoches, Tex.: Northwestern University Press, 1987.

Thrapp, Dan L. *The Conquest of Apacheria.* Norman: University of Oklahoma Press, 1967.

———. *Al Sieber—Chief of Scouts.* Norman: University of Oklahoma Press, 1964.

———. *Encyclopedia of Frontier Biography.* 3 vols. Glendale, Calif.: Arthur H. Clark Co., 1988.

Upton, Emory. *Infantry Tactics Double and Single Rank Adapted to American Topography and Improved Firearms.* New York: D. Appleton and Co., 1874.

Utley, Robert M. *A Clash of Cultures: Fort Bowie and the Chiricahua Apaches.* Washington, D. C: National Park Service, 1977.

———. *Frontiersmen in Blue: The United States Army and the Indian, 1848–1865.* New York: Macmillan Co., 1967.

———. *Frontier Regulars: The United States Army and the Indian, 1866–1891.* New York: Macmillan Publishing Co., 1973.

———. *The Indian Frontier of the American West, 1846–1890.* Albuquerque: University of New Mexico Press, 1984.

Walker, Henry Pickering. *The Wagonmasters: High Plains Freighting from the Earliest Days of the Santa Fe Trail to 1880.* Norman: University of Oklahoma Press, 1966.

Wallace, Edward S. *The Great Reconnaissance: Soldiers, Artists, and Scientists on the Frontier, 1848–1861.* Boston: Little, Brown and Co., 1955.

Western Apache Raiding and Warfare. Edited by Keith H. Basso. Tucson: University of Arizona Press, 1993.

Winther, Oscar Osburn. *The Transportation Frontier: Trans-Mississippi West 1865–1890.* New York: Holt, Rinehart and Winston, 1964.

Wister, Owen. *Owen Wister Out West: His Journals and Letters.* Chicago: University of Chicago Press, 1958.

Wooster, Robert. *The Military and United States Indian Policy, 1865–1903,* Lincoln: University of Nebraska Press, 1995.

———. *Nelson A. Miles and the Twilight of the Frontier Army.* Lincoln: University of Nebraska Press, 1993.

Young, Otis E. *The West of Philip St. George Cooke, 1809–1895.* Glendale, Calif.: Arthur H. Clark Co., 1955.

———. *Western Mining.* Norman: University of Oklahoma Press, 1970.

ARTICLES

Albrecht, Elizabeth. "Estavan Ochoa: Mexican-American Businessman." *Journal of Arizona History,* 4 (1963): 35–40.

Ball, Eve. "The Apache Scouts: A Chiricahua Appraisal." *Arizona and the West,* 1 (1965): 315–28.

Byars, Charles. "Documents of Arizona History: Gatewood Reports to His Wife from Geronimo's Camp," *Journal of Arizona History,* 7 (1966): 76–81.

"Colonel Bonneville's Report: The Department of New Mexico in 1859." Edited by Henry P. Walker. *Arizona and the West,* 22 (1980): 343–62.

Clum, John P. "Fighting Geronimo: A Story of the Apache Indian Campaign of 1876." *Sunset Magazine,* 11 (1903): 36–41.

Cramer, Harry G. III. "Tom Jeffords—Indian Agent." *Journal of Arizona History,* 17 (1976): 265–97.

Crook, George. "The Apache Problem." *Journal of the Military Service Institution,* 7 (1886): 257–69.

Cruse, Thomas. "The Fight at Cibicu, and Nock-ay-del-Klinne, Apache Medicine Man." *Winners of the West* (July 30, 1934).

Cunningham, Bob. "Blame the Bootlegger—Accounting for Geronimo's Last Escape," *The Smoke Signal,* 59 (Spring 1993), 165–172.

Daly, H. W. "The Capture of Geronimo." *Winners of the West,* (December 30, 1933).

———. "The Geronimo Campaign," *U.S. Cavalry Journal,* (October 1908): 68–291.

De la Garza, Phyllis. "Apache Kid," *True West* (August 1995): 14–19.

Dorr, L. L. "The Fight at Chiricahua Pass in 1869 as Described by L. L. Dorr, M. D." Edited by Marian E. Valputic and Harold H. Longfellow. *Arizona and the West* 13 (Winter 1971): 369–78.

Duffen, William A. "Overland Via 'Jackass Mail' in 1858: The Diary of Pochion Way." *Arizona and the West,* 2 (1960): 1229–46.

Eaton, George O. "Stopping an Apache Battle." *Cavalry Journal,* (July-August 1933): 012–18.

"The Ending of the Apache War." *Harpers Weekly,* 30 (1886): 266–67.

Farley, John F. "Early Day Indian Fighting in New Mexico." *Winners of the West.* (September 30, 1935).

Gale, Jack C. "Hatfield under Fire, May 15, 1886: An Episode of the Geronimo Campaigns." *Journal of Arizona History,* 18 (1977): 447–68.

———. "Lebo in Pursuit." *Journal of Arizona History*, 21 (1980): 11–24.

Gatewood, C. B. "Son of Heroic Gatewood Tells How Apache Chief Surrendered." *San Diego Union*, August 4, 1933.

Gatewood, Charles B. "Geronimo." *Missouri Republican*, November 22, 1886.

Hall, J. C. "In the Wild West." *National Tribune* (October 20, 1887): 1

Hazen, Eli W. "Notes of Marches Made by Co. E, 1st Inft. C.V." N.d., copy in the files at Fort Bowie National Historic Site.

Hunter, Thomas Thompson. "Early Days in Arizona." *Arizona Historical Review*, 3 (1930): 105–20.

Irwin, B. J. D. "The Fight at Apache Pass." *Bisbee (Arizona) Daily Review*, February 4, 1934.

Kane, Randy. "An Honorable and Upright Man: Sidney R. De Long as Post Trader at Fort Bowie." *Journal of Arizona History*, 19 (Autumn 1978): 297–314.

Keyes, Edward. "Some Recollections of Arizona and Cochise." *The United Service* (July 1890): 98–101.

Kibby, Leo P. "A Civil War Episode in California-Arizona History." *Journal of Arizona History*, 2 (1961): 20–23.

McChristian, Douglas C., and Larry L. Ludwig. "Eyewitness to the Bascom Affair: An Account by Sergeant Daniel Robinson, Seventh Infantry." *Journal of Arizona History*, 42 (Autumn 2001), 277–300.

Moran, George H. R. "Arizona Territory—1878: The Diary of George H. R. Moran, Contract Surgeon, United States Army." Edited by E. R. Hagemann. *Arizona and the West*, 3 (1963): 249–61.

Mulligan, Raymond A. "Sixteen Days in Apache Pass." *The Kiva*, 24 (1958): 1–13.

Murray, Richard Y. "Apache Pass, 'Most Formidable of Gorges.'" *Corral Dust: Potomac Corral of the Westerners*, 6 (1961):17–24.

Myrick, David F. "The Railroads of Southern Arizona: An Approach to Tombstone," *Journal of Arizona History*, 8 (1967): 155–70.

Nalty, Bernard C., and Truman R. Strobridge. "Captain Emmet Crawford Commander of Apache Scouts 1882–1886." *Arizona and the West*, 6 (1964): 30–40.

Neifert, William W. "Trailing Geronimo by Heliograph." *Winners of the West* (October 1935).

Noggle, Burl. "Anglo Observers of the Southwest Borderlands, 1825–1890: The Rise of a Concept." *Arizona and the West*, 1 (1959): 105–31.

Oury, W. S. "A True History of the Outbreak of the Noted Apache Cachise in the Year 1861." *Arizona Star*, starting June 28, 1877, copy at University of Arizona Library.

"Overland via the 'Jackass Mail' in 1858: The Diary of Phocion R. Way." Edited by William A. Duffen. *Arizona and the West*, 2 (1960): 35–53 and 147–163.

Park, Joseph F. "The Apaches in Mexican-American Relations, 1848–1861." *Arizona and the West*, 3 (1961): 1229–46.

Pettit, James S. "Apache Campaign Notes—'86." *Journal of the Military Service Institution*, 7 (1886): 331–38.

Radbourne, Allan. "The Naming of Mickey Free." *Journal of Arizona History*, 17 (1976): 341–4.

———. "Salvador or Martinez: The Parentage and Origins of Mickey Free," *English Westerners Society Brand Book*, 14 (January 1972): 2–26.

Robbins, Rebecca. "Some Reflections on the Heliograph." *Periodical: Journal of the Council on America's Military Past*, 12 (1983): 24–31.

Robinson, Daniel. "The Affair at Apache Pass." *Sports Afield*, 17 (August 1896): 79–83.

Rolak, Bruno J. "General Miles' Mirrors: The Heliograph in the Geronimo Campaign of 1886." *Journal of Arizona History*, 16 (1975): 145–160.

Russell, Don. "Chief Cochise vs. Lieutenant Bascom: A Review of the Evidence." *Winners of the West*, (December 1936): 1–3, 7.

Ryan, Pat M. "John P. Clum: 'Boss with the White Forehead.'" *Journal of Arizona History*, 5 (1964): 48–60.

Sacks, Benjamin H. "The Creation of the Territory of Arizona," *Arizona and the West*, 2 pts., 5 (1963): 29–62, 109–48.

———. "New Evidence on the Bascom Affair." *Arizona and the West*, 4 (1962): 261–78.

Schoenberger, Dale T. "Lieutenant George N. Bascom At Apache Pass, 1861." *Chronicles of Oklahoma*, 51 (1973): 84–91.

Serven, James E. "An End to the Apache Warpath." *The Smoke Signal*, (Fall 1970): 26–44.

———. "The Military Posts on Sonoita Creek." *The Smoke Signal*, (1965): 26–48.

Sharp, Jay W. "Reluctant Apache Warrior Tzoe Joined General Crook's Forces and Became Known as 'Peaches.'" *Wild West*, 10 (December 1997): 12–18, 88.

Smith, Ralph A. "The Scalp Hunter in the Borderlands, 1835–1850." *Arizona and the West*, 6 (1964): 5–22.

Sonnichsen, C. L. "Tom Jeffords and the Editors." *Journal of Arizona History*, 29 (1988): 117–30.

Spring, John A. "A March to Arizona from California in 1866, or: Lost in the Yuma Desert." *Journal of Arizona History*, 3 (1962): 1–6.

Stevens, Robert C. "Colonel John Finkle Stone and the Apache Pass Mining Company." *Arizona Historical Review* 6 (1935): 74–80.

Sweeney, Edwin R. "Cochise and the Prelude to the Bascom Affair." *New Mexico Historical Review*, October 1989: 427–46.

Teal, John W. "Soldier in the California Column: The Diary of John W. Teal." Edited by Henry P. Walker. *Arizona and the West*, 13 (1971): 33–82.

Turcheneske, John A. "The Arizona Press and Geronimo's Surrender." *Journal of Arizona History*, 14 (1973): 133–147.

Tyler, Barbara Ann. "Cochise: Apache War Leader, 1858–1861." *Journal of Arizona History*, 6 (1965): 1–11.

Utley, Robert M. "The Bascom Affair: A Reconstruction." *Arizona and the West*, 3 (1961): 59–68.

———. "Captain John Pope's Plan of 1853 for the Frontier Defense of New Mexico." *Arizona and the West*, 5 (1963): 149–63.

———. "The Surrender of Geronimo." *Journal of Arizona History* 4 (1963): 1–9.

Vandenberg, Hoyt Sanford Jr. "Forsyth and the 1882 Loco Outbreak Campaign." *The Smoke Signal*, 60 (Fall 1993): 174–95.

Van Orden, Jay. "C. S. Fly at Canon De Los Embudos: American Indians as Enemy in the Field, A Photographic First." *Journal of Arizona History*, 30 (1989): 319–46.

Wagoner, J. J. "Overstocking of the Ranges in Southern Arizona during the 1870s and 1880s." *Journal of Arizona History*, 2 (1961): 23–27.

Walker, Henry P. "Colonel Bonneville's Report: The Department of New Mexico." *Arizona and the West*, 22 (1980): 343–62.

———. Wagon Freighting in Arizona." *The Smoke Signal*, (Fall 1973): 182–204.

Ward, C. H. "A Trip to the Cavalry Camps in Southern Arizona." *Cosmopolitan*, (October 1888): 109–14.

Watson, Richard F. "Story of the Apache Kid." *Winners of the West* (July 1939).

Way, Phocion R. "Overland via 'Jackass Mail' in 1858: The Diary of Phocion R. Way." Edited by William A. Duffen. *Arizona and the West*, 2 (1960): 35–164.

Wharfield, H. B. "Footnotes to History: The Apache Kid and the Record." *Journal Arizona History*, 6 (1965): 37–46.

Williamson, Dan R. "Bowie in 1886." *Belt* (October 1929).

Winther, Oscar Osburn. "The Southern Overland Mail and Stagecoach Line, 1857–1861." *New Mexico Historical Review* 32 (1957): 81–106.

Woodward, Arthur. "Side Lights on Fifty Years of Apache Warfare, 1836–1886." *Journal of Arizona History*, 2 (1961): 3–14.

Yohn, Henry I. "The Regulars in Arizona: Interviews With Henry I. Yohn." *Journal of Arizona History*, 16 (1975): 119–26.

NEWSPAPERS

(Prescott) *Arizona Miner*

(Tucson) *Arizona Weekly Star*

Army & Navy Journal

(Tubac) *Weekly Arizonian*

(Tucson) *Arizona Citizen*

(Washington, D.C.) *Daily Morning News*

Bisbee (Arizona) *Daily Review*

Boston Evening Transcript

Daily New Mexican

Denver Post

Harpers Weekly

Las Cruces (New Mexico) *Borderer*

(St. Louis) *Missouri Republican*

New York Herald

Rio Grande Republican

Sacramento Daily Union

(San Francisco) *American Flag*

Santa Fe Gazette

The Santa Fe New Mexican
Silver City (New Mexico) *Herald*

THESES, DISSERTATIONS, AND OTHER UNPUBLISHED PAPERS

Burgess, Opie Rundle. "Fort Bowie's Colorful Past." Warren, Arizona. Copy at Fort Bowie National Historic Site.

De Stefano, William. "Tom Jeffords, Capitalist." Paper presented at the Arizona-New Mexico Historical Convention, Tucson, 1995.

"Diary of Corporal Alexander Grayson Bowman, Company B, Fifth Regiment, California Volunteers, October 18, 1861–February 22, 1865." Transcribed by Mary Linda Simanton, history seminar, Catalina High School, Tucson. Copy in Fort Bowie National Historic Site files.

Lominac, Karen, and Kathy Luczai. "The Butterfield Stage Station and the Chiricahua Indian Agency: An Investigation of Their Locations in Apache Pass." unpublished typescript in files of Western Archeology Center, Tucson, 1978.

Miller, Darlis. "Across the Plains in 1864 with Additional Paymaster Samuel C. Staples." Master's thesis, Kansas State University, 1980.

Murray, Richard Y. "The History of Fort Bowie." Master's thesis, University of Arizona, 1951. Copy at Fort Bowie National Historic Site.

Spude, Robert L. "The Santa Rita del Cobre, The Early American Period, 1846–1886." Typescript in possession of the author.

Wrattan, George M. "The Surrender of Geronimo." Oral account told to Dr. S. M. Huddleson. Typescript in Fort Bowie National Historic Site collections.

Index